METHODS OF RESEARCH IN SOCIAL PSYCHOLOGY

METHODS OF RESEARCH IN SOCIAL PSYCHOLOGY

SECOND EDITION

Elliot Aronson
University of California, Santa Cruz

Phoebe C. Ellsworth
University of Michigan

J. Merrill Carlsmith
Late Professor of Psychology
Stanford University

Marti Hope Gonzales
University of Minnesota

McGRAW-HILL PUBLISHING COMPANY

New York St. Louis San Francisco Auckland Bogotá Caracas Hamburg
Lisbon London Madrid Mexico Milan Montreal New Delhi Oklahoma City
Paris San Juan São Paulo Singapore Sydney Tokyo Toronto

This book was set in Times Roman by the College Composition Unit in cooperation with Black Dot, Inc.
The editors were Susan Badger and Laura D. Warner;
the production supervisor was Denise L. Puryear.
The cover was designed by Rafael Hernandez.
R. R. Donnelley & Sons Company was printer and binder.

METHODS OF RESEARCH IN SOCIAL PSYCHOLOGY

1 2 3 4 5 6 7 8 9 0 DOC DOC 8 9 4 3 2 1 0 9

ISBN 0-07-002466-9

Library of Congress Cataloging-in-Publication Data

Methods of research in social psychology/Elliot Aronson...[et al.].—2nd ed.
    p.   cm.
  Rev. ed of: Methods of research in social psychology/J. Merrill Carlsmith, Phoebe C. Ellsworth, Elliot Aronson. c1976.
  ISBN 0-07-002466-9
  1. Social psychology—Methodology.   2. Social psychology—Research—United States.   I. Aronson, Elliot.   II. Carlsmith, J. Merrill, (date). Methods of research in social psychology.
HM251.M4535   1990
302'.072073—dc20   89-12811

ABOUT
THE AUTHORS

ELLIOT ARONSON received his A.B. from Brandeis University in 1954, his M.A. from Wesleyan University in 1956, and his Ph.D. from Stanford University in 1959. He has taught at Harvard, the University of Minnesota, and the University of Texas, and is currently Professor of Psychology at the University of California at Santa Cruz.

He has won numerous teaching and research awards, among them Distinguished Teaching Awards at both the University of Texas and the University of California, the Distinguished Teaching Award in Psychology from the American Psychological Association (APA), and the American Association for the Advancement of Science (AAAS) Prize for Distinguished Research in Sociopsychology, and he was the first recipient of the Donald Campbell Award for Distinguished Research in Social Psychology. Past president of APA's Division of Personality and Social Psychology, and past chair of the National Academy of Science Committee on Energy Conservation, he has written and edited numerous books, including *The Social Animal, The Jigsaw Classroom, The Handbook of Social Psychology* (with Gardner Lindzey), and *Energy Use: The Human Dimension* (with Paul Stern).

PHOEBE C. ELLSWORTH received her A.B. from Harvard in 1966 and her Ph.D. from Stanford University in 1970 (J. Merrill Carlsmith was her graduate adviser). She has taught at Yale and Stanford, where she won the Dean's Award for Distinguished Teaching in 1984, and is now Professor of Psychology at the University of Michigan. Her primary research interests are the relation between cognition and emotion and, entirely separate, Psychology and the Law. She has worked in both the laboratory and the field, using true experiments, quasi-experiments, surveys, simulations, polygraphs, videotape recorders, paper-and-pencils, and her own eyes, both as treatments and as measures.

J. MERRILL CARLSMITH received his A.B. from Stanford University in 1958 and his Ph.D. from Harvard University in 1963. The classic Festinger and Carlsmith study, "Cognitive Consequences of Force Compliance," was his senior honors thesis, for which he won the Sigma Xi Award for Outstanding Student Research. He taught for two years at Yale, then returned to Stanford, where he remained until his untimely death in 1984.

He was a brilliant teacher of research methods and statistics, and won the Dean's Award for Distinguished Teaching in 1980. He was author of numerous journal articles and a major textbook, *Social Psychology* (with Jonathan Freedman and David Sears). He was a gifted experimenter and an incisive critic, and his contributions to the second edition were sorely missed.

New to the second edition, MARTI HOPE GONZALES received her A.B. from Southwest Texas State University in 1977 and her M.A. from Trinity University in 1979. In 1987 she received her Ph.D. from the University of California at Santa Cruz, where Elliot Aronson was her graduate adviser. Her introduction to the hazards of experimental research came in 1975, when as a novice experimenter she was bitten by one of her three-year-old subjects. Despite that inauspicious beginning, she has continued to teach and conduct social psychological research. She has taught at Southwest Texas State University and the University of California at Santa Cruz, and is currently Assistant Professor of Psychology at the University of Minnesota. Her current research interests are varied, ranging from applied research in energy conservation to basic experimental and archival research on self-presentation.

To Leon Festinger

Sometimes directly, sometimes indirectly,
he taught us how to do it.

CONTENTS

FOREWORD

New scientific fields are often the breeding grounds for controversy and crisis. Debates regarding basic methods and ultimate goals—as well as general theories and specific findings—are common as new disciplines seek to establish their identities. In this formative period, schools of thought emerge; central questions for study are identified, and tools and methods for addressing these issues are devised. Frequently, these early schools of thought can be seen as deriving from the seminal work of individual pioneers and their followers in the field. As a result, "insiders' " histories of the early days of such fields typically read much like intellectual genealogies.

Certainly this has been true of social psychology in its first half-century as an experimental enterprise. In the beginning, as it were, there was Kurt Lewin—in many respects, the "father" of modern social psychology. Out of Lewin's laboratory, after his move to this country, emerged Leon Festinger, the preeminent theorist in social psychology for the two decades following Lewin's death, and the man to whose memory this volume is appropriately dedicated. Elliot Aronson, in turn, began his career as a graduate student in Festinger's lab at Stanford, as did Merrill Carlsmith as an undergraduate. After their move to Harvard, Aronson continued as Carlsmith's mentor. Together they produced a series of elegant and influential experimental studies of cognitive dissonance and attitude change processes that remain classics to this day.

From their productive collaboration, as well, came the famous *Handbook of Social Psychology* chapter from which the first edition of this book derived. In that chapter, Aronson and Carlsmith tried—for the first time in the history of the field—to illuminate the pragmatic issues that arise in the actual "doing" of experimental social psychology. Many previous sources, to be sure, were available for students who wanted to learn about the formal properties of various research designs or the statistical analysis of experimental data. Aronson and Carlsmith's was the first attempt, however, to articulate the immense store of "tacit knowledge" that is required for the effective implementation of general design principles, and for the realization of abstract theories in successful experimental research in social psychology—to codify the "oral traditions" that had been passed informally from one generation to the next.

Perhaps even more significantly, Aronson and Carlsmith set for themselves a higher standard. Where other books on research methods had sought to inform students about how to avoid sources of bias and invalidity, the *Handbook* chapter aspired to teach something about the process of designing and implementing experiments that were not only technically correct but also elegant, interesting, and important. Their goal, in short, was to inspire others in the design of future classics—experiments with a significant "tale to tell" of the sort for which they, themselves, were so well known.

In elaborating this brief primer on experimental methods into the first edition of this book, Aronson and Carlsmith were joined by Phoebe Ellsworth. Continuing the chain, Ellsworth had collaborated with her mentor, Carlsmith, on studies of nonverbal behavior at Stanford, and had then gone on to make important contributions of her own in the areas of emotion and psychology-and-law. Together, the three offered students a guide to both the art and the science of social psychological experimentation. Their efforts provided not only an effective theoretical rationale for experimentation, but also a detailed look at its practice in social psychology—from the initial elicitation of informed consent to the administration of the postexperimental interview.

Although it is a pleasure to welcome this second edition of *Methods of Research in Social Psychology,* it is hard to do so without some sadness. Merrill Carlsmith died in 1984, at the age of 48. His untimely death was a personal tragedy to his friends and colleagues, and a significant loss to the field. More recently, as this Foreword was being prepared, Leon Festinger also passed away. His demise in some ways marks the end of an era in social psychology.

It would be equally difficult, however, not to greet this revision with joy, as well. In the authorship of the book, we see again the proverbial passing of the mantle as Aronson and Ellsworth are joined by Marti Hope Gonzales, a recent student of Aronson's, who has just embarked on her own career in social psychology. In the substance of this volume, we find the continuing intellectual legacy of Carlsmith, Festinger, and Lewin—ready to inform and to inspire yet future generations of researchers.

Mark Lepper
Stanford University

PREFACE

In the early 1970s when we (Carlsmith, Ellsworth, and Aronson) first decided to expand the Aronson-Carlsmith chapter on experimental methodology in the *Handbook of Social Psychology* (1969) into a book, social psychology was in the midst of a crisis. At the heart of the crisis was a persistent questioning of the viability of the experimental method as used by social psychologists. In the preface to the first edition of this book, we wrote:

> During the past few years, the experimental method seems to have lost favor in the hearts of many social psychologists. Many of us have grown weary of reading about brief and lifeless encounters between strangers who cross each other's paths once— or not at all—in an antiseptic laboratory and then are rushed into isolation in order that they may fill out seven-point scales which confirm the small hypotheses of a limited mind. Like a faltering dictator who has extended himself beyond the range of his competence, the experimental method is increasingly subject to vituperative attacks by some who were once staunch supporters, but who now speak with the revolutionary rhetoric of a new convert. We welcome the questioning inherent in this development; we don't like dictatorships, and we feel that the field sorely needs a more representative methodology.

We wrote the first edition, in part, to reaffirm our belief in the importance and viability of the experimental method, to help our colleagues expand their options into new and different experimental procedures, and to demystify the experimental method in the minds of graduate students so that they might learn the skills that would help them take their places as creative and knowledgeable practitioners of what we regard as an important and noble art. In discussing the criticisms, we wrote:

> Many of the criticisms are well taken, and we have attempted to incorporate them in our remarks (e.g., the repeated emphasis on the importance of multiple methods). Yet we feel that much of the criticism of experimentation has been directed at non-

essential attributes: the college sophomore, the laboratory, the trivial tasks, the seven-point scales, and so on. An experiment is simply a form. Its single essential attribute is random assignment of subjects to conditions, and when this random assignment is possible and not ridiculous, it confers an important benefit—a certain minimum guaranteed level of confidence that the treatments caused the observed differences in behavior. Experiments are not unique in providing information about causal relationships, but they are wonderfully efficient compared to the alternatives currently available in social science. Many of the proposed "alternatives," such as the movement to field settings, are not incompatible with the experimental method. Others, such as the development of quasi-experimental designs, rely on the experiment as a standard against which the value (and potential shortcomings) of the quasi-experimental approximations can be assessed. An understanding of the experimental method is in some sense fundamental to an intelligent understanding of the advantages and disadvantages of the alternatives. The whole point of learning "methodology" is to be able to choose the most appropriate method for answering a particular question; our recent awakening to the recognition that the experiment may not always be the best method should not lead us to the absurd conclusion that it is never the best method.

More than a decade has passed since we put those thoughts on paper. The crisis appears to be over. But we have not changed our basic stance. As in the first edition, we will continue to make as strong a case as we can for the elegance of the experimental method, and for its improvement. As we stated in the first edition, within this basic form of the experiment, an infinite number of possibilities exist; it is our aim to help the reader explore some of those possibilities. Indeed, some of these possibilities have begun to merge with greater frequency during the past ten years.

For example, while the high-impact experimental procedure (in the tradition of Milgram, Asch, and Festinger & Carlsmith) remains the hallmark of experimental social psychology, contemporary research on *social cognition* has led to an increasingly popular methodological paradigm known as the "judgment experiment." In the judgment experiment, subjects are asked to recognize, recall, classify, evaluate, or reason about stimulus materials presented by the experimenter. Such experiments typically emphasize control and systematic variations in the stimulus environment; in these procedures, impact on subjects is important only insofar as the stimuli capture and hold their attention and elicit meaningful responses. Of course, there is considerable variation in the extent to which subject involvement is engendered by the experimental task, but what judgment studies have in common is the emphasis placed on stimulus control when subjects are asked to serve as *observers*.

Another important change has taken place since the first edition of this book: There has been a sharp increase in the number of researchers in social psychology who have turned their primary attention from basic experiments to social issues and problems confronting people outside the laboratory. Such *applied* social psychological research brings investigators face to face with the complexities of "real-world" phenomena. Although the impact of these phenomena—school desegregation, the arms race, the AIDS epidemic, the energy crisis—exceeds that of laboratory experiments, it is often difficult to assess their powerful effects experimentally. Much of what happens to people outside the laboratory is beyond the researcher's control, and it is often difficult to assign people randomly to treatments or conditions. For these reasons, applied researchers often forgo pure experimentation in favor of such alternatives as quasi-experiments, surveys, interviews, and systematic observations.

Accordingly, we have expanded our treatment of experimental and non-experimental methods of research in this second edition. Of course, we hasten to add that some things *haven't* changed. In our judgment, the controlled experiment *still* remains the single most powerful tool for enabling investigators to disentangle just what causes what, and is the standard against which other research methods continue to be measured. Therefore, it is the controlled experiment—in its myriad guises—that remains the focus of this edition.

A knowledge of experimental methodology is worthwhile, even for people who do not intend to conduct experiments. We are constantly bombarded with information from the print and electronic media, much of which contains explicit or implicit assertions about human social behavior. From Dear Abby to Phil Donahue, from Dr. Ruth to Ted Koppel, commentators are continually telling us about how we humans behave and why we behave as we do. It becomes the task of consumers of this information to separate the wheat from the chaff—to separate reasonable journalistic conclusions or interpretations from inferences that are biased or just plain wrong. Not all of our readers are going to do experiments; but the analytical skills involved in designing and conducting experiments are an important set of tools for examining assertions in this arena. Experiments are the product of a particular way of reasoning about the social world. It is our contention that knowing *how* to think is even more important than knowing *what* to think. There are no valid answers unless and until we find the correct way to formulate the question. It is that conviction that prompted us to write the first edition, and that fuels this effort.

As in the first edition, it is our goal to demystify the process of planning and conducting social psychological research by discussing in a sequential fashion the concerns, problems, pitfalls, and joys that researchers encounter from the time they first conceive of an idea or formulate a question to the time they close up shop, answer in hand.

In the first edition, we mentioned that we were indebted both to our students and to our professional colleagues whose ideas and suggestions contributed directly to our thinking. If anything, this debt has increased over the years, and we appreciate the many helpful comments and suggestions for the second edition provided by the following reviewers: Shelly Chaiken, New York University; Mykol Hamilton, University of California–Los Angeles; and Edward E. Jones, Princeton University. We are also grateful to the Center for Advanced Study in the Behavioral Sciences, where we sat on the terrace and planned both the first and second editions.

While handing out bouquets, we would like to take this opportunity to acknowledge the great debt we owe to our teachers. In this regard, it is particularly meaningful that we dedicate this volume to Leon Festinger; in the history of social psychology, he was arguably the greatest teacher of how to do experiments. He blazed a magnificent trail for those of us who followed him, by finding ways to ask important questions in a scientifically precise manner. As far as we know, Festinger never taught a course on how to do experiments; yet, because of the ground he broke, just about everyone doing experiments in social psychology is indirectly in his debt. For the authors of this volume, the debt is a bit more direct: one of us (E.A.) worked closely with Festinger for three years as his graduate research assistant; one of us (J.M.C.) worked with him as an undergraduate (and with Aronson as a graduate student); the others (M.H.G. and P.C.E.) can trace their lineage to Festinger by way of Aronson and Carlsmith, respectively. Festinger never taught a course on social psychological experimentation; he taught by example, and by critically looking over the shoulders of students who feel his presence even some thirty years later! We believe that the kind of mentor-student relationship that Festinger practiced is the best way to learn the art of experimentation. We offer this volume as a supplement—and as homage—to the apprenticeship model.

We made the decision to dedicate this book to Leon some time ago—as a surprise "gift" to that great and good man. Recent events have rendered the dedication particularly poignant: As the book was about to go to press, we were deeply saddened to learn of Leon Festinger's sudden death at the age of 69. Our sense of loss, both personal and professional, is immeasurable.

Elliot Aronson
Phoebe C. Ellsworth
Marti Hope Gonzales

METHODS OF RESEARCH IN SOCIAL PSYCHOLOGY

INTRODUCTION

A college student stands waiting outside the door of an empty classroom. It is the hour scheduled for a psychology experiment, and he is to be a subject. Standing with him are seven or eight other students, also waiting for the experimenter. One of them—the person who first called him up and told him about the experiment—is a friend. He doesn't know any of the others. Now that the moment has arrived, the student is a little nervous. He has never been in a psychology experiment before; he wonders whether the experimenter is going to ask him a lot of personal questions. What if the experimenter decides to probe his Freudian impulses in front of the other people? He looks around at the other subjects and comforts himself with the thought that he can't possibly be made *too* conspicuous. After all, they're all in the same boat.

The experimenter arrives, unlocks the classroom door, and asks the subjects to be seated in the front row. The student—seeing that his friend already has people sitting on both sides of him—takes one of the last remaining seats, near the end of the row. The experimenter then addresses the group, explaining that the experiment involves a test of perceptual judgment and that their task will be to match lines of equal length. Propping up two large, white cards in the chalk tray of the blackboard, the experimenter turns to the subjects and gives them instructions:

> This task involves the discrimination of lengths of lines. You see the pair of white cards in front. On the left is a single line; on the right, three lines of differing lengths are numbered 1, 2, and 3 in order. One of the three lines at the right is equal to the standard line at the left; you will decide in each case which is the equal line. You will state your judgment in terms of the corresponding number. There will be twelve such comparisons. As the number of lines is few and the group small, I shall call on

1

each of you in turn to announce your judgment, which I shall record here on the prepared form. Please be as accurate as possible. Let's start at the right and proceed to the left.

The student listens to these instructions and feels relieved, smiling to himself over his foolish speculations about Freudian questions. The experiment is simple and straightforward, and, at least on the first set of cards, the matching line is obvious. It is number 3. The student is even spared the embarrassment of having to speak first, since his seat is the next to the last in the row.

The first subject calls out his judgment: "It is line 3."

Then the second, third, and fourth subjects respond—and so on—until it is the student's turn. He says "3," and the person in the last seat agrees. It is an easy task; the judgment is unanimous. The experimenter removes the cards and replaces them with a new pair, with new standard and comparison lines. The student glances up and sees that again the matching line is number 3. The first subject calls out, "line 3," and the others follow suit. The student calls out "3" in his turn and watches the experimenter remove the second pair of cards. It is an easy task, but tedious. Ten more trials to go, and already he feels bored. Some personal questions would at least have been more stimulating.

"This one is line 2," announces the first subject.

The student stops daydreaming and returns his attention to the task. He glances up at the new set of cards. The matching line is obviously number 1. With a smirk, he turns to the person sitting next to him, but this person is staring calmly ahead at the cards and seems not to have noticed the first subject's careless mistake. The student checks the lines again; there is no doubt that number 1 is correct.

"Number 2," announces the second subject.

Now the student is getting nervous again. He squints at the line, but line number 2 is plainly shorter than the standard line. The second subject must be a real conformist, just repeating the first subject's answer, even though it was wrong. The student looks up at the experimenter, who is proceeding just as though everything were normal, pointing at the third subject for a judgment. The student leans forward a little to hear what the subject will say.

"Line 2."

Now the student is forced to think about what to do when his own turn comes. Suppose that the other three subjects also say it's line number 2. He will look like an idiot if he says it's number 1 after six people have already agreed that it was number 2. Maybe someone will save him. Maybe someone else will think it is number 1, so that he won't be the only deviant. But it *is* number 1. It's a simple question of fact—there is only one right answer, and it's obvious. So what could be the matter? He turns to the person next to him and whispers, "*What* were the instructions again?"

"You're supposed to pick the one that's the same length as the standard."

"Oh yeah, that's right."

"Number 2," calls out the subject next to him.

The experimenter is pointing at him now—it's his turn. He squints at the lines one more time, but there's no doubt.

"Number 1," he murmurs.

"What's that?" asks the experimenter. "I couldn't hear you."

"Well, it looks like number 1 to me," says the student, shrugging his shoulders.

He looks down at his shoes, but he can hear the group fall silent. He knows that they are all staring at him—the experimenter too—wondering why his judgment was the only one that was different. Maybe he's got some weird visual defect. But maybe—it's just possible—they were *all* sheep, following the first guy's mistake. Maybe by now the first subject is laughing because he sees what's happened, and all the others are feeling embarrassed because they don't have the courage to call it as they saw it. Maybe now that he has spoken for what he believed, the last subject will have the courage to do it, too. He looks up a little. The experimenter is pointing at the last subject.

"Number 2," says the last subject.

A new pair of cards is placed at the rack, and the student studies them intently. It's line number 3—clearly. He moves his head from side to side in case it's some kind of optical illusion based on the angle of vision. Number 3 it is, and he would defend his judgment no matter what. He waits apprehensively for the first subject's judgment.

"Line 1."

The experiment continues for eight more trials. Sometimes—to the student's immense relief—there is no argument; everyone else agrees with him. But more often, the group is unanimously against him. Unanimously. He is tense and acutely self-conscious, his confidence in his judgment shaken. How can it be that he sees a simple thing like that *differently* from everybody else? Maybe something is wrong with him. Maybe it is a special test to pick out crazy people. He dreads his turn. Once or twice he has called out the same number as the others, even though it didn't look that way to him. Thinking of the silence and the stares, seeing himself as the center of the trouble, he has convinced himself that there was room for doubt about the lines. But it doesn't make him feel any better. He feels he has betrayed himself by abandoning his own personal viewpoint. Whether he yields to the group or remains independent, he feels like a freak.

At the end of the experiment, the experimenter asks him to stay for a few minutes and asks him about his reactions. The experimenter then tells him that all members of the group were cooperating with the experimenter by giving wrong answers on some of the trials, calling two obviously different lines equal. The experiment was a study in social psychology designed to learn about reactions to group pressure, to find out how people feel and what they do when the evidence of their senses is contradicted by the unanimous judgments of their peers.

The subjects in this experiment conducted by Solomon Asch (1951) were deceived, and they were upset. They were led to believe that their own perceptions were seriously at variance with those of other people. In this experiment, the subjects are put into a state of conflict, and they must decide whether to go along with the judgment of the others or to stand alone. In either case, they experience misgivings, discomfort, and distress. If they resist, they feel they may suffer from scorn or ridicule from the others. If they yield, they may feel that they are cowards or conformists. This feeling may be intensified rather than relieved when, at the close of the session, the experimenter reveals that the entire situation was prearranged. Far from removing the discomfort, the experimenter may be adding insult to injury. The yielders may leave the experiment with reduced self-respect. They may believe—perhaps for the first time—that they lack the courage to stand up for their beliefs. Is it fair of the social psychologist to make people feel this way? The use of noxious or deceptive situations by an experimenter raises many ethical issues which cannot be taken lightly.

The problem of group pressure in society—pressure strong enough to move individuals to act against their beliefs and values—also raises many *social* issues which cannot be taken lightly. Asch was deeply concerned with the conditions that lead some people to yield or to resist when confronted with powerful group pressures. He believed that he could not answer questions about these conditions unless he placed people in a situation in which real group pressures were operating.

Why, though, did Asch decide to study group pressure by means of an *experiment?* Why did he bother to set up a special situation and train a large group of students to play the role of a unanimous majority and go to all the trouble involved in conducting a laboratory experiment, when there are hundreds of groups in the world outside of the laboratory whose members exert pressure for conformity? Why not simply observe one of these groups or ask people to think of situations in which they were under strong social pressure and to describe how they behaved? What are the characteristics of the experiment, as opposed to other forms of research? There are many ways of carrying out research in social psychology, and in Chapter 1 we discuss some of the advantages and disadvantages of experiments as research tools.

How could Asch be sure that what he was really studying was group pressure? How could he be sure that the experience was realistic to the subject? What does it mean to be "realistic" in an experiment? What would it mean if someone else did the experiment a little differently and got different results? How do we know whether the results that we get in an experiment have anything to do with the social situations outside the laboratory? There are some very serious problems with the use of the experimental method in an area as complex as social psychology; we examine some of these problems, as well as some partial solutions, in Chapter 2.

Why did the Asch experiment involve so much deception? Why did he tell the subjects a false story about perceptual judgment, train a large group of people to give incorrect responses, and pretend that the whole experiment was something different from what it was? What are the consequences of deceiving subjects? Are there ways of studying social processes without using deception? The use of deception in social psychological research raises serious and controversial issues—among them ethical issues about deception's potentially undesirable effects. In Chapter 3 we address some ethical quandaries faced by experimenters who use deception, and we evaluate some of the alternatives suggested by social psychologists. There are additional ethical issues, as well, for example, when participants in social psychological research are made to experience physical or psychological pain or are induced to confront unpleasant aspects of themselves. There are no fixed and ready solutions to these kinds of dilemmas faced by researchers, but we shall discuss some factors to consider in making the most humane and methodologically sound decisions.

In order to qualify as an experiment, a piece of research must have at least two different treatments. In the Asch experiment, some subjects made their judgments in the presence of a unanimous majority (treatment 1), and others made their judgments alone (treatment 2). Asch knew that the unanimous majority had a powerful effect on subjects' responses, because the subjects who had to make their judgments in the group made many more errors than those who had to make their judgments alone. But many other things might have affected the amount of conformity displayed by subjects. The results might have been different if the size of the majority had been different, if the perceptual task had been easier or harder, if the majority had not been completely unanimous; one can think of many variables that might have affected the results of the experiment. Should Asch have included these variables in his experiment? How many different kinds of situations should an experimenter study in an experiment? Should the same people be exposed to all the different situations in which the experimenter is interested, or should each subject be involved in only one of the experimental situations? Often a situation has many different elements. How can the researcher arrange an experiment to rule out the possibility that some extraneous element of the situation is responsible for the results? Given that only a limited number of subjects are available, how can the experimenter get the greatest amount of valid information about the experimental question? These and other questions have to do with the form of a research question—the underlying *design* of an experiment—and they are discussed in detail in Chapter 4.

Asch chose a true experimental design to answer his question about the effects of peer pressure on conformity. Not all researchers, however, limit their designs to experiments. Sometimes the nature of the research question or practical demands of real-world settings preclude the use of experiments, and researchers settle instead for alternative methods. What are some of these alternative methods of research? What situations dictate their use? What limitations are inherent in their use? How might these limitations be partially overcome? In Chapter 5, we shall take a brief detour from our focus on the controlled experiment and introduce the advantages and disadvantages of various nonexperimental methods of research in social psychology.

Assuming that an experiment is the method of choice for a researcher, how does he or she create or choose a setting for the experiment? How does the experimenter create a realistic situation in the laboratory in which to embed the treatments and measures? How does the experimenter describe the experiment to the subjects when they walk in the door? When is it necessary to have an elaborate scenario, and when will a simpler, more straightforward situation do just as well? Are there some questions better answered outside the laboratory? Should experimenters choose to conduct an experiment in the field, what real-world situations constitute an appropriate setting? What problems and concerns are unique to choosing a setting for a field experiment, and how can they be solved? Questions about creating or choosing settings, and about the stagecraft involved in some social psychological experiments, are discussed in detail in Chapter 6.

Asch chose to create a setting in the laboratory and used a group of peers who unanimously disagreed with the subject. Why did he choose this method? When a social psychologist wants to study the effect of a complicated social variable such as aggression or group pressure or authority, how is this variable created in the laboratory or the field? How can the experimenter be sure that the situation has an impact on the subject? In Chapter 7 we describe the techniques that social psychologists use to translate conceptual variables into systematically varied stimulus events.

After the subject has been exposed to the events created in the experiment, the experimenter wants to know how these events have affected the subject. How does the experimenter find out? What is measured? Should the experimenter ask the subjects, or simply observe the way they behave? If the experimenter chooses the latter technique, what exactly should be observed and recorded? How can the experimenter tell if what is being measured is what was intended? In Chapter 8 we examine the advantages and disadvantages of various kinds of measures used to study social behavior, some of the problems involved in measuring complex responses, and the questions that the social psychologist considers when choosing a measure.

Subjects in social psychological experiments are usually people, and they respond to the experimental situation with the same motivations and concerns that influence people's behavior outside the laboratory. Subjects—like most of us—want to look competent and attractive; they may want to impress the experimenter; they may want to win the experimenter's goodwill by doing what they believe is expected of them. How does the experimenter know whether the subjects are responding to the experimental situation, are just doing what they believe the experimenter expects them to do, or are simply trying to look good? How did Asch know whether his subjects were conforming to social pressure from their peers—as he intended—or to subtle social pressure from the experimenter himself, which he did not intend? How can the experimenter prevent various sources of bias? In some respects, subjects in experiments do not behave like people outside the experimental situation. Subjects in experiments are willing to do all sorts of things that they rarely do in other contexts.

How can we be sure that the subjects' behavior resembles what they would do in an analogous situation outside the experiment? How do we know that they are not doing what we ask them to do simply because they *are* in an experiment? Questions about the subjects' motivations, the experimenter's biases, and the situation's demand characteristics are examined in Chapter 9.

What happens when the experiment is over? The experimenter wants to know how subjects feel, what they thought of their experience, whether they interpreted the situation as the experimenter intended, and why they responded as they did. The subjects, however, will want to know what the experiment was all about, and how well they did. If deception of any kind has been employed in the experiment, subjects may find themselves embarrassed at having been "duped" or may even feel angry at having been "lied to" when the experimenter reveals the particulars of the deception and reasons for it. The subjects may also need some reassurance if the experimental situation was difficult, confusing, painful, or embarrassing. At the end of the experiment, the experimenter and subjects have a talk. Ideally, all the questions on both sides are answered, and the subjects leave feeling that the experience was valuable and rewarding and that they have made a real contribution to the research enterprise. In Chapter 10 we discuss this delicate and important conversation between subject and experimenter and present some ideas that may help to ensure that it accomplishes all its goals.

An experimenter's professional responsibilities do not end upon successful completion of an experiment. As a scientist, the experimenter wants to share her or his newfound knowledge with peers, for that is how social psychology—like other sciences—advances. Professional journals are the primary vehicles by which the results and implications of experiments are communicated. So, once the subjects have left the experimental setting enlightened, and once the data have been analyzed, it is the task of the experimenter to write up a report of the experiment. Typically, before the report appears in a social psychological journal, it is reviewed by experts in the field and, if necessary, revised by the experimenter before it is published. In psychology, there is a standard format experimenters use to communicate their findings. What form does the report take? How is it organized? What is included, and what is omitted? Is one particular style of writing preferable to another? Who is the intended audience? In Chapter 11 we will share our recommendations—and those of other researchers in social psychology—for writing an accurate, thorough, and engaging report once an experiment has been completed.

CHAPTER 1

AN INTRODUCTION TO EXPERIMENTS

WHY METHODOLOGY? WHY EXPERIMENTS?

"I'm not planning to do any psychological research myself, so why should I study research methods?" This is a question students ask us from time to time, and it deserves some answers.

The first answer is that you never know when you might be called upon to carry out some "research." No matter what field you enter, you may feel a need to improve your performance or that of your subordinates. You will inevitably run up against problems, and you may have to try out different ways of solving them. People in business are constantly striving to figure out ways to improve sales or productivity; doctors test new ways to persuade patients to follow their advice; lawyers try out new strategies for successful argument or negotiation. An understanding of the logic of research design is as useful in improving the informal research questions that continually arise in our professional and personal lives as it is in designing formal research studies.

The second answer is that understanding how to do research prepares us to *evaluate* the research we read about. In this information age, we are inundated with communications from the press and television media: If parents share custody of their children after divorce, the children will be better off than if only one parent has custody; coconut oil raises cholesterol and olive oil lowers it; bottling up one's emotions leads to illness; "back to basics" education results in higher S.A.T. scores; and so on and so on. As consumers of this information, we face the task of figuring out what claims to believe, of separating reasonable journalistic conclusions or interpretations from inferences that are biased or just plain wrong. An understanding of research methods prompts the consumer to ask "How do they know?" when faced with news of a new discovery and provides the tools to answer that question. Quite often it turns out that "they" don't know.

Finally, studying the methods of social psychological research can improve people's reasoning ability more generally. Darrin Lehman and his colleagues (Lehman, Lempert & Nisbett, 1988) found that training in social psychology improved students' ability to reason about everyday problems. Because the topics studied by social psychologists are quite similar to the problems we face in everyday life, learning to think about them the way researchers do creates skills that can be transferred to real-life problems.

"Why does your book place such a heavy emphasis on the *experiment,* when there are quite a few other methods for conducting psychological research?" This is a question our colleagues ask us from time to time, and it, too, deserves an answer.

The reason is that a true experiment is the best method for finding out whether one thing really *causes* another. Very often our questions are questions about causality. Does happiness *cause* people to behave more kindly? Does back-to-basics education *cause* higher S.A.T. scores? Does violent television programming *increase* aggression? Does enforced cooperation *reduce* racial prejudice? A well-conducted experiment can provide a definitive answer to questions like these, at least in its own particular context. Finding out whether the results apply in other contexts typically requires further research.

But the experiment is not the only method in the researcher's repertoire, and sometimes the student of human behavior chooses a different strategy. There are three common reasons for conducting nonexperimental research. The first is that the researcher is not interested in a question about cause and effect. A pollster, for example, may be interested in predicting who is going to win the next election, without caring *why* one candidate will be favored over another. Or, a researcher may simply want to demonstrate the *existence* of some phenomenon: that people from all over the world use the same facial expressions to communicate emotions or that people are prone to certain kinds of mistakes in reasoning—for example, they overestimate the "normality" of their own tastes and behavior (Ross, Greene & House, 1977), they can't resist coming up with logical explanations of events that are really random (Feller, 1968; Ward & Jenkins, 1965), they overestimate the likelihood of events that are vivid and more easily called to mind (Gregory, Burroughs & Ainslie, 1985; Sherman et al., 1985). For questions that do not involve causality, the experiment is not essential, although it may be very useful.

The second reason for conducting nonexperimental research is that in some situations an experiment would be unethical or impossible. If we want to know whether marriages of dissimilar people are more likely to end in divorce than marriages of similar people, we have to study the question nonexperimentally. We cannot force a hundred women to marry men who resemble them and a hundred others to marry men who are totally unlike them. There are a host of topics—mental illness, powerful emotions, the deterrent effect of the death penalty—that we are morally unwilling to impose upon people. There are a host of others—gender, race, birth order—that we can't impose upon people. Because many extremely important questions involve qualities that cannot be controlled experimentally, researchers have devised increasingly sophisticated ways of conducting nonexperimental research to reveal causes. We will discuss some of these methods later on. They range from nearly worthless to fairly close approximations of true experiments, but they are all approximations. The better approximations *are* better because they are more fully informed by an understanding of the logic of the true experiment. Because the true experiment is the standard by which studies of cause and effect are evaluated, and because it is impossible to understand the virtues and shortcomings of the varieties of nonexperimental research without a thorough understanding of experimental research, we begin with experiments and emphasize them throughout this book.

The third reason that researchers do nonexperimental research is to *supplement* experimental research, so that the advantages of one kind of research can compensate for the shortcomings of the other: Two methods are better than one. Suppose you want to find out whether there is racism in criminal sentencing. You might first do an experiment, giving jury-eligible citizens a series of cases which differ only in that half the defendants are black and half are white. Thus, some subjects would hear about an armed robbery committed by a white man, and others would hear about the exact same events, only the perpetrator would be black. If the subjects recommended longer sentences for the black defendants, you could be sure that this was because they were black. This would be an enormously important finding, one very difficult to prove in any other manner. Nonetheless, your study would be open to criticism that your subjects were not *really* sentencing anybody and that their experience differed from that of real jurors in innumerable ways. So you might go out and collect data on hundreds of real trials, recording not only the race of the defendant but all the other factors that might lead to harsher sentencing—what the crime was, who the victim was, and so on. If blacks received longer sentences in this study, you wouldn't know for certain it was because they were black. It could be some other factor you failed to take into account—for example, the quality of the attorney. But you would know that your experimental results hold up in the real world. The two studies together are more persuasive than either alone: The first tells you that race influences sentences; the second tells you that real jurors behave like your subjects.

THE NATURE OF EXPERIMENTS

A scientific investigation starts with a question. Why do people yield to group pressure? Do people like something better if they have had to work hard to get it? How does a steady diet of violent television shows affect a person's behavior? Any question can be studied scientifically, provided that it involves something that can be observed. After formulating the question, the scientist must decide exactly what to observe in order to answer it. For many questions, the scientist's next task will be to find a situation in which to observe the phenomenon. A researcher who is interested in the effects of different kinds of college curriculum on graduates' subsequent success, for example, will have to specify the types of curriculum that might make a difference. For some questions, the scientist may even have to wait for circumstances in which to make observations. Social psychologists who want to study people's responses to a natural disaster will have to wait for a flood, tornado, earthquake or other calamity to happen. Similarly, astronomers must wait for the earth to move into a particular position before they can make specific observations.

An experiment differs from other types of scientific investigation in that rather than searching for naturally occurring situations, the experimenter *creates* the conditions necessary for observation. There are several advantages to this procedure. First, by setting up the conditions, the experimenter has a better chance of capturing exactly what was intended. For example, Solomon Asch deliberately set up his experimental group so that the subject was faced with several other people who steadily and consistently disagreed with him about an apparently obvious judgment. It is hard to imagine a natural situation which so clearly and forcefully pits the evidence of one's senses against the evidence of one's peers.

Second, the experimenter can *control*—and thus systematically *vary*—conditions in order to study the same general situation with and without the crucial element. In studying the effects of group pressure, Asch arranged his experiment so that all subjects were members of a group in which the members' task was to judge the lengths of lines. In some groups the members called out their judgments so that everybody could hear them, and of course the subject had to let everybody hear his judgment, too. Since expressing his true opinion meant making a spectacle of himself by announcing the only deviant opinion in the group, there was a great deal of pressure toward conformity in these groups. In one group (the control group), the members simply wrote down their judgments, so the subject had no idea what the other members were saying and thus experienced no group pressure. If Asch had used a non-experimental procedure, he would have had to try and find naturally occurring groups working on similar tasks in similar settings but differing in that some groups were characterized by high amounts of pressure on the individual and others were pressure-free. It is often extremely difficult, if not impossible, to find natural situations which are alike in all respects except the one that interests the experimenter.

Finally, and most important, the experimenter has the power to decide which individuals will be exposed to which conditions. Outside the experiment, people who are more independent may choose groups in which less pressure is exerted; less independent people may like to have their decisions made for them and so prefer groups with obvious pressure. Thus, if the individuals in the groups with the most pressure conformed more to their groups, this finding might not be due to the group pressure but to the fact that the people who chose those groups were more conforming to begin with. In an experiment, the experimenter assigns subjects to treatments *at random.* Thus, whether a person happens to be a member of a group that exerts pressure is due to chance alone and not to any prior differences among subjects. If the subjects in the group that exerts pressure make more errors in their judgments of the lines, the experimenter *knows* that this difference was caused by the group pressure and not by any prior differences in the individuals who were members of the two types of group. Because the experimenter can assign subjects to treatments at random, the experiment, unlike other procedures, can provide a strong basis for making statements about causality.

Experiments have certain general features in common. Because much of this book will be concerned with the actual procedures of experimentation, it is important to start out with a general overview of these procedures, introducing and defining the terms that we will be using in subsequent chapters. In order to make this presentation more concrete, we will turn again to the Asch experiment as an example of how an experiment is put together. Having looked at the Asch experiment through the eyes of the subject, we will now reexamine it from the point of view of the experimenter.

The experimenter begins with an idea, or a question, or a hypothesis. The idea may derive from a theory, from doubts about the validity of some previous experiment or theoretical formulation, from a concern with a social problem, or simply from curiosity about some kind of behavior. Asch was generally interested in the conditions of submission to group pressure, which he felt to be a problem involving important social issues. He was dissatisfied with earlier social psychological accounts, because they tended to give the phenomenon a label, such as "suggestion," which explained little, and because they paid too little attention to the processes that enable a person to *withstand* group pressure. Thus, like most experimenters, he was interested in the problem for a variety of reasons.

Independent and Dependent Variables

The next step is to translate a concern for a general problem area into a specific question. Asch's specific question was: What are "the social and personal conditions that induce individuals to resist or to yield to group pressures when the latter are perceived to be *contrary to fact?*" (Asch, 1965, p. 393), and he started out with one "social condition"—the presence of a unanimous majority. In many experiments the basic question is stated as a **hypothesis**, or prediction about the outcome of an experiment. Either way, an inquiry is made about a causal sequence. The antecedent event, or "cause," in the proposed sequence is called the **independent variable,** because the experimenter creates it and controls its variation; it is independent of all other causative influences. The experimenter is sometimes said to *manipulate* the independent variable. In the initial Asch experiment, the independent variable was group pressure—specifically, the pressure assumed to be exerted by a unanimous majority which gave false judgments. The "effect" in the causal sequence is called the

dependent variable, because the experimenter expects its value to depend on the changes introduced in the independent variable. In the Asch experiment the dependent variable was the number of errors the subject made in the direction of the false judgments of the majority.

Technically, a **variable** is any attribute which can assume different values among the members of a class of subjects or events but which has only one value for any given member of that class at any given time. Thus, height is a variable within the class of human beings (and other things); within the class as a whole height can assume a large range of values, but at any given moment a given human being can be only one height. Some variables, such as height, are *continuous* and can assume any value within some finite range. Others, such as virginity, are *discrete* and can assume only a limited number of values—in the case of virginity, only one of two: presence or absence. In a psychology experiment the independent variable is usually a stimulus event, and the dependent variable is a response made by the subject.

The values of the independent variable (or variables) that the experimenter chooses to use define the experimental **conditions.** At least two values of the independent variable are necessary in order to demonstrate that the variable is having an effect, since in an "experiment" with only one value of the independent variable, it is impossible to determine whether the results (the measurements of the dependent variable) have anything to do with the presence of the independent variable. In the Asch experiment there were two values of the independent variable: presence of group pressure (in the form of a unanimous majority) and absence of group pressure. In a study of this sort, in which there are only two conditions defined by presence *versus* absence of the independent variable, the subjects who receive the independent variable (those who had to make their judgments in the face of unanimous opposition) constitute the **experimental group,** and those who do not receive it constitute the **control group.**

Having formulated a question or hypothesis, the experimenter must decide how to turn it into a set of experimental procedures. One of the most important parts of this transformation involves translating the concepts of the hypothesis into specific, observable events. This substitution may be viewed as the **empirical realization** of the conceptual or abstract variables contained in the question. An abstract concept such as "group pressure" is "made real" in terms of the events actually experienced by the subjects—thus the term "empirical realization." Usually in social psychology the process of creating an empirical realization is intimately bound up with decisions about the overall staging and context of the experiment. Thus, in the Asch experiment the impact of the group pressure depended on a great many elements of the situation—the apparent simplicity of the task, the public announcements of the members' judgments, the unanimity of the judgments by the other "subjects," and the consistency of those judgments through time. Certainly, this was an extreme form of group pressure, unlikely to be encountered outside the laboratory, and Asch intended it to be so. In many real-life situations, people are able to avoid the dilemma created by a contradiction between their own beliefs and the norms of a group. For one thing, the ambiguity of some situations allows people to avoid even perceiving that there is a dilemma. Also, the fact that people typically are not required to state their opinions publicly may allow them to assume that they are not the kind of people who yield to others. In addition, it is often possible to explain away discrepancies by referring to factors outside the situation or by assuming that the majority are motivated by a desire to persuade others or to play devil's advocate and don't "really mean" what they are saying. Asch wanted to remove these extraneous defenses in his empirical realization of the concept "group pressure" in order to study it in the pure case, forcing the subject to face the dilemma and to resolve it by yielding or by standing firm. Once having determined what happens in this extreme case, he could then make the situation less extreme and compare the results with those obtained in the initial experiment.

In Asch's experiment the empirical realization of the dependent variable followed naturally from the rest of the situation; the conceptual dependent variable, yielding, was simply realized as the number of times a subject went along with the group and gave the wrong answer.

For the kind of complex variables studied by social psychologists—variables such as guilt, anxiety, self-esteem, and group pressure—there is no one "right" empirical realization. Some are better than others, and in Chapters 7 and 8 we will discuss some of the characteristics of a good empirical realization and some of the techniques for creating one. More than one empirical realization may capture essential features of some variable such as "group pressure," but they may emphasize different features. An experimenter interested in studying how people evade facing the dilemma posed by conflicting group and personal values, for example, might create a situation in which the pressure was less obvious or in which the subject could attribute the group's disagreement to some external factor. This experimenter's data on yielding might look very different from those obtained by Asch. Such was the case in an experiment by Lee Ross, Günter Bierbrauer, and Susan Hoffman (1976), in which the experimenters manipulated possible *reasons* for the incorrect judgments of confederates. They found that when the subjects could find some *reason* for the difference between their perceptions and the majority answer—even if it was not a very convincing reason—they no longer yielded. Of course, their results did not invalidate Asch's findings about the effects of group pressure. When different empirical realizations of a concept produce different kinds of behavior, it is an indication that the original conceptual variable—in this case, group pressure—is too general and needs to be differentiated into a number of less general related variables. Ross and his colleagues showed that if people can convince themselves that the majority is responding to a "different situation," they will be much less likely to give in to group pressure. By this process of differentiation, social psychologists arrive at a more detailed and comprehensive understanding of a general category of behavior—such as people's susceptibility to group conformity pressures.

Sources of Error

Before actually beginning to run the experiment, the experimenter must also consider various types of *error* that might arise. Although we are interested in varying only the independent variable, in practice it is impossible to design an experiment in which nothing except the independent variable affects the outcome. This is true primarily because we are dealing with human beings. Anything besides the independent variable that affects subjects' behavior is a source of error. Subjects bring personal variables into the experiment—age, background, alertness, intelligence, and so on. Subjects may differ with respect to their experience with the type of independent variable being manipulated and with the dependent variable being measured. For example, the average number of errors made by a subject in the Asch experiment was 3.84 (out of 12 trials), but there was wide variability; some subjects never gave in to the group, and others displaced their estimates toward the majority in more than half the trials. Asch made a point of analyzing individual differences among subjects that might have affected their tendency to yield. One factor that often differentiated between the yielders and nonyielders was self-esteem, with the yielders showing "primary doubt and lack of self-confidence" (1965, p. 397). Variables such as these are called **subject variables;** since the experimenter can exert no direct control over them, they are typically sources of error.

Two types of error can affect the outcome of an experiment. The first type, called **random error,** refers to extraneous variables whose *average* influence on the outcome is the same in both (or all) conditions. Subject variables and minor events that occur during particular experimental sessions contribute to random error, as do all the other extraneous influences on the subject's behavior which are not controlled by the experimenter and which are equally likely to occur in any of the conditions of the experiment. In this sense, random error constitutes the "noise" in the system, from which the experimenter is trying to extract a meaningful "signal" or *consistent* type of variation produced by the treatments administered.

If a given source of random error tends to raise the subjects' scores in one condition, it will also raise the scores of those in the other conditions. This will decrease our confidence in the actual numerical levels of the scores (since they will all be artificially inflated), but it will not decrease our confidence in the *differences* between the two conditions, since both sets of scores are raised by the same amount.

If, as is more usual, a given source of random error simply increases the range of scores in both groups, it is possible that this increased variability will obscure the effects of the independent variable, and the experimenter may erroneously conclude that the treatment had no effect. Had the investigator been able either to eliminate more of the random error (reduce the noise) or to use a stronger treatment (generate a stronger signal), the treatment difference might have been large enough to show up against the noisy background.

The second type of error, called **systematic error** (constant error), is much more dangerous. Whereas random error typically increases the baseline variability in both conditions, systematic error tends to influence all the scores in one condition in the same direction and to have no effect, or a different effect, on the scores in the other condition. Thus, systematic error can affect the size of the difference between the two conditions, thereby distorting the experimenter's source of information about the effects of the independent variable and possibly vitiating the results of the whole experiment.

Obviously, it is in the experimenter's best interest to attempt to reduce both kinds of error, but of the two types, it is more important to eliminate systematic error. If there is too much random error in an experiment, a true relationship between the independent and dependent variables can be obscured, so that the experimenter might erroneously conclude that the variables are unrelated. *Systematic* error, however, can make it look as though two variables are related, when in fact they are not; thus, the experimenter concludes that the hypothesis has been confirmed when it has not. In the first case, the experiment will not be published, and the worst that can happen is that the experimenter will fail to discover an interesting phenomenon which a more carefully controlled experiment would have revealed. In many cases, the experimenter is interested enough in the hypothesis to attempt another experiment on the same topic, improving the procedure, so that the true relationship does not remain buried for long. In the case of systematic error, however, the experimenter often publishes the spurious finding, and it remains in the literature, influencing experimental work for a long time and stimulating efforts that could more productively be directed elsewhere. Unfortunately, social psychology is far from being an exact science, and once such a spurious finding becomes part of the literature, it can be very difficult to disprove.

One way of eliminating systematic error is to convert it to random error. Different sources of variability, such as subject variables, the experimenter's behavior, time of day and distractions and extraneous events within the experimental setting, are not in *themselves* automatically random or systematic influences. Whether they affect the subject's responses randomly or systematically depends on whether certain experimental precautions have been taken. For example, suppose that some extremely nearsighted subjects in the Asch experiment were unable to see the lines well enough to judge them accurately. If for some reason all these subjects were placed in the experimental group, their inability to judge the lines accurately would spuriously increase the number of errors made by subjects in that group and perhaps cause the experimenter to draw unwarranted conclusions about the effects of group pressure. Perhaps the experimenter unintentionally biased the data by assigning all the nearsighted subjects to the experimental group; perhaps they were all friends and came to the experiment together, and the experimenter happened to be running only the experimental group that afternoon. Whatever the reason, anything that results in the overrepresentation of subjects of a given type in one experimental condition is a potential source of systematic error. If the experimenter had assigned each subject to the experimental or control group *at random,* however, the error would be *random* error. It would be highly un-likely that all nearsighted subjects would end up in the experimental group, and thus the increased misjudgments made by these subjects would be bal-anced out by similarly inflated misjudgments made by their counterparts in the control group.

Random Assignment of Subjects to Treatments

In general, **random assignment** is one of the experimenter's most important tools for ruling out the dangers of systematic error. It is so important, in fact, that it is considered the criterial attribute for defining a study as an *experiment.* The most common variety of random assignment is the random assignment of subjects to experimental conditions, as in the example of the nearsighted sub-jects mentioned above. The experimenter's goal is to make sure that none of the myriad extraneous factors which might affect a subject's behavior in the experiment—such as nearsightedness, intelligence, or a bad mood—is more likely to be associated with one of the experimental conditions than with the other (or others). Since the conditions are defined by the independent-variable treatments, they must be kept free of any extraneous factors that may cause differences between them in order for the experimenter to conclude that the differences were *caused* by the independent variable alone. If subjects in one condition were more nearsighted, or intelligent, or unhappy, the experimenter could not conclude that the independent variable was affecting their behavior; any differences that show up in the behavior of the subjects in the two condi-tions might be due to differences in the type of subject assigned to the condi-tions in the first place.

Assigning subjects to conditions at random means that each subject who walks in the door has an equal chance of being placed in any one of the ex-perimental conditions. If there are two conditions, each subject has a 50:50 chance of being in either one.[1] Thus, nearsighted subjects have a 50:50 chance of being in the experimental group or the control group, intelligent sub-

---

[1] With two conditions, one method for random assignment is simply to flip a coin, assigning "heads" to the experimental group and "tails" to the control group. A table of random numbers is a better and safer tool for random assignment and has the advantage of being adaptable to any number of conditions. A table of random numbers is simply a table in which the digits 0 to 9 are arranged in random order in a long sequence. The experimenter decides arbitrarily that each ex-perimental group will correspond to a number or type of number. With two groups, you might decide that the odd numbers will represent the experimental group and the even numbers the con-trol group. Then you pick a place on the table to begin, again arbitrarily. If the first number you come to is odd, the first subject is assigned to the experimental group. You continue through the table in order until you have run as many subjects as you want. With three conditions, you might decide that the numbers 1 to 3 will correspond to the first condition, 4 to 6 to the second, and 7 to 9 to the third (ignoring zero). If it is important to come out with an equal number of subjects in all groups, a table of random permutations is used. In this kind of table, the numbers 0 to 9, for ex-ample, are put in random order once, so that all ten digits appear. Then the next ten digits are 0 to 9 again, in some other random order. This assures that after every ten subjects you will have equal numbers in the experimental and the control group.

jects have a 50:50 chance, unhappy subjects have a 50:50 chance, and so on for *every* kind of characteristic that can differentiate among subjects. The end result is that there will be roughly equal numbers of nearsighted subjects in the experimental and control groups, likewise for intelligent subjects, unhappy subjects, and so on for *all* kinds of traits. By randomly assigning subjects to conditions, the experimenter can be sure that *no* subject variable is more likely to occur in one condition than in the other and thus that no subject variable is a source of systematic error.

We can look at random assignment in another way—as the "great equalizer." Because random assignment ensures that all extraneous factors that might influence the subject's behavior in the experiment are approximately equal in the two (or more) conditions, we would expect that if we *left out* the experimental treatments and ran both groups of subjects as control groups, the average scores of these two groups on the dependent-variable measure would be the same. Not every subject would have the same score, of course. Even in Asch's control group, in which there was no group pressure, 5 percent of the subjects made errors of judgment. With random assignment, we can assume that in a group of subjects exposed to group pressure, about 5 percent of them would have made mistakes even without the pressure. Since in the Asch experiment 74 percent of the subjects who were exposed to group pressure made at least one mistake, we can conclude that the independent variable had a large effect.

Factors other than subject variables can cause systematic error, if they are associated with some conditions more than with others, and these factors may also be eliminated by random assignment. For example, if there is more than one experimenter, it is important that each experimenter run about the same number of subjects in each condition. If one experimenter ran subjects only (or mostly) in the experimental group, and the other experimenter ran subjects mostly in the control group, differences between these two conditions could be due to differences in the personalities or techniques of the two experimenters. Thus, subjects should be assigned to experimenters at random.

Holding Variables Constant

Although random assignment is essential for eliminating systematic error, it cannot reduce the amount of random error, or "background noise," in the experiment. If the treatment is only one of a large number of factors influencing the subject's behavior in important ways, its influence may not be strong enough to stand out above the variability introduced by all the other extraneous factors. A common means of controlling random error is to *hold* important extraneous variable *constant* at a single level (or to reduce the possible levels to a more limited range). In his initial experiment Asch always used the same sets of lines (holding stimulus materials constant) and always used a unanimous majority of seven accomplices (holding size of group constant). In regard to our hypothetical example of the nearsighted subjects, Asch might also have given all subjects eye tests before they participated in the experiment and eliminated those who couldn't see well, thus holding visual acuity constant at 20-20. The principle behind the technique of holding a variable constant is that the less an extraneous variable is allowed to vary, the less it can affect the dependent variable. Of course, it is never possible to control all sources of random error; the experimenter must use judgment in deciding which extraneous factors are most likely to produce large fluctuations in the particular dependent variable being measured.

In all social psychological experiments some factors are held constant, and others, typically considered less important, are allowed to vary at random. Although holding variables constant may appeal to our sense of tidiness, it does have some drawbacks in that it places limits on the conclusions that can be drawn from the experiment. By preventing a variable from affecting the subjects' behavior in a given experimental setting—by holding it constant—we give up the possibility of finding out whether that variable would have affected subjects' behavior had it been allowed to vary. Sometimes the experimenter doesn't care much whether it would have had an effect, because it is not relevant to the particular enquiry. Often, the investigator *knows* it would have had an effect but wants to eliminate this effect in order to observe the effect of some other variable against a clear background. For example, it is frequently found that women are more likely to receive help than are men, especially the kind of "chivalrous" assistance elicited in experimental studies of helping behavior. In addition, men are more likely to help women than they are to help other men, although women are as likely to come to men's aid as to women's (Eagly & Crowley, 1986). Now suppose an experimenter wants to study something else that might influence people's willingness to help others—for example, to find out whether feeling happy makes people more helpful. An experimenter who runs subjects of both sexes—or who uses both male and female confederates—can expect to find very different levels of helping, depending on the gender combination of needy person and helper, and this complicated "background" may make it very difficult to tease out the effect of a happy mood. Therefore, in conducting experiments on helping behavior, investigators often hold the sex of the subject and/or sex of the "needy" confederate constant—for example, using only male subjects and male sufferers.

Although this procedure is valuable, holding a variable constant at some level restricts the generality of the experimenter's conclusions to situations involving that particular level. The helping researcher only knows that happy men are more likely to help other men; whether they are more likely to help women, and whether women's moods affect their helpfulness, remain unanswered questions. After Asch's initial experiment, it was clear that subjects tended to conform to the judgments of a unanimous majority of seven. But what about a unanimous majority of six? Or five? Or three? We might be tempted to make an educated guess, but conclusions from the actual experiment performed would have to be limited to majorities of seven. We have no information about the importance of the size of the majority in inducing conformity, and thus we cannot generalize to majorities of other sizes.

Now, suppose that Asch had not bothered to hold the size of the majority constant but had let it vary, say, between three and eight. If group size were *not* an important variable affecting conformity, he would have obtained basically the same results as he did with the constant majority of seven. As a result of his experiment, he could have generalized the conformity effect to a wider range of majority sizes. If group size *were* an important variable, however, some of his majorities would have induced subjects to make many misjudgments, and other majorities might not have induced subjects to conform at all. Thus, many *more* of the subjects in the experimental group would have behaved like members of the control group, making no errors at all, and the variability *within* the experimental group would have been increased. There would have been a large increase in random error, and it is quite possible that the overall effect of group pressure would have gone undetected. Allowing a potentially important factor to vary at random is a gamble. If it "pays off"—if the experiment produces significant results—the experimenter is more confident of the generality of these results than if the factor had been held constant. If the experiment does not show any difference between the groups, background error may have obscured a true difference that would have been apparent had the experimenter held the variable constant. Holding variables constant, then, is the safer procedure, although allowing them to vary at random is *potentially* more informative.

Systematic Variation

Besides holding a variable constant and allowing it to vary at random, the researcher has a third choice—varying it *systematically,* adding it to the experiment as a second independent variable. In effect, the experimenter asks a direct question about the additional variable instead of hoping to pick up some relevant information indirectly, as happens when the variable is allowed to vary randomly. In the Asch experiment, this would be equivalent to having several different groups of subjects who were exposed to group pressure, some subjects being assigned to a condition in which the majority consisted of seven people, some to a majority of six people, some to a majority of eight people, and so on. By comparing the number of errors made by subjects in each of these conditions, the experimenter gains a much surer understanding of the relation between size of majority and conformity than is possible by with either of the other methods.

In fact, Asch did vary the size of the majority systematically in a later experiment. Some subjects were members of pairs—they were faced with only one other person who gave wrong answers. Other subjects had to face a majority of two; others, majorities of three, four, or eight; and finally, some subjects were members of very large groups in which the size of the majority ranged from ten to fifteen. Asch found that subjects could hold their own against a single other person who disagreed with them; no subject made more than one mistake, and most made none at all. When the majority consisted of two, conformity began to show up, subjects averaging 1.53 errors. With three people in the majority, the effect increased to its full strength, with subjects making an average of four errors. Larger majorities, even those of ten to fifteen, did not produce effects stronger that did a majority of three.

Interactions

Another advantage of varying more than one independent variable at a time is that this technique can provide information about how one independent variable *interacts* with the other. An **interaction** is a situation in which the independent variable has *different* effects, depending on the value of some other variable. If the other variable is also experimentally varied, the data will show the interaction. But if the other variable is either held constant or allowed to vary at random, information about the interaction may be suppressed.

To take a hypothetical example, suppose that Asch had run an experiment in which there were two independent variables—majority size and similarity of the people in the majority to the subject. To simplify things, we will imagine that only two levels of each of these variables are used; thus, the experimenter has (1) majorities of two and (2) majorities of four, and these majorities are made up either of people very similar to the subject or of people very dissimilar to the subject. Each subject is randomly assigned to one of these four types of groups.

Given this design, we can envision several possible patterns of results. If the size of the majority has a large influence on the number of errors the subject makes but the similarity of the group makes no difference, the results would look something like those shown in Figure 1-1. This graph illustrates a *main effect* for majority size and *no effect* for the similarity variable. (A main effect is an effect caused by a single variable.) In other words, large majorities (defined here as four people) cause people to conform more than do small majorities (defined here as two people), and they have this effect whether or not the members of the majority are similar to the subject.

We can also envision a situation in which people tend to conform to the judgments of those who are similar to them but are able to maintain their independence when they perceive the others as dissimilar, regardless of how many others there are. In other words, we can imagine a situation in which there is a *main effect* for similarity, with majority size having no effect. This situation is illustrated in Figure 1-2.

Or, we can envision a situation in which both the size of the majority and its similarity to the subject make a difference. For example, subjects may tend to agree with similar people more than with dissimilar people, and they *also* tend to agree with large majorities (four people). There are then *two main effects,* one for similarity and one for majority size, as shown in Figure 1-3.

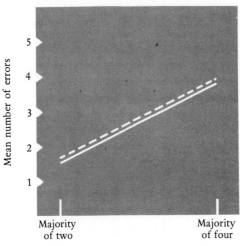

FIGURE 1-1
Main effect for group size; no effect for similarity.

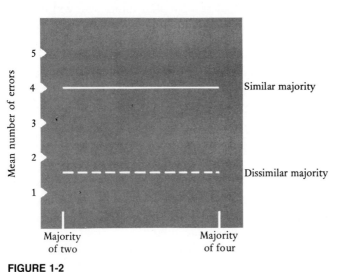

FIGURE 1-2
Main effect for similarity; no effect for group size.

In each of the three figures, the two lines have the same slope. This means that each variable has a constant effect, independent of the effect of the other variable. In Figure 1-3, the effect of increasing the majority size from two to four is to increase the number of errors by an average of two, regardless of whether the group is made up of people who are similar or dissimilar to the subject. The effect of making the group similar instead of dissimilar is to raise

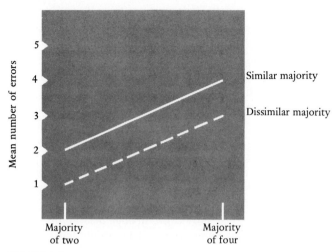

FIGURE 1-3
Main effect for group size; main effect for similarity.

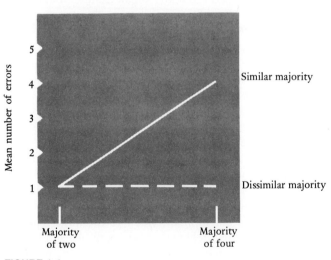

FIGURE 1-4
An example of an interaction between majority size and similarity.

the number of errors by an average of one, regardless of whether the majority size is two or four.

In an *interaction,* the slopes of the two lines will differ. This means that the effect of one independent variable (or both) is not constant, but varies depending on the value of the other independent variable. In Figure 1-4 we see one type of interaction that might exist in our hypothetical example. Majority size has an effect, but only when the group is similar; the effect of majority size depends on the value of the other independent variable, similarity of the group. It takes a *large* group of *similar* people to get the subject to make many mistakes. Neither small groups nor dissimilar groups have any effect. By varying two variables at once, their combined effects are readily apparent.

What would have happened if the experimenter had held one of the variables constant? Obviously, part of the picture would be missing. For example, if similarity had been held constant—if only similar groups had been used—the experimenter would have found a strong effect and might therefore be tempted to overgeneralize, lacking the evidence of the effects of majority size in *dissimilar* groups which is available in Figure 1-4. In effect, the experimenter would not know whether the effects of majority size were those of Figure 1-1, Figure 1-3, or Figure 1-4, having only the data for similar groups, and these data are the same in all three situations. However, if only *dissimilar* groups had been used, the experimenter might have erroneously concluded that majority size does not affect conformity.

The experimenter would also obtain an incomplete picture of the situation by holding majority size constant, varying only similarity. Holding majority size constant at four, for example, the experimenter might assume that similar groups always tend to produce more conformity; at two, the experimenter might give up the whole line of research, since the results would indicate that similarity makes no difference.

What would have happened if similarity had been allowed to vary at random? Since the groups that were more similar would tend to influence the subject strongly and those that were less similar would have only a weak influence, we would expect to get an effect somewhere in between the strong effect for all-similar groups and the zero effect for all-dissimilar groups. Figure 1-5 shows what the data might look like.

Whether or not the experimenter decides that the data conform to a particular hypothesis about the effect of majority size, it is clear that less information is available than if similarity had also been varied. An experimenter who examines the data closely may note that the effect of majority size is not very uniform, as it would be were there a single main effect. In the large-majority condition, some subjects conform a great deal and some not at all, and the experimenter might be led to conduct further experiments, introducing other variables, to find out why. However, if the diluted effect of group size does not attain significance, the investigator might decide that the hypothesis was no good and therefore abandon the study of majority effects.

Artifacts

Although there are inherent difficulties in both strategies—holding variables constant and allowing them to vary at random—both are necessary techniques in any social psychological experiment, since there are so many possible variables that affect social behavior that it is impossible to vary them all system-

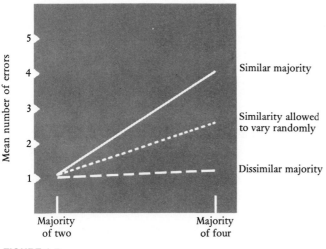

FIGURE 1-5
Results of a hypothetical conformity experiment, with similarity
allowed to vary at random.

atically in a single experiment. Some random error, as well as many limitations
on the generality of the findings, are inevitable. It is crucial, however, to make
sure that no other variables change *with* the independent variable, always taking on one range of values in the experimental group and another in the control
group. Such variables can be sources of systematic error in that they can cause
differences between the two groups, differences which are mistakenly attributed to the independent variable. An extraneous variable that varies along with
the treatment is said to be *confounded* with the independent variable. When
the extraneous variable is a relatively trivial methodological event, the error is
often called an **artifact.**

To take a hypothetical example, if the subjects in the experimental group
undergo a complex and interesting experience during the presentation of the
independent variable, but subjects in the control group simply come into the
lab and sit and wait for the same amount of time, differences between the two
groups could be caused by the boredom of the control subjects rather than by
the effects of the independent variable on the experimental subjects. If in the
Asch experiment the lines to be judged were flashed on a screen and removed
before the judging started, subjects in the control group would be writing down
their judgments immediately after the stimulus disappeared, but subjects in the
experimental group would have to wait until all the "subjects" before them
had given their answers. This longer delay between seeing the lines and giving
their judgments might have caused the subjects to forget which line was really
longest and thus could have operated to increase the number of errors made,
even in the absence of group pressure.

Two special kinds of artifact are **demand characteristics** (changes in the subjects' behavior simply from the experience of being in an experiment) and **experimenter bias** (changes in the subjects' behavior resulting from subtle hints unintentionally given off by the experimenter which let the subjects know how they are expected to respond). These two types of systematic error will be treated in detail in Chapter 9.

Alternative Explanations

Sometimes, the whole experimental procedure may allow for two substantively different and theoretically interesting interpretations of the results. In other words, the variables are not well enough defined so that the expected results *necessarily* indicate the validity of the experimenter's hypothesis. Someone reading the experiment may think of an *alternative explanation* which also fits all the experimental data.

A tradition of research on the *risky shift* illustrates what we mean by the term "alternative explanations." In the 1950s, many people believed that groups were more cautious than individuals in making decisions; that is, members of a group would be more level-headed and would tend to avoid extreme behavior. James Stoner (1961) set out to test that proposition. Briefly, he had people read about fictitious characters who had to make a choice between two alternatives: to take a risk or to adopt a more conservative stance. Participants were asked to decide how much risk they would advise the character to take. After they made their decisions individually, participants met in groups to discuss the situations and to reach agreement on what the group would advise. Were group decisions after discussion more cautious than the individuals' earlier decisions? Surprisingly not. By and large, groups recommended that the characters adopt a riskier strategy than did the average individuals, hence the term "risky shift."

These unexpected results initiated a whole line of research on group decision making in many different countries and with people of all ages from all walks of life. Investigators using Stoner's choice dilemma found consistent evidence of the risky shift. It seemed to be an amazingly robust finding. Eventually, however, some researchers uncovered the existence of a *conservative shift*. That is, under some circumstances, group decisions are more conservative than the average individual decision. Given these conflicting findings, it became the task of investigators to explain them. Are groups *really* more willing to take risks than are individuals?

Careful study revealed that group decisions are not always more risky than individual decisions; neither are they always more conservative. There is one reliable characteristic of group decisions, however: They tend to be more *extreme* than the average individual decision. That is, if individuals initially tend to favor conservative solutions to choice dilemmas, they are likely to shift to an even more conservative position when they get together as a group. Similarly, if individuals tend to favor risky solutions, group decisions are likely to shift to a more risky position. Thus, the risky shift demonstrated by Stoner and the conservative shift demonstrated by others were both examples of a more general tendency of group discussions to exaggerate individual group members' initial inclinations. This more general phenomenon has been labeled *group polarization*.

The preceding story serves as an example of a "reasonable" explanation for research findings and an even *more* reasonable alternative explanation. The story also has a moral: Researchers should try to anticipate alternative explanations and design experiments that will rule them out by adding extra control groups, by changing the design, or, if these are not feasible, by collecting additional data which may help to discriminate between two plausible explanations. For example, had Stoner and others used two kinds of choice dilemmas—yielding both conservative and risky decisions by individuals prior to group discussion—or had investigators used different measures of risk taking, this interesting group phenomenon might have been understood sooner.

If some potentially interesting variables have been held constant or allowed to vary at random, the experimenter often decides to run a *replication* of the experiment, this time systematically varying one or more of these variables to find out what effect it has within the context of the experimental situation. Or, if an alternative explanation has been suggested, the experimenter may run a replication in which the conditions are changed in such a way as to rule out the alternative explanation. A **replication** is nothing more than a repetition of the experiment. In a **direct replication** the experimenter tries to make the conditions exactly the same as they were in the original experiment in order to see if the experimental effect is a stable (or reliable) one. If the replication is successful—if the results in the two experiments are the same—the experimenter will be more confident that the observed effect is a stable one that will be consistently achieved in the same conditions. We hasten to add, however, that direct replications are relatively rare in social psychological research. More often, investigators replicate and *extend* previous research; that is, direct replications are typically only part of a study in which additional variables are studied as well.

In a **systematic replication** the experimenter *varies* some quality of the original situation in order to resolve ambiguities or to add new information about the variables controlling the subjects' behavior. Asch's follow-up experiment with different majority sizes may be viewed as a systematic replication of the original experiment. It provided additional information about the relationship between the size of the erroneous majority and its effectiveness in inducing the subject to conform.

NONEXPERIMENTAL METHODS OF RESEARCH

So far, we have been discussing research that falls into the category of the *experiment*, a study in which the investigator has some control over the independent variables and can assign subjects to conditions at random. By *manipulating some variable*, the experimenter creates differences in the experiences of two or more groups of subjects; and by *assigning subjects to the groups at random,* the experimenter creates groups which are equivalent in all respects except their experience with the independent variable. The experimenter can be reasonably sure that any differences in the behavior of the subjects in the groups are due to the differences in the treatments, since the random assignment of subjects to conditions has ruled out everything that might have made the two groups different to begin with. If the experiment has been conducted properly, the investigator can legitimately say that the treatments *caused* differences in behavior. Thus, Asch was justified in claiming that in his experiment, unanimous majorities *caused* many people to distort their judgment so as to correspond more closely to the majority judgment.

Only in an experiment can we *control the independent variable* and *assign subjects randomly* to conditions. For this reason, the controlled experiment is the only research method that allows us to make unequivocal cause-effect statements. The experiment is thus an extremely important method of conducting empirical research, but it is by no means the only method. It is true that in other kinds of research we invariably sacrifice the chance to make definite statements about causality, but below this rigorous standard extends a long continuum of methods, ranging from those that are simply suggestive, providing ideas in the same way as a novel or a newspaper article might, to designs that may provide a tenable scientific basis for inferring causality, designs hardly distinguishable from experiments.

Correlational Studies

Many important and interesting questions are not amenable to experimental research, because the experimenter cannot control the presumed antecedents or cannot assign subjects at random. Instead of introducing treatments, the researcher makes observations of events as they occur in nature. This does not mean that the research is "unscientific"; anyone who lacks faith in the development of a science through the exclusive use of correlational methods need only look at the history of astronomy. It does not even mean that statements of cause and effect are forever destined to be regarded as questionable. We do not raise our eyebrows and ask for experimental evidence when we read that eclipses of the moon are caused by the earth passing between the moon and the sun or that the odd footprints scattered across some outcroppings of Connecticut red sandstone were made by dinosaurs. When measurement of naturally occurring phenomena provides enough evidence that supports a theory and none that refutes it, causal statements are made and accepted, regardless of the scientist's inability to control the phenomena under investigation.

There are also many problems in psychology which cannot be studied experimentally. Every researcher faces ethical issues; for certain questions, ethical considerations may rule out the use of experimentation altogether. We do not feel free to assign subjects at random to conditions that might damage them physically or psychologically. For moral reasons, we are unwilling to tell someone that he or she is about to die, to remove people's frontal lobes, or to study the causes of psychosis by driving people crazy. Instead, we must find people who are already suffering in these situations and look to see if they are also characterized by other variables that we believe to be causes or consequences. For example, cigarette manufacturers frequently claim that there is no direct evidence showing that cigarette smoking *causes* lung cancer or heart disease in humans. They are right. This is because researchers are loath to randomly assign humans to ''smoking'' and ''nonsmoking'' conditions in order to demonstrate to skeptics that smoking cigarettes endangers life. Instead, they simply look to see if people who smoke are more frequently diagnosed with lung cancer or heart disease than people who do not smoke. Actually, in the case of research on smoking, researchers have done much more than ''simply look.'' The simple observation was made decades ago, and hundreds of studies were conducted in attempts to separate the effects of smoking from the effects of diet, stress, personality type, and a host of other variables. The Surgeon General finally found the evidence convincing enough to declare that smoking *causes* the diseases that smokers get more often than nonsmokers. Without the experimental method, the demonstration of causal relationships generally requires a great deal of patience and effort and is often costly.

Studies in which the investigator is looking for a relationship between two variables which can be measured—but which cannot be controlled—are called **correlational studies.** When one variable causes another, the two will inevitably be correlated. However, the reverse is not true; discovering that two variables are correlated can never (without other evidence) provide unequivocal proof of causality. We might hypothesize, for example, that children who watch hours of violent television shows every day are more violent and aggressive than children who don't. Since we cannot assign some children at random to homes that encourage them to watch violent television shows and others to homes that prohibit them, we may decide that a correlational study is the most suitable method for studying this hypothesis. In such a study, we might observe children from 100 households, measuring the amount of violent television they watch. We might also measure the children's aggression: the frequency with which they fight with their siblings, break toys, throw tantrums, and so on. Suppose that our hypothesis was confirmed and that on the whole, the children who watched the most violence on television were also the most aggressive (a high positive correlation). Would we be able to conclude from these data that the children's aggression was *caused* by the violent television shows? No. There are all sorts of other things that could have led to the same high positive correlation.

First, it is possible that the causal relationship is exactly the opposite of the one we have hypothesized. Perhaps children who are more aggressive *to begin with* prefer watching television characters punch, shoot, stab, or otherwise harm one another more than do children who are less aggressive. An even more common situation is that of a third-variable correlation; the two observed variables—*X* and *Y*—are correlated because both of them are highly correlated with (and maybe caused by) a third variable—*Z*—which we don't know about and haven't measured. Returning to our aggressive children, a third variable would exist if some other factor encouraged them both to view violent television shows and to behave aggressively. For example, it is possible that in homes where parents are frequently absent children have the opportunity to watch a lot of violent television shows and to engage in aggressive, destructive acts with no restraints. That is, the observed positive correlation may occur because parents are not at home to impose limits on television watching and aggressive behaviors. Or perhaps the relationship exists because parents who are themselves aggressive allow their children to watch violent fare on television, use corporal punishment, and condone aggressive behavior in their children. Plausible explanations for the observed positive correlation are limited only by our imaginations.

Thus, in a correlational study we can never be sure what the independent and dependent variables are. A correlational study can neither guarantee that the causal variables have been isolated nor provide the experimenter with control over the phenomena being studied. A correlational study does, however, allow the researcher to find out whether the phenomenon is *predictable* from knowledge about some other variable. Converging evidence from a large number and variety of correlational studies, all of which provide support for the same general theory, can ultimately satisfy scientists about causal relationships, as in the cases of eclipses and dinosaurs.

Basically, a correlational study consists of two sets of measurements, one of each member of a pair of variables which the scientist believes to be related: height and weight, extent of brain damage and extent of language loss, college board scores and grades in college, self-confidence and attractiveness, and so on. The degree of relationship between the two variables is tested mathematically and expressed as a **correlation coefficient** (symbolized as *r*). The value of *r* ranges from +1.00 to −1.00. A perfect **positive correlation,** +1.00, indicates that as one variable increases a constant amount, the other does too; by knowing how much of one variable is present, one can predict the exact value of the other. An *r* of −1.00 (a perfect **negative correlation**) also allows one to make exact predictions, but in this case the higher the value of one variable, the lower the value of the other (e.g., the *higher* the horsepower of a car, the *lower* the amount of time necessary to reach 60 miles per hour). An *r* of 0 indicates no relationship; knowing the value of one variable does not tell us anything about the value of the other (e.g., horsepower and color of the car). As *r* moves from 0 to +1.00 through the range of positive correlations or from 0 to −1.00 through the range of negative correlations, our ability to predict improves; the variables are more strongly related.

Very seldom do correlations among variables of interest to social psychologists approach +1.00 or −1.00. To cite but two examples, the correlation between general attitudes toward birth control and use of the birth control pill is only +.08 (Davidson & Jaccard, 1979) and the correlation between environmental attitudes and recycling behaviors is +.39 (Heberlein & Black, 1976). Although the magnitude of these correlation coefficients is not impressive in an absolute sense, it is worth noting that when the implications of even a "small" relationship are important, it is often worthwhile to pursue research. For example, the correlation between watching television violence and aggressive behavior ranges from +.10 to +.20 across a wide range of studies (Freedman, 1988): a relatively "weak" relationship. However, few people would argue that violence and aggression are not serious social problems. Thus, it is of both theoretical and practical import to determine if viewing television violence actually causes aggression. Moreover, if indeed it does, it is also important to determine how to explain that causal relationship and to arrive at ways to offset the deleterious effects of televised violence on aggressive, socially destructive behavior. Complex social variables such as aggression have many causes. It is completely unreasonable and simplistic to expect any single predictor variable to have a very high correlation with aggression. Even a history of actual aggressive behavior is an imperfect predictor. It is worthwhile, though difficult, to pursue even weak correlations if they keep turning up to find out whether a variable such as viewing televised violence is part of the reason some people are violent. The problem, of course, is to distinguish between weak-but-reliable correlations and imaginary ones.

Quasi-Experimental Designs

Of course, in the world outside the laboratory, there *are* phenomena that are easier to control than the movement of the planets, dinosaurs, or even what children watch on television. Social psychologists frequently design and implement interventions in government, industry, and educational settings and measure the effect of those interventions. However, despite control over the treatment or intervention, researchers are sometimes unable to assign individuals randomly to experimental and control conditions; they may be required to utilize only one group or to use intact, preexisting groups.

Studies that have independent variables and dependent variables but do not use randomization to assign subjects to groups are called **quasi-experiments** (Cook & Campbell, 1979). Because random assignment is not used, the groups compared are likely to differ in many ways aside from the treatment. In the absence of the "great equalizer," the groups are **nonequivalent,** and the researcher must determine which differences, if any, between these nonequivalent groups are due to the effects of the treatment and which are due to other differences between the groups. Without random assignment, one cannot say with certainty that the independent variable is the sole cause of some outcome, so the investigator has to "play detective" and logically and/or statistically eliminate as many rival causes as possible.

There are many varieties of quasi-experiments. Sometimes researchers use only one group to measure the effects of their intervention. Measures might be taken at some time before an intervention and again at one or more points after the intervention. Participants' behaviors or characteristics *before* the treatment can then be compared to their behaviors or characteristics *after* the treatment. For example, medical researchers may measure the physical and psychological functioning of a group of patients *before* the administration of a new drug and at various times *after* the administration of the drug. This strategy allows for a comparison of the patients' functioning before and after the drug is prescribed. Should symptoms subside, the researchers can be *somewhat* confident that the drug was the cause of improvement.

Or, unable to create groups by random assignment, a researcher may use two groups that already exist, giving the treatment to one but not to the other. These two groups can then be compared on dependent variables designed to measure the effects of the treatment. For example, researchers may be interested in improving employee morale in a corporation. Two different departments within the organization can be used to assess the effects of an intervention designed to improve employee morale. Before the treatment is implemented in one department, the morale of employees in both departments is measured (e.g., attitudes toward the organization, ratings of job satisfaction, absentee rates). Thereafter, employees in one department receive the ''morale-boosting'' treatment, and employees in the comparison group carry on as usual. The effectiveness of the treatment is then assessed by administering the same dependent measures to employees in both departments after those in the experimental group receive the treatment. If employees exposed to the treatment show improved morale compared to employees in the comparison group, results are *suggestive* of the efficacy of the intervention. We hasten to add, however, that such a conclusion is still open to debate, because we can't be sure that it was our intervention *alone* that caused improvement in employee morale.

Whatever form they take, quasi-experiments differ from true experiments in that subjects are not randomly assigned to treatment or control conditions. In Chapter 5, we will provide a more detailed description of situations in which quasi-experiments are either necessary or preferred, examples of various quasi-experimental techniques, and obstacles to valid causal inferences associated with them. For now, let us return to the experiment.

THE ADVANTAGES OF EXPERIMENTATION

The implication that the experiment is to be preferred over other techniques has provided an undertone to much of our discussion so far. It is now time to examine this implication explicitly and to ask why one should bother to attempt an experiment in the first place. Certainly, there are disadvantages to the social psychology experiment. It is often difficult to design. Hours of critical and creative thought go into selecting the appropriate empirical realizations of the experimenter's concepts. Alternative explanations must be eliminated, and stimulus materials and dependent measures must be carefully selected or developed. It is also likely to be laboriously time-consuming. Permission to proceed must first be secured from human subjects committees; subjects must be recruited; numerous "dress rehearsals" must be conducted with pretest subjects to ensure that the instructions are understandable and that the stimuli and events are interpreted appropriately. Once the experiment is finally up and running, it is not unusual for the experimenter and one or more assistants or confederates to spend an hour or more with each subject. The experimenter frequently has to make elaborate preparations to set the stage, to motivate the subject, and (in certain kinds of experiments) to deceive the subject. After expending all this time and effort, the investigator may obtain only a single datum: perhaps something as simple as a yes or no answer to a single question. Once the data have been collected—questionnaire responses, subject ratings of stimulus materials, overt behaviors, and so on— they must be scored, coded, and prepared for statistical analysis.

Furthermore—and this is perhaps the most common criticism—the experiment is usually far removed from the real-life phenomena in which the experimenter is supposedly interested. To the layperson it may seem ludicrous for psychologists interested in the formation and change of basic attitudes and important values to study children picking out toys or eating spinach, or college students guessing the lengths of lines, deciding how much they like a group on the basis of an "interaction" consisting entirely of written messages, or using 7-point scales to rate a person who appears on a videotape.

Those of us who conduct experiments firmly believe that these disadvantages are outweighed by the benefits of experimentation. In attempting to explain the reasons for this belief, we will examine one laboratory experiment in some detail and compare it with other approaches that might have been used to answer the same question. For illustrative purposes we have chosen the classic experiment by Elliot Aronson and Judson Mills (1959) which demonstrates not only the advantages of the experimental approach but some of the pitfalls as well. Aronson and Mills set out to test the hypotheses that a person who undergoes a severe initiation in order to be admitted to a group will find the group more attractive than if little or no initiation were required. To test this hypothesis, they conducted the following experiment.

Sixty-three college women were recruited as volunteers to participate in a series of group discussions on the psychology of sex. This format was a ruse, created in order to provide a setting in which subjects could be made to go through either mild or severe initiations in order to gain membership in a group.

Each subject was tested individually. When a subject arrived at the laboratory, ostensibly to meet with her group, the experimenter explained that he was interested in studying the "dynamics of the group discussion process" and that, accordingly, he had arranged these discussion groups for the purpose of investigating these dynamics, which included such phenomena as the flow of communications and who speaks to whom. He explained that he had chosen "The Psychology of Sex" as the discussion topic in order to attract a large number of volunteers and that this had proved to be a successful device, since many college students were interested in this subject. There was, however, one major drawback: Many of the volunteers were embarrassed and found it more difficult to participate in the discussion than they might have if the topic had been a more neutral one. He explained that his study would be impaired if any group member failed to participate freely. He then asked the subject if she felt she could discuss this topic without difficulty. The subjects invariably replied in the affirmative.

These instructions were used to set the stage for the initiation. The subjects were randomly assigned to one of three experimental conditions: a severe-initiation condition, a mild-initiation condition, or a no-initiation condition. The no-initiation and the mild-initiation conditions constituted the control groups. As soon as the subjects in the no-initiation group told the experimenter that they had no qualms about discussing sex, they were told that they could join a discussion group. It was not that easy for the subjects in the other two conditions, however. The experimenter told these subjects that he had to be absolutely certain that they could discuss sex frankly before he could admit them to a group. Accordingly, he said there was a special test which he was using as a screening device to eliminate those women who would be unable to engage in such a discussion without undue embarrassment. In the severe-initiation condition, this embarrassment test consisted of having each subject read aloud (to the male experimenter) a list of twelve obscene words and two vivid descriptions of sexual activity from contemporary novels. In the mild-initiation condition, the women were merely required to read aloud a list of relatively inoffensive words related to sex. This elaborate procedure constituted the empirical realization of the independent variable.[2]

Each of the subjects was then allowed to ''sit in'' on a group discussion, being carried on, she was told, by the members of the group she had just joined. This group was described as one that had been meeting for several weeks; the subject was told that she would be replacing a group member who had to leave because of a scheduling conflict.

To provide all subjects with an identical stimulus, the experimenter had them listen to the same tape-recorded group discussion. At the same time, the investigators felt that it would be more involving for the subjects if they were made to believe that this was a live, ongoing group discussion. In order to accomplish this while justifying the lack of visual contact necessitated by the tape recording, the experimenter explained that since people found that they could talk more freely if they were not being looked at, each subject sat in a separate cubicle, talking through a microphone and listening through head-

---

[2] Remember that this experiment was carried out in the mid 1950s when female undergraduates were unaccustomed to seeing (much less verbalizing) explicit obscene words and descriptions of sexual activity. As in most social psychological research, the independent variable must be understood in the cultural context of the time and place, a point discussed more fully later.

phones. Since this explanation was consistent with the other aspects of the cover story, all the subjects found it convincing.

It was important to discourage the subject from trying to "talk back" to the tape, since if she did so she would soon realize that no one was responding to her comments. In order to accomplish this, the experimenter explained that it would be better if she didn't try to participate in the first meeting, since the other group members had done some reading for the meeting, and therefore the subject would not be able to participate on an equal footing. He then disconnected her microphone.

At the close of the discussion, the experimenter returned and explained that after each session, all members are asked to rate the worth of that particular discussion and the performance of the other participants. He then presented her with a list of rating scales. This was the measure of the dependent variable. The results confirmed the hypothesis. The women in the severe-initiation condition found the group much more attractive than did the women in the mild-initiation and the no-initiation conditions.

This experiment certainly has some of the disadvantages mentioned earlier. Most striking is the fact that the experimenters constructed an elaborate scenario bearing little relation to the real-life situations in which they were interested. The "group" which the subject found more or less attractive was, in fact, nothing more than a few prerecorded voices coming in over a set of earphones. The subject was not allowed to see her fellow group members or to talk with them. This is obviously a far cry from group interaction as it occurs outside the laboratory. Moreover, the use of deception raises both ethical problems and more pragmatic questions, such as whether the deception was successful.

The authors' hypothesis could have been investigated more directly and perhaps more easily by employing nonexperimental methods. For example, one might try to study it cross-culturally, rating the severity of the initiation rites into manhood in different cultures and correlating these with some index of the extent to which adult males like their group. A still more direct and perhaps simpler method would be to do a correlational study of existing fraternities. One might first observe whether the fraternities required initiations for membership. If initiations were required, one might rate them for severity. At a later time, one could return and interview the members of the various fraternities to find out how much they liked one another and their particular fraternity. If it turned out that the men in the fraternities requiring severe initiations liked their group better than did those in other fraternities, this would seem to provide far greater support for the hypothesis, since the evidence would have been gathered in a natural setting.

Unquestionably, this procedure has certain advantages. First, it is simpler than a laboratory experiment. It is unnecessary to recruit volunteers, tape-record a discussion, or go through an elaborate rigmarole designed to deceive college women. In addition, it is the real thing. Rather than a series of separate individuals, each listening alone to a tape recording of disembodied voices for a short time, the fraternity situation involves real people living together in real groups over a relatively long time, developing strong positive or negative feelings toward one another. Moreover, there would be little question that the initiation we label as severe would in fact be a severe initiation. In the most extreme instances, the initiation would most certainly be far more severe than anything we could attempt in the laboratory.

However, there are some problems with this approach. First, the stimulus objects, that is, the fraternities themselves, vary a good deal in their inherent attractiveness. The severity of initiation, although hypothesized to be a cause of attractiveness, is certainly not the only cause. Obviously, groups have many characteristics which people find more or less attractive. Some groups are attractive because their members are friendly, perceptive, intelligent, athletic, "nice," generous, handsome, witty, and so on. Others are unattractive because members are dull, stupid, too loud, too quiet, too outgoing, too inhibited, and so on. In such a complex stimulus situation, the severity of initiation, although important, might be only one drop in a large bucket. Thus, because there is great variation among the fraternities in these and other attributes, it might be very difficult to demonstrate differences between severe-initiation fraternities and mild-initiation fraternities, even if initiation were the most important single determinant of attractiveness. In terms of our discussion earlier in this chapter, all these attributes of the fraternities are extraneous sources of random error. Since these sources of random error will undoubtedly affect the dependent variable—a liking for the fraternity—they can act to obscure or distort the effect of the independent variable, severity of initiation.

One of the great advantages of the experiment is that in the laboratory, the experimenter can often exert a great deal of control over such extraneous variables and thus ensure that the stimuli in the experimental conditions are similar. Thus, in the initiation experiment described above, the group whose attractiveness was to be judged was identical for all subjects. By holding constant all aspects of the group, Aronson and Mills succeeded in eliminating all the extraneous factors which may cause one group to be more attractive than another. In other words, they succeeded in minimizing random error, markedly increasing the odds that they would be able to successfully detect the effects of their independent variable, severity of initiation. Thus, although some degree of realism was sacrificed, one of the great gains was the achievement of considerable control over extraneous variations in all characteristics of the group to be rated. By reducing noise, they were better able to detect the signal.

This control, although highly desirable, is not in itself the major advantage of an experiment. There is one advantage that is far more important—the random assignment of experimental units (subjects) to experimental conditions. Let us suppose that the extraneous variation mentioned above was not great enough to obscure the relationship between severity of initiation and attractiveness. In other words, suppose we conducted a study of existing fraternities and discovered that the members of severe-initiation fraternities did find one another more attractive than did members of mild-initiation fraternities. If this occurred, we would have to consider the possibility of alternative explanations.

The inability of such a correlational study to specify causes and effects is a fundamental weakness. If the hypothesis is supported by the data, the experimenter usually wishes to assert as a conclusion to the study that the independent variable caused differences in the subjects' behavior—in the Aronson and Mills experiment, that severe initiations *cause* increased liking for the group into which one is initiated. In our fraternity example there are a variety of other possible, and indeed plausible, explanations which involve different causal sequences. The simplest explanation for these results might involve a relationship which is the reverse of the one we have proposed. Rather than severe initiations causing high attractiveness, it may be that high attractiveness causes severe initiations. The more attractive group may perceive that they are attractive and may attempt to maintain this pleasant situation. Perhaps out of a desire to prevent the group from being diluted, they may try to discourage applicants and make it difficult for people to get into the group by requiring a severe initiation. Or perhaps only highly desirable fraternities can afford to require severe initiations, because only they can be sure of getting enough applicants who are willing to put up with it. One could list many other reasons why the attractive groups might tend to have more severe initiations. The point is that any such reason points to an explanation for our data which involves a causal sequence that is the exact opposite of the one we hypothesized. Since this study necessitates the investigation of groups that were in existence before we arrived on the scene, there is no clear way to determine from these data which of the two hypotheses is correct.

This analysis should provide a clear understanding of what is meant by the statement that correlation does not prove causation. Whenever we observe that variable X (e.g., severity of initiation) is correlated with variable Y (e.g., attractiveness of a group) we cannot be sure whether X caused Y or whether Y caused X. In our laboratory experiment, of course, there is no ambiguity. We know what caused X—the experimenter. Consequently, in observing that Y is correlated with X, the experimenter can be certain that Y cannot have caused X; X must have caused Y.

But let's return for a moment to the study of fraternities. We might decide to circumvent the above problem by actually intervening in the initiation rites of two existing fraternities by conducting a quasi-experiment. We might first find two comparable fraternities which typically practice relatively severe initiations. Further, we might even be successful at persuading members of one of these two fraternities to reduce the severity of their typical initiation rites. The result would be two fraternities—one that continues to use *severe* rites of initiation and the other that now uses *mild* rites of initiation. Now that we have two (nonequivalent) groups, we can compare new members' ratings of attraction to their respective fraternities. If members who experienced severe initiations like their new fraternity more than those who experienced mild initiations, can we justifiably conclude that differences in attractiveness were due solely to our treatment? Not necessarily. First, our two fraternities no doubt differ on dimensions aside from our initiation intervention. Moreover, although our quasi-experiment has provided us with more control than a correlational study, we still were unable to *randomly assign* prospective fraternity members to one or the other fraternity, and therefore we cannot be absolutely certain that the members of fraternity A did not differ from the members of fraternity B in some systematic way that we didn't anticipate.

Let us elaborate upon that point: Recall from earlier in this chapter that in correlational studies, there is the possibility that an observed correlation between X and Y is simply produced by some third variable which affects both of them. The same problem holds for our quasi-experiment above: There may be other variables that are correlated with both rites of initiation and members' liking for their fraternity. Again, the true experiment circumvents this pitfall. In an experiment, it is extremely unlikely that an adventitious third variable is correlated with the two variables under consideration. The reason for this is apparent when we look at the defining characteristic of an experiment. In an experiment, the experimenter both has control over what treatment each subject receives and determines that treatment by assigning subjects to conditions at random. If the subject receives a treatment that has been determined truly at random, it is virtually impossible for a third variable to be associated with that treatment. Consequently, such a third variable cannot affect the dependent variable. In the real-life fraternity example, the demon which is of constant concern to the investigator is the possibility that the independent variable, severity of initiation, has not been randomly assigned to the various subjects. Insofar as some unknown third variable affects applications to a fraternity with severe-initiation practices, that third variable might also affect how attractive the group will be to its new members.

One plausible third-variable correlation in the real-life fraternity example involves differences in the amount of the subjects' initial motivation. For example, it is reasonable to assume that some people may simply want to be in a fraternity without caring much about *which* fraternity, whereas other people will be motivated to join a specific fraternity, perhaps because they have reason to feel that they will be happier with the members of that group. If a specific fraternity has a reputation for requiring severe initiations prior to admission, those people who have a strong desire to join that particular fraternity will be willing to go through the initiation in order to join. However, people who simply want to belong to a fraternity, with no particularly strong feelings about which one, will be much more likely to choose a fraternity that imposes little or no initiation. After all, if a man does not care which fraternity he joins, why would he bother to go through a severe initiation to get into a particular fraternity? Consequently, a fraternity that requires little or no initiation will initially attract many people who have no special desire to be in that specific fraternity as well as some people who do have a great desire to be in that specific fraternity. However, a fraternity that requires a severe initiation will *pri-*

marily attract those people who have a strong desire to be in that specific fraternity, a desire strong enough to allow them to endure the initiation. Therefore, any relationship between attractiveness and severity of initiation may be strictly a function of a disproportionate number of highly motivated people joining the severe-initiation fraternity. This problem is averted by the experiment. Random assignment of subjects to conditions not only guarantees that no unknown variable is causing the severe initiations to be administered by only one particular kind of group but also prevents the possibility that systematic motivational differences or personality characteristics among the potential joiners will cause the observed relationship.

Finally, in most laboratory experiments, one can vary the independent variable in a systematic manner, thus allowing for the isolation and precise specification of the important differences. If one were to study fraternities with different initiations, the likelihood would be that the various initiations would differ both qualitatively and quantitatively on a large number of dimensions. Suppose that the fraternity requiring a severe initiation asked its pledges to perform many demeaning jobs, to wear funny clothes, to submit to severe physical punishment, to expose themselves to danger, and to eat insects. In order to be sure which aspect of this complex treatment was causing the increased attractiveness, it would be ideal to have another fraternity that asked pledges to do all these things *except* submit to severe physical punishment. Instead, the ideal second fraternity would ask pledges to submit to mild physical punishment. Such a fraternity probably does not exist, but if we were creating initiations experimentally, we could produce an appropriate fraternity identical in all respects to the other one, except severity of physical punishment.

In sum, the major advantage of an experimental enquiry is that it provides us with unequivocal evidence about causation. Second, it gives us better control over extraneous variables. Finally, it allows us to explore the dimensions and parameters of a complex variable.

SOME PROBLEMS WITH EXPERIMENTATION IN SOCIAL PSYCHOLOGY

In discussing the advantages of the experiment in Chapter 1, we presented a rosy picture of the information to be gained and the pitfalls to be avoided in using the experimental method. Although it is true that only the experiment can provide an adequate basis for drawing causal inferences, there is no guarantee that it always succeeds in doing so. In an area as complex as social psychology, some very serious difficulties can arise in the application of the experimental method.

In Chapter 1, we also discussed controlled experiments as if they are all alike—in terms of the experiences of subjects who participate in them, and in terms of the variables of interest to experimenters. This was a bit of an oversimplification, one we would like to remedy before turning to a discussion of problems inherent in designing and conducting experiments in social psychology.

In what many believe to be the heyday of social psychological experimentation (the 1950s and 1960s), subjects often found themselves enmeshed in live events in the laboratory, events which frequently unfolded in ways very different from what they were initially led to expect. For example, Solomon Asch's (1951) subjects found the accuracy of their perceptions challenged by judgments of other people present in the room; Stanley Milgram's (1963) subjects found themselves asked to deliver an escalating series of electric shocks to a nearby confederate; and some subjects in Elliot Aronson and Judson Mills's (1959) experiment—believing themselves to be prospective participants in a study of a group discussion processes—were asked to recite a list of graphic and obscene words and passages in a manner aimed at arousing embarrassment. Although those events were not representative of the kinds of experiences subjects encounter outside the laboratory, few would doubt that they were intense and involving for subjects. Experimental manipulations had impact.

More recently, however, experimental methods have changed. In part this shift in emphasis reflects a response to ethical concerns about the use of treatments that tormented the subjects and about the deception involved. And in part this shift is due to the fact that the questions *being asked* have changed. For example, early research on attributions has expanded to address the more general ways in which we perceive, encode, recall, interpret, or reason about social stimuli. Experimenters in this **social cognition** tradition have studied both the accuracies in our processing of social information, and our biases and shortcomings. One methodological consequence of this shift in focus has been an increase in experiments in which subjects become (more or less) dispassionate observers of social information—often provided via written, audiotaped, or videotaped stimuli—as opposed to unwitting *participants* in live events. In these **judgment experiments,** subjects are less like actors who find themselves unexpectedly on stage as the plot unfolds and more like members of the audience asked to sit back and attend to, reason about, and respond to what is going on up on stage (or in some cases, the contents of the scripts before them).

Of course, in these experiments, there is considerable variation in the extent to which subjects become involved and actively engaged. For example, consider a task posed to subjects by Amos Tversky and Daniel Kahneman (1973). Subjects read about an imaginary man named Jack. Some subjects were asked to assume that Jack was randomly selected from a group of 100 men, 30 of whom were engineers; other subjects were asked to assume that Jack was randomly selected from a group of 100 men, 70 of whom were engineers. Half of the subjects in each of these two groups were given no other information before they were asked to estimate the probability that Jack was an engineer; the other half were given descriptions of Jack—descriptions that were representative of stereotypes most people hold of engineers. Using paper and pencil measures, Tversky and Kahneman found that subjects made use of base-rate information (i.e., 30 percent versus 70 percent odds) in estimating probabilities that Jack was an engineer when there was no other information provided but that they ignored this "statistical" information when they were provided with a stereotypically "engineerlike" description.

Contrast this method with a different experiment on the power of vivid information over statistical summaries conducted by Gene Borgida and Richard Nisbett (1977). Briefly, some subjects were exposed only to statistical summaries of the performance of a professor of a learning and memory course. Others were exposed to both the summaries and two face-to-face testimonials in which alleged former students expressed their opinions of the professor's course performance. Even in the face of statistical summaries provided by over 100 students, subjects were disproportionately influenced by the verbal reports of only two other students.

Both are social cognition experiments; both addressed shortcomings in the processing of social information. But the treatment in the second experiment was more involving and engaging. Thus, there *are* differences in the amount of impact produced by treatments in judgment experiments: At the extreme end of the continuum, they are hardly distinguishable from treatments employed by Asch (1951) or Aronson and Mills (1959). However, it is safe to say that most judgment experiments have in common an emphasis on control and systematic variation in the stimulus materials about which subjects—as processors of social information—reason or make judgments.

In subsequent chapters on experimental design, and independent and dependent variables (Chapters 4, 6, and 7, respectively), we will discuss ways in which the methods, goals, and concerns of those who conduct judgment experiments differ from those of researchers whose experiments are generally more impactful. Thus far, however, we have used terms such as ''impact'' and ''control'' somewhat casually. Let us elaborate upon the meaning and implications of those terms as they relate to problems and concerns encountered by social psychological experimenters.

IMPACT AND CONTROL

Consider first the question of **control,** one of the fundamental advantages we claimed for the experimental method. There are several limitations on the kinds of control that can be achieved in a social psychology experiment. Some of these limitations may be overcome by new approaches; others may be inevitable in the study of certain kinds of questions which interest social psychologists.

One of the major limitations of control that concern us is the extent to which unmeasured individual differences (subject variables) may obscure the results of an experiment. In the ideal experiment, two identical units (corn plants, rocks, rats, children, or fraternities) are exposed to different experimental treatments. It is a philosophical truism that no two units are ever exactly alike, but the experimenter strives to make them as nearly identical as possible. This ideal can be approximated much more satisfactorily in most other sciences, and even in some other areas of psychology, than is possible in social psychology, because in social psychology the ''units'' are human beings. Our subjects differ from one another in their genetic makeup, life histories, learned personality characteristics, values and attitudes, abilities, and immediate and distant past experiences. Any and all of these differences can have a large impact on the way in which subjects perceive and respond to our experimental treatments.

An experimenter who studies animal behavior can often minimize these differences by using a single known genetic strain and by keeping the experimental subjects in similar, stimulus-controlled environments (sometimes throughout their lives), so that unknown past experiences probably will not cause large amounts of variability in behavior when animals are exposed to the experimental situation. An experimenter who studies the parameters of human learning (often using new and unfamiliar nonsense syllables in order to eliminate the effects of differences in subjects' experiences with real words) can reduce the problems of intersubject variability by using each subject in all of the experimental conditions. In other words, each subject becomes his or her own control. Since the extraneous subject variables (e.g., verbal facility, real differences in short-term memory, task motivation) are the same in all conditions, they cannot be responsible for differences in the subject's performance from one condition to another.

At present, such solutions are rarely possible in social psychology. Typically, social psychologists have no control over, and little or no information about, the genetic strain or the preexperimental experiences of their subjects. Of course, in some kinds of social psychological experiments, each subject can be used as his or her own control, that is, be exposed to all levels of a given independent variable, as in the learning studies described above. Experiments in which subjects are asked simply to observe and respond to social stimuli frequently expose subjects to more than one treatment. Such experiments *can* and very often *do* provide valid results if differences between or among treatments to which subjects are exposed are not so obvious as to give away the experimenter's hypothesis and if exposure to one treatment does not "change" the subject in ways likely to contaminate his or her responses to additional treatments.

However, in social psychology it is often impossible to use each subject as his or her own control, because many experimental treatments cannot be presented to the same subject one after the other. If a person has been asked to read a list of obscene words and then listens to a group discussion, we assume that this experience will have a strong effect on her response to a second condition, in which she is asked to read a list of only slightly taboo words before listening to the same group discussion. Having told a subject that *The National Enquirer* reports that the use of condoms is an effective strategy for curtailing the spread of AIDS, it is difficult to estimate the effect on the same subject of the same communication subsequently attributed to the U.S. Surgeon General. The effects of some experiences may be inherently nonerasable, even if subjects do not guess our hypothesis and change their behaviors accordingly. We do not know for sure that this is the case with any particular social psychological treatment, but it is a sound assumption that such effects cannot be wiped out within the time limits of a typical experiment. Again, however, we have neither the means nor the knowledge to achieve perfect control over the variables affecting the behavior we are studying. Random assignment of subjects to conditions will ensure that differences among subjects will not be a source of *systematic* error. But it is still possible that this variability will create enough *random* error to obscure the effects of the experimental treatment—so that the experimenter will not be able to detect a signal (the effects of treatment) amid the noise of random error (extraneous variability in subject characteristics).

What about control over the *stimulus situation?* We argued that one great advantage of studying the effects of initiation by means of an experiment was that all subjects could be exposed to the same discussion group. A high degree of control was achieved in that situation, since the group was tape-recorded, and all subjects listened to the same discussion. Often, though, since we are studying social situations, it is necessary to introduce the experimental treatment as one event in a continuous interaction between the subject and other people. When this is the case, the stimulus situation may vary greatly from one subject to the next, since the other members of the group must modify their behavior a little in response to each subject. Furthermore, since we are ultimately interested in social processes that occur in everyday life, we often present subjects with a situation that is familiar to them in some respects—one that is like other situations they have encountered outside the experiment. Consequently, our stimulus situation is certain to *interact* (Chapter 1) with individual differences among the subjects which arise from their differing past experiences in similar situations. There is bound to be more variation in the way different subjects perceive and respond to the experimental situation than would be the case if we could use unfamiliar stimuli such as nonsense syllables. Even if the events in our experimental situation could be kept perfectly constant for each subject (for example, by the use of tape recordings), the subject's *interpretation* of these events could be influenced by prior experiences beyond our control, and thus the "same" situation would seem very different to different subjects. For example, if one experimental condition requires that a confederate rebuff the subject, the experience of rejection might provoke very different reactions in different subjects, depending on their prior experience in similar situations. A subject who had recently been rejected by her lover might be more upset by the experimental situation than one who was more secure in her social relationships. The social psychologist is not in control of such sources of variability and usually doesn't even know what they are.

The Compromise between Impact and Control

There is an interesting problem inherent in conducting social psychological experiments. The experimenter must choose a stimulus situation which closely approximates the meaning of the conceptual independent variable, while minimizing the amount of extraneous variability resulting from differences in the subjects' interpretations of the situation. On the one hand, the experimenter wants the experimental situation to be meaningful and involving to the subjects—in a word, the treatments should have impact. On the other hand, a situation which the subject finds meaningful and involving is also likely to trigger a wealth of memories and influences from the past which can affect the subject's interpretation of present circumstances. From the experimenter's point of view, these memories and influences constitute extraneous variability and jeopardize control over the effects of the independent variable. The choice of an empirical realization of one's conceptual variable—and an appropriate stimulus situation in which to apply it—always represents a compromise between impact and control, in which a little of each is sacrificed.

The problem is not amenable to a general solution. It arises in a different guise every time a new experiment is designed, and it requires a new solution for each new experimental question. We can indicate some of the factors the experimenter should take into consideration and present a few examples of compromises which particular experimenters have reached for particular problems, but we cannot present a general rule; none exists. The manifestation of the conflict between impact and control will be different for each new experiment, as will the specific methodological problems raised by the conflict.

The problem of finding effective empirical realizations of conceptual variables is exacerbated by the relatively narrow limitations imposed on the types of experimental treatment a social psychologist can use. Ethical considerations, restrictions of time, subjects' knowledge that they are in an experiment—all these factors combine to reduce the experimenter's control over the variables and the treatment's impact on the subjects. In many social psychological experiments, we see subjects for only an hour or two, with no control and not much knowledge of their behavior before they enter the laboratory or after they leave. Within that short period we attempt to expose them to a complex social stimulus. The range of possible stimuli we feel free to use is sharply restricted by ethical considerations; there are many interesting questions which we cannot study directly because they require doing things to people which we are not willing to do (see Chapter 3 for a more complete discussion of the ethical issues involved). As a consequence, the treatment actually used often represents a compromise between (1) the experimenter's desire to maximize the intensity and effectiveness of the stimulus (so that it will be strong enough to override the variability due to individual differences among subjects) and (2) the experimenter's genuine concern for the subject's welfare.

For example, consider the experiment on severity of initiation in Chapter 1. There are many possible ways to provide a severe initiation which would be more powerful than the technique actually employed. The initiation used by Aronson and Mills was rather bland in comparison with the initiations administered in primitive societies and even in some college fraternities. Because of restrictions on the amount of impact possible in an experimental setting, individual differences among subjects loom large relative to the effects of the experimental treatment, and consequently these differences tend to have a substantial influence. If a severe initiation is indeed one of the determinants of liking for a group, we suspect that no matter who the subject is, or what experiences he has had, a slow and painful circumcision would affect his feelings about the group into which he is being initiated. The effect of the initiation on each subject's attitude toward the group would be so strong that differences in attitude due to subject variables or to minor fluctuations in the initiation procedure would be trivial by comparison, and we would be highly confident that we had located a major determinant of attitude toward the group. But reading a short list of obscene words is such a comparatively mild initiation that its effects may not be strong enough to show up against a background of variations in attitude resulting from existing individual differences in the values, beliefs, and experiences of the subjects.

In an experiment on animal learning, it is usually fairly easy to have an impact on the subject, to force the animal, if you will, to pay attention to the treatment and to take the situation seriously. For a pigeon at 75 percent of free-feeding body weight, learning a response that will produce food is important. It can certainly be argued that it is possible to set up a social psychology experiment in which the subject is as concerned about successful performance as is our hypothetical pigeon. In order to do so, however, the situation must be a very realistic one for the subject. Realistic and meaningful social experiences tend to be complex, and any two such experiences (treatments) tend to differ on a large number of dimensions. It is very difficult to create two equally realistic situations which differ *only* in terms of the independent variable the experimenter intends to manipulate; in order to make both situations equally plausible to the subject, the experimenter usually allows certain other differences between them. But once such differences are allowed, it is always more difficult to understand precisely what the experimental treatments comprise. In other words, as we increase realism in an attempt to have a greater *impact* on the subject, we frequently sacrifice *control*.

For a psychologist interested in human behavior, there are several possible ways of dealing with this fundamental dilemma. Some psychologists, as we have seen, are willing to sacrifice a great deal of control in order to study situations with unrestricted impact and realism, that is, in naturally occurring situations. Their research is necessarily nonexperimental; accordingly, their conclusions about cause and effect can never be definite. Other psychologists decide to use animals as subjects and are thus able to achieve a high degree of both impact and control; in making this choice, however, they can no longer be very certain that their results will be relevant to human behavior. In addition, many social variables believed to be tremendously influential in human behavior cannot be studied in lower organisms, or at best only indirectly. The experimental social psychologist is reluctant to sacrifice either relevance or control. Rather than dealing with the problem once and for all by choosing a research strategy that will maximize one at the expense of the other, the experimenter attempts to live with this dilemma which manifests itself differently in every new experimental situation.

Exactly what is the nature of this dilemma? On the one had, the experimenter wants maximal control over the independent variable, with as few extraneous differences as possible between or among treatments. The experimenter wants to specify as precisely as possible the exact nature of the treatments administered and their effects on the subjects. This leads the experimenter to try to develop highly specifiable empirical realizations, in which the differences between treatments are simple and clear, in which all manipulations are standardized—in short, to approximate the methodology of a traditional verbal-learning experiment. On the other hand, if the experiment is controlled to the point of sterility, it may fail to involve the subject, may produce little impact, and therefore may not affect his or her behavior to any measurable extent.

The Impact-Control Dimension: Two Examples

As an example of this dilemma, let us first consider an experiment that is representative of a category of social psychological research that scores high on the dimension of control. The experiment (Hovland & Weiss, 1951) is a classic and is one of a series of studies on attitude change carried out by Carl Hovland and his associates at Yale. In most of the previous work on attitude change, several of the variables which might be assumed to affect attitudes had been allowed to vary simultaneously. One of the major purposes of Hovland's research was to isolate and control these variables to assess their separate influences on the subjects' attitudes.

In this experiment, Hovland and Walter Weiss (1951) were interested in discovering whether a highly credible communicator can change people's attitudes more than a less credible communicator can. The general design of the experiment involved presenting the same communication to two groups of subjects, in one group attributing the communication to a highly credible source and in the other group attributing it to a source of low credibility. Five days before the actual experiment, the subjects filled out a long questionnaire, which included questions about their attitudes on the issues that were later used in the experiment, as well as questions asking for their evaluations of the "trustworthiness" of a large variety of sources, including those that were later used in the experiment. The subject's possible tendency to agree with affirmative statements was controlled by preparing one communication that took an affirmative position and one that took a negative position on each of the issues used in the experiment. Both the positive and negative communications contained the same number of facts on the topic and the same background information as their "evidence." Four different topics were used, with eight different communicators (four "trustworthy" and four "untrustworthy"). Two of the topics were "the feasibility of atomic submarines at the present time (1950)" and "the desirability of selling antihistamine drugs without prescriptions." For the former topic the high-credibility source was J. Robert Oppenheimer and the low-credibility source was *Pravda*; for the latter, the high-credibility source was a prestigious medical journal and the low-credibility source was a mass circulation pictorial magazine. (See Table 2-1 for a summary of the topics and sources used in their experiment.)

The subjects, participating in the experiment as part of a regular class, believed that they were providing "live" classroom data for a survey of the role of mass media as a vehicle of communication. Each subject received a booklet containing four articles: an affirmative article on topic A attributed to a trustworthy source, a negative article on topic B attributed to an untrust-

TABLE 2-1
TOPICS AND SOURCES USED IN
CARL HOVLAND AND WALTER WEISS'S (1951) EXPERIMENT

| | Source credibility | |
Topic	High	Low
Antihistamine drugs: Should the antihistamine drugs continue to be sold without a doctor's prescription?	*New England Journal of Biology and Medicine*	Mass circulation monthly pictorial magazine
Atomic submarines: Can a practicable atomic-powered submarine be built at the current time?	J. Robert Oppenheimer	*Pravda*
The steel shortage: Is the steel industry to blame for the current shortage of steel?	*Bulletin of National Resources Planning Board*	Syndicated anti-labor newspaper columnist
The future of movie theaters: As a result of TV, will there be a decrease in the number of movie theaters in operation by 1955?	*Fortune* magazine	Syndicated movie gossip columnist

worthy source, an affirmative article on topic C attributed to an untrustworthy source, and a negative article on topic D attributed to a trustworthy source. The four topics were different for different groups of subjects. When they had read the booklets, the students handed them in and were given attitude questionnaires on the topics they had read about. The experiment was highly controlled in that there were few extraneous or ambiguous events during the experimental session that could have affected any particular subject's responses.

The results of the experiment were statistically significant, but surprisingly weak. Although the average difference in perceived trustworthiness between the high- and low-credibility communicators was very great (78.2 percent more subjects perceived the high-credibility source as trustworthy than the low-credibility source), the differences in attitude change were much smaller than one might expect, given this large difference in perceived trustworthiness. The net attitude change was only 14.1 percent greater for high-credibility communicators than for low-credibility ones.

Similarly weak effects are characteristic of other highly controlled experiments. A reasonable conjecture is that these weak effects are due to the fact that the impact of such a manipulation—reading a series of four brief articles for a classroom survey—is too small to have much influence on behavior. It may have been dull and uninvolving for the subjects to read communications on issues of little direct consequence to them. To show a strong effect, it would have been much more desirable to have the communicator present, delivering a dramatic speech with flair and passion, perhaps even interacting and arguing with members of the audience.

Now let us glance at an example of a series of experiments by Henry Murray (1963) that score high on the dimension of impact. The subject was first given a month in which to write out a description of his personal philosophy, including all the important principles he had chosen to live by. At the end of the month, the subject brought this exposition into the lab, and a copy was given to a talented young lawyer. In return, the subject received a copy of the lawyer's description of *his* philosophy. The experimenter asked the subject and the lawyer (actually an accomplice) to spend the next couple of days reading over each other's description and then to return to the lab for a debate on the respective merits of their two philosophies. On the appointed day, the subject and the lawyer returned. They were both told that there would be three stages to the debate: First, they would have a chance to ask each other questions and to clarify various aspects of their philosophies; then, the lawyer would have a chance to criticize the subject's philosophy; and finally, the subject would have a chance to criticize the lawyer's philosophy. The first stage of the debate passed as expected, with a friendly interchange in which the two asked questions about each other's written statements. Then, it was the lawyer's turn to criticize the subject's ideas, and he launched into a scathing attack on the subject and his philosophy, becoming "far more vehement, sweeping, and personally abusive" (Murray, 1963, p. 29) than the subject had been led to expect.

It is reasonably clear from Murray's report that impact was achieved. But at what price in control? In these studies it is difficult to determine just which aspect of the treatment was affecting the subjects' responses. Perhaps different subjects were responding to different things. The point we are trying to make is not that one method is uniformly better than the other but that the two goals of a social psychology experiment, impact and control, are in continuous tension: As one goal becomes preeminent, the other tends to be sacrificed.

Looking at this problem another way, we may say that one of our important experimental goals is to design a treatment that will have a strong enough effect to show up clearly against a background of extraneous variability. Some investigators have attempted to deal with the problem by reducing the possible sources of extraneous variability. For example, they have used subjects as their own controls and administered all levels of a highly controlled independent variable to everyone. By using precise manipulations such as written paragraphs, however, they have made subjects mere passive readers of a standardized message. In doing so, these investigators have tended to reduce the power of the independent variable they were studying, running the risk that the effect would be obscured by even the very small amount of extraneous variability that was left. The other alternative—strengthening the impact of the variable being studied—often results in a concomitant increase in the possible sources of extraneous variability. Impactful manipulations are often vivid and complex, and the components to which people attend are likely to vary considerably across subjects. Furthermore, the use of impactful manipulations frequently precludes using subjects as their own controls. Thus, the effect of the independent variable *relative* to background error may not change much across the different available procedures; as one increases, so does the other.

Often, a good compromise can be worked out. In a study of communicator credibility such as the one mentioned above, we might achieve the best of both worlds by using a film or videotape of a dramatic and articulate communicator. If we used the same tape in both conditions and made it clear to the subject that the communicator had great credibility in one condition and little credibility in the other, we would have a high degree of control. Moreover, such a tape would probably have a great deal of impact on the subjects—perhaps not as much as a live, interacting communicator, but almost certainly more than a printed message. Control has been achieved, in the sense that we are certain that subjects in both conditions have received identical stimuli and that we can reproduce our experimental conditions exactly.

MULTIPLE MEANING AND SYSTEMATIC REPLICATION

As we suggested above, with a little work and ingenuity, experimenters can and often do strike an acceptable compromise between experimental impact on the one hand and experimental control on the other. This kind of general procedural solution may appear to be completely satisfactory, but the problem of impact versus control goes deeper. Attaining impact may not only result in a diminution of experimental control due to differences in the presentation of the treatment from one subject to another but may also—even when the treatment is held constant—lead to an increase in the number of possible conceptual constructs associated with the independent variable. If we gain impact by elaborating the treatment to make it striking and complex, the experimental effect may be caused by any one of the elements we have added rather than the "pure" independent variable we originally had in mind. In other words, even when all subjects have received the identical stimulus, if the stimulus is rich and complicated and meaningful, we may not know which of the many components of the stimulus was responsible for observed changes in the subjects' behavior. We shall call this problem the problem of multiple meaning, because, quite literally, certain experimental treatments allow for a multitude of interpretations.

Multiple Meaning

The problem of multiple meaning is one of the most perplexing and pervasive problems in social psychological experimentation, primarily because the experimental treatments that have the most meaning and impact for the subjects tend to involve a complex bundle of stimuli, and consequently these treatments can be interpreted in more than one way. It is a sobering experience to go through any issue of a social psychology journal from cover to cover, listing alternative explanations for each experiment. It is a rare article that does not suggest at least one interpretation which differs from the one proposed by the author. It is even more sobering to try to redesign the experiment in a manner that is free of alternative interpretations. In some cases the most plausible alternative explanations can be ruled out by a slight change in the design or the manipulations, but these are uncommon.

In examining a completed experiment, one of the first and most important questions to be asked is: What is the defining difference between the two (or among the ten) experimental conditions? What is happening in condition A that makes the subjects behave differently (on some dependent variable) from the subjects in condition B? It is usually possible to list several differences. But this is not what the investigator originally had in mind. The investigator had a concept of a single, abstract variable such as guilt, self-esteem, or fear, felt it was theoretically important, and believed, according to the hypothesis, that this variable caused the observed differences in the subjects' behavior. We have referred to this abstract variable as the conceptual variable (Chapter 1). But in building an experiment, it is impossible to manipulate conceptual variables directly; each conceptual variable must be translated into an experimental procedure. The description of the actual procedure constitutes the empirical realization of the conceptual variable (see Chapter 1). The problem is that there is no necessary one-to-one correspondence between a conceptual variable and its empirical realization. This problem exists even with apparently simple conceptual variables, such as hunger. A frequently used empirical realization of hunger is the percentage of free-feeding body weight. When we say that in an experiment one pigeon was at 75 percent of free-feeding body weight while another was at 100 percent, we also say that the reason for observed behavioral differences is hunger. How do we make this leap? There are several differences between birds at 75 percent of free-feeding body weight and birds at 100 percent. How can we be sure that differences in their performance are attributable to hunger rather than to physical weakness or anxiety about food? To return to the severity-of-initiation experiment, what is the distinction between the different experimental conditions? Is it, as the investigators assert, that the subjects in the severe-initiation condition have made a greater expenditure of unpleasant effort than the subjects in the other conditions have? Could it not have been the result of having passed a demanding test? Or was it that the subjects who read the obscene words were sexually aroused? One can list a great many differences among the experimental conditions. Thus, although the researchers in the severity-of-initiation experiment had a great deal of control over the manipulation of experimental conditions and the presentation of the stimulus to be judged, their interpretation of the results is open to question because their empirical realization of the conceptual variable (unpleasant effort) contained multiple meanings.

Let us restate the problem in general terms. In any given experiment, the experimental treatments differ in many ways. We want to isolate some conceptual variable which "explains" or "accounts for" observed differences in the subjects' behavior. Actually, in the design (or planning stage) of experiments, the problem usually arises in the reverse order. We wish to study the effects of a particular conceptual variable (for example, unpleasant effort). There are many ways to translate this abstract conceptual variable into a concrete experimental operation. If we have our subjects read a list of obscene words, how can we be sure that this operation is, in fact, an adequate empirical realization of the abstract conceptual variable Aronson and Mills originally had in mind?

This problem is not unique to social psychological research. It does tend to be more acute in this area, however, partly because we often (though not necessarily) design extremely complex treatments in order to produce situations that will have sufficient realism and impact for the subject. There is a sense in which the complex social situation used in the severity-of-initiation experiment lends itself to many more possible interpretations than does the use of a pigeon at 75 percent of free-feeding body weight. But this is not the whole story, for simpler variables may also possess multiple meanings. Thus, if instead of asking subjects to read aloud a list of obscene words, Aronson and Mills had asked them to perform some exhausting physical task, this, by itself, would not have made the results much clearer. For although this empirical realization would have ruled out sexual arousal as an alternative explanation, it would have opened up a Pandora's box of other alternative explanations which did not arise in the original experiment, for example, interpretations based on physical fatigue. (Fatigue may make a person more acquiescent, or perhaps fatigue reduction is a pleasant experience which happens to occur at the same time as the stimulus to be judged.) Similarly, if electric shock had been used, it would have opened the door for yet another set of interpretations, this time based on fear and fear reduction.

Conceptual variables in social psychology are often words taken from everyday language, such as "aggression," "emotion," and "guilt." Sometimes these terms have a specified meaning for social psychologists, a shared meaning that is more strictly defined than is the same term in everyday use. But this is not usually the case. One social psychologist may believe that aggression involves hurting people, another may define it in terms of the intent to hurt, and still another may include the mere wish to hurt. Since the term is a common and familiar one, each of the three psychologists may assume that the term "aggression" means the same thing to the other psychologists, since "everybody knows" what aggression is. Thus, the defining characteristics of many concepts in social psychology may not be clearly delineated by the investigators. Obviously, different conceptual variables can lead to different empirical realizations and can suggest the measurement of different behaviors. Therefore, it may be difficult to compare the results of two different experiments, both designed to investigate "aggression." But this is not the whole problem. Even if investigators share the same conceptual definition of a psychological process, they may arrive at very different empirical realizations of the concept in their research. One person's may be derived from a theory, another's from logical inferences from previous experimental results, and still another's from intuition. There are no rules in social psychology for creating empirical realizations of conceptual variables.

Refining Conceptual Variables: Systematic Replication

The absence of such translation rules in social psychology means that relatively few standard methods exist for manipulating or measuring any given conceptual variable. This is less true in some other areas of psychology. Seventy-five percent of free-feeding body weight is interpreted as an empirical realization of hunger rather than of physical strength, because so many experiments have been performed in a manner that increases our confidence in this particular empirical realization. Essentially, there are two properties we demand of a series of experiments before we are convinced that we are dealing with a unitary conceptual variable: *First,* we ask for a number of empirical techniques that differ in as many ways as possible, having in common only this basic underlying conceptual variable. Each of these techniques must then be applied in the same experimental paradigm. If all the techniques yield the same result, we become more convinced that the common underlying variable is, in fact, the variable that is producing the results.

Neal Miller (1957) presents one example of the use of this kind of research program in relation to hunger. In different experiments, Miller manipulated several different procedures that might be thought to influence hunger. These procedures included a bilateral lesion in the region of the ventromedial nuclei of the hypothalamus (the brain's "hunger center"), injection of enriched milk directly into the stomach, and normal intake of milk through the mouth. If different empirical realizations are systematically compared in this way, we gain: (1) the ability to compare the results across many different experiments; (2) information about the validity of the conceptual variable; and possibly, as occurred in the case of hunger studies, (3) important information that leads to changes in the concept of the variable studied.

Similarly, if we want to be sure that the degree of unpleasant effort is the key variable in the severity-of-initiation experiment, the experiment should be repeated, using a number of different methods to produce unpleasant effort. In order to eliminate overlap between conceivable alternative interpretations, these methods should be as different as possible from one another. That is, if we suspect that in the original experiment sexual arousal might have been the variable responsible for our observed differences, it is important that the second technique not involve sexual arousal. Perhaps the initiation could consist of some exhausting physical exercise. If both these techniques produce similar results, we have ruled out sexual arousal, as well as a large number of related interpretations. We have also ruled out alternative explanations based on fatigue, since fatigue was not a factor in the first experiment. But both these experiments might have in common the feeling of a job well done. Therefore, a third experiment should be conducted, using still a different method that eliminates this explanation. This technique of "purification" can go on indefinitely, but as the number of such systematic replications becomes larger and more diverse, we gain additional confidence that we understand the conceptual variable that underlies all of them. Given that conceptual variables taken from everyday language are often ill-defined, we will probably end up with a variable that is more sharply delineated than it was when we started. We may discover important new aspects of the variable, and we may also discover that some aspects which we had thought were important are really unnecessary. This kind of integrated program of systematic replication is more than a technique for confirmation; in a very real sense it can be a technique for discovery.

For example, Anthony Greenwald and his colleagues (1986) provide a provocative case history of the *sleeper effect* which demonstrates the value of systematic replications as tools for discovering the sources of inconsistencies across experimental results. Their research program also demonstrates that with tenacity, insight, and ingenuity, experimenters can and often do reconcile these inconsistencies, providing for greater understanding of conceptual variables. The *sleeper effect* refers to the diminishing effects of a source's credibility over time; that is, with the passage of time, perceivers may dissociate a source from the specific content of his or her message. Consequently, the persuasiveness of a low-credibility message may actually *increase* over time, while the persuasiveness of a high-credibility source may *decrease* over time. For example, subjects who initially disagree with a communication from *Pravda* may with the passage of time dissociate that nontrustworthy source from the message about the feasibility of nuclear-powered submarines. Consequently, they may believe the message *more* at a later time than they did initially. The converse may be true with regard to the same message attributed to a high-credibility source such as J. Robert Oppenheimer. If the association of Oppenheimer and his message about the feasibility of nuclear-powered submarines weakens over time, then subjects will believe his message less than they did initially.

Although Carl Hovland and his associates at Yale University (Hovland, Lumsdaine, & Sheffield, 1949; Hovland & Weiss, 1951; Kelman & Hovland, 1953) found evidence of the sleeper effect, in subsequent research some investigators *could* demonstrate the sleeper effect, and others could *not*. How can we account for these discrepancies? These are the kinds of perplexing results which excite and intrigue experimenters, and throughout the 1970s and into the 1980s numerous researchers attempted to pin down the source of conflicting findings. Is there a sleeper effect? Under what conditions does it manifest itself, and under what conditions does it not? Across studies, different empirical realizations were used to systematically vary messages and information about source credibility. For example, the impact of the messages was increased, and advancing technology enabled experimenters to take more sensitive dependent-variable measures. Finally, the mystery was solved. Whether the sleeper effect was found depended on a very simple operation: If source credibility information was presented *prior* to the message, no sleeper effect; if source credibility information was presented *after* the message, the sleeper effect obtained (see for example, Gruder et al., 1978; Pratkanis, Greenwald, Leippe, & Baumgardner, 1988). Thus, because the robustness of a social psychological phenomenon can hinge on minor experimental variations that to the undiscerning eye may seem inconsequential, systematic replications are invaluable for uncovering the source of inconsistent results and can ultimately enhance our understanding of conceptual variables.

The program of research we described above is concerned with replication across experiments. The same principle may also be applied within a single experiment. For example, in the study of communicator credibility outlined in Table 2-1, instead of simply using Oppenheimer's statement about the feasibility of atomic submarines as the high-credibility communication, Hovland and Weiss devised four different issues with four different highly credible communicators (and, correspondingly, four different communicators with low credibility). Thus, there was more than one specific empirical realization of the conceptual variable "credibility" within the context of the single experiment. Had the authors used only the Oppenheimer communication, they would have had no way of determining whether the effect was due to credibility or to some attribute peculiar to Oppenheimer. Using more than one credible source was a means of providing increased confidence in the effects of the conceptual variable (credibility) independent of individual characteristics of particular communicators. Paradoxically, this suggests that control—in the sense of having all stimuli identical for every single subject—may not be desirable, because it becomes impossible to separate the results from extraneous features of the specific stimuli used. The principle is the same as that involved in systematic replication. When we use several empirical realizations of a conceptual variable, and they all have the same effect on the subjects, we gain confidence in the crucial role played by the conceptual variable. Why? Because other aspects of any given empirical realization will typically be characteristic of that realization but not of all the others. The more unlike two different empirical realizations are in their superficial irrelevant features, the more confident we are that their underlying point of similarity, that is, their representation of the conceptual variable, is responsible for similarities in the subjects' behavior.

Of course, the use of several different empirical realizations of the conceptual variable does not guarantee this pattern of ideal results. When the different empirical realizations all have the same effect on the subjects, our confidence in the importance and generality of our conceptual independent variable is greatly increased. But what if one or more of our empirical realizations does not produce the same results as the other ones? Obviously, this sort of partially successful experiment does not allow the experimenter to feel confident or fully knowledgeable about the conceptual variable. Instead, mixed results of this sort raise questions and provide the experimenter with an opportunity to explore the meaning of the conceptual variable. The investigator can compare the successful empirical realizations with the unsuccessful ones in an attempt to discover what differentiates them.

By performing a manipulation check or taking some other relevant measure (such as the pretest of "perceived trustworthiness" administered by Hovland and Weiss, 1951), the experimenter can carry out an **internal analysis,** that is, systematically study the relationship of some tangential variables (such as the specific personification of a credible communicator, or the specific topic about which he or she writes) to the central variables of the hypothesis. Studying inconsistencies in one's experimental results can lead to new ideas and hypotheses which suggest further research and can ultimately result in a more solid understanding of the conceptual variables. An experimenter who uses only one empirical realization of the independent variable may never be led to the new questions and insights into the conceptual variables, and thus the results of the experiment may be limited in generality to the single situation used. In short, the use of several different empirical realizations is likely to provide more information than the use of a single empirical realization, whether or not the experiment is "successful."

The *second* procedure for demonstrating that we are dealing with a unitary conceptual variable is to show that a particular empirical realization of the conceptual variable produces a large number of different outcomes, all of which are theoretically tied to the independent variable. In the first procedure, we used the same dependent variable measure to see if different empirical realizations of the conceptual independent variables produced the same effects. In this second procedure, we test the effects of the same empirical realization on several dependent variables (or several different manifestations of the same conceptual dependent variable, each of which should be affected, according to our original conceptualization). Again, we can point to Miller's (1957) examples. In one study he compared volume of food consumed, stomach contractions, rate of bar pressing in order to obtain food, and amount of quinine tolerated in the food. Obtaining the predicted results on each of these various measures of hunger lends support to the notion of a single, unitary variable. Similarly, if it can be shown that asking a subject to read a list of obscene words not only makes her like the group she joins but also produces a variety of other outcomes that are theoretically associated with effort and are *not* associated with any one alternative explanation such as sexual arousal, we are more confident that the single, unitary variable involved in the experiment is effort. For example, if our concept of the effects of unpleasant effort implies that it will lead people to seek social support for engaging in the laborious task, our confidence would be increased by an experiment that showed that subjects who recited a list of obscene words were more likely to seek social support for their behavior than subjects who did not recite such a list aloud to the experimenter.

These solutions are not entirely new; similar techniques have been discussed at length by Egon Brunswik (1956) and Donald Campbell and his colleagues (Campbell, 1957; Campbell & Stanley, 1966; Cook & Campbell, 1979; Cook, Leviton, & Shadish, 1985), but they have not been used consistently in social psychological experimentation; in fact, they are seen only rarely. Far more frequent are single, isolated studies which stand in the literature as the only evidence for some process, with no indication that the leap from the conceptual variable to its supposed empirical realization was justified. Also frequent are experiments in which the only grounds for comparability are the authors' claims to be studying the same conceptual variable. Given the vagueness of such variables, there is really no basis for comparison between two experiments which use totally different operations for the independent variable, organize their manipulations around different situations, and measure different dependent variables.

Difficulties of Systematic Replication

Why is the technique of systematic replication used so rarely? The most general answer is that it is often difficult or unfeasible. In many cases it is hard to modify a particular empirical realization of the independent variable without changing the entire experimental situation. The independent variable not only must be conceptually solid but also must make sense to the subject. Thus, a replication of the severity-of-initiation study might necessitate a major change in the context of the experiment. If the subjects were asked to perform 30 push-ups (instead of reading obscene words), one could hardly maintain the format of a group discussion on the psychology of sex without straining the subjects' credulity. Even the most naive of subjects would have second thoughts about doing push-ups as a screening device for a discussion of sex. Thus, one must often redo the entire experiment, changing not only the particular operations used in setting up the independent variable but also the general sctting, the experimental instructions, the stimulus to be rated, and sometimes the measurement of the dependent variable.

This means that we can seldom perform the systematic replication we were aiming for at first; we are forced into the awkward position of letting a large number of factors vary simultaneously. The problem is much more serious if our new experiment differs from the old one in terms of both the independent variable and the dependent variable, since there is no empirical basis for claiming that the two experiments have anything to do with each other, and the whole argument must rest on the plausibility of the experimenter's theoretical claims for a connection between them. If the two experiments show that both reading obscene words and doing push-ups have an effect on attraction to a group, we are more confident about the centrality of the concept of negative effort than we are if one experiment shows that reading obscene words leads to attraction to a group and the other shows that doing push-ups leads to seeking social support. The latter two experiments have no actual behaviors in common. We may believe the theoretical connection between them put forth by the authors, but we would have more confidence in the conceptual variable if both versions could be shown to produce the same behavior. Similarly, our confidence that the two behaviors are related would be strengthened if there was evidence that they were both affected by the same empirical realization of the independent variable.

Even when one of the variables is the same, or very similar, a replication involving many procedural changes is a gamble; the amount of new information gained is largely a function of whether the replication is successful. If this hypothetical second experiment does not produce similar results, what can we conclude? Which of the many changes was the crucial one? Should we conclude that the independent variable was not "really" degree of effort, but some other variable that systematically affected the results? This conclusion would be unjustified, for it is possible that some new variable existing in the second situation is obscuring the relationship. When more than one procedural change is made, an unsuccessful replication is not readily interpretable and thus can rarely add anything to an understanding of the variables studied. However, if such a conceptual replication *does* produce similar results, the gain in interpretation is that much greater. The successful replication not only increases our confidence in the reliability of the original finding but also provides some positive assurance about the validity of our conceptual variable as one that has general effects rather than effects peculiar to the original situation. We would have good evidence that neither the particular method of manipulating the independent variable (or of measuring the dependent variable, if the independent variable is held constant) nor the specific stimuli, nor the particular context, nor the experimental procedure of the first experiment was causing the result.

Noteworthy in this regard is a conceptual replication of the initiation experiment by Harold Gerard and Grover Mathewson (1966). Their experiment was constructed to differ from the Aronson-Mills study in many respects. For example, Gerard and Mathewson gave their subjects electric shocks as an initiation instead of having them read obscene words; the test was introduced as a measure of emotionality rather than as a test of embarrassment; the tape recording was that of a group discussion of cheating rather than one of sex. The dependent variable was still a measure of the attractiveness of the group, although the actual measurement technique differed slightly. Their results confirmed the Aronson-Mills (1959) interpretation: People who underwent painful electric shocks in order to become members of a dull group found that group to be more attractive than did people who underwent mild shocks.

As useful as it is, the Gerard-Mathewson experiment is only one link in a chain of replications necessary to attain complete confidence in a conceptual variable. Since the process of confirming the role of a conceptual variable is really a process of eliminating alternative hypotheses, it is necessary to reconstruct a procedure several different times in order to perform a series of systematic replications. The task of eliminating all possible alternative explanations may become extremely time-consuming. The experimenter is often forced to decide whether to allocate several months or even years to pinning down a single conceptual variable or to move to a new area of interest. Quite frequently, experimenters will attempt a compromise, moving into a novel experimental situation that overlaps somewhat with the previous zone of operation. They hope that the new data will have some relevance for the interpretation of the old, and vice versa. For example, in 1959 Stanley Schachter published a series of studies dealing with affiliation. His basic finding was that people are more motivated to affiliate with others when they are afraid.

Schachter interpreted this finding in terms of social-comparison theory; that is, when people are unsure about the appropriateness of what they are feeling (as they were in the emotionally arousing high-fear condition), they want to see what other people are feeling in order to evaluate their own reactions. Thus, they are motivated to affiliate with others. Although Schachter acknowledged that there were many gaps remaining in our understanding of the psychology of affiliation, he moved on to a new area, and his next series of studies (e.g., Schachter and Singer, 1962; Schachter and Wheeler, 1962) was concerned with the determinants of emotional states. This new research was closely connected with the old, however, in that Schachter felt that when objective cues are absent, social comparison is an important determinant of how people interpret their own emotional arousal. Thus, people in an agitated state may look around to see what emotion other people in the same situation are feeling and use this information in deciding what their own agitation means. Although not specifically concerned with affiliation, the fact that social-comparison theory is supported in a distinctly different context may increase our confidence in the importance and generality of social-comparison processes, and thus indirectly in their applicability to the affiliation situation.

This procedure of moving into an overlapping area is by no means a completely satisfactory solution for the underlying problems, since it does not lead directly toward the development of standard empirical realizations of conceptual variables, and it does leave gaps in our knowledge of the area abandoned by the researcher. Nevertheless, our confidence in a given interpretation increases if several such studies all point in the same direction.

Other Methods for Discovering the Meaning of Conceptual Variables

A slightly different method for increasing confidence in the empirical realization of a conceptual variable involves carrying out an experiment specifically designed to refine the meaning of the variable rather than to replicate a specific experimental relationship between variables. Such an experiment should be aimed at producing a different kind of data which will still be consistent with the original conceptual interpretation. For example, in the severity-of-initiation study, it would have been possible to carry out another experiment using mild initiations and severe initiations but decreasing the desirability of the group so that some subjects would be unwilling to undergo the initiations. Evidence that more subjects refused to read the list of words in the severe condition would increase our certainty that the difference between the two conditions did involve negative effort. Obviously, this must be a separate experiment, since one cannot collect data about the effects of severity of initiation if more than a few subjects refuse to be initiated.

Another way of getting information about the role of some conceptual variable in producing the observed results is to attempt to measure the hypothetical intervening processes involved. For example, in the severity-of-initiation experiment, the conceptual variable of unpleasant effort implies that the subjects felt very uncomfortable when reading the words; another alternative explanation assumes that they felt sexually aroused. To the extent that we can obtain some direct evidence about the presence of either of these two processes, we gain confidence in one or the other interpretation.

Self-report Measures

One type of measure frequently used as an indication of the subjective aspects of a conceptual variable is the self-report. For example, after attempting to manipulate unpleasant effort, an experimenter might simply ask how the subject feels—whether the experience was unpleasant and effortful, or sexually arousing, or something else. Subjective reports, however, are of limited value and must be used with caution, since they present serious problems of interpretation. The major problem is that frequently the subject may be either unable or unwilling to comment on ongoing processes.

For example, in a classic experiment (Aronson & Carlsmith, 1963), children were threatened with either very mild or very severe punishment for playing with a desirable toy. In this experiment the conceptual variable was cognitive dissonance. Children who obeyed the experimenter and refrained from playing with the toy (and all children did obey) should experience dissonance between the cognition that they wanted to play with the toy and the cognition that they were not playing with the toy. The experimenters hypothesized that when the threat was severe, the dissonance would not be very strong, since the children had a very good reason for not playing with the toy (i.e., they would be severely punished for playing with it). In the mild-threat condition, however, the children did not have such a good reason for obeying, since the threatened punishment was not severe; therefore, they should experience a great deal of dissonance. The experimenters predicted that in the mild-threat condition the children would reduce the dissonance by deciding that the toy wasn't so desirable after all and that the reason they weren't playing with it was that they didn't particularly want to play with it. This prediction was confirmed. The experimenters in this study believed that the major variable affecting the children's opinion of the toy was cognitive dissonance, but they did not wish to assert or imply that the children were consciously aware of this dissonance *or* that they could have reported it if asked.

The difficulty involved in using subjective reports as valid indicators of underlying processes emerges even more clearly in the well-known experiment by Bibb Latané and John Darley (1966) in which subjects were placed in a room that gradually and inexplicably began filling with smoke. When the subjects were alone in the room, they usually escaped immediately. But when two calm confederates were sitting in the room, the subjects remained there for as long as six minutes while smoke poured into the room. When questioned afterwards, almost all subjects staunchly maintained that they were not paying any attention to the other people in the room. On the basis of their behavior, however, we are convinced that they were paying attention.

Another problem with subjective reports is the ever-present possibility that simply asking a subject to report on some process may interfere with the process. Research on the sensations and emotions of subjects under the influence of psychedelic drugs is very difficult, since euphoria often turns to annoyance when the experimenter's questions break into the world of private experience. A more subtle type of interference occurs when the experimenter's question accelerates the process. If this happens, it is possible that by the time the subject formulates a reply, the process has run its course, leaving no conscious traces. For example, even if the children in the mild-threat condition of the Aronson and Carlsmith (1963) experiment were able to report their feelings, it is likely that as the experimenters called their attention to the cognitive conflict, they would also be forcing them to *resolve* the conflict. The children could do this by deciding that they didn't really like the forbidden toy anyway. Therefore, they wouldn't want to play with it—hence, no conflict. Indeed, this result was the predicted outcome of the experiment. However, it was predicted to result from the children's choice not to play with the toy rather than from their reflections about the situation. Had they forced the children to think about the conflict, the experimenters would have had no way of knowing whether the decrease in liking for the forbidden toy was the spontaneous result of choosing not to play with it, *or* the product of a conscious rationalization constructed to answer their question. In such a case, it is not only likely that the subject's answer to the question would come too late to reflect the conflict but also possible that the question itself would become an artifact that could be responsible for the predicted results. In a replication of the mild- and severe-threat study, Merrill Carlsmith and his colleagues (1969) showed that simply asking a question that forced the child to think about the conflict actually did affect the results of the experiment. After the experimenter had given the mild or severe threat and left the child alone with toys, a "janitor" came into the room, ostensibly to move a chair. In the control condition he simply remarked on how nice the toys were, but in the experimental condition he also pointed to the forbidden toy and asked, "How come you're not playing with this toy?" and then left the room before the child could answer. It turned out that simply asking the question had quite a noticeable effect on the results. By forcing the subjects' attention toward the toy, the question increased their subsequent derogation of the toy. Thus, it can be risky to attempt to gather information about how the subject is feeling simply by asking a question, because it may be impossible to tell whether the subject's behavior on the dependent-variable measure is due to the treatment, the question, or a combination of the two. Even though the experimenter wants to draw conclusions about the effects of the treatment, it may be impossible to disentangle these effects from the possible effects of the question, and therefore the experimenter may be unable to interpret the results of the experiment.

A more obvious situation in which a question can act as an artifact is an experiment that employs deception. In this context, asking subjects to report on an internal process is very likely to make them aware of the purpose of the experiment. For example, consider Solomon Asch's experiment on group pressure (1951), in which the other "subjects" in the group repeatedly made unanimous but erroneous judgments. Suppose that in the course of the experiment, Asch had asked how the subject felt each time he was in conflict with his peers. It is likely that the subject would have begun to suspect the true purpose of the experiment. Moreover, even if the question does not give away the purpose of the experiment, the answer may be worthless because the context of the question makes it clearer to the subject what the experimenter expects—or conversely, what answer it would be best to avoid giving. For example, in the severity-of-initiation study, since the subject was told that reading the obscene words was a test to eliminate people who showed excessive embarrassment, she was aware that the experimenter expected her to be a little embarrassed. Many subjects tend to be very cooperative; thus, if they are sure they know what the experimenter wants to hear, they will frequently say it. However, subjects may have purposely claimed not to be embarrassed in order to ensure gaining membership in the group.

There are limitations in a person's ability to engage in direct introspection. For example, a series of experiments by Richard Nisbett and Timothy Wilson (1977) has revealed that subjects are often woefully inadequate in accessing and reporting the higher-order cognitive processes that mediate their behaviors. That is, subjects are often unaware of the effects of a stimulus, such as an independent variable, on their subsequent responses. But that doesn't stop most subjects from *assuming* that they know. Because subjects often tell us more than they really know, it is risky to take an introspective report as *conclusive* evidence of the effects of an independent variable (our treatments) on the dependent variable (subjects' responses).

These comments are not meant to imply that subjective, introspective reports are of no value. Often, they are very valuable in helping to frame hypotheses for experiments. Gordon Allport's well-known statement, "If we want to know how people feel—why not ask them?" is not without merit. While it is risky to take a subject's introspective report as final data, the report can and frequently does provide clues as to what kinds of variables to manipulate and what kinds of questions to ask in subsequent experiments. Moreover, during pretesting subject self-reports can be solicited immediately after the manipulation of the independent variable. These subjective reports occasionally provide information which may lead to a modification of the experiment or a follow-up experiment. In the pilot stages of an experiment, for example, careful questioning of subjects may reveal inadequacies in the procedure that must be corrected. It may become apparent that subjects are responding to some aspect of the situation which the experimenter had not noticed or had dismissed as unimportant or that subjects do not understand the instructions. By systematically collecting such information in pilot tests and revising experimental procedures when necessary, experimenters increase the odds that the independent variable is operating in the way they believe it will. This must be done cautiously; given the findings of Nisbett and Wilson (1977), there is no sure guarantee that *even* in carefully conducted interviews after pilot testing, subjects will be able to describe their feelings and perceptions adequately.

The utility of self-report measures depends on a variety of factors. First, if the experiment and the question are relatively simple and straightforward, as in a psychophysics experiment, self-report measures may be relatively more trustworthy. Second, if it is unlikely that the subject will guess what answer the experimenter expects (i.e., if the experimenter has no particular expectation) or will ascribe more positive consequences to one possible answer than to another, we may be more confident in the truthfulness of subjective reports than if these conditions do not hold true. Finally, if the experimenter is interested in subjective reports per se, without making assumptions about the veridicality of their correspondence to hypothesized internal processes, such reports can constitute a perfectly legitimate source of data. Thus, the utility of self-report measures depends on what kind of question the experimenter is trying to answer, whether deception is being employed, what kind of experience the subject is being asked to report, and whether there are differences in the perceived consequences of various different answers the subject might make. In general, however, let us repeat that subjective reports are often of little value and should not be relied on too heavily. Moreover, if they are collected in the course of an experimental session, they may distort the subjects' response on any subsequent dependent variable. For example, a subject in the Asch experiment who had become suspicious after being asked for a subjective report might subsequently have shown great independence of judgment; by contrast, if the question had not been asked, the subject might have conformed throughout all the trials.

Nonverbal Cues

A more subtle method for gauging whether the subjects are experiencing the internal state associated with the conceptual variable is to record such nonverbal indications as facial expressions, body movements, or changes in speech patterns. As an example, consider again the two alternative possibilities raised for the effects of reading the obscene words and passages in the severity-of-initiation study: discomfort versus sexual arousal. If subjects were uncomfortable or embarrassed, they might stutter (Mahl & Schultze, 1964), bite their nails (Krout, 1935), smile or laugh, or avoid the experimenter's gaze (Edelmann, 1987). If they were sexually aroused, their voices might get more husky, and they might spend more time touching or stroking their hair, arms, or legs (Fast, 1970; Hall & Hall, 1971). This type of measure offers two main advantages over self-report measures: (1) Many nonverbal behaviors are less subject to conscious control and censoring (Ekman, 1985; Duncan, 1969; Ekman & Friesen, 1969, 1975; Ekman, Friesen, & O'Sullivan, 1988; Ekman,

Friesen, O'Sullivan, & Scherer, 1980; Mehrabian, 1969), and (2) nonverbal behaviors can be measured without drawing the subject's attention to the fact that a measurement is being made. In many cases, however, the correspondence between various types of nonverbal behavior and processes that interest social psychologists has not been fully validated; thus, the use of such measures at the present time involves some ambiguity. Nevertheless, nonverbal cues are currently under intensive investigation by social psychologists and others, and we may hope that future research will enable us to place more reliance on the use of such measurement procedures. Physiological measures, such as heart rate and galvanic skin response (GSR), may also be employed by social psychologists, although to date these measures typically reflect a general *level* of arousal without differentiating among different *types* of arousal.

Changes in Design

Still another procedure for solving some of the problems of interpreting the conceptual variable involves the use of a more sophisticated design. For example, as mentioned above, the experimenters' conceptual variable in the mild- and severe-threat experiment implied the existence of a negative drive state (dissonance) following the subject's decision not to play with a desired toy in the face of a mild threat. According to the theory, the child's liking for the toy should diminish when the threat of punishment is mild but not when it is severe, since a severe threat should provide ample justification for relinquishing even a very desirable toy. Although Aronson and Carlsmith found the predicted result, they did not test for the existence of this negative drive state. It is doubtful that any of the nonverbal or physiological measures currently available would be subtle enough to discriminate between the negative drive produced by dissonance and the straightforward negative affect produced by the threat. Nevertheless, some indirect evidence bearing on the dissonance interpretation could have been provided by a more sophisticated design.

Such a design was used in a subsequent experiment by Jonathan Freedman (1965). Essentially, Freedman replicated Aronson and Carlsmith's results, using the same independent variable but a different dependent variable (number of children in each condition who played with the toy once the threat was removed, and the length of time they did so). He also employed two additional conditions, in which the child no longer had the opportunity to choose to relinquish the forbidden toy. Freedman's experimental conditions were the same as those of Aronson and Carlsmith—he issued either a mild or a severe threat of punishment for playing with the toy, then left the room, allowing the children to decide to abide by the sanction and therefore, supposedly, to experience dissonance in the mild-threat condition. In these conditions, like those in the Aronson-Carlsmith experiment, Freedman found great differences between the mild-threat and the severe-threat treatments. In the two additional control groups, Freedman issued either a mild threat or a severe threat for playing with the toy, but then he stayed in the room, so he could watch the child. Thus, the child did not have to decide whether to leave the toy alone; since the experimenter was standing right there, keeping a watchful eye, the child knew that he could not play with the toy. Having no choice in the matter, the child would experience no dissonance. Since there was no dissonance, one would not expect any difference between the severe and mild conditions. The results were consistent with this reasoning; these two conditions were not different from each other, and both were very similar to the results in the severe-threat conditions when the experimenter did leave the room. Thus, dissonance reduction was observed only in the condition designed to produce dissonance—the unsupervised mild-threat condition. (Figure 2-1 provides a pictorial representation of this interaction.)

Thus, by modifying the experiment to include two conditions in which dissonance was not expected but in which the rest of the procedure was left unchanged, Freedman's experiment led to increased confidence in the conceptual variable "cognitive dissonance." In general, a conceptual variable can often be illuminated by including additional conditions which resemble the original conditions operationally but which cannot be interpreted in terms of the conceptual variable. Such a procedure reduces the need for exhaustive systematic replications.

SUCCESSFUL AND UNSUCCESSFUL REPLICATIONS

In Chapter 1 we distinguished between two types of replication. In a **direct replication,** the experimenter tries to repeat the original experiment exactly. If the

FIGURE 2-1
The effects of experimenter presence and severity of threat on proportion of children playing with forbidden toy. (*Freedman, 1965.*)

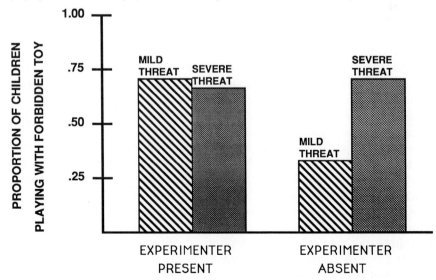

results are the same as those of the first experiment, we gain confidence that the relationship under study is reliable and stable and is unlikely to be obscured by uncontrolled or unknown variables, so long as the experimental conditions are kept the same. In a **systematic replication,** some aspects of the situation are deliberately varied or left uncontrolled: The conditions are not exactly the same as those of the original experiment. If such a replication is successful, we not only gain confidence in the reliability of the phenomenon but also obtain evidence that the result is not unique to the specific conditions of the original experiment.

In social psychology almost all replication is necessarily systematic rather than direct. Even though the second experimenter may have been trying to reproduce the original experiment exactly, in practice there are bound to be some differences. At the very least, the experimenter is different; frequently, the subject population is different as well. In addition, because social psychological manipulations tend to be complex and unstandardized, there are typically minor (perhaps even major) changes in the instructions, tone of voice, emphasis, and so on. Often, the methodological descriptions included in published experiments do not provide sufficient information to enable one to carry out an exact replication, and the new experimenter fills in the gaps by guesswork and intuition. Thus, when a replication succeeds in producing the same effect as that found in the original experiment, we gain some confidence not only in the reproducibility of the finding but also in its generality. We have good evidence that the original finding is a solid one, not dependent on extraneous factors unique to the first study. This increases our confidence that the conceptual variable was responsible for the outcome.

When such a replication fails, however, interpretation of this failure is subject to the same uncertainty that we mentioned for conceptual replications in which the experimenter deliberately alters the conditions of the original experiment. Even though the second experiment may be intended as a direct replication, the passage of time and the use of a different experimenter and new subjects preclude the complete achievement of this goal, and usually there are more important procedural differences between the two experiments as well. Thus, it is difficult to draw firm inferences. The most we can say is that something about the original experiment was not accurately specified and seems to have a decisive effect on the results. Failure to replicate limits the **generality** of a finding but has no implication for the validity of the variables involved.

One obvious—but frequently overlooked—problem about failures to replicate is that negative results are easily produced by factors irrelevant to the truth or falsity of the basic hypothesis. If an effect cannot be obtained, it may be that the effect does not exist or that one or both of the investigators are ignorant of relevant influential variables. But it may also be that the second experimenter is not skillful enough to attain it. In social psychological experiments, the experimenter's behavior often constitutes a crucial part of the treatment: The experimenter can contribute to the impact of the independent variable or nullify it, can run the experiment rigorously or sloppily, can pick up or overlook cues of boredom or suspicion. All these variations in the experimenter's behavior—and many others besides—can affect the outcome of a social psychological experiment in which the independent variable is typically contained in the context of an interpersonal interaction. Hence, there is a certain asymmetry between positive and negative results. If an experiment cannot be faulted in terms of the use of adequate techniques to preclude bias, positive results carry their own proof of competence; negative results must be supplemented.[1]

In better established sciences, it is not uncommon for failures to replicate to be interpreted as indications of incompetence on the part of the experimenter who has attempted the replication. When a biology student (or even a professional biologist with a reputation for excellence) cuts a planarian in two and both halves die instead of regenerating, no doubt whatsoever is cast on the results of previous experiments in which the experiments were successful in obtaining new worms from fragments of old ones. Nor does the experimenter feel that he or she has happened upon a hitherto unknown strain of nonregenerating planaria. Instead the experimenter concludes that human error—failure to provide enough food or water for the nonregenerating halves, mangling the worm when cutting, or making some other mistake—has caused the nonreplication of results.

Even in previously unexplored areas of research, experiments in the "hard" sciences often contain inherent proofs of competence. If one experimenter extracts a hormone from the brain of a rat in an experiment designed to study the effects of injection of that hormone into an opposite-sex rat of the same litter, an experimenter who wishes to replicate the study can demonstrate competence by successfully extracting the same hormone. Social psychology experiments rarely contain such built-in competence gauges; often, the second experimenter has no way of even knowing how similar the replication experiment is to the original. In part because of these ambiguities, social psychologists commonly make a particular type of "attribution error" in interpreting failures to replicate.

Specifically, experimenters frequently attribute a failure to replicate to some intentional change in the procedure. The credibility of this claim depends on the use of a design which includes a successful "direct" replication. Suppose, for example, that Jones, a hypothetical psychologist at Yale University, produces a specific experimental result, using Yale undergraduates as subjects: He finds that insulting subjects' performance on a task makes them aggressive toward the experimenter. Smith, at the University of Illinois, criticizes these results, maintaining that they were not a function of the conceptual variable proposed by Jones but were merely a function of some artifact in the

---

[1] This statement is not meant to imply that positive results prove the validity of the conceptual variable. Many "successful" experiments are open to more than one interpretation (see the discussion of alternative explanations in Chapter 1). It is also possible that the results of the first experiment were caused by bias. Techniques for avoiding bias are discussed in Chapter 9.

procedure. Smith decides, for example, that the insult was irrelevant and that Jones's subjects were aggressive because the insult *frustrated* them by interrupting them when they were close to finishing the task. Smith then attempts to repeat Jones's procedure in all respects except one; he changes the procedure slightly, giving the subjects a stack of magazines to leaf through instead of a real task, in order to eliminate the artifact. He fails to replicate and concludes that his experiment demonstrates that Jones's results were due to task interruption. This is only one of many possible conclusions. Smith's failure to replicate could have been caused by any number of things and is therefore uninterpretable. It could have been a function of any of countless minor variations in the procedure, such as tone of voice, the precise wording of the insults, the elegance of the experimental room, or cues of friendliness or authority from the experimenter.

Most of this ambiguity could be eliminated by use of a balanced design that includes a "direct" replication of the conditions run by the original experimenter. That is, suppose that Smith's design had included a repeat of Jones's conditions with the supposed artifact left in, and his results in these conditions approximated those of Jones's experiment. If he had found no effect in the conditions without the supposed artifact, or if he found differences in the opposite direction, one could be sure that this result was not merely a function of incidental or unintentional procedural differences. That is, if Smith's subjects become aggressive when the insult interrupts a task, but not when they are reading magazines, Smith's results are directly comparable to Jones's. If Smith fails to obtain results similar to Jones's in the supposedly exact replication, however, we would have to conclude that there was some more important, unknown factor in the variables used in the original experiment, that it was limited to a particular population, that Jones had unconsciously biased his data, that Smith was less skillful at delivering the insult, and so on. An unbalanced replication design is not worthless. If it achieves results similar to those of the original experiment, it can extend the generality of the phenomenon; if its results are dissimilar, it can indicate that the generality of the phenomenon is limited and needs further specification. In cases of failure to replicate, however, such designs are often misleadingly overinterpreted and held as evidence against the validity of the original experimenter's conceptual variable.

Failure to replicate may be an important indication of the lack of generality or validity of the first experiment. It may also demonstrate the incompetence of the second experimenter.

Cross-Cultural Replications

The problem of replication is compounded when a social psychologist attempts to study a phenomenon cross-culturally. It is becoming increasingly common for psychologists to conduct studies using members of different cultures or subcultures as subjects, with the goal of testing the generality of a phenomenon. Sometimes, the experimenter will have a specific hypothesis about cultural differences and may predict that due to some environmental difference, members of a particular culture or subculture will behave in different ways in response to the conceptual variable. The goal is a laudable one, but attaining it is fraught with difficulties. Even if it were possible to perform a direct replication in another culture, such a study might well be meaningless. Subjects from another culture may interpret the experimental situation differently, so that the "same" manipulation will not mean the same thing. We may be able to guess what will arouse guilt, anger, or embarrassment in a sample of U.S. college students, but we have no basis for assuming that the same treatments will work for ghetto children or nuns or Australian aborigines. To assume that differences in their responses to the experiment represent true differences in their responses to the conceptual variables would be foolhardy.

Accordingly, the experimenter may find it necessary to change the procedure, perhaps only by translating it into another language, perhaps by using different techniques. However, in changing the experimental techniques, the investigator still cannot be sure that any observed differences represent true differences in the subject populations; they may simply be a result of the changed method. Colleagues in psychology will be quick to pick up the potential artifact introduced by using different techniques for different groups of subjects; anthropologists will point out that it is specious to speak of using the "identical" method in a culture whose members will interpret it according to wholly different assumptions.

Although there is really no solution to this problem, we should not abandon such research or rely merely on anecdotal evidence for the generality or specificity of a phenomenon. There is no way to tell which of psychology's theories are widely applicable and which are culture-specific without trying them out in fundamentally different cultural or subcultural settings. The researcher willing to accept this challenge should put a great deal of effort into devising an experiment that will be conceptually equivalent to the original study in terms of the experience and expectations of the new subjects.[2]

In order to know what changes to make to achieve equivalence, the researcher should consult a professional who has studied the culture. In writing up such research, the experimenter should describe the method in more than usual detail, specifying changes made in the experiment and providing a rationale for introducing them. Best of all—though most time-consuming—the experimenter should attempt to replicate the study more than once in each culture, using variations of the treatment within cultures. If all studies within each culture produce similar results, whereas consistent between-culture differences emerge across a number of experiments, the experimenter can be confident that the difference between populations is a true one.

---

[2] The issues raised by the use of "conceptually equivalent" experiments are similar to those raised by the use of a flexible administration of the independent variable (see Chapter 7).

EXPERIMENTAL REALISM VERSUS MUNDANE REALISM

In this chapter we have used the term realism or realistic experiment rather loosely. There has been a great deal of confusion concerning this concept, largely because "realism" has more than one meaning. Aronson and Carlsmith (1968) proposed a broad distinction between two senses in which an experiment can be said to be realistic. In one sense an experiment is realistic if the situation is realistic to the subjects: if they believe it, if they are forced to attend to it and take it seriously, in short, if it has impact on them. They called this kind of realism **experimental realism.** The term "realism" can also be used to refer to the similarity of events occurring in a laboratory setting to those likely to occur in the real world. They called this type of realism **mundane realism.** The mere fact that an event looks like one that occurs in the real world does not imply that it is important in the study of human behavior. Many events that occur in the real world are boring or uninfluential. Thus, it is possible to put a subject to sleep if an experimental event is high on mundane realism but remains low on experimental realism.

Mundane realism and experimental realism are not polar concepts; a particular technique may be high on both mundane and experimental realism, low on both, or high on one and low on the other. Perhaps the difference between experimental and mundane realism can be clarified by citing a couple of examples in which a high degree of experimental realism was achieved but little mundane realism. Let us first consider Solomon Asch's (1951) classic experiment on group pressure, in which subjects were asked to judge the length of lines and were confronted with unanimous and contradictory judgments from a group of peers. For most subjects this experiment seems to have contained a good deal of experimental realism. Whether subjects yielded to group pressure or remained independent, the vast majority went through a rather painful experience that caused them to squirm, sweat, and exhibit other signs of tension and anxiety. They were involved, upset, and deeply concerned about the evidence of their senses. We may assume that they were reacting to a situation that was as "real" for them as any of their ordinary experiences. But the experiment was hardly realistic in the mundane sense. Recall that the subjects were judging a very clear, physical event. In everyday life one rarely encounters a situation in which direct and unambiguous sensory evidence is contradicted by the unanimous judgments of peers. Although the judging of lines is perhaps not important or realistic in a mundane sense, since it does not immediately remind us of a real-world situation, one cannot deny the impact of having one's sensory input contradicted by everyone else in the group.

Another example is the procedure employed by Stanley Milgram (1973) in his studies on obedience. In these experiments Milgram instructed the subjects to give a series of electric shocks to a person, ostensibly as part of an experiment on learning. Unbeknownst to the subject, no shocks were actually dispensed. After each "incorrect" trial, the subject was asked to increase the intensity of the shocks by pressing the next of a continuous series of levers labeled from "Slight Shock" at one end to "Danger: Severe Shock" near the other end. The majority of the subjects continued to increase the shock level to the maximum, despite the fact that the "recipient" (actually a confederate), who was closeted in the next room, indicated that he was in severe pain, pounded on the door, and finally fell silent. Since the confederate's silence constituted an incorrect response on the "learning task," the subjects were asked to keep increasing the intensity. Most obeyed. Milgram provides a vivid description of the effects this procedure had on the typical subject who complied with the instruction. The subject sweated, stuttered, trembled, burst into uncontrollable nervous laughter, and showed many other signs of an extreme loss of composure. There is no doubt that a high degree of experimental realism had been achieved. We suspect that few of these subjects easily forgot the experience they had had in the "contrived," "artificial" conditions of the laboratory. Yet there is no doubt that similar experiences do not happen to most people in the real world.

On the other hand, consider a series of experiments by Daniel Wegner and his colleagues (1981) which, although high on mundane realism, are low on experimental realism. In one experiment, subjects read fictitious newspaper headlines about candidates running for city council seats in a distant city. Some headlines were neutral statements about the candidates (e.g., "George Armstrong Arrives in City"); others were direct incriminating statements (e.g., "Andrew Winters Connected to Bank Embezzlement"); others were denials of alleged wrongdoing (e.g., "Karen Downing Not Associated with Fraudulent Charity"); and still others were incriminating questions (e.g., "Is Bob Talbert Linked to Mafia?"). After reading the headlines, subjects provided their impressions of the candidates. By participating in this experiment, subjects were doing something that they frequently did in everyday life: reading headlines in a newspaper. Thus, the experiment had a great deal of mundane realism. But nothing much was happening to the subjects. Very few U.S. college students are profoundly affected by reading headlines about a remote city council election in another state. The procedure did not have a great deal of experimental realism.

Studies of the effects of attitude similarity on attraction by Donn Byrne and his colleagues (e.g., Byrne, 1961, 1969, 1971; Byrne & Nelson, 1965; Byrne & Rhamey, 1965) are examples of social psychological experiments that while precisely controlled are low on *both* experimental and mundane realism. Briefly, in these experiments, potential subjects are asked to complete questionnaires designed to assess their attitudes on various topics—such as belief in God, premarital sex, smoking marijuana, and welfare legislation—prior to arriving at the laboratory. When a subject arrives, he or she is provided the same questionnaire—which has allegedly been completed by another student. In actuality, the questionnaire was completed by the experimenters prior to the subject's arrival to reflect varying degrees of attitude similarity between the subject and the fictitious other. The subject reads the completed questionnaire and is then asked to evaluate the other using a six-item questionnaire within which two attraction measures are embedded. Thus, in these experiments, attitude similarity is operationalized as the proportion of attitudes held in common by the subject and the bogus other (typically 0, 50, or 100 percent similar attitudes). Attraction is operationalized as the sum of scores on two attraction measures (subjects' personal feelings about the other and desire to work with the other in an experiment).

Outside the laboratory when we are exposed to strangers for the first time, seldom if ever do they hand us a checklist of their attitudes on various topics so we can get to know them better; neither do new acquaintances hand us a scale on which we are to check how much we like them, or how much we'd like working with them in an experiment, hence the low mundane realism of the studies conducted by Byrne and his colleagues. Furthermore, it is highly unlikely that exposure to scales on which another has placed X's to indicate his or her attitude will be experimentally real in the sense of being engrossing and impactful for subjects.

Contrast this procedure with Murray's (1963) study of stressful interpersonal disputations, in which a skilled confederate attacked the subject's general philosophy of life. The latter study lacks the precision that Byrne and his colleagues have achieved. At the same time, Murray's experiment is high on both types of realism. There is no doubt that this procedure had a substantial impact on the subject (experimental realism). At the same time, this type of confrontation has mundane realism: It does occur frequently in the lives of university students in seminar discussions and similar situations.

Occasionally a critic will argue that experiments in social psychology are artificial and therefore worthless. One argument suggests that the mere fact that a subject enters a laboratory lends an unrealistic atmosphere to the proceedings and that data obtained through laboratory experimentation are therefore invalid. We believe that this argument stems fundamentally from a confusion between experimental and mundane realism. If the purpose of an experiment is to capture the essence of a phenomenon such as conformity, obedience, or attraction, the experiment must have experimental realism. Some experiments are so deficient in experimental realism (however high they may be in mundane realism) that they do not even capture the subjects' attention, let alone influence their behavior. A major objective of this kind of laboratory experiment is to have the greatest possible impact on the subjects within the limits of ethical considerations and requirements of control. The situation encountered by subjects in such an experiment must be so interesting, involving, and believable that its effects will transcend the influence of the subjects' knowledge that they are in an experiment. It is difficult to argue that the subjects in the Asch experiment, the Milgram experiment, or the Aronson-Mills experiment were able to step back and say, "Hey, I'm only in an experiment." What was happening to the subjects was real, nontrivial, and impactful. Whatever one might say about these experiments, no one would ever suggest that the subjects were *bored*.

Mundane Realism and Impact

Thus, if experimental realism is high, the situation will be meaningful for the subjects, regardless of how far removed it may be from their experience outside the laboratory. If an experimental procedure already has impact, it is unnecessary to make it occur in a real-world setting. In certain situations, however, increasing mundane realism will also increase impact. Occasionally, the requirements of an experiment are such that adding mundane realism is the only way to achieve impact. The atmosphere of an experiment is conducive to neither the convincing manipulation of certain variables nor the effective elicitation of certain types of behavior. For example, many social psychologists have discovered that when subjects know that they are in an experiment, convincing them that someone is angry at them or getting them to express aggressive behavior is difficult. Most subjects know that such behavior is inappropriate within the confines of an experimental situation. Consequently, if one performs an experiment that requires the manipulation or expression of hostility, an approach that has mundane realism may be necessary.

For variables such as aggression, which are difficult to deal with in the laboratory, the field experiment provides an excellent alternative. An experiment by Mary Harris (1974) provides an example of the creative employment of mundane realism in the field. In this experiment, men and women confederates approached people standing in line at various restaurants, stores, ticket windows, and banks and cut in front of them. After cutting in line, the confederates either said "Excuse me" or said nothing, and surreptitiously recorded the verbal and nonverbal responses of the unsuspecting subjects. A number of Harris' predictions were confirmed: Subjects near the front of the line exhibited more verbal and nonverbal aggression than did those near the back of the line (presumably because they were closer to their goal and thus were more frustrated when the confederates stepped in front of them); the male confederate was on the receiving end of more aggression than the female confederate; and confederates who said "Excuse me" were less likely than those who said nothing to elicit aggression from subjects.

There is little doubt that the field setting of this experiment added impact that would have been lacking in a more artificial setting. But this is due to the difficulty of achieving experimental realism by using this procedure in the laboratory, where subjects might judge the other person's intrusive behavior as inappropriate behavior for a psychology experiment and might even suspect that person of being an accomplice. Many events that occur every day in the real world—those high on mundane realism—are likely to be interpreted differently if they occur in the context of a laboratory experiment, and thus an experimenter's claim that a high degree of mundane realism increases the relevance of the findings may be ill-founded if experimental realism has been sacrificed. However, if a laboratory experiment has experimental realism, and if other aspects of the experiment are well controlled so that the intrusion of such factors as acquiescence, experimental demands, and/or evaluation apprehension are minimized, we contend that there is no need for an experiment to strive for mundane realism.

Internal and External Validity

Before we elaborate our position further, we should discuss an important distinction made by Donald Campbell (1957) between internal validity and external validity of an experimental effect. According to Campbell, an experimental result has **internal validity** if within the experimental situation there is a significant difference between or among the effects of the conditions of the experiment (assuming, of course, that the experiment is free of extraneous variables whose effects might be confounded with those of the treatment). In other words, the treatment has a significant effect, and there is no reason to believe that it is due to an artifact; one can assume that differences in dependent variable measures are due to the manipulation of the independent variable, and the independent variable alone. Internal validity may be increased by having a well-controlled, well-designed experiment that allows the experimenter to rule out confounding extraneous variables as alternative explanations of the result and that reduces random error so that significant results are more likely. Internal validity may also be increased by selecting procedures and operations that have a great deal of experimental realism for the subject. Internal validity may suffer (although not necessarily) if the subject sees through the experiment, does not take it seriously, or responds "like a subject" rather than like a person. Many strategies for increasing internal validity are clear and are discussed throughout this book. We will discuss specific threats to internal validity in more detail in connection with quasi-experiments in Chapter 5, for those designs present special problems for researchers concerned with enhancing the internal validity of their research.

    External validity refers to the generality of an effect, to the populations and settings to which it can be applied. External validity may be maximized by increasing the heterogeneity of the sample and the experimental situations, by conducting a series of studies to purify the empirical realization of the conceptual variable, and/or by using a multiplicity of response measures. And *both* internal validity and external validity can also be enhanced by increasing the experimental realism of the situation. Let us elaborate briefly. First, if subjects are not engaged in experimental procedures but rather have time to sit back and speculate about the experimenter's hypothesis, they can exercise a number of options: They may decide to become "cooperative" subjects and comply with what they imagine the experimenter expects. They may decide to become "contrary" subjects and assert their independence by behaving in opposition to what they imagine the experimenter expects. Or they may "put on a good face," working to appear smarter, kinder, more sensitive, or more socially skilled than the average person, regardless of their speculations about the experimenter's specific hypothesis. All these strategies constitute potential threats to the *internal* validity of an experiment. Second, if subjects have the opportunity to speculate about the true hypothesis and are cooperating, acting contrary, or putting on a good face for the experimenter, results obtained are generalizable only to similarly cooperative, contrary, or socially desirable experimental subjects. Thus, these options represent a potential threat to the *external* validity of the study as well.

According to Campbell, the optimal design for an experiment in a social setting is one that maximizes both internal and external validity. But of the two, internal validity is, of course, the more important, for if random or systematic error makes it impossible for the experimenter even to draw any conclusions from the experiment, the question of the generality of these conclusions never arises. However, the extent to which a laboratory experiment has external validity is not easy to determine. Although one can gain confidence in the external validity of an experiment if one follows the procedures listed above, there are several sources of difficulty in attempting to generalize. Most of these focus on the problem of defining the variables involved in the complex situations that obtain in the world outside the laboratory. Even if a laboratory situation were an exact analogue of some process occurring in the outside world, we could not be sure that the same variables would operate in the two situations. One cannot guarantee generalizability simply by providing an experiment that has a high degree of mundane realism.

TRIVIALITY: THE ARTIFICIAL, THE OBVIOUS, THE IRRELEVANT, AND THE NONGENERALIZABLE

One common criticism of social psychology is intimately related to the issues of realism and validity we have been discussing here. The catchword of this criticism is "triviality." The argument that experimentation is too picayune to reflect reality is not directed solely toward social psychologists; the image of the scientist spending a lifetime in the laboratory, ignoring the world in order to confirm one tiny fact, has been applied to all varieties of scientist. However, questions about triviality are raised especially often about social psychology. Since the subject matter of social psychology is human interaction and everyone has had direct experience with human interaction, many people who would not presume to judge the importance or relevance of an experiment in physics feel quite confident about their ability to judge an experiment in social psychology. We do not wish to assert that social psychology is an esoteric specialty about which no one but a psychology Ph.D. can make a valid statement. We merely wish to point out that instant dismissal of an experiment on the grounds of "triviality" is at best an oversimplified response, no matter who makes it.

The term "triviality" is used to refer to at least three distinct though related types of perceived deficiency, as illustrated by the following example. One of social psychology's most strongly established findings is that one's liking for a person increases with familiarity: if the other individual lives nearby, if the two see each other often, and so on. If a social psychologist reports this finding to someone, the person may say, "My feeling for the guy next door is one of unmitigated repulsion, and I see him every day. Familiarity works only in the lab, where everything else is equal, and a person has nothing to lose." Or, the person may retort, "So what else is new? You did two years' worth of experiments to find that out? People have known that since the beginning of time." Or the response may be, "What about violence in the streets?" Any and all of these comments may be brought forward as evidence of triviality.

Artificiality

The first of these criticisms is that research is trivial because it is artificial or inapplicable. This is the issue we have been discussing throughout the last section. We have seen that the idea that an experimental situation should be an exact analogue to a real-life situation is based on a false premise, namely that the same variables will operate in the same way in two different situations. Since we have no justification for accepting this premise, the time and effort necessary to create a would-be replica of some real-world situation are likely to be misplaced and might better be devoted to establishing a situation that has experimental realism. The goal of any scientist is to discover the basic, underlying variables that affect the behavior of whatever is being studied. In order to do this, the researcher must limit the situation to manageable proportions by holding many variables constant and focusing only on a few aspects of the situation. Usually, this requires some sacrifice of mundane realism in order to acquire the control necessary for interpretable results (internal validity). Often, there is simply too much happening in a real-world situation, or even in a convincing experimental analogue, for the influence of the important variables to be clearly apparent. Galileo arrived at his laws of motion by rolling innumerable smooth, round balls down innumerable smooth, inclined planes, not by watching boulders roll down mountains and certainly not by building an exact-scale model of a mountain in his laboratory and rolling pebbles down it. Once the relevant variables and their principles of operation are known for a relatively simple situation, it is then possible to study how they interact with other variables in a more complex situation. If these variables and principles are not isolated, the apparent generality conferred by a situation high in mundane realism is spurious, since we have no way of defining the conditions in which the experimental effect will hold true.

In a sense, the concern about artificiality in social psychology results from our very failure to isolate relevant variables and their principles of operation. For many individual experiments in social psychology, as we have mentioned, plausible alternative explanations can be suggested, and often these alternative explanations are based on some "trivial" artifact the experimenter seems to have overlooked. In part, this reflects a lack of control in the particular instance. In part, it reflects the more general fact that in social psychology we lack confidence in our empirical realizations because they have not been purified through systematic replication. If we have not precisely defined the requirements for the empirical realizations of a given conceptual variable, we cannot specify the conditions in which it will have a predicted effect, and thus we cannot make statements about generality at this stage. Given this state of affairs, to ask for a general statement which will apply to a given real-world situation is to ask for a guess, not a fact.

In any specific experiment, investigators choose a procedure—based on knowledge of theory, careful observations of the world, or simple intuition— that they believe is an empirical realization of the conceptual variable. All experimental procedures are contrived in the sense that they are invented. Indeed, it can be said that the art of experimentation rests to a great extent on the investigator's skill in contriving the procedure that is the most accurate realization of the conceptual variable and that has the greatest impact and credibility for the subject. At the same time, this introduces the disquieting possibility that the experimenter may unwittingly be selecting a particular example of the conceptual variable, not because it seems to be the most accurate rendition of the conceptualization, but because the investigator has a hunch that it will work; this hunch may be based in part on specific features of the treatment completely unrelated to the conceptual variable.

For example, if we look only at Milgram's first study (1963) on the antecedents of obedience, we may hesitate to generalize his results very far—say, to the behavior of the German people in the 1930s and 1940s. But this is not because Milgram's experiment was artificial and lacked mundane realism. Rather, on the basis of that experiment alone, we are not convinced that the effect would have been as strong in slightly different circumstances. For example, we may feel that the scientific trappings of the original experiment may have increased the subjects' tendency to obey. The same problem arises with respect to generalization from any experiment. No matter how similar or dissimilar the experimental context is to a real-life situation, it is still only one context; we cannot know how far the results will generalize to other contexts unless we carry on an integrated program of systematic replication. After his first experiment, Milgram performed a series of well-executed systematic replications (1973) which have gradually increased our knowledge of the extent to which his initial finding can be generalized. Our confidence in the generality of the finding would be increased still further if the same conceptual variable (obedience) were operationalized in the context of scenarios even more different from the situation in the original experiment.

This is not to say that mundane realism has no value or that criticism of an experiment for artificiality is never meaningful. As previously mentioned, moving outside the laboratory can often increase the experimental realism of a situation. Moreover, although mundane realism does not increase our overall confidence in the external validity of any given data, it may increase our confidence in the applicability of the data to a given setting. An investigator who is interested in answering a question about the operation of a variable in a particular setting, rather than in attempting to delineate more general principles, would be well advised to conduct the experiment in that setting or one that resembles it. For example, consider the experiment by Donald Taylor, Paul Berry, and Clifford Block (1958) which showed that brainstorming was an ineffective technique of problem solving. The applicability of these findings to industrial settings was questioned by proponents of brainstorming primarily because the investigators studied college students rather than industrial employees. Subsequently, Marvin Dunnette, John Campbell, and Kay Jaastad (1963) obtained similar results in a study of industrial employees in an industrial setting. Because of the change in setting and subjects, it seems reasonable to conclude that the later study is more applicable to industrial situations. However, the results of this study, taken alone, clearly have no greater external validity than do those of Taylor, Berry, and Block; one set of results is more applicable to one situation, the other to a different situation. We would be able to generalize to a greater extent if either group of experimenters had based its conclusions on the study of a heterogeneous sample of subjects, a wide variety of problems, a wide variety of settings, or a wide variety of response measures.

Sometimes, people feel that results must be specific to a laboratory situation, because they seem implausible or unreasonable in the light of everyday experience. Contradictions between social psychological findings and "the wisdom of experience" are due partly to differences in the kinds of questions and comparisons that are relevant to psychology and to everyday life. For example, Peter Lewinsohn and his colleagues (1980) asked both depressed and nondepressed individuals to complete questionnaires in which they rated their own personal competencies. Later, trained coders unobtrusively observed subjects as they interacted with others and rated them on those same social competency dimensions. Self-ratings of both depressed and nondepressed people were compared with observer ratings. Surprisingly, for nondepressed subjects there was a greater discrepancy between self- and other ratings than there was for depressed subjects: It seems that depressed people are more realistic and accurate (if not self-congratulatory) in inferring how they are evaluated by others. Nondepressed people, however, seem to move through the world blithely unaware of the extent to which others fail to share their positive (but illusory) self-evaluations.

To many people, this finding may seem implausible. One of the main reasons for this implausibility is that the psychologist is using a different basis for comparison than the average person. A person imagining the last time he or she felt sad or depressed may assert that friends and loved ones bent over backward to provide words of support, praise, and reassurance; how could these significant others really believe that he or she was not deserving of such kind overtures? And this recollection may be an accurate reflection of a few isolated instances in *one* person's life. The psychologist, however, compares many questionnaires filled out by many different subjects, some of whom are chronically depressed, not just temporarily "blue." Looked at from the psychologist's point of view, there is a good deal of evidence for a kind of "depressive realism." That is, the negative self-ratings of chronically depressed subjects were more closely related to observers' ratings than were the more positive self-ratings of nondepressed subjects. The fact that depressed people are more accurate in assessing others' evaluations of them may not "ring true" to the average person, however, because the average person (by definition) is not depressed *and* because social convention often dictates that we spare others our candid evaluations of them.

Thus, plausibility should never be the criterion for judging scientific research. If it were, we would find it much more difficult to discover new phenomena. One of the basic purposes of setting up an experiment in controlled conditions and making the best possible measurements is to free ourselves from the chains of plausibility as a criterion. It may be that in social psychology, as in other branches of science, some findings are accepted as "true" but as useless or injudicious for individuals to attempt to apply to everyday life. For example, we know from research in physics that a table is made up of a certain volume of molecules mixed with an even greater volume of empty space; for the purposes of everyday life, it is useful to assume that a table is a solid object and to put things down on it without worrying about whether they might fall through. Likewise, some humanists have advanced the idea that certain psychological findings might better be ignored in everyday life rather than taken as suggestive of new modes of behavior:

> Psychology has split and shattered the idea of a "person," and has shown that there is something incalculable in each of us, which may at any moment rise to the surface and destroy our natural balance. We don't know what we are like. We don't know what other people are like. How, then, can we put any trust in personal relationships, or cling to them in the gathering political storm? In theory we cannot. In practice we can and do. Though A is not unchangeably A or B unchangeably B, there can still be love and loyalty between the two. For the purpose of living one has to assume that the personality is solid, and the "self" is an entity, and to ignore all contrary evidence.[3]

"Common Knowledge"

The second form of the triviality criticism is that the research finding is common knowledge. In some ways, this is the exact opposite of the implausibility criticism, but both originate from the same initial assumption: namely, that everyday observation is reliable and valid. The comments made regarding questions about implausibility are relevant here. Strong additional evidence of the inadequacy of so-called common knowledge as a criticism of experimental results is that often the same results are judged "implausible" by one everyday observer and "common knowledge" by another. For example, do "birds of a feather flock together," or do "opposites attract"? Common knowledge, like the work of Aristotle, contains many true observations and many false ones. Unfortunately, experience does not provide standards for distinguishing between them; that is the business of the controlled experiment.

---

[3] E. M. Forster, "What I Believe," in *Two Cheers for Democracy* (London: Edward Arnold, 1951), pp. 77–78.

Irrelevance

The third form of the triviality criticism is that the content of the experimental finding is of small importance in relation to the somber spectrum of social problems confronting us and which—by implication—we should be confronting. In Chapter 1 we discussed this problem, indicating the dilemma that often exists in the choice between accurate (and often less applicable) research in the laboratory and applicable (and often less accurate) research in the field. In this chapter we have pointed out that it is very difficult to apply psychological findings to real-world behavior if we are ignorant of the operational principles of the variables involved and that in order to discover these principles it is necessary to study small portions of the relevant behavior in a controlled and often simplified situation. If we are unaware of how the variables work, we cannot expect much success in applying them in a real-world situation, in which countless other variables may be operating. Indeed, unless and until we have some idea about relationships among variables, it would be presumptuous and irresponsible to intervene in the real world. Sometimes, psychological variables have been understood well enough to be applied outside the laboratory, and some of these instances provide irrefutable evidence that the apparent importance of a laboratory experiment may be a less relevant consideration than the control achieved. For example, Morton Deutsch (1949) conducted research to study the consequences of cooperation versus competition and suggested that the objective outcomes of these two different situations have implications for the *feelings* between the participants. Briefly, he suggested that people in competition will be hostile and suspicious in their dealings with one another; people who cooperate will be more friendly and concerned with one another's welfare. In the aftermath of unsuccessful desegregation efforts, Aronson and his colleagues (Aronson, Stephan, Sikes, Blaney, & Snapp, 1978; Aronson & Osherow, 1980; Bridgeman, 1981) noted that one source of the failure of these efforts to reduce interracial hostilities lay in the competitive structure of the traditional classroom. In schools in Texas and California, they trained teachers to use a cooperative educational technique known as the "Jigsaw Classroom." Briefly, in such classrooms, students are required to cooperate with one another in order to master course material. Material to be learned is divided among members of mixed-race "jigsaw groups," and students teach one another. In order to learn from others, students must *cooperate,* attend to their colleagues, and become good interviewers; in fact, it is in their best interest to do so. The jigsaw intervention produced many positive effects: Children in the jigsaw classrooms grew to like one another better, developed a greater liking for school, and developed an enhanced sense of self-esteem compared with children in traditional classrooms. Moreover, increased liking among children in the jigsaw classrooms crossed racial and ethnic boundaries, and minority children increased their academic performance without jeopardizing the performance of majority group children.

More recently, research in social cognition and persuasion has been used to induce consumers to use energy more efficiently (Gonzales, Aronson &

Costanzo, 1988). Prior to this relatively simple but successful intervention, utility companies and policy makers had devoted literally millions of dollars to energy conservation campaigns, for the most part with limited success. Briefly, Gonzales and her colleagues made use of recent laboratory research in social cognition in training energy auditors to be more effective and persuasive communicators in their interactions with utility customers. Consumers exposed to presentations by trained home energy auditors *did* change their energy use behaviors significantly more than consumers exposed to the typical audit presentation. The auditor training program was based in large part upon the type of social psychological research that is most often the butt of the triviality criticism: namely, highly controlled paper-and-pencil studies of the ways in which subjects process and reason about social information. Thus, attempting to judge the "importance" of psychological research on the basis of the topic studied or the specific methods employed is risky at best.

The purpose of this section has not been to demonstrate that the various forms of the triviality criticism are totally pointless or misguided. It is true that generalizing from the laboratory is often a mistake. Without testing our predictions in more complex settings we cannot say whether variables will continue to be influential. It is also true that social psychologists have been somewhat conservative about stepping out into the confusion of the world and attempting to apply their techniques and test their variables. However, social psychology has progressed to the point where such valuable excursions are increasingly common: in educational, legal, business, and health care settings, to name but a few. We hope to see social psychologists *continue* to take risks, and to grapple with the complications of real-world settings.

Triviality and Generalizability

Let us assume for a moment that we were able to design a series of methodologically flawless laboratory experiments free of artifacts and alternative explanations. Let us also assume that the hypothesis of interest was widely acknowledged to be of tremendous social import. Finally, let us assume that we were able to "start simple" and then build increasingly more complex situations (high on both experimental and mundane realism) in order to approximate the intricacies of the real world. Is the ability to *generalize* to other people, places, and times in the real world—to ensure that our findings are *"externally valid"* as the term is traditionally used—necessarily the standard against which the value of experiments in social psychology should be assessed? Not always. Numerous important experiments, many of them "classics" in social psychology, have been conducted by researchers whose goals were not to generalize to other subjects, other operationalizations, or other settings. And this does not diminish the magnitude of their contributions to understanding behavior, for their goals were not to *make* generalizations but rather to *test* them.

This argument is forcefully made by Douglas Mook (1983). He cites as an example the classic experiments on attachment in rhesus monkeys conducted by Harry Harlow (1958). Recall that Harlow found that contact comfort (provided by "mothers" made of cylinders covered in warm terry cloth) was a more powerful determinant of attachment in infant monkeys than was food (provided by "mothers" made of bare wire frames to which bottles were affixed). Especially when frightened, rhesus infants ran and clung to the terry cloth mothers—evidence that young monkeys "love" their mothers, not because they provide food, but because they provide comfort. How would such a study rate on the question of external validity? Miserably. Orphaned rhesus monkeys reared in a laboratory are hardly representative of the entire population of rhesus monkeys, much less human infants. Furthermore, the research setting was most certainly artificial: How many infant monkeys encounter mother figures made of wire and a baby bottle or a cylinder covered by terry cloth warmed by a light bulb? It would have been ludicrous for Harlow to have concluded that in the wilds of Africa, orphaned rhesus infants would prefer terry cloth mothers to wire mothers when forced to choose. Such external validity was not Harlow's concern. His goal was to challenge a then current model of mother love, *not* to determine the monkeys, locations, or time to which his particular findings would generalize.

The generalizability of any research finding is suspect whether it is based upon a laboratory experiment or on one conducted in the field; whether the subjects are U.S. college students or Chinese factory workers. Bringing the research out of the laboratory does not necessarily make it more generalizable or "true"; it simply makes it different. The question of which method—"artificial" laboratory experiments *versus* experiments conducted in the real world—will provide the more generalizable results is simply the wrong question. The generalizability of *any* research finding is limited. This limitation can be explicated only by systematically testing the robustness of research results across different empirical realizations of both independent and dependent variables via systematic replication to test the extent to which different translations of abstract concepts into concrete realizations yield similar results.

Finally, social psychological experimenters are scientists just as physicists, chemists, astronomers, and biologists are. As such, our efforts need not be, indeed, *should not be,* solely directed toward determining whether results from one or another specific experiment will hold across different samples, different locations, or different points in time. Our efforts are best directed toward testing the accuracy or implications of abstract theoretical propositions. If our experiments are internally valid, and if we are mindful of the value of a window between our laboratories and the world outside, we need not concern ourselves with issues of triviality or artificiality. Those scientists who are interested in testing the external validity of a laboratory experiment in a specific situation—energy conservation in the home, prejudice reduction in the classroom, AIDS reduction among intravenous drug users in big city slums—need to test that finding in the specific situation in which they are interested. If it has internal validity, the laboratory experiment can serve as a flexible blueprint for these scientists' applied empirical research.

ETHICAL ISSUES

The experience of subjects in psychological experiments is not always pain-less. Subjects may suffer anxiety, frustration, self-doubt, and sometimes even physical pain for the sake of the experimenter's research. Sometimes subjects may agree to participate in an experiment without knowing about all the pos-sible negative consequences; sometimes, experimenters find themselves in the uncomfortable position of lying to subjects about the true purposes and the ex-act nature of the experiment.

When is it justifiable to make subjects suffer, or to deceive them, in order to gain fundamental knowledge about some social process? Ethics in the context of social psychological research raise complex problems due to the tension that exists between two sets of related values that are held in our society: on the one hand, a belief in the value of free scientific inquiry; on the other, a belief in human dignity and a person's right to privacy and protection from harm. In our opinion, the dilemma raised by the conflict between these two sets of values cannot be shrugged off either by making pious statements about the inviolability of human dignity or by pledging glib allegiance to the cause of science. They are problems that every social psychologist faces, not just once, but whenever an experiment is constructed and conducted. It is impossible to set forth a single set of specific rules and regulations governing all experi-ments. In each instance the researcher must carefully consider the importance of the experiment and the extent of the potential injury to the participants be-fore deciding on a course of action.

We hasten to add that ethical issues can and do arise even when deception is not used and when experimental procedures are not anticipated to be pain-ful, uncomfortable, embarrassing, or extreme. Sometimes even an apparently benign procedure can profoundly affect subjects in ways experimenters could not have foreseen, however sensitive, caring, and insightful they might be. For example, consider a series of "social dilemma" experiments conducted by Robyn Dawes, Jeanne McTavish, and Harriet Shaklee (1977). Typically in these investigations, subjects are faced with the decision to cooperate with others, or to "defect." When everyone cooperates, everyone benefits financially; but when one or more participants choose to defect, the deserters receive a high payoff, and those who choose to cooperate lose money. The rules of the game are fully explained to all subjects at the outset of the experiment and subjects' responses are anonymous. No deception is involved. This scenario seems innocuous enough.

However, 24 hours after one experimental session, an elderly man called the experimenter. He had been the sole defector in his group, thereby winning $19 while everyone else won only $1. He wanted to return his winnings to be divided equally among the other (cooperative) participants. During the conversation, he reported that he felt miserable about his greedy behavior and that he hadn't slept all night. After a similar experiment, a woman who cooperated while others defected revealed that she felt gullible and had learned that people were not as trustworthy as she had earlier believed. Thus, despite careful planing by the investigators, these "social dilemma" experiments had powerful effects on subjects—effects that could not have been easily anticipated. Our point is simple but important: *No code of ethics can anticipate all problems,* especially those that arise when subjects discover something unpleasant about themselves or others in the course of their participation.

In recent years students of human behavior have become increasingly concerned with ethical issues. Debates about research ethics range far beyond the narrower questions examined in this chapter. Some of the issues raised are the rights and responsibilities of the researcher who wants to study differences between subcultures or ethnic groups; the obligation of the researcher to consider the broader societal implications of the research; the possibility of free choice when the subject is captive, as in research on prisoners; the accountability of the researcher for the subsequent use and misuse of the research data by others. We cannot begin to deal with all these issues here, despite their obvious importance to the researcher. Clearly, researchers will need to examine their own planned research in terms of these concerns, and they may want to consult writers who have considered the problems of research ethics in greater depth, including sources such as Herbert Kelman (1968), Allan Kimmel (1988), Arthur Miller (1972b), Thomas Murray (1982), Robert Sears and his colleagues (1967), and the American Psychological Association (APA) (1953; 1981; 1982). In addition, the Department of Health and Human Services and one of its agencies, the National Institutes of Health (NIH), have been issuing comprehensive guidelines and regulations for research with human subjects. The prospective experimenter should study these guidelines before undertaking research. In this chapter we limit ourselves to some more narrowly focused concerns facing the experimenter in social psychology. Such a limitation should not be taken as an invitation to ignore the broader problems but rather as another example of the emphasis of this book on the more mundane and practical questions to be faced by the researcher.

Thus, our aim is largely descriptive. We attempt to describe the nature of some practical ethical questions faced by social psychologists and the ways in which they attempt to resolve these problems in a manner consistent with the value they place on scientific inquiry and—just as important—on human dignity and well-being.

PAIN AND SUFFERING

The study of certain psychological processes, such as responses to fear or punishment or frustration, depends on the successful arousal of some discomfort or distress in the subjects. Physical pain is involved in studies in which electric shock or other stressful stimuli, such as ice-cold water or loud noise, are used. Psychological discomfort is more common in social psychological research and more various in its manifestations; the psychological pressure applied by the unanimous majority in the Asch experiment is a good example. The stress may be temporary, or it may involve some risk that the subject will continue to worry or suffer after the experiment has ended. It may affect some subjects adversely, but not others. In general, the unifying feature of this variety of treatments is that they all involve the subject in an experience which is actually or potentially distressing.

In most cases, the experimenter who is contemplating a treatment which may be painful or upsetting to the subjects first seeks out ways to answer the question without using stressful procedures. Of course nonstressful alternatives will usually reduce the impact of an experiment. If the purpose of the stress is simply to create impact for its own sake, or to raise the subject's level of involvement, it may be possible to eliminate the stressful procedure without notably altering the question under study.

Even though the researcher may make every effort to find an innocuous treatment, it is not always possible. At least at our present state of knowledge, valid answers to many social psychological questions depend on experimentation which causes subjects some psychological discomfort, such as anxiety, embarrassment, annoyance, or insecurity. One simply cannot fully investigate the effects of anxiety except in situations which make people anxious, and for the greatest clarity of inference, the experimenter must be able to schedule that anxiety. An experiment might require subjects to submit to painful electric shocks, perform monotonous tasks, experience embarrassment, act aggressively toward another person, tell lies, resolve a moral dilemma, eat grasshoppers, or any of hundreds of other stressful procedures ranging from mild inconvenience to high levels of unpleasant arousal. When stress is an integral part of what the experimenter is trying to understand, it may be extremely difficult or impossible to remove the stress without eliminating the whole phenomenon of interest.

Although painful or unpleasant procedures are sometimes necessary, their use always raises serious ethical problems for the researcher. Each experimenter must decide how to deal with these problems; however, we would like to summarize our ideas about this issue and to offer a few tentative recommendations. These suggestions are the product of a series of discussions in which we tried to formulate our own thoughts and to make our opinions explicit. We considered the problems we faced in our own research and attempted to reconstruct our concern about the welfare of the subjects and the modifications we had made to deal with this concern and assuage our consciences. We discussed experiments that were planned but rejected for ethical reasons. We argued. What follows does not represent a fundamental agreement, for none was ever reached. Instead, it represents a tentative consensus on a few points and a presentation of the issues and arguments involved in a few other areas. None of these suggestions is particularly original; they have been presented elsewhere by other researchers, and to some extent they represent the kinds of ideas that are generally discussed by social psychologists who are concerned with these issues.

First of all, when the stressful procedures are free of deception, the problem is less acute, because the experimenter can warn the subject in advance, and the subject can decide to withdraw from participation in the study. We feel that whenever stressful procedures are used, it is a good idea to give the subject as much information about the experiment as possible. When there is no need for deception we recommend that the subject be informed of the likely extent of the discomfort or inconvenience and be given a free choice as to whether to participate in the experiment. We also believe that once the subject has consented to participate in an experiment involving a given amount of discomfort, the experimenter must not go beyond the limits agreed to by the subject; otherwise, the whole idea of voluntary consent is undermined. In addition, subjects should be allowed to quit at any time during the experiment, and they should be explicitly informed of this option at the outset. Of course, it may be extremely difficult for the subject to refuse to participate or continue in the experiment, for fear of looking like a coward, of ruining the experiment, or for any number of other reasons. Thus, the ethical problem is not completely removed because the subject may not feel entirely free to choose what to do, although there is more choice than in an experiment in which important information is distorted or withheld. We believe that the experimenter should do everything possible to make sure that the subject has a real choice; for example, one strategy might be to employ a confederate who does refuse to participate in the experiment. In addition, the experimenter should observe the subject carefully. Any unusual signs of distress should be grounds for terminating the experiment. When the experiment is over, the investigator should interview the subject to make sure that there are no lingering ill effects (see Chapter 10).

These ideas are similar to those set down in codes of research ethics under the rubric "informed consent" (U.S. Public Health Service, 1969; American

Psychological Association, 1982). Before the subject agrees to participate, "the investigator informs all participants of all aspects of the research that might reasonably be expected to influence willingness to participate and explains all other aspects of the research about which the participants inquire" (American Psychological Association, 1982, Principle 9, p. 5). Allowing the subject to leave in the middle of an experiment is another aspect of the same principle. A description of an experiment is obviously much less "informative" than actual participation is; the subject who, on the basis of experiences in the study, decides not to continue in the experiment is essentially withdrawing consent as a consequence of the additional information.

How much discomfort may an experimenter inflict on a subject in the name of science? This question is not easily answered. The reasons for this should be clear: First, one cannot easily quantify the psychological discomfort caused by an experimental procedure, as is clear from our previous description of the unforeseen discomfort encountered by subjects in the experiment by Dawes, McTavish, and Shaklee (1977). Moreover, in many cases, the amount of psychological stress is as much a function of the incidental demeanor of the experimenter as of the actual procedure involved. The experimenter may approach the subject with respect and sympathy, communicating interest and concern and expressing gratitude for the subject's help in providing important information; this kind of considerate regard may lead many subjects to accept difficult procedures as justifiable. However, the experimenter may ignore the subject's individuality, communicating both a desire to reduce observations to a number and a lack of concern about the subject as a person. Subjects so treated may feel that even quite innocuous experiments were not worth their time and trouble.

The experimenter sets the tone, and the general atmosphere for the subjects may be largely independent of the experimental treatments. Unless the experimenter is careful, even the most innocent-looking procedure can cause a subject to feel uneasy or inept. Because the experimenter-subject relationship is, by nature, one of unequal status, it is relatively easy for an experimenter—wittingly or unwittingly—to make a subject feel small and powerless. This is one reason that it may be difficult for the subject to drop out of the experiment. It is also the reason why it is difficult to determine the actual amount of discomfort caused to a subject simply by looking at the "method" section of a published report. In the hands of a careful, caring experimenter, a procedure that appears harmful may produce little stress. Similarly, in the hands of an arrogant or insensitive experimenter, a procedure that appears innocuous enough may upset the subject a great deal.

In examining our own research ideas and those of other social psychologists, we often consider the unpleasantness of the subject's experience in terms of the value of the experiment. On one hand few experimenters would cause even a small amount of discomfort to a subject "just for the hell of it," that is, without a clear idea of what they were looking for in the experiment. On the other hand, many experimenters would be willing to burden subjects with some strain if the experiment were an important one and if there were no other way of performing it. It is commonly accepted that the merits of a proposed experiment should be a factor in deciding whether to employ a potentially stressful procedure (American Psychological Association, 1982; Freund, 1967; Kelman, 1968; Ring, 1967; Rubin, 1970). But in practice, it is almost as difficult to arrive at an objective judgment of the ultimate importance of an experiment as it is to judge the extent of the subject's discomfort. Most experimenters have a strong feeling that their own experiments are important, but others may not agree. All universities now have a committee on human subjects which reviews all proposed research with an eye to just these issues. Such a committee provides a good check on the sometimes overoptimistic views of a prospective experimenter but cannot serve as a substitute for the experimenter's careful thought about the issues. A good rule of thumb is to place the degree of discomfort at the mildest possible level which is consistent with the hypothesis; although this may be far from ideal scientifically, it is a reasonable and necessary compromise.

The degree of stress the experimenter is willing to allow should also be a function of the number of precautions taken. Thus, a second rule of thumb is to make sure that the level of stress or discomfort is low enough so that the experimenter is confident that any ill effects can be erased or resolved. A given degree of stress may be within reasonable bounds if the experimenter has guarded against serious consequences. For example, consider Stanley Milgram's experiment (1963) in which subjects believed that they were giving severe electric shocks to a person who beat on the wall and begged to be let out of the experiment. Participation in this experiment was obviously an extremely disturbing experience for many subjects, and some writers (e.g., Baumrind, 1964) have questioned the ethics of Milgram's procedures. Milgram himself recognized the danger that serious psychological consequences might result and took special precautions to prevent them (see Milgram, 1964). After the experiment was over, Milgram introduced the subject to his "victim" and discussed the experiment with him at length, reassuring him that his behavior was perfectly normal. Later on, when the whole series of studies had been completed, Milgram sent out a five-page report about the experiments to all the subjects, along with a follow-up questionnaire designed to find out how they felt about their participation in the experiment. Finally, Milgram conducted a further follow-up study in which the 40 subjects "most likely to have suffered consequences from participation" were interviewed by a psychiatrist in order to find out whether there were any lingering ill effects resulting from their experience in the research. The psychiatrist found no evidence of deleterious effects in any of the subjects (Milgram, 1964, p. 850).

Finally, an experimenter who plans to expose subjects to some negative experience should take special precautions to make sure that the experiment is *scientifically* acceptable. For example, experiments conducted as casual classroom exercises or as undergraduate research projects are less likely to be methodologically sound studies which advance the science of psychology, and we believe that the use of ethically questionable procedures is therefore inappropriate in these contexts. If the experiment is conducted solely for purposes of pedagogy and the experimenter is not interested in really learning something about social behavior, *or* if the study is carried out so negligently that nothing *can* be learned from looking at the results, there is no justification for putting subjects through an unpleasant experience.

DECEPTION

Most of the research we have discussed thus far has involved deception. Social psychologists have long considered it necessary in some kinds of experiments to withhold information from subjects. Indeed, experimenters often find themselves in the troublesome position of concealing the truth from their subjects in order to *reveal* a truth about human behavior. Sometimes experimenters deliberately attempt to mislead their subjects. The experimenter's independent variable often involves some particular psychological state, such as fear or anger, which cannot be aroused effectively unless the subjects believe in the eliciting events. It would be difficult to make subjects really angry, for example, if they were informed that the experimenter was following a script designed to infuriate them. Many dependent variables involve behaviors which subjects might not want to perform if they knew how the experimenter planned to interpret the behavior. The obedient behavior of the subjects in the Milgram (1973) experiment is a good example of this kind of dependent variable. Had the subjects known that their behavior would be compared with the obedient behavior of Nazi officials who were "only following orders," they might have been much more likely to resist the experimenter's influence. Finally, the experimenter often desires to keep the subject uninformed of the purposes of the study, so that the results of the research can be generalized to uninformed people in similar situations outside of psychological experiments.

In most social psychological experiments, the subject is kept partially ignorant of the true purpose of the experiment; the deception is in not telling the whole truth about what is going on. In some experiments, the deception is more elaborate, involving a carefully staged production with a large cast, a well-rehearsed script, and a variety of misleading embellishments. The use of deception in social psychology has raised methodological questions, which we shall discuss in Chapter 6, and ethical questions, to which we now turn.

The ethical questions raised by the use of deception include the invasion of the subjects' privacy by eliciting information which they do not intend to share and the violation of their expectations of openness and honesty on the part of the experimenter. The subjects' understanding of the situation is incomplete or false, and thus it is impossible for them to give their fully informed consent. For this reason, we believe that the experimenter should try to find a procedure which will answer the question without deceiving the subjects; that is, one that is *not* chosen on purely methodological grounds. Even if a deceptive procedure seems the most appropriate for the experimental question, we believe that other procedures should be considered as well, and if a technique which uses less deception will do almost as well, it is usually preferable. But, more often than not, these efforts will be fruitless; some questions invite bias due to the defensiveness or cooperativeness of subjects, and deception is the best practical technique for avoiding this kind of bias. In essence, the problem is that if we are completely open and honest in describing our procedures to the subjects, we may create pressures which make it practically impossible for them to be completely open and honest with us. For example, it is hard to imagine an experimenter collecting valid data on the effects of group pressure on conformity (as in the Asch experiment) by announcing the purpose of the experiment in advance.

And the dilemma is even more difficult. Even if we begin by choosing a nondeceptive technique, sooner or later we may have to validate our procedures by using deception. For example, Craig Smith and Ellsworth (1985) theorized that different emotions are caused by different ways of interpreting the situation. Encountering a filthy derelict asleep on the street, one person may experience disgust, a second sorrow, and a third guilt because of their differing interpretations. Smith and Ellsworth began their investigations by asking people to remember and talk about emotional experiences they had had. No deception was involved, and the critic might argue that no "real" emotions were either. In follow-up research Smith and Ellsworth studied subjects who were actually experiencing emotions: They were about to take a difficult exam (fear, hope), or they had just received their grade (joy, anger). Again there was no deception, and this time the emotions were real, but there was no random assignment and little control. The theory that the different interpretations *cause* the different emotions has still not been given an adequate test, and it is hard to imagine that such a test could be carried out without deception. Still, it was perhaps preferable to begin with the nondeceptive studies. If neither the memory study nor the uncontrolled "real-life" study had shown a speck of support for Smith and Ellsworth's ideas, they might have decided that there was no point in "validating" these ideas in a deception experiment.

What specific problems are posed by the use of deceptive techniques? If deception is used, the experimenter is not only misleading the subjects but also invading their privacy by extracting data under false pretenses. This often involves an outright lie: The experimenter presents the subject with a largely untrue "cover story." But deception occurs in more subtle forms as well. If a cover story about one or more aspects of the experiment is a sin of commission, a failure to inform the subject of the true purpose (or sometimes even the existence) of the dependent variable measure is an analogous sin of omission. Thus, a projective technique such as the Rorschach or the Thematic Apperception Test (TAT) is a deceptive device unless the subject is forewarned about what it is really supposed to measure. In using the TAT, psychologists typically present subjects with a set of pictures and ask them to write stories about each picture, ostensibly as a test of creativity. If the psychologist then takes the stories and uses them to make inferences about unconscious sources of conflict and anxiety in the subject's personal life, the subject's privacy has been invaded. Told beforehand that the test was an instrument designed to uncover specific aspects of his or her underlying personality dynamics, the subject might have written different stories or even refused to take the test.

Deception is also involved when the experimenter gives a veridical picture of the general purpose of the test, but fails to mention its special purpose, for example, to gauge the subject's current level of sexual arousal. A simple interview often contains an even more subtle element of deception. As Edward Shils (1959) has pointed out, interviewers express concern about the establishment of "rapport" with the respondents. Techniques for establishing rapport frequently involve procedures for gaining the confidence of the respondents by behaving in a pseudo-friendly manner, thus seducing them into "voluntarily" revealing themselves under false pretenses.

The social psychological experiment usually involves more brazen forms of deception than simply pretending to be friendly. Often, the deception is innocuous, designed to either ascertain the subject's reaction to a particular untrue event or merely keep the subject from guessing the true purpose of the experiment. An example of innocuous deception is the typical communication-persuasion study (e.g., Hovland and Weiss, 1951), in which the experimenter deceives the subject by attributing a statement to a false source. We consider this innocuous because, so far as the subject is concerned, it is usually of little consequence whether a particular communicator did or did not make a particular statement.

Is deception that is truly innocuous harmful to subjects—even if there are no stressful or difficult aspects to the procedure? Most critics of social psychological experiments take it for granted that simply lying to subjects produces harm to them or to their perception of the psychological enterprise (Baumrind, 1985; Kelman, 1968), but, in fact, there is no empirical evidence to support the claim that deception per se is any more harmful than nondeception experiments. In a recent review of the literature, Christensen (1988) points out that follow-up interviews of subjects in deception experiments consistently reveal that surprisingly few subjects feel that they were harmed by the deception. Indeed, interestingly enough, in those rare instances where the effects of deception have been studied systematically, the general finding is that subjects are actually happier with deception experiments than with nondeception experiments. For example, Smith and Richardson (1983) found that subjects who participated in deception experiments reported that they enjoyed the experience more and received more educational benefit from them than subjects who participated in nondeception experiments. This may be because deception experiments are usually more interesting than nondeception experiments. It may be because experimenters are more likely to talk to subjects about their experiences after an experiment involving deception. It may be that in *most* experiments the major "harm" that might befall a subject is boredom, and subjects in deception experiments are less bored!

It has been suggested that we should not take our subjects' statements at face value when they say they didn't mind (or even liked) a deception experiment because they are only trying, consciously or unconsciously, to please the experimenter (Baumrind, 1985). It is true that we should ask these questions carefully in the course of a genuine conversation (see Chapter 10). But if we do so, then we should also respect our subjects enough to take what they say seriously, and not prejudge their responses because of our own attitudes about deception.

But this should not lull us into complacency, because not all deception experiments involve procedures that are innocuous. Suppose the deceptive procedure leads the subject into a situation that causes anguish, distress, or discomfort. When this happens, we are on dangerous ground; all the ethical problems discussed in the first part of this chapter become even more problematic because the use of deception wholly or partly precludes the use of the basic safeguard of the nondeceptive stressful experiment: namely, the informed consent of the subject. In the Asch experiment, a subject had no way of knowing that an apparently straightforward "perceptual judgment" study would lead to a situation of being forced to decide between being a publicly visible deviant or a sellout to personal convictions. We might consider that the increased self-awareness provided by the experiment was a valuable educational experience, but it is an experience which the subject, when volunteering for an experiment on visual perception, could not foresee. It was not part of the bargain. We would argue that any procedure that induces subjects to confront some unpleasant aspects of themselves should raise researchers' deep ethical concern. Although the researcher might insist that such procedures are "therapeutic" or "educational" for subjects (indeed, many *subjects* have made this point), this reasoning does not, in and of itself, justify the procedure. First, the experimenter could not possibly know in advance that it would be therapeutic for all subjects. Second, even if experimenters were omniscient in that regard, they have no special right to expose unsuspecting people to disturbing facts about themselves in the name of education, even when personal insights thereby obtained might be "good for them."

It could be argued that the results are good or useful for society even though the procedure may be harmful to some of the subjects. Again, this does not in and of itself justify the procedure unless the subjects themselves are in a position to weigh societal benefits against individual discomfort. It should also be clear that an ex post facto defense is not adequate. That is, suppose an experimenter puts a subject through some very stressful experiences and then finds *afterward* that all subjects attest that they are glad they participated and would still have agreed to participate if they had been properly informed in advance. Some subjects might be attempting to justify having gone through an arduous experience (see Aronson & Mills, 1959). Once a stressful experiment is over, an ex post facto endorsement is ambiguous at best.

Earlier we used the word "bargain." This word was not chosen casually, for it is this concept which is at the heart of the ethical dilemma faced by experimental social psychologists. Whether or not deception is innocuous, if subjects have not consented in advance to allow the experimenter to manipulate and observe a specific aspect of their behavior, their privacy is being invaded. They no longer have the opportunity to decide what personal information they will disclose to the experimenter. This is no less true if they volunteer for an experiment which might appear to be *more* unpleasant than the real one. For example, in Stanley Schachter's experiments on affiliation (1959), the subjects volunteered for an experiment in which they were told that they would receive some painful electric shocks. This did not happen; instead, the experimenter observed how their *fear* of the shock affected their tendency to affiliate. The subjects almost certainly sighed in relief when they were told that they weren't going to be shocked after all. Nevertheless, they had not been forewarned that the experimenter was going to observe the effect of fear on their desire to be with other people. They had no opportunity to decide whether they wanted to participate in an experiment on fear and affiliation, because they did not find out that that was what the experiment was about until after they had already participated.

During the past several years, moral philosophers have entered the controversy and have suggested some solutions to the problem of informed consent. Although creative, these suggestions strike us as impractical in the extreme. One example will suffice. Soble (1978) has suggested a technique known as "Prior General Consent Plus Proxy Consent." In this technique, the experimenter first obtains the general consent of the subject to participate in an experiment that may involve extreme procedures. The subject then empowers a friend to serve as a proxy, that is, to examine the details of the specific procedure in advance and to make a judgment as to whether the subject would have consented if given the choice. If the proxy says "yes," the experimenter may proceed. Although this technique may be ethical in the most technical sense, it has some obvious ethical and methodological flaws. First, subjects are still agreeing to something they cannot possibly understand: The proxy can be wrong. Second, it is reasonable to assume that most proxies will make conservative errors, that is, they will try to protect the welfare of the subject by being more cautious than the subject would have been. If that is the case, and a substantial number of proxies say "no," we may end up with a sample of extreme and unknown bias. Third, this cumbersome and rather dramatic procedure may have more impact on the subject than the actual experiment, thus distorting the subjects' responses (Adair, Dushenko & Lindsay, 1985). Finally, one may have ethical qualms about placing this burden of responsibility on the proxy.

Although it is not always possible in social psychological experiments to obtain the subject's informed consent, at least it is possible to ensure that the personal information obtained in studies entailing a partial invasion of privacy will be kept completely confidential. Confidentiality is by no means a remedy for the ethical problems of social psychological experiments, but it is an important safeguard. In experiments in social psychology the subject can remain anonymous, except to the experimenter. That is, social psychologists tend to be interested in general principles of human behavior rather than in the behavior of any specific individual: in aggregate data, not individual responses. Consequently, only the experimenter will ever be aware that a particular person behaved in a certain manner. Moreover, the experimenter has absolutely no interest in linking the person to the behavior. At the close of the session, the subject's data can be transferred to a coded data sheet that contains no names, so that no one can know whose data they are. The very impersonality of this process is a great advantage, because it precludes the misuse of the data thereby obtained. We recommend that any experimenter conducting social psychological research take these precautions to protect the subjects' anonymity. Both before and at the close of the session the experimenter should make sure that the subject understands that all personal information will be kept anonymous.

ALTERNATIVES TO DECEPTION

In the 1960s and 1970s, debates raged concerning the ethics of the use of deception in social psychological experiments. Battle lines were drawn between opponents and proponents of deception research. Opponents described deception experiments as "confidence games" (Forward, Canter, & Kirsch, 1976) and noted numerous possible dangers of this method (e.g., Kelman, 1967). Some critics also questioned the use of deception on methodological grounds. For example, they challenged the validity of responses provided by hoodwinked subjects and even accused experimenters of deceiving themselves in assuming that subjects are taken in by their clever stratagems. They suggested alternatives such as role playing. On theoretical and methodological grounds, proponents pointed to the many inadequacies of these alternatives to deception (e.g., Aronson & Carlsmith, 1968; Cooper, 1976; Freedman, 1969; West & Gunn, 1978). As Joel Cooper (1976) so colorfully noted, the debate came to resemble cowboy movies of yesteryear in which the villainous black-clad "bad guys" shot it out with the heroic "good guys" dressed in pristine white. Of course, just who were the "good guys" and who were the "bad guys" is not always clear, for the ethical and practical issues involved in assessing the morality and practicality of deception experiments are myriad and complex. This, indeed, is the definition of a dilemma. Are we "good guys" if we protect the subject from experiencing an hour's worth of anxiety or are we "good guys" if we wrestle with our own conscience in order to discover something that might help us understand an important societal phenomenon such as obedience or conformity or racial prejudice?

As we noted earlier, the use of deception *does* raise serious questions about the rights of subjects and the invasion of their privacy. When deception is employed, crucial information is withheld from subjects, or specious information is provided to them. Under such circumstances, it is impossible for subjects to provide consent that is truly informed. Accordingly, the investigator should not embark on a deception experiment without first exploring the possibilities for studying the same question or testing the same hypothesis without deception. Going beyond this recommendation that specific alternative procedures be considered for specific experiments, some psychologists have proposed more *general* procedures as an adequate substitute for deception across a variety of experimental situations. Some research has been done to evaluate the efficacy of these alternative procedures (e.g., Holmes & Bennett, 1974; Miller, 1972a; Willis & Willis, 1970). Despite "mixed results," however, interest in the potentialities of these new, nondeceptive techniques has increased with the concern about the ethical implications of traditional deception experiments.

Role Playing

Perhaps the most frequently cited alternative technique is the **role-playing** situation, simulation, or "as-if" experiment, in which subjects are asked to behave as if they were in a particular situation. Typically, the experiment is explained to the subjects in advance, and they are asked to behave as they would behave if the situation were real instead of experimental or as if they did not know the purpose of the research. This approach attempts to enlist the subjects' aid in actively and conscientiously collaborating with the experimenter. An increasing number of psychologists concerned about the dehumanizing aspects of deception research recommend the role-playing approach.

An early example of this approach is provided in a study by Milton Rosenberg and Robert Abelson (1960). These investigators asked each subject to play the role of the owner of a department store. The subjects were then presented with a set of attitudes that, as a store owner, they were supposed to hold. These attitudes were purposely arranged so that an inconsistency of one sort or another appeared somewhere in the set. For instance, all subjects were told they should set a positive value on keeping sales high; one group was then told that they should feel negatively toward modern art and positively toward Fenwick, the manager of their rug department. (Other groups were fed different attitudes about Fenwick and modern art). All subjects were then given beliefs to the effect that (1) displays of modern art reduce sales; (2) Fenwick plans to use a display of modern art in the rug department; and (3) under Fenwick's management the volume of rug sales has increased. Finally, the subjects were asked to estimate their new attitudes after assimilating this information. As predicted, the results showed that people choose the simplest paths toward resolving unbalanced cognitive structures.

This experiment has the great virtue of not requiring deception. It also has a fairly high degree of mundane realism, in the sense that these things might actually happen to people, whether or not they own a department store. Indeed, it is frequently argued (Brown, 1962; Kelman, 1968; Schultz, 1969) that this procedure is actually a better technique for carrying out experiments than are the more elaborately staged experiments of the kind we have been discussing—that is, experiments in the tradition of Asch, Milgram, or Aronson and

Mills. As Brown (1962, p. 74) put it, "We believe that a role-playing subject will behave in a way that corresponds more closely to the life situation than a hoodwinked subject will."

There are some very serious difficulties with this point of view, however, and these difficulties are similar to the problems arising from introspective reports, which we discussed earlier. First, when we ask subjects to predict how they would behave in a given situation, they may well be unable to do so in a veridical fashion. If they have not actually experienced a similar situation, their basis for predicting what they would do is probably no better than the experimenter's. Second, even if they *have* experienced a similar situation in the past, they face at least two additional cognitive tasks: (1) to recall accurately the last time they were in a similar situation; and (2) to decide what they should say or do in the *current* situation, given their assumptions about what the experimenter expects, and their desire to appear competent, psychologically healthy, and otherwise socially desirable.

In an experiment that involves deception, it is possible to arrange events which have an impact on the subject. The subject, involved in an ongoing situation which requires a response, often must act without sufficient time to think things over and without fully understanding the implications of various alternative responses. In a simulation study, the subject is typically not faced with the same impact or the same pressures, and it is asking a great deal to request that the subject pretend to be in a new and unfamiliar situation and to make correct inferences about how he or she would behave. Regardless of how well motivated, the subject can only guess. Jonathan Freedman (1969, p. 111) forcefully points out the basic difficulty with these kinds of data:

> The argument comes down to the simple truth that data from role-playing studies consist of what some group of subjects guess would be their reactions to a particular stimulus. The subjects are giving their intuitions, their insights or introspections about themselves as others. If you are studying the myths and values of a society this data would be useful. If you want to know how people behave, it is, at best, suggestive. If you are interested in people's intuitions, fine; if you are interested in their behavior . . . , you must ordinarily use the experimental method. Just because a significant number of subjects have the same intuition about something does not make them correct. We must rely on real data, not on opinion surveys. Consensus is not truth.

Essentially, the problem boils down to the fact that we have no way of knowing whether the subjects' guesses are accurate. In many situations we might actually expect subjects' statements about themselves to be inaccurate. First, if asked to predict their behavior in a completely unfamiliar situation, subjects may have no idea what they would do. Second, even if they were able to predict accurately how they would behave in some hypothetical situation, they might decide that this behavior would be too peculiar, and they would therefore give the experimenter a more reasonable response. We have no reason to assume that a subject will perceive the consequences of telling the truth as more attractive than the consequences of giving a "good," or "reasonable,'' or ''intelligent'' answer. In general, we might predict the subject's perception to be just the reverse. The response might stem from fear that the experimenter might think the subject strange for responding in an apparently unconventional way. Or, it might stem from a desire to help the experimenter. Thus, a response may well reflect what the subject thinks most people would do, even though that is contrary to what the subject would in fact do.

Let us be more concrete. Suppose that we ask a male subject to role-play a situation in which he is seeking a date. We tell him to predict for us how he would respond when faced with a choice between a moderately attractive woman and a stunning woman. Let us imagine that in a real situation this particular subject would, out of shyness, a low level of aspiration, or bad prior experience with stunning women, choose the moderately attractive woman. Being reasonably self-aware, he realizes that he would make this choice. Nevertheless, he might feel that most people would choose the very stunning woman. In order to appear normal and to avoid having to make embarrassing explanations, he might tell us that he would choose the very stunning woman. Thus, when the prevalent belief in the folk culture is that most people do X, a subject may respond ''X,'' knowing that she or he does not do X but believing that it is an accurate description of human behavior the experimenter wants the subject to provide.

Several investigators have suggested that subjects are very sensitive to and concerned about the experimenter's opinion (Riecken, 1962; Rosenberg, 1965). Others have shown that subjects tend to be cooperative and ''help'' the experimenter whenever possible (Orne, 1962). Finally, subjects often perceive an experiment as a testing situation and are motivated to ''look good'': to conform to the image of a healthy, intelligent, mature person (Silverman, Shulman, & Wiesenthal, 1970). Harold Sigall, Elliot Aronson, and Thomas Van Hoose (1970) found that this motivation to present a favorable image tends to override the desire to help the experimenter or confirm the experimental hypothesis. In their experiment, subjects in one condition were faced with a situation in which ''cooperation'' demanded one response and ''looking good'' demanded the exact opposite response. Subjects did not cooperate in this condition. The authors concluded that ''subjects looked as though they were cooperating only when such 'cooperation' resulted in good, effective behavior'' (1970, p. 7; see also Greenberg and Folger, Chapter 6). It should be clear that the problem is a particularly sticky one when, as in the case of the Rosenberg-Abelson (1960) experiment, the actual hypothesis involves a course of action which makes sense for most people. In this kind of experiment, we are always faced with the possibility that our data are nothing more than the opinions of a sample of people about how most people would behave in a given situation—as Freedman (1969) has noted, it would be establishing truth by taking a poll.

Although the simulation experiment may possess a certain degree of mundane realism (see Chapter 2), it is usually totally lacking in experimental realism. We can conceive of a continuum of realism ranging from a situation in which subjects merely play a role, attempting to predict how they would behave in some situation, to the other extreme, a situation in which subjects are totally unaware of being in an experiment and instead are faced with a social situation to which a response must be made. Let us illustrate this continuum by giving some examples of how the Asch experiment might have been carried out in different ways.

At one end of the continuum one could describe the situation and ask the subjects to predict how they would behave. Our guess is that many fewer people would conform in this situation than in the experiment as Asch ran it. Indeed, to take a parallel case, Milgram (1973) asked a group of undergraduates (from the same population used to recruit the actual subjects in some of the experiments) to predict how many subjects would obey the experimenter and continue delivering shocks until the highest level had been reached. The highest estimate was 3 percent whereas in the actual experiment 65 percent of the subjects typically persevere through the entire series. A group of psychiatrists asked the same question were no better than the students at predicting the behavior of subjects exposed to the experimental situation (Milgram, 1973).

Returning to the Asch study, a slightly more realistic technique might be to show the lines to the subjects and provide them with false information about how all previous subjects had responded. If they believed the experimenter, this information might cause them some concern, but there would be little pressure on them to conform. More realistic yet would be the situation used by Morton Deutsch and Harold Gerard (1963) and by Richard Crutchfield (1955), in which the subject sees the ostensible responses of the other subjects light up on a panel. Asch's own technique is still more realistic. Here the subject is faced by a number of confederates, all of whom state their judgment while the subject watches, leaving the subject to state a judgment while being watched by them. Even more realistic would be a situation in which the subject was not in a laboratory and was unaware that an experiment was being carried out but was faced with the same type of contradiction as in the Asch experiment. Here, mundane realism would increase the experimental realism of the situation.

It is reasonable to argue that as experimental realism and deception increase, the ethical problems become more serious. Precisely because we may be discovering aspects of behavior which the subject might not wish to disclose (or might not even be aware of), we must worry about the fundamental ethical problems. To us, it does not seem reasonable to argue that role-playing experiments, which mitigate these problems, are also superior methodologically. The reason that a dilemma exists for the experimental social psychologist is precisely that the methodological adequacy of an experiment tends to be inversely related to the protection of the subject's right to withhold information. Enough data have already been collected on this question to indicate that it is foolish to assume that role playing or self-reporting automatically provides an accurate representation of the subject's behavior in a corresponding real-life situation. In a classic study conducted more than 40 years ago, La Piere sent out questionnaires to a large number of hotel owners, asking whether they accepted Chinese guests. More than 90 percent of the hotel owners who returned the questionnaires indicated that they would refuse accommodations to Chinese. La Piere then traveled about the country, accompanied by a Chinese couple, and visited the same hotels to find out how well their stated policies corresponded with their actual practices. He found, to his surprise, that the Chinese couple was accepted by 99 percent of these hotels. La Piere concluded that a self-report "may indicate what the respondent would actually do when confronted with the situation symbolized in the question, but there is no assurance that it will" (1934, p. 236).

It has been argued that simulation studies have demonstrated their usefulness in that they have succeeded in producing orderly results (Kelman, 1968). But order is no substitute for validity. It is quite possible that people's ideas about behavior are simpler and *more* orderly than their actual behavior. Indeed, there are convincing reasons—both theoretical and empirical—to expect this to be true. Social cognition researchers (e.g., Markus & Zajonc, 1985; Nisbett & Ross, 1980; Tversky & Kaheman, 1973, 1974) have cogently argued that there are strong simplifying strategies or biases built into the ways people interpret and reason about the social world. One such bias is that we tend to assume much more interpersonal consistency than actually exists (Kelley, 1967). That this bias extends to perceptions of behavior in experimental situations is demonstrated in a study by Anthony Doob (1967), in which he found that subjects' guesses about how people would behave in an experiment were "more orderly than the data that were produced by these same subjects when they did not know that it was all make believe" (p. 31). Thus, subjects' honest verbal responses may show a gratifying consistency while bearing little resemblance to their own behavior in an actual situation.

Another example of the inaccurate simplicity of role-playing subjects' responses lies in their ability to mirror only "obvious" findings obtained via deception experiments. That is, subjects might well be able to "predict" the main effects of one or another independent variable, but subjects are seldom capable of predicting the more subtle interactive effects of two or more independent variables (Miller, 1972a). For example, Richard and Yolanda Willis (1970) compared the responses of role-playing and involved subjects in a conformity experiment. They found that role-playing subjects duplicated the responses of subjects who were actively engaged in events in the laboratory only when the main effect of one independent variable was assessed. The subtle effects of a two-way interaction which influenced involved subjects were totally lost on subjects who only played the role of someone responding to conformity pressures.

What if a role-playing study does produce results similar to those found in a previous deception experiment? Some investigators have succeeded in obtaining data from role-playing experiments that replicate the results of the corresponding deception experiments (e.g., Bem, 1965; Greenberg, 1967). For example, Bem has carried out successful role-playing replications of several cognitive dissonance experiments, including the Festinger and Carlsmith forced-compliance experiment. In Bem's role-playing simulation of this study, subjects were told that they were participants in an experiment designed to "determine how accurately people can judge another person" (1968, p. 250). The subjects listened to a tape recording that described the experience of Bob, a subject in one of the conditions of the Festinger-Carlsmith experiment. The tasks were described, and the subjects were told that Bob had accepted an offer of $1 or $20 to tell the next subject (and occasional future subjects) that the tasks were fun and exciting. The subjects then heard a tape recording supposedly of Bob telling the waiting subject about the tasks. After listening, they were given the same scales that the subjects in the original study had filled out and were asked to rate the tasks as Bob would have rated them. The new subjects accurately guessed how the subjects in each condition of the original experiment had responded. Thus, Bem successfully replicated the Festinger-Carlsmith study without using any deception.

There are problems with this line of research, however, that indicate that even successful replication does not prove that role-playing studies have the same meaning as their non-role-playing counterparts. Although Bem was successful in deciding which aspects of the situation to make salient in order to replicate the original results, other authors, providing additional information about the experiences of the subjects in the original experiment, were not able to replicate these results (e.g., Jones, Linder, Kiesler, Zanna, & Brehm, 1968). Whether a role-playing study produces results equivalent to those of an experiment apparently depends on subtle features of the role-playing situation. Without the original study as a criterion, there is no way of guessing the adequacy of the simulation. We cannot know in advance whether the results of role-playing study will correspond to those of a comparable study that does not involve role playing. Thus, in order to be sure of the validity of a role-playing study, it is always necessary to perform the corresponding non-role-playing experiment, and the purpose of simulation as a substitute for deception is defeated.

A Role for Role-Playing Studies

We do not mean to condemn all uses of role-playing studies. They are useful for generating new ideas and hypotheses, for exploring subjects' beliefs about the way people behave, for studying the accuracies and inaccuracies in their processing of social information, and for making inferences about the salience and influence of various aspects of an experimental situation. Indeed, the present burgeoning interest in attribution and other varieties of social cognition research is primarily concerned with people's beliefs about behavior and the ways they use and misuse social information in making inferences or decisions. Of course, even in these kinds of studies, it is impossible to be sure that a person's social belief or social judgment corresponds to such beliefs or judgments in the face of actual behavior *unless* we examine her or his responses in both situations. For example, the goals of subjects in social judgment studies are often different from their goals in their interactions with other people (Swann, 1984). In the laboratory, they are often exposed to social information and asked to make global predictions or judgments in order to answer the experimenter's question. However, in the real world—and in the typical impactful deception experiment—people are less motivated to make accurate global predictions, and more motivated to make accurate specific predictions in order to respond adaptively to the behavior of others. Furthermore, subjects asked to make social judgments in the sterility of the well-controlled laboratory situation are exposed to different information than is provided by live interactions. This discrepancy in the amount and kind of social information conveyed to subjects (in role-playing versus impactful deception experiments) can serve as a kind of experimental artifact, one which generates systematic differences between the behavior of role-playing subjects and involved subjects, differences which, according to some (e.g., Funder, 1987; Swann, 1984), tend to underestimate people's ability to process social information accurately.

Finally, we should make it clear that the kind of role-playing situation we are most concerned about is the situation in which the subjects are told *what variables* the experimenter is interested in and asked to say, or act out, how they would respond to those variables. This is asking for an opinion on our hypothesis, and may have a direct impact on the internal validity of the study. The situation in which subjects are asked to play a role (for example, to participate on a mock jury, *unaware* that the experimenter is manipulating jury composition, or the attractiveness of the defendant, or some other variable) is less risky. Here the external validity of the study is an open question (can we generalize these results to real juries?), but the internal validity (can we trust our results?) is not subject to the distortions of role-playing subjects.

In the future perhaps we will have a way of knowing in advance when subjects' role-playing or social judgments *in* the laboratory are similar to behaviors or judgments *outside* the confines of the social psychological laboratory. Such a comprehensive theory of role playing would enable researchers to delimit the validity of role-playing studies. According to Freedman (1969):

> If such a theory were proposed, extensively tested and supported by data, it would presumably be possible to have considerable confidence in appropriate role-playing studies. If we trusted the theory, we would trust the data that came from those role-playing studies which it predicted would coincide with experimental studies. Under these circumstances, role-playing could substitute for experimental procedures.

Unfortunately, we are a long way from having such a theory. For the time being, since we don't know when we can trust simulations, we cannot regard them as adequate alternatives to non-role-playing experiments or as reliable predictors of subjects' behavior when faced with the stimulus in question.

Mutual Disclosure

A second type of alternative to deception that has been suggested (Jourard, 1968; Kelman, 1968; Schultz, 1969) is simply to increase the amount of truthful communication between the experimenter and the subject during the course of the experiment. At the most conservative level, application of this principle might simply involve disclosing to the subject that full information about the experiment will be given only after it is over, asking the person to behave "normally," and reiterating that all the relevant information will be given and any questions answered at the end of the experiment. This is a reasonable suggestion, which essentially involves making the "contract" between the experimenter and the subject explicit. At the other extreme is Sidney Jourard's (1968) proposal for free experimenter-subject dialogue, in which the experimenter first discloses the general purpose of the experiment, a personal conception of the meaning of the experimental operations and the dependent variable measures, and assumptions about what they reveal and then solicits the subject's statement of the meaning of the operations and measures. The basic rationale behind this procedure, for which there is some evidence (Jourard, 1968), is that the amount and validity of a subject's self-disclosure to the experimenter is a function of the amount of the experimenter's disclosure. The subject's role is one of "collaborator" rather than of "object"; in some ways this role is similar to that of subjects in Wundt's and Titchener's early studies of consciousness.

This collaborator role is also similar to the situation we have recommended for pilot experiments and postexperimental interviews. A great deal of mutual benefit can be derived from a free and open dialogue between the experimenter and the subject. In addition, from the experimenter's point of view, such an interaction is also frequently less strenuous and more gratifying than carrying out a deception experiment, and it is with some wistfulness that we read suggestions for the application of this technique throughout an experiment. But we have reservations. Most important is the probability that the addition of a supportive, self-revealing dialogue to a given stimulus situation will change the whole nature of that situation. Jourard himself suggests that such dialogues are rare and valuable occurrences in everyday life. If this is so, the inclusion of such an event in an experiment will inevitably have a profound effect on the subject's perceptions and interpretations of the situation, and we would not be justified in generalizing the subject's reactions to the same situation experienced alone. Most experimenters in social psychology want to be able to generalize to real-world situations in which subjects cannot ask the meaning of things that happen to them or the intentions of people they meet and also expect to receive a full an honest answer before they have to respond. If they could, they might respond differently. If, as social psychologists, we are interested in how people behave when they have insufficient time or motivation for the conscious analysis of the nature of the stimuli or the implications of their response alternatives, when there is no omniscient helper whom they can ask for explanation, when they have no opportunity to explain and qualify the meaning of their behavior, we have to let subjects fend for themselves in the experimental situation. After the experiment is over, we can engage in a mutually revealing dialogue with the subjects, trading interpretations, explaining our purposes to each other, and perhaps achieving a relationship of the sort Jourard describes.

This is not to say that the method of mutual disclosure is inappropriate for experimentation in social psychology. There are questions that may be profitably explored using this technique, just as there are situations in which role playing can be usefully employed. Indeed, to do justice to Jourard, he is basically concerned with a different question from those we have been discussing in this book. We have been dealing with questions involving the conditions and variables that typically affect human behavior, whereas Jourard is concerned with the atypical instances when behavior is not controlled by the usual constraints. The procedure he suggests may be a means of creating such instances. As such, it could be a useful and valuable technique, but it is obvious that it is not universally applicable to social psychological problems. No single technique will answer all questions, and one of the most important steps in conducting a study is to find a procedure that is appropriate for the question asked.

DEBRIEFING

Whether or not deception is employed, the experimenter is obliged to go to great lengths to protect the subjects' welfare. An important opportunity for doing so is the postexperimental session. In a typical deception experiment, the experimenter will (and should) spend more time with the subject after the experiment is over than during the experimental session itself. Much of this time is spent in describing the nature of the experiment and the reasons for the deception.

But it is not that simple. Debriefing following a deception experiment is not simply a matter of exposing a subject to the truth. There is nothing magically curative about the truth; indeed, if the truth is harshly or hastily presented, it can hurt the subject more than no explanation at all. There are vast differences in how debriefing sessions are conducted, and these differences are of crucial importance in determining whether a subject is uncomfortable after the experiment.

Many effective debriefing techniques exist. Here, we will talk about those aspects of the debriefing session that are designed to minimize the uneasiness caused by the use of deception. Perhaps the most essential aspect of the process is that the experimenter communicate both sincerity as a scientist seeking the truth and awkwardness about the fact that it was necessary to resort to deception in order to arrive at the truth. No amount of postexperimental gentleness or sensitivity is as effective in relieving a subject's discomfort as an honest account of the experimenter's *own* discomfort in the situation. Although no one enjoys being deceived, much of the displeasure may stem from a feeling that one's deceiver is feeling smug about it. Therefore, we recommend that the experimenter frankly explain that the deception was necessary (if it really was, the subject will understand this) and express regret about this necessity. The experimenter should make it clear to the subject that there was no other way to test the experimental question in a satisfactory manner. It is also important to provide the subject with an account of the experiment and the reasons the experimenter thinks it is worthwhile, in order to allow the *subject* to decide whether it was valuable. Obviously, it would be presumptuous for the experimenter to make light of the subject's uneasiness or to suggest that everyone shares the opinion that the scientific ends justify the means. The experimenter has no right to assume that this commitment to science is shared by the subject.

Although a careful and thorough debriefing procedure is costly in terms of time and effort, it is well worth the price; it is our experience that the vast majority of subjects gain understanding of the complexity of experimentation and actually become enthusiastic about the research process in general, and about the specific experiment in which they participated, as a direct result of the debriefing process. Debriefing also has the advantage of serving an educational-didactic purpose, which results in some compensation to the subjects for their services. We will discuss our recommendations for the content of the debriefing session in more detail in Chapter 10. For now, let us sum up by saying that whether or not deception is employed in an experiment, a sensitive and thorough debriefing is an essential component of any study. Moreover, whether or not subjects experience pain, discomfort, or embarrassment during the course of their participation, they have contributed to our understanding of human social behavior. Experimenters are ethically if not morally obliged to "return the favor" by explaining to subjects the questions in which we are interested and the reasons underlying the methods we used to answer them and, finally, to relay to subjects just what it is they have helped us discover about social behavior. After all, yet another way to conceive of social psychological experiment is that of an opportunity for the exchange of knowledge between subject and experimenter.

THE RELATIONSHIP BETWEEN THE SUBJECT AND THE EXPERIMENTER VIEWED AS A CONTRACT

Suppose deception has been employed. No matter how skillfully the experimenter may explain the treatments and reestablish rapport with the subject at the close of the experiment, the fact remains that the subject has been deceived, and no amount of restoration can erase the experimenter's dishonest behavior. Most experimental social psychologists are uncomfortable with this ethical burden but are willing to accept it. They feel that if a deception experiment is the only way to discover something of real importance, the truths so discovered are worth the lies told in the process, so long as no harm befalls the subject. The experimenter can also take comfort in the knowledge that in most cases the subject, although not aware of the true purpose of the experiment, at least is aware of *being in* an experiment. The person knows that his or her relationship to the experimenter is that of subject. Indeed, the two principals are—in effect—parties to an experimenter-subject contract. The possibility that deception will be used can be considered one of the implicit clauses in this contract. A significant number of subjects—although not aware that there is deception in a given experiment and certainly not cognizant of the nature of that deception—nevertheless have an inkling that things often are not what they seem in psychological experiments. This is not to imply that the subject is simply playing a game with the experimenter or is spending time in the experiment generating specific hypotheses about the nature of the research. The situation is much more ambiguous. Although aware that some of the relevant information is missing, the subject may simply experience the situation without stepping back during the actual experiment to analyze the experimental events. This behavior is somewhat similar to that of the "faithful subject" described by Stephen Weber and Thomas Cook (1972). Thus, in debriefing subjects, most of us will hear an occasional person say, "Yes, I had a feeling that there might be something more involved in the experiment, but I didn't know what it might be." In short, subjects are not shocked or even surprised that they were deceived. They seem to accept deception as part of an implicit bargain. Many experimenters find it desirable to make this implicit clause explicit by telling the subject in advance that some aspects of the experiment cannot be explained at that time and may be slightly different from what they appear to be. Indeed, Weber and Cook find that this sort of introduction may enhance the probability that subjects will adopt the "faithful subject" role.

In a few experiments, investigators have used the supposed "debriefing" session as a suspicion-free opportunity to introduce further experimental manipulations. We are opposed to this procedure on both moral and practical grounds. One of our major objections to the use of a false debriefing session to introduce deceptive manipulations is that the possibility of deception in the midst of the debriefing is *not* a part of the implicit contract. Most subjects assume that a distinctly different phase of their interaction with the experimenter is signaled by the experimenter's announcement that the experiment is over, a phase in which complete honesty is to be expected. Most experimenters encourage this assumption. If experimenters continue to violate this aspect of the contract, subjects will have no way of knowing for sure when the experimenter is telling the truth and when expressed sincerity might be a further ploy. Similarly, they will be unable to be certain when it is safe to disclose their inner thoughts about the experiment without these thoughts being used as data. This is clearly unethical. On a practical level, once subjects realize they have been deceived, if they know that it is possible for a debriefing session to serve as a clever contextual device for fooling them *again*—perhaps even for eliciting their inner feelings in order to *use* them as part of the experiment—they will understandably hesitate to reveal much to the experimenter during the postexperimental session.

This might seem like hairsplitting. Isn't deception simply deception? Shouldn't we be consistently "for" or consistently "against" it? We don't think so. We believe that the implicit contract is important, and an illustration will clarify our position. Suppose that a subject volunteers for an experiment on group problem solving and that the experimenter assigns a routine task to a male and a female subject. In the course of their performance of that task, the experimenter leaves the room, and the female subject, who is very attractive, begins to flirt with the male subject. Suppose further that the woman is really a confederate of the experimenter and that the purpose of the experiment is to observe the subject's response to flirtation. Admittedly, such a situation is highly deceptive. But this is tempered by the fact that the subject came into the room willingly in order to participate in a psychological experiment. Compare this with a situation in which the confederate approaches the subject outside a classroom—in the dining hall or in his dormitory—and engages in the same kind of flirtatious behavior. As soon as he makes a pass, the young woman explains that it was all an experiment and hands him a 25-item questionnaire. The latter situation has certain naturalistic advantages, but many experimental social psychologists might prefer to avoid it on the grounds that the subject has not entered into a contractual relationship. If the questionnaire is the dependent variable measure, the subject can, of course, refuse to answer the questions. But if the dependent variable is some behavior which the confederate observes before telling the subject about the experiment, even that protection is denied him. This procedure is more extreme than either a naturalistic observation study in which subjects' behaviors are observed without their knowledge but is not manipulated, or a laboratory deception experiment, in which subjects have tacitly invited the experimenter to observe their behavior but are unaware of which aspects are being revealed. The naturalistic flirtation study raises additional ethical problems, since the concept of the experimental contract is no longer applicable.

ETHICS IN THE FIELD

From the foregoing, it should be apparent that the experimenter who wants to conduct an experiment in the field faces an additional ethical problem that does not arise in laboratory experimentation: The subjects are often unaware that they are in an experiment. The field experimenter cannot take comfort in the concept of a contractual understanding. It may not be possible to obtain informed consent. The problem is serious and perplexing, and the experimenter should consider the consequences with care.

Before considering different aspects of this problem in detail, we should point out that the line between a successful laboratory experiment in which deception is employed and a field experiment in which the subjects are unaware that they are subjects is not always as clear as it may seem. To some extent one technique slides into the other. Some of the most effective laboratory manipulations are those in which we succeed in presenting the independent variable as an event unrelated to the experiment, a nonce event that has nothing to do with the research or the experimenter's purpose. If the experimenter is completely successful, the subject will see the treatment as something which happens outside the context of the experiment and will be unaware of the dependent variable measure. The situation is analogous to a field experiment: If the manipulation of the independent variable and the measure of the dependent variable are seen as unrelated to the experiment, subjects will be unaware of being a subject during the very time that their behavior is influenced or measured—in other words, during the real experiment. The subject may, in fact, be unaware that the experimental "contract" is still in effect. The problem is not quite as extreme in the laboratory as it can be in a field experiment, since the subject has at least agreed to provide data for the experimenter, but the two situations are more similar than might appear at first glance. Indeed, in some laboratory experiments the subject may believe that the most crucial parts of the experiment are not parts of the experiment at all.

For example, in a classic experiment by Leon Festinger and Merrill Carlsmith (1959), the subject was required to spend an hour working on a dull, repetitive task: turning pegs a quarter turn at a time or packing spools in a box, and starting over again from the beginning each time the task was completed. At the end of the hour, the experimenter, somewhat agitated, came in and explained that the subject scheduled for the next hour was supposed to be given a positive expectation about the enjoyability of the task and that the assistant who normally provided that expectation by describing the task in glowing terms had not shown up. Apparently as a last-ditch measure, the experimenter then asked if the subject would perform the assistant's job and tell the next subject that the task was fun and exciting. Subjects were paid either $1 or $20 to take on the role of substitute assistant for the next subject and for any future occasions when the regular assistant could not make it. After describing the experiment to the "next subject" (actually a confederate), subjects were asked to indicate their own opinions of the task. The experimenters predicted that subjects who had been paid only $1 would like the task more, since the only way to reduce the inconsistency between their unfavorable initial impressions and their favorable verbal descriptions of the same task was to decide that the task was not so bad after all.

In many cases field research may use as a dependent variable information in the public domain. In such cases, the subject's lack of informed consent may not be a serious problem. For example, G. W. Hartmann (1936) studied the effects of different types of political advertisements by using one type in one voting precinct and another in a different precinct. The percentage of people voting for a particular candidate in a particular precinct is publicly available. Moreover, there is certainly nothing to prevent an experimenter from circulating political advertisements (especially if they are consistent with private beliefs and conform to normal standards for political campaign material).

The factors that should be taken into consideration in deciding whether to run a given deception experiment apply equally well to field experiments.

First, there is the availability of alternative modes of studying the same question. This is not always a useful consideration in the decision of whether to conduct a field experiment, however. Often, the decision to do a field experiment instead of a laboratory experiment is reached after alternative procedures have been considered or actually used. In some cases the investigator decides on the field experiment after concluding that there is no adequate way of conducting a given study in the laboratory. For example, recall the field experiment by Harris (1974) in which she measured the amount of aggression displayed by people when confederates stepped in front of them as they stood in line in banks, stores, and restaurants. Subjects in the field were undoubtedly less self-conscious than subjects who might have had a similar experience under the watchful eye of an experimenter. It is therefore likely that their responses to the intrusion were more genuine and therefore more valid. Thus, the possibility of an alternative mode has already been explored independently of ethical considerations. In addition, in some cases the investigator is specifically interested in the applicability of some theory or findings *outside* the laboratory, in which case any nonfield alternative will be irrelevant. Nonetheless, the additional ethical problems of field research should be considered in choosing a setting; if they raise any serious questions, the possibility of a laboratory setting should be explored.

Second, there is the consideration of the merit of the research. As we have mentioned repeatedly, the importance and merit of an experiment are difficult qualities to measure. The best we can do here is to advise that the experimenter be aware of the ethical problems involved and weigh benefits of the proposed experiment against them.

Third, there is the consideration of confidentiality or anonymity of the results. Here, the field experiment has a slight advantage. In a laboratory experiment it is *possible* (though, as we have said, highly unethical) that the experimenter might reveal to someone how a specific person behaved in the experiment. It is also *possible* that this information could have negative consequences for the person. Consider, for example, the subject who delivered the strongest shock in the Milgram experiment. As long as *someone* knows that he did so, that subject's protection is not totally guaranteed. In some field experiments it is impossible for a given person to be associated with a given behavior, simply because not even the experimenter knows the subjects' names. Anonymity can be more easily ensured in such instances.

For example, Anthony Doob and his colleagues (1969) conducted a series of field experiments in a chain of discount houses in order to find out whether the "introductory low price offer" really does increase the final sales of a product. Using an argument similar to that of Aronson and Mills (1959), they reasoned that if customers initially bought the product at a higher price, they would have expended more negative effort and should therefore like the product more and continue to buy it more. The researchers divided the stores into pairs matched on gross sales and randomly assigned one of each pair to the "introductory low price" conditions and the other to the regular price condition. Thus, in one of the experiments, a new brand of mouthwash was introduced at $.25 a quart in half the stores and at $.39 a quart in the other half. Nine days later the price was brought up to $.39 for all stores. These researchers found—as predicted— that in subsequent weeks more mouthwash was sold in the stores that had *not* used the introductory low price offer. The dependent variable in the experiment was amount of sales, recorded by the buyers as they replenished the stock. There was no way for the experimenters to know which subjects had returned to buy the increased-price mouthwash and which had switched brands; no one even knew who the subjects were. Thus, this experiment ensured complete anonymity for subjects.

Finally there is the consideration of the level of risk involved in field experiments. On the whole, we recommend much lower levels of stress than are allowable in the laboratory; in field experiments in which debriefing is impossible, the level of stress should be negligible. There are many occasions when nature provides noxious experiences, and one alternative for the social psychologist who wishes to study real-world responses to stress is simply to wait for naturally occurring stressful events. An in-between situation arises when it is known that some event is going to happen—a remedial-reading program in a school for example, or a new type of therapy at a hospital—and the psychologist is called in to decide who gets the treatment. Since it is both ethical and methodologically sound to assign subjects at random to treatments whose effects are unknown (see Chapter 1), such a situation can provide useful data on variables that the psychologist otherwise could not or would not control.

However, if the treatment involves some event that is not particularly stressful—some ordinary event that could happen to the subject every day, such as a price change in the local brand of mouthwash—the only difference between this occasion and a hundred similar occasions is that this one is part of a systematic study, and we do not believe that the ethical problems raised by conducting a field study are any more serious than those of many laboratory studies. In both cases, experimenters have an obligation to terminate the research immediately upon seeing any bad effects on the subjects, regardless of what prior evidence might have led them to expect.

In discussing the ethical questions raised in field research, some investigators have suggested the use of modified field studies as an ethically preferable alternative to laboratory deception research. For example, as early as 1967, William McGuire suggested that the social psychologist should take advantage of "natural manipulations" outside the laboratory, employing the best applicable quasi-experimental design for a specific problem in order to approach valid cause-and-effect inferences when random assignment of subjects to manipulated conditions is impossible or inadvisable. This procedure avoids the problems raised by the experimenter's responsibility for events that may be harmful or disturbing to the subject. It is not free of ethical problems, however, for it can exacerbate the problems of invasion of privacy, especially when subjects are unaware that their behavior is being observed for research purposes. Methodologically, it has the advantage of demonstrable "generalizability" and if subjects are unaware, nonreactivity (i.e., freedom from artifacts due to subjects' knowledge that their behaviors are being measured). For example, if we take advantage of an earthquake or other natural disaster to observe who chooses to affiliate with others, we know that our results apply to at least one nonlaboratory situation, and we can be sure that the subjects' behavior was not caused by their perceptions of what was desirable from the experimenter's point of view. However, this method has the disadvantage of precluding proof of causality, since we do not have control over the "treatment." Once this limitation is accepted, however, field research using quasi-experiments in natural settings and supported by social psychological predictions, conceptions, and theories can offer a useful alternative to laboratory experimentation.

A different means of modifying field experiments has been suggested by Herbert Kelman (1968, p. 225), who raises the possibility of designing field experiments "in which, with full cooperation of the subject, specific experimental variations are introduced. The advantages of dealing with motivations at a real-life level of intensity might well outweigh the disadvantage of subjects knowing the general purpose of the experiment." Although it is difficult to be sure just what sort of event Kelman has in mind, his recommendation seems to mirror the advantages and disadvantages of McGuire's suggestion. That is, the problem of deception and invasion of privacy is eliminated, since the experimenter obtains the subject's fully informed consent and even cooperation. However, the experimenter is manipulating the subject's behavior and introducing potentially distressing or harmful stimuli at a real level of intensity. Generalizability to noncooperative subjects is questionable, and reactivity is likely to be maximal, but if adequate steps can be taken to counteract the dangers of bias and reactivity, the basic design does allow for causal inferences.

The experimenter who employs this procedure because of the advantages of obtaining the subject's informed consent should make an effort to ensure that the subject's consent is in fact freely given. In some contexts, requests made by a psychological experimenter are, by virtue of the experimenter's role, difficult to refuse, even though the subject may have qualms about participating. For example, in attempting to set up a control group for an experiment designed to study the amount of social control exerted under hypnosis, Martin Orne (1962) tried to find a task so boring and pointless that nonhypnotized subjects would either refuse to do it or soon stop working at it. He was unable to find such a task. Subjects willingly spent hours performing page after page of trivial addition and, according to task instructions, ripping up each page as soon as they had finished. Orne concludes that "a particularly striking aspect of the typical experimenter-subject relationship is the extent to which the subject will play his role and place himself under the control of the experimenter. Once a subject has agreed to participate in a psychological experiment, he implicitly agrees to perform a very wide range of actions or requests without inquiring as to their purpose, and frequently without inquiring as to their duration" (1962, p. 77). Although Orne did not use situations that would actually result in a "severe physical pain or exhaustion," there is no a priori reason to believe that subjects would feel free to refuse to participate in these situations either. Thus, the experimenter who wishes to expose consenting subjects to intense experiences should consider very carefully the meaning of their consent and perhaps allow them an opportunity to refuse gracefully, for example, as we mentioned earlier, by having a confederate present who does refuse the request. By introducing the confederate, of course, we are reintroducing deception into the research. The irony of this procedure is that we are here using deception to make sure that the subject is perfectly free to give an honest refusal.

Which of these two methods of field research an experimenter chooses will depend on their appropriateness for the particular problem to be studied. Each poses a different problem: the possibility of invasion of privacy in the method suggested by McGuire, and the possibility of unwilling "informed consent" in the Kelman procedure. There is no consensus on which of these possibilities is the more dangerous. Some investigators feel that the use of noxious conditions in social psychological experiments is the more serious problem (e.g., McGuire, 1967); others imply that the invasion of the subject's privacy is more important.

ETHICS IN EXPERIMENTS WITH CHILDREN AS SUBJECTS

The use of children as subjects in experimental social psychological research raises some of the same ethical problems as the field experiment does. Typically, the subjects are unaware that they are in an experiment, unaware even that experiments exist. They are completely "naive" subjects, and often this naivete is exactly what attracts the social psychologist to the nursery school in the first place. In general, such an experimenter is not particularly interested in contributing to developmental psychology but simply wants to conduct an experiment involving a deception so transparent that it would be unlikely to convince the proverbial college sophomore. Or the experimenter may be interested in studying some form of behavior which is less strongly inhibited in children than in college students, such as the physical expression of aggression. Or finally, the social psychologist may feel that children are more malleable, more easily influenced than adults. This very malleability, however, may imply that the consequences of the experiment may be more profound with children and thus that even greater caution is necessary.

Another similarity between research with children subjects and field research is that effective debriefing is often neither possible nor particularly desirable. Usually, with very young subjects, the experimenter employs some other means of ensuring that the children do not leave the experimental situation with any feeling of anxiety or inadequacy. It is a good idea to play with the subjects and talk to them and make every effort to make sure that they are feeling happy and contented at the end of the experimental session (see Smith, 1967).

The issue of informed consent is typically met by obtaining consent from the parents and/or from the person in charge of a university-administered nursery school, when the parents have delegated the responsibility of providing informed consent to this person. This second system is often a very good arrangement, since the nursery school administrator usually has enough knowledge of psychological research and enough concern for the welfare of the children to make "informed consent" a meaningful term, and in addition the experimenter can be assured that the parents do not object to having their children participate in experiments. It is a good idea for the investigator to take steps to make sure that the parents really are informed about the particular experiment, however, since they are in a position to know whether a given manipulation might have unexpected undesirable effects on their child. If the real reasons for deceiving the subjects is that it is necessary that they be ignorant of the true purpose of the experiment, there should be no reason for withholding this information from the parents. In the interests of both the child and the psychologist, the parents should be informed in advance.

But of course no one except the child knows what it is really like to go through the experiment, and the child has not given any informed consent. As with field experiments, then, the experimenter should use only very low levels of arousing experimental manipulations and should watch the child at all times to be able to terminate the experiment immediately if the child shows any signs of untoward distress. As with field situations, one useful rule of thumb for choosing stimulus situations for research with child subjects is to choose the sorts of situations which most children are exposed to anyway in their everyday lives. For example, in attempting to arouse fear in a nursery school setting, Merrill Carlsmith, Mark Lepper, and T. K. Landauer (1974) showed children a clipping from the Walt Disney cartoon *The Legend of Sleepy Hollow*. Although the sequence shown was frightening, it was assumed to involve a kind and level of fear that the children could cope with, since it was from the same movie that large numbers of children have seen and enjoyed on their own.

INSTITUTIONAL GUIDELINES

There are no absolute rules set down in a code that can provide instant answers to any of the ethical questions raised here. As mentioned previously, both the U.S. Public Health Service and the American Psychological Association have set out codes that, although they establish some guidelines, are necessarily full of ambiguities. The consensus of these reports is that each proposed research study must be considered separately. And we agree. This consideration begins with the individual experimenter, who weighs the consequences of alternative courses of action and makes a choice. If the experiment involves the infliction of physical or psychological discomfort or the use of deception, how valuable will the results of the research be? How much will the subjects suffer? If the planned research is not carried out, what will be lost? If the design is altered by removing the deception or the possibility of the subjects' distress, how will this alteration affect the validity of the results?

Probably few psychologists would demand that deception or the use of unpleasant treatments be eliminated altogether. What is being recommended, as a minimum standard, is that the investigator be aware of the ethical implications of these procedures. The scientist must be concerned about the health and welfare of subjects. Thus, we recommend that whenever possible, the experimenter should avoid the use of deception or any methods that cause discomfort to the subject. If there is a reasonable way of constructing a given experiment to avoid these problems, the experimenter is obligated to find it. We agree with other commentators (for example, Kelman, 1968) in deploring the fact that many novice experimenters in social psychology, in assuming that extreme measures are inevitable, do not first attempt alternative solutions in which the amount of deception or discomfort necessary is slight or nonexistent. Such solutions may be difficult to find, but nonetheless the experimenter has an obligation to try to find them.

CHAPTER 4

EXPERIMENTAL DESIGN

ASKING THE QUESTION

In later chapters, we will concentrate on the experimenter's translation of conceptual variables into concrete events, and on the arrangement of these events into a meaningful sequence. That is, we will discuss how best to present the independent variable and to measure the dependent variable. On the one hand, decisions about how to manipulate the independent variable, how to measure the dependent variable, and how to integrate the two in a situational context may be viewed as decisions about the *content* of the research question. The experimental design, on the other hand, may be viewed as the *form* of the question. As the poet may express the same message in the form of a sonnet or a limerick, so the experimenter can ask the same question in a variety of ways. And just as the sonnet form is a more appropriate vehicle for some messages than is the limerick, some types of experimental design may be more appropriate than others for certain questions.

Specifically, the *design* of an experiment refers to the selection and arrangement of conditions. For example, in the Aronson-Mills experiment on severity of initiation, the design included three conditions: mild initiation, severe initiation, and no initiation. This same design—with one group receiving a low level of the independent variable, a second group receiving a high level, and a third, or "baseline," group not exposed to the independent variable at all— may be used in a wide variety of situations bearing no resemblance in content to the severity-of-initiation study. The same design appears in the Festinger and Carlsmith (1959) experiment, for example, in which subjects were offered money to tell another person that a dull task was exciting. One group was offered $1 to tell the lie, a second group was offered $20, and a third group was not asked to lie about the task. Similarly, an experimenter who deprives one group of rats of food for 10 hours, a second group for 48 hours, and lets the rats in a third group have all the food they want is using the same design as is a doctor who prescribes 10 mg of a drug to one group of patients, 100 mg to a second group, and no drug (or a placebo) to a third. The content of the questions is quite different, but the form is the same: Does X affect Y, and does a great deal of X affect Y differently from a small amount of X?

It has been stated that "when one simply asks a question of nature, the answer is always positive," since "even an experimental manipulation that produces no change in the dependent variable can provide useful and often important information" (Sidman, 1960, p. 9). The problem is that "simply asking a question of nature" is not always simple. A question may take many different forms. Some versions of a question may be intrinsically ambiguous, some may be rhetorical, and some may be moot. It is also possible to ask a leading question, so that one particular answer is more likely than another, whether or not it is the true answer. Although all these forms of a question are useful in certain contexts, none is desirable for an experiment. The goal of empirical research is to ask clear and usually specific questions that will elicit unambiguous, unbiased, and informative answers. An ideal design poses the experimenter's question fairly, thoroughly, and economically.

How does one ask a question of nature? The first step is to make the question concrete and explicit. Saying that one is interested in social change or attitudes or guilt is not enough. Sooner or later, the question usually takes the form, "Does X affect Y?" or some more complicated version of the same thing. In this chapter we will concentrate primarily on questions about causality and on designs that allow the experimenter to infer that changes in the independent variable *cause* changes in the dependent variable. In Chapter 1 we briefly discussed correlational and quasi-experimental designs that can provide useful information when random assignment, and therefore causal inference, is not possible. Conceptually, an experiment is designed to investigate a causal relationship between two variables: Does the amount of unpleasant effort expended lead to a higher evaluation of the results of that effort? Does fear bring about a need to affiliate with others?

Chapters 6 through 8 will deal specifically with the ways in which theoretical independent and dependent variables are translated into concrete events and placed in a realistic situation. After the research question has been identified, and before subjects arrive to participate in those events, the experimenter must consider *how to ask* the question. What comparisons should be made? How many different groups should be run, and what should they be? Should the subjects be pretested before they are exposed to the independent variables? Should each subject receive only one treatment, or more than one? How many levels of the independent variable are needed, and how many measures of the dependent variable? A number of general principles should be taken into consideration when making these decisions, several of which are discussed below, but the most important factor should be the question itself. A clearly thought out question is the most important step toward finding the "right" design. In considering various experimental designs, the experimenter should continually ask: Would the results of this design answer my question? If not, why not?

One useful technique for gauging the adequacy of a potential design is to imagine different possible patterns of results. An experimenter often has a specific hypothesis about how the data should look and gets results that do not correspond to the hypothesis. By considering other possible outcomes before conducting the experiment, the experimenter can build in other conditions or other measures that may help to explain such outcomes. Conversely, by simply viewing the experiment as a "success" only if the outcome confirms the hypothesis, the experimenter may be at a loss to explain unpredicted results and may have to carry out another experiment—with a whole new design—to obtain the information that, with a little prior thought, could have been collected within the context of the original experiment.

For example, Ellsworth and Carlsmith (1968) conducted an experiment in which they predicted that eye contact would intensify the dominant emotion in an interaction. According to their hypothesis, subjects praised during an interview would like the interviewer more if she looked them in the eyes than if she avoided looking at them, whereas in a negative interaction the subjects would *dislike* her more if she maintained eye contact. This prediction was generally confirmed, but the specific pattern of results was somewhat unexpected. Subjects in the negative condition without eye contact liked the experimenter a great deal—as much as did subjects in the positive condition with eye contact. It would be a distortion of these results to say that looking at a person while saying negative things intensifies dislike, since when the interviewer said negative things and looked away, there was no evidence of dislike. The experimenters had some speculations about this unexpected pattern of data. For example, they speculated that when people are embarrassed about some imagined weakness or defect, they want to avoid close social interaction with others, so they like people who keep their distance. Had the experimenters considered the possibility of this pattern of results before they started the research, they might have asked subjects questions that could have provided some information about this possibility. Or, they might have designed the experiment to contrast conditions in which negative aspects of the interview were either very personal or quite impersonal. Instead, the only way this pattern of results could be explained was to design a whole new experiment to test their speculations (Ellsworth, Friedman, Perlick, & Hoyt, 1978). For some complex questions, considering all conceivable patterns of results is obviously difficult. Nonetheless, it is important to remember that relatively minor changes can often open the door to a great deal of relevant information. An experimenter who thinks only in terms of the confirmation of the hypothesis may miss many opportunities to gain insights when the hypothesis is incomplete or just incorrect.

Even when the outcome is exactly as predicted, there are likely to be alternative explanations for the pattern of results obtained. Once again, it is worth-while to think ahead, to take the part of a critic of the finished experiment, and to try to find confounding variables that might have produced the predicted outcome. Often, it is possible to alter the design so as to rule out many of the plausible alternative explanations, for example, by holding variables constant or by adding new conditions to the experiment.

Typically in social psychology, as in the case of the Ellsworth and Carlsmith study, additional conditions are added to the experiment in replications carried out after the original experiment has been completed, either because the experimenter did not think of a particular alternative explanation in time to account for it in the initial experiment or because the addition of conditions would make the experiment too complex and unwieldy. Although it is preferable to account for alternative explanations in advance, the basic method of adding conditions to rule out extraneous influences is the same whether the conditions are run at once or in stages and may be illustrated by the following example in which two experiments were run in a row.

The purpose of the experiments was to find out whether people who are allowed extra time to perform a task spend more time on a subsequent task than do people who are required to complete the first task in a minimum amount of time. The amount of time allowed for the first task was the independent variable; the amount of time spent on the second task, with no restrictions imposed, was the dependent variable. In the initial experiment (Aronson & Landy, 1967), a secretary burst into the room while the experimenter was giving the instructions and reminded him that he was urgently needed to help set up some equipment and that it would take about five minutes (in the "minimum time" condition) or fifteen minutes (in the "excess time" condition). The experimenter asked the subject to do the task while he was off working on the equipment and said that he would be back in five (or fifteen) minutes. The investigators felt that since the amount of time allotted depended on the time necessary to set up the equipment, the subject should perceive it as unrelated to the demands of the task itself. It was possible, however, that the experimenter might have given the impression that the subject should be finished by the time he returned, and thus that the task should take less than five minutes in the minimum-time condition. If this were true, the fact that the subjects who spent less time working on the first task also spent less time working on the second might have been due to their perceptions that five minutes was the appropriate amount of time to spend on a task of that sort. Thus the results might not have been due to the availability of excess time but rather to perceived task requirements.

The second experiment (Landy, McCue, & Aronson, 1969) consisted of two conditions designed to rule out this alternative explanation. Instead of having the available time for the first task controlled by the experimenter, it was controlled by a confederate, who provided distractions designed to either hurry or delay the subject. The results replicated those of the first experiment; on the second task, when the confederate was not there, subjects who had been hurried on the first task took less time than did subjects who had been delayed by the confederate. The results of this replication indicate that neither perceived task requirements nor differences in the nature of the distractions could have accounted for the excess time effect. Viewing the first and second experiments as part of a single design, we can see how the addition of conditions can greatly clarify and strengthen the results by ruling out alternative explanations.

To summarize, a suitable experimental design results from knowing what the question is and anticipating potential problems and ambiguities. These considerations are important at each stage of the design of an experiment. Often during the course of planning an experiment, an experimenter thinks of additional variables that might affect subjects' behavior in the situation that has been set up. Each time this occurs, the experimenter has to decide whether to build the new variable into the experiment, to rule it out, or to measure it. Certain problems and ambiguities recur in social psychological research, and experimental designs have been worked out expressly to deal with them. Some of these problems are discussed below, along with the appropriate designs, and this discussion may provide a set of guidelines for avoiding error in future experiments. Nonetheless, designing an experiment involves much more than the perfunctory selection of the prefabricated design that comes closest to answering one's own question. Frequently, none of the common designs is quite right, and the experimenter must extrapolate the principles and come up with a new design.

CONTROL GROUPS

The simplest experimental design consists of two groups: an experimental group that is exposed to the experimental treatment, and a control group that is not given the treatment. In Chapter 1 we discussed the importance of control groups and the inevitable ambiguity that arises in attempting to interpret the results of studies which lack a control condition. The basic principle of experimental design is to "design the experiment so that the effects of the independent variables can be evaluated unambiguously" (Underwood, 1957, p. 87). Without a control group, it is impossible to be sure how subjects would behave if they were *not* exposed to the independent variable, and thus it is impossible to arrive at an unambiguous evaluation of the effects of the independent variable.

In order to be confident that any differences we observe in the behavior of experimental subjects and control subjects are due to the treatment, it is important that there be no *other* differences between the two groups. This means, first, that the subjects should come from the same population and should be randomly assigned to the experimental and the control groups (see pp. 17–18). Examples that fail to meet this criterion are easy to find: the 8 A.M. introductory psychology class is used as the experimental group, the 2 P.M. class as the control group; experimental subjects are run by one (perhaps more experienced) experimenter, control group subjects by another; the experimental group consists of volunteers, and the "control group" is simply data from the files of all the students in a given class; the experimental subjects are juvenile offenders, and the control subjects are other adolescents from the same high school. In all these examples, other differences exist between the experimental subjects and the control subjects. Because the assignment of subjects to conditions is not random, extraneous differences could account for differences in the way subjects in the two groups behave in the experiment. Random assignment makes extraneous differences between groups so improbable that we can safely assume that there are none.[1]

When background data are available, or if other information indicates the similarity of the two groups prior to the treatment, we can use these data to check on the equivalence of the two groups, as a sort of guarantee of the effectiveness of random assignment in the particular case. However, the probability that nonequivalent groups will result from random assignment is generally so small (depending on the total number of subjects in the experiment) that it is safe to assume equivalence, and it is unnecessary to introduce special tests to make sure that this is so. Although the results of such a test may seem like a reassuring extra guarantee, in many social psychological experiments a test administered before the manipulation of the independent variable may threaten the validity of the experiment by sensitizing the subjects to the variables being manipulated or measured. Such sensitization could threaten the experiment's internal validity by changing subjects' responses to the treatment, or it could threaten external validity by raising the possibility that the results of the experiment apply only to pretested subjects. However, if some sort of preliminary measure is already an integral part of the experiment for subjects in all conditions, it is certainly useful to examine the responses to the test to see if there are any systematic differences.

Although random assignment can ensure that the experimental group and the control group are equivalent before the experiment begins, it cannot keep them that way if *during* the experiment they have very different experiences prior to the introduction of the independent variable. In order to be certain that differences in the subjects' behavior on the measures of the dependent variable are due to the experimental treatment, the experimenter tries to keep the experiences in the two groups identical, *except* for levels of the independent variable. In some experiments, this similarity of experience can be achieved by postponing the assignment of subjects to the experimental or control group until just before the treatment is introduced. These subjects may receive the initial instructions, hear the same description of the study, and experience all the events that occur before the treatment *without* being assigned to conditions, thus ensuring that they will be treated alike up to that point.

For example, in the Festinger and Carlsmith (1959) experiment, subjects came into the laboratory, received instructions about the ostensible purpose of

---

[1] More precisely, statistical techniques allow us to assign a probability (significance level) to the possibility that the observed differences were due to initial differences between the groups.

the experiment, worked on the boring task, heard that there was another experimental condition in which an accomplice of the experimenter gave the subjects a glowing description of the task, saw the experimenter called away in a crisis, heard about the accomplice who failed to show up and the "next subject" already getting impatient in the waiting room, received an urgent request to fill in for the accomplice, and finally learned that they would be paid $1 or $20 for doing so. The independent variable defining the conditions was the amount of money offered. Subjects in this experiment could have been randomly assigned to either condition at any time, from before they even entered the laboratory until the moment before the experimenter actually mentioned the money. The later in the sequence the random assignment is made (or, equivalently, the later the experimenter *knows* the condition to which the subject has been assigned), the greater our confidence that subjects in the two conditions will have had the same experience when the independent variable is actually introduced. Nothing can cause the behavior of subjects in the experimental and control groups to diverge up to the point when they are randomly assigned to conditions; afterward, there may be several possible causes, only one of which is the independent variable.

Even when subjects must be assigned to conditions at the beginning of the experiment, it is possible to hold constant many variables that might otherwise affect their behavior differently in the two groups. First, the experimenter wants to keep the *activities* of the groups as similar as possible. Suppose, for example, that subjects in the experimental group spend half an hour working on interesting tasks and interacting with other people and that somewhere embedded in this lively sequence of events is the independent variable. If the control-group subjects simply sit in a chair and wait during the same half hour, we are not justified in attributing differences in the behavior of the two groups to the independent variable. One or another of the tasks, the social interaction, or even the boredom of the subjects in the control group might be responsible for the differences.

Likewise, it is important that the control-group subjects be given the same background *information* as is given to the experimental-group subjects, except for information that is an integral part of the treatment. Thus, in the Schachter (1959) studies of affiliation, subjects in the experimental and control groups were given the same description of the purpose of the research, the same outline of the procedure, and the same rationale for their opportunity to choose whether they preferred to wait for the shocks alone or with other subjects. The only element of the presentation that differed for the two groups was the description of the severity of the shock they were to receive, and this constituted the fear-inducing independent-variable manipulation. Using preprogrammed tapes, as in the severity-of-initiation study (Aronson & Mills, 1959) is another important means of keeping the activities and information of experimental and control subjects the same.

In the ideal social psychological experiment, the experiences of experimental and control subjects take the same amount of time, involve interaction with the same people, require the same information, and include the same activities, except for the introduction of the treatment. When this goal is achieved, we are confident that differences in their behavior are attributable to the independent variable. Given the complexity of many social psychological treatments, however, it is sometimes difficult to construct one single control group that will achieve all of these goals. For any control group the experimenter can think of, there is some alternative explanation that might account for differences in the behavior of the subjects in the two groups. Often, it is possible to solve this problem by using more than one control group, each designed to rule out a different alternative explanation.

For example, suppose that an experimenter is interested in the ways in which speakers modify their communication when they can't see the person they are talking to. The conceptual independent variable is visibility. The obvious experiment involves two conditions: one in which the speaker and listener sit face to face across a table, and one in which an opaque barrier is placed between them. But even in this very simple experiment, there are difficulties in isolating the independent variable. Is it visibility that affects communication, or is it the knowledge that the other person is paying attention? Only in the full-visibility condition does the speaker know whether the listener is paying attention. This design can be modified by adding a control group in which the listener behind the barrier gives verbal or vocal indication of paying attention. Thus there may be three conditions: visible (with attention implied), invisible (attention implied), and invisible (no information about attention). Depending on the experimenter's theoretical concerns, still more elaborate designs may be constructed. For example, attention might also be varied in the visible condition.

In the visibility example, the experimenter discovered that the independent variable was multifaceted when searching for an appropriate control group. Often, experimenters are interested in multifaceted independent variables to begin with, or in the combined effects of two or more independent variables. In these cases the simple, zero-treatment control is not sufficient, and sometimes it may even be appropriate. For example, Table 4-1 provides a visual representation of an experimental design used by Stanley Schachter and Jerome Singer (1962). They hypothesized that people infer that they are experiencing a particular emotion if they are physiologically aroused *and* if there are environmental cues signaling that particular emotion. If either the arousal or the cues are missing, the emotion will not be experienced; both components are essential. Schachter and Singer's main treatment group was given an injection of epinephrine to produce unexplained physiological arousal and was exposed to a confederate who exhibited blatant signs of euphoria or anger. The researchers' prediction was that the experimental subjects would interpret their arousal as happiness when the confederate was euphoric, as anger when the confederate was angry. A control group in which subjects received no injection and saw no confederate would not have been very helpful in this experiment, since there would have been a great many differences between their

TABLE 4-1
EXPERIMENTAL AND CONTROL GROUPS IN
THE SCHACHTER AND SINGER EXPERIMENT (1962)

Group	Experience	Controls
Experimental: Injection with no information	Subjects injected with epinephrine, told the injection was harmless and told to expect no side effects	
Control group 1: Placebo with no information	Subjects injected with saline solution, told the injection was harmless, and told to expect no side efects	Controls for physiological arousal and experience of getting an injection
Control group 2: Injection with information	Subjects injected with epinephrine and told to expect shaking hands, rapid heart rate, and flushed faces	Controls for expectation of the source of physiological arousal
Control group 3: Injection with misinformation	Subjects injected with epinephrine and told to expect numb feet, itching sensation, and slight headache	Controls for the provision of any information as to source of physiological arousal

experiences and those of the experimental group which could account for differences in the emotions they felt at the end of the experiment.

In fact, no single control group includes all experiences of the experimental group except the "critical one." Several control groups are needed for an adequate test of the hypothesis. Schachter and Singer included one control group which was exposed to a euphoric or angry confederate and which received a placebo injection instead of the epinephrine; presumably, these subjects should not feel the emotions modeled by the confederates, since the component of unexplained physiological arousal was absent. In addition, this group controlled for the experience of getting an injection. If this group had behaved differently from the experimental group, the researchers could have concluded that the physiological arousal brought about by the epinephrine was a crucial factor. A second control group was designed to test that part of the hypothesis stating that the physiological arousal must be *unexplained*. Like the experimental group, this control group received an injection of epinephrine, but this time the experimenter explained to the subjects exactly what physiological symptoms would be caused by the drug. Schachter and Singer predicted that these subjects would not use the confederate's behavior to infer an emotion, since they had no need to look for an "emotional" explanation of their physiological arousal, having already been provided with a perfectly adequate pharmacological explanation. However, this control group had *some* information, whereas the experimental group had none, thus raising the possibility that receiving information—any information, whether correct or incorrect—would cause differences between this group and the experimental group. So a third control group, which received *false* information about the symptoms caused by the drug, was added; thus the subjects in this group had received information, but their actual physiological symptoms remained unexplained. It has been suggested that still other control groups were necessary to provide an adequate test of this complex independent variable, but the general implications should be clear: If the purpose of control groups is to allow the experimenter to arrive at an unambiguous assessment of the effects of the independent variable, more than one control group may be necessary. The control group(s) to be used should be dictated by the experimenter's question and the conceptual independent variable, even if this results in a design that does not fit standardized models.

FACTORIAL DESIGNS

In factorial designs, two or more independent variables are tested so that every level of one variable occurs with every level of the other(s), each different *combination* of levels defining a condition. The simplest type of factorial design, and one of the most commonly used in social psychological experimentation, is the 2 × 2 ("two by two") factorial, in which each of two different independent variables is tested at each of two levels. The hypothetical experiment we used to demonstrate the nature of an *interaction* in Chapter 1 is an example of a 2 × 2 factorial design. In that experiment, one independent variable was the size of the unanimous majority that disagreed with the subjects' judgments of the lengths of lines; the two levels of this variable were (1) majority of two, and (2) majority of four. The other independent variable was the similarity between the dissenting group and the subject, and the two levels of this variable were simply (1) similar, and (2) dissimilar people in the group. Several other examples of 2 × 2 designs have also been discussed in other contexts, for example, the experiment by Freedman (1965), in which children were issued either a mild or severe threat not to play with a toy and in which the experimenter either left the room or remained. Both levels of each factor (variable) were combined with each other, resulting in a 2 × 2 design, or four conditions in the experiment: "experimenter issues mild threat and leaves," "experimenter issues a severe threat and leaves," "experimenter issues mild threat and stays," and "experimenter issues severe threat and stays."

This type of design can provide a great deal of information in a very efficient manner. Unlike a simple two-group design, it can provide information about the generality of a phenomenon. For example, in the hypothetical experiment in which both the size and the similarity of the unanimous majority were varied, we can examine the effects of majority size in two different situations (similar and dissimilar groups), thus obtaining information equivalent to that available from conducting two separate two-condition experiments. If the number of errors subjects make increases with larger majorities, regardless of the similarity of the group, we have evidence that the generality of this effect is not limited to one particular kind of group.

At the same time, a 2×2 design allows us to examine the effects of group similarity to find out whether it has any effect on judgment errors and whether this effect generalizes to both majority sizes. This information is also equivalent to that obtainable from two separate two-condition experiments, but it is important to note that they are *not* the same two experiments that we would carry out to test the effects of group size. In order to obtain valid information about the generality of both group size and group similarity, we would have to run four separate two-condition experiments: eight conditions in all, or twice as many subjects as we need to discover the same information by means of a 2×2 design.

To illustrate this point diagrammatically, imagine that we are interested in the effects of large versus small groups and that in our basic two-condition experiment, we are going to hold similarity constant, that is, both groups will consist of people who are similar to the subject. If we run 10 subjects in each condition, the design is as follows.

Condition 1 $n = 10$	Condition 2 $n = 10$
Majority of two (small)	Majority of four (large)
(Both groups similar to the subject)	

In order to find out whether this effect generalizes to dissimilar groups, the experimenter might replicate the study, using the same design but with groups which were dissimilar to the subject:

Condition 1 $n = 10$	Condition 2 $n = 10$
Majority of two (small)	Majority of four (large)
(Both groups dissimilar to the subject)	

One possible pattern of results for these two experiments might be:

EXPERIMENT 1

4 errors	6 errors
Majority of two (small)	Majority of four (large)
(Both groups similar to the subject)	

EXPERIMENT 2

3 errors	5 errors
Majority of two (small)	Majority of four (large)
(Both groups dissimilar to the subject)	

In the first experiment subjects make four errors with the small majority and six errors with the large majority; in the second experiment, in which the group is dissimilar, they make three errors with the small majority and five errors with the large majority. We can conclude that pressure from large majorities produces more errors than does pressure from small majorities and that this result holds up regardless of whether the majority is made up of people who are similar or dissimilar to the subject.

Now, what can we conclude about the effects of *similarity* of the group on number of errors? Since subjects in the first experiment made an average of five errors, and subjects in the second experiment made an average of four errors, it might look as though similar majorities tend to raise the number of errors by one. Although it may be tempting to draw this conclusion, we must beware of doing so, because it is not justified by the research we have carried out. Many reasons besides group similarity might have caused subjects in the second experiment to make one less error than subjects in the first experiment. It is later in the year, and subjects may have become suspicious about looking like conformists in a psychology experiment; the experimenter might be more relaxed and less able to induce a high degree of tension; the confederates might be different people, or they might be bored and less able to create effective group pressure. Similarity of the group has never actually been varied within the context of a single experiment, and thus any differences that might be attributable to similarity might equally well be attributed to any of the other factors that inevitability distinguish two different experiments.

In order to assess the effects of similarity, we would have to conduct two *more* experiments, this time holding group size constant and allowing similarity to vary, as follows:

EXPERIMENT 3

Number of errors	Group
4	Similar to subject
3	Dissimilar to subject
[Majority size constant at two (small)]	

EXPERIMENT 4

Number of errors	Group
6	Similar to subject
5	Dissimilar to subject
[Majority size constant at four (large)]	

If, as is indicated in these charts, the subjects in experiment 3 make four errors with the similar group and three errors with the dissimilar group, and if the subjects in experiment 4 make six errors with the similar group and five errors with the dissimilar group, we will have perfectly replicated the results of the first two experiments, and we will now be able to have confidence in the generality of both similarity and majority size.

However, we will have used four separate experiments and 80 subjects to do so. If we use a 2×2 factorial design, we can achieve the same confidence with one experiment and 40 subjects, as follows.

	Majority size	
Group similarity	**Large (4)**	**Small (2)**
Similar to subject	$n = 10$	$n = 10$
Dissimilar to subject	$n = 10$	$n = 10$

The same results obtained by the four smaller experiments, when presented as the results of the factorial design, would look like this:

	Majority size		
Group similarity	**Large (4)**	**Small (2)**	**Average**
Similar to subject	6	4	5
Dissimilar to subject	5	3	4
Average	For large majorities: 5.5		
	For small majorities: 3.5		

The effect of majority size can be seen by comparing the *column averages* (5.5 for large majorities and 3.5 for small majorities); larger majorities increase the number of errors by two. The effects of similarity can be seen in the *row averages* (5 and 4); similar groups increase the number of errors by one. As described in Chapter 1, this set of results corresponds to two main effects: Both majority size and similarity have an effect on the number of errors, and this effect is the same regardless of the value of the other variable. In other words, both variables have been shown to have an effect, and both these effects have been shown to have some generality.

Factorial Designs and Interactions

In Chapter 1 we examined the concept of **interaction,** pointing out that an interaction occurs when the effect of one independent variable depends on the value of the other. For example, the effect of group size on the number of errors subjects make might depend on whether the group was made up of people who were similar or dissimilar to the subject. When the other people are similar, a large group of them might induce the subject to make more errors, but when the other people are dissimilar, the subject might be relatively unaffected by their misjudgments, regardless of how large the group is. Such a finding would limit the generality of the conclusion that pressure from large groups produces more conformity than does pressure from small groups. Indications of the limits of the generality of a hypothesis are useful to the social psychologist interested in understanding the phenomenon, who in this case, for example, might be led to further insights and research into the question of why large groups of similar people are able to make the subject deny sensory evidence. The ability of the factorial design to indicate interactions is one of its greatest advantages. When no interactions exist, it provides increased evidence for the generality of whatever main effects are found; when interactions do exist, it helps the experimenter to refine and elucidate the variables.

Often, an experimenter chooses to use a factorial design on the basis of a specific prediction involving an interaction. For example, Ellsworth and Carlsmith (1968) predicted that eye contact would have different effects on recipients, depending on whether the general atmosphere of the conversations in which they were engaged were positive or negative. Thus the two variables involved in the prediction were amount of eye contact and atmosphere of the conversation. The authors expected that in a comfortable, positive atmosphere, subjects would like the experimenter better if she looked at them a great deal than if she rarely looked at them. When the atmosphere was uncomfortable, however, subjects were expected to prefer the experimenter who did not look at them very often. Thus the authors were making an interaction prediction: High amounts of eye contact should enhance liking in a positive situation but should diminish liking in a negative situation. They used a 2 × 2 factorial design with high versus low eye contact and complimentary versus critical conversation as the levels of the variables, and their prediction was generally confirmed. To be able to predict when a variable will have one kind of effect and when it will have a different effect indicates a substantial understanding of the variable. In order to test such a prediction, a factorial design is necessary, and this is perhaps one of the main reasons for its popularity.

The 2 × 2 is the simplest factorial design, but there are many others, as the number of independent variables (factors) and the number of levels of each variable are increased. For example, the experiment on group pressure might have used groups of two, four, and six members. Crossed with the two levels of similarity, this would have resulted in six conditions: three similar groups of different sizes and three dissimilar groups of different sizes. This design is called a 2 × 3 design, with two levels of similarity and three levels of group size. Had we also used three different levels of similarity (very similar, moderately similar, and dissimilar) we would have had a 3 × 3 design, or nine conditions in all.

In addition to increasing the number of levels of each factor, it is also possible to add new variables to a factorial design. For example, if we want to know how conformity is affected when the majority is *not* unanimous, we might want to include conditions in which one member of the group gives the answer in judging the lines. If we now added the variable of unanimity versus nonunanimity to our original design, we would have two levels of group size, two levels of similarity, and two levels of unanimity. This would result in a total of eight conditions, as follows:

	Small majority (2)		Large majority (4)	
	Group similar to subject	Group dissimilar to subject	Group similar to subject	Group dissimilar to subject
Unanimous	1	2	5	6
Nonunanimous	2	4	7	8

This design is referred to as a 2 × 2 × 2 (unanimity × similarity × group size) design. It permits the experimenter to test for the three different main effects, for interactions between any pair of variables (three different *two-way interactions*), or for an interaction among all three variables, within the context of a single experiment. Had we conducted the same experiment with three different group sizes, we would have had a 2 × 2 × 3 design; adding a third level of similarity would make it a 2 × 3 × 3 design, and so on.

Control Groups in Factorial Designs

In none of the factorial designs we presented above—or, for that matter, in any pure factorial design—is there one group designated the "control group." A separate control group is often not used with a factorial design. The comparison of interest is typically between different values of the independent variable, not between its presence or absence. On occasion, the experimenter may want to know how the various conditions in the design differ from a situation in which no treatment at all is given. For example, in our basic 2 × 2 design on group pressure, suppose that the small number of errors occurred when the group was *small* and *dissimilar*. Suppose that subjects exposed to pressure from a small, dissimilar group made an average of two errors in judging the lines. How can we tell whether this number reflects the operation of a small but nonetheless real degree of group pressure or is within the range of errors people would make judging the same lines in the absence of any pressure at all? Within the context of the 2 × 2 factorial design, we cannot answer this question. In order to understand how far our treatments shift the behavior from "normal," we need a group that receives *no* treatment, as an indicator of what is "normal" is in this situation. In this case, we might add a control group similar to Asch's original control group, in which subjects simply judged the lines in private without pressure of any kind. If these subjects made no errors, we would know that even small, dissimilar groups are capable of exerting a certain amount of effective pressure. However, if subjects in our additional control group made an average of two errors, we could conclude that groups have to be either large or similar (or both) in order to induce subjects to conform. When a control group is added to a factorial design, the assignment of subjects to the control group is, of course, part of the same random-assignment procedure as is used for the subjects in the various experimental groups.

In many factorial experiments a control group is useful for providing a baseline measure against which to assess the effects of all the treatments. Whether such a group is useful for any particular experiment depends on the experimenter's question, that is, on the variables being studied. For example, consider a field experiment by Ellsworth, Carlsmith, and Alexander Henson (1972). Briefly, this study investigated the extent to which being stared at motivates people to "escape" another's fixed gaze. A confederate stood on a street corner and (at random) either (1) gazed intently at a motorist stopped at a red light or (2) merely glanced at the driver and then looked away. When the light turned green, the confederate used a stopwatch to time how long it took the driver to proceed through the intersection. In this experiment, the independent variable was the presence or absence of a stare, and the dependent variable was the length of time it took the driver to move across the intersection once the light turned green. For a moment, let's suppose that the threatening properties of staring may depend on whether the person staring is male or female. To test this possibility, we set the experiment up as a 2×2 (stare $\times$ confederate gender), as follows:

	Stare	No stare
Male starer		
Female starer		

It is hard to think of a baseline control group that would be useful in this experiment. The experiment itself contains conditions (the no-stare conditions) in which a person is simply standing on the street corner, not looking at the driver, and this seems to approximate the normal state of affairs fairly well. We could add an additional control group in which no one was standing on the street corner (we could conceal the experimenter who times the driver's speed) in order to get an absolute baseline. But this control group would not really tell us anything about the effects of staring, which is, after all, what we are studying. It could tell us whether the presence of a person on the street corner affects the speed with which the driver crosses the intersection, but this is rather remote from our original question. In designing a factorial experiment, the experimenter tries to consider whether a baseline measure makes sense in terms of the question. Sometimes the experimenter will find that adding a control group will make a substantial addition to the conclusions that can be drawn, sometimes that all the relevant controls are contained within the factorial design, and sometimes that several additional control groups are necessary for an understanding of the results of the experiment. There are no hard and fast rules in this area. It is important to ask what additional information is important and what type of control group(s) can provide that information.

An example of a 2×2 design that did add an extra control group is provided by a follow-up to the experiment on staring. Ellsworth and Ellen Langer (1976) tested the hypothesis that in certain kinds of situations, people would *approach* a person who was staring at them. The general situation involved a woman who needed help and who either stared at potential helpers or looked away. When the nature of the victim's trouble was clear, investigators predicted that her stare would elicit approach and assistance. But when the victim's predicament was ambiguous, they predicted that staring would not be likely to elicit helpful behavior; they felt that as subjects became less and less sure of the appropriate response, their tendency to flee would become stronger. Thus the investigators were making an interaction prediction in a 2×2

design. The subject was told that the victim seemed to have lost a contact lens (clear condition) or that she seemed not to be feeling well (ambiguous condition), and the victim either stared at the potential helper or looked down at the ground. In this experiment, the investigators felt that it would be useful to include an extra control group, one in which the subject was not told anything about the victim. The purpose of having this control group was to find out whether the stare alone elicited any approach in this general situation and to add a condition that would be similar to the situation in the street-corner experiment. As predicted, the stare increased help in the clear condition, but not in the ambiguous condition; when no information at all was given, no one approached the starer. The situation in the control group could be regarded as one of total ambiguity, as in the earlier experiment on staring.

PERCENTAGE OF SUBJECTS HELPING

Behavior of victim	Nature of problem		
	Clear	Ambiguous	No information
Stare	83	25	0
No stare	58	42	

THE NUMBER OF CONDITIONS

From our discussion of factorial designs, it is clear that there is theoretically no limit to the number of conditions that can be used in a single experiment. In principle, one could conduct a $6 \times 7 \times 8 \times 9 \times 10$ factorial design, though in fact most experiments in social psychology are far less elaborate. But what *is* a "good" number of conditions to run? We can imagine a variety of research strategies that might be used to study a phenomenon. At one extreme, experimenters might remain confined almost entirely to the simple two-condition experiment with experimental group and control group, perhaps occasionally conducting a 2×2 if they suspect that there may be an important interaction effect. The results of each experiment would serve as a stimulus to the next one, and bit by bit, over a long series of experiments, an experimenter will expect to arrive at an understanding of the phenomenon. At the other extreme, an experimenter might collapse a whole series of studies into one big experiment, with many levels of many different variables included in a grand design. By careful analyses of the data from this experiment, the experimenter might hope to arrive at the same level of understanding as the first experimenter achieved. However, such a complicated kitchen sink approach is not advised when there are no reasons to anticipate meaningful interactions between or among variables. Especially when experimenters embark on a whole new line of research, they might be "jumping the gun" in including a plethora of independent variables in their designs.

In attempting to decide what conditions are needed, two basic considerations will affect the size of the experiment. The first involves the number of *levels* of the independent variable to be used; the second, the number of independent variables to be tested.

Levels of the Independent Variable

Two levels of the independent variable are necessary to determine whether it has an effect. In the simple two-condition experiment, these levels may be zero in the control group and some other (often arbitrarily chosen) amount in the experimental group. This was the situation in the original Asch experiment, in which the control group was exposed to no group pressure, and the experimental group was exposed to a unanimous majority of six or seven, a number that Asch presumably thought would be "big enough" to make a difference if group pressure really was a relevant variable affecting judgments of fact.

If differences are observed between the two conditions of this basic design, the experimenter can conclude that the independent variable does affect the behavior under study and also can get some information about how it affects the behavior, by seeing whether the behavior is increased or decreased compared to the no-treatment control group. Often, especially in the initial stages of the exploration of a phenomenon, this is all the experimenter wants to know from the experiment. The experimenter is interested in finding out whether there is "something there" and so picks the level of the independent variable that he or she thinks is most likely to produce changes in the subjects' behavior and pits it against a total absence of the independent variable. If a relationship is found, the experimenter can then go on to more elaborate designs, using many levels of the independent variable (and perhaps additional independent variables) to find out exactly *how* the independent variable affects the behavior—for example, whether the relationship is linear, curvilinear, exponential, or whatever.

The simple two-condition experiment is thus a potentially informative starting point for research and is relatively cheap in terms of time and effort. It can be something of a gamble, however. If the experiment reveals *no* difference between the experimental group and the control group, the experimenter really does not know very much. It is possible that the independent variable would have no effect at any level, but the two-condition experiment certainly does not provide sufficient evidence to draw this conclusion. There is also the possibility that larger or smaller amounts of the independent variable might have had an effect, that the experimenter happened to hit what Benton Underwood (1957) calls a "dead spot" in choosing which value of the independent variable to use. Had a number of different levels of the independent variable been sampled, the experimenter might have discovered a relationship that would not have been apparent in a two-condition experiment.

Whether an experimenter feels that a two-condition experiment is an adequate first step in exploring a phenomenon depends to some extent on expectations about the way the independent variable will operate. Some variables, such as motivation and general level of arousal, are known to have a curvilinear relationship with certain dependent variables, such as problem solving. At very low levels of motivation or arousal, the subject may not be sufficiently involved in the task to give it full attention, and performance is correspondingly mediocre. At medium levels of motivation, the subject may do exceedingly well, reaching peak performance. At very high levels of motivation or arousal, performance is likely to deteriorate; at this level of arousal the subject can no longer approach the task systematically and therefore does less well than if motivation had been less strong. With dimensional variables such a these, when prior research or intuition suggest that different amounts of the variable will have markedly different effects, perhaps conforming to some complex function, the investigator often finds it desirable to use several levels of the independent variable, in an attempt to "catch" the point at which the effect is strongest and to get a more detailed picture of the form of the relationship than would be possible with a two-condition experiment. Even with variables that have been studied extensively, sometimes brand new phenomena can be discovered by pushing the independent variable to previously untried limits—for example, the discovery of superconductivity of materials at exceptionally low temperatures.

However, some variables may not seem like such plausible candidates for a dimensional model. For example, Jack Brehm and Ann Cole (1966) were interested in how subjects would react to a person who performed an unsolicited favor for them. The favor—buying the subject a Coke—was the independent variable; in the control group the confederate did not do anything for the subject. The experimenters were interested in the favor as an all-or-none variable: Either the confederate did or did not buy the subject a Coke. Indeed, it is difficult to conceive of "half a favor." In cases like this, in which the variable is an event that either does or does not happen, the investigator often considers two levels of the independent variable appropriate for an initial study designed to find out whether a phenomenon exists. This does not mean that the experimenter believes that there is *no* dimensionality involved: If during the course of a half-hour interaction, the subject were given *three* gratuitous Cokes, we would not expect the benefactor to be regarded in the same way as the single-favor confederate. Nor would we expect the subject's response simply to be three times as strong. For one thing, the subject would probably begin to suspect that the confederate had peculiar ulterior motives. The three-favor condition is only superficially regarded as a point on the same dimension as the one-favor condition. Psychologically, a whole new set of variables is probably involved. The subject may now perceive the confederate as a possible lunatic or lecher, a perception that has little to do with the experimenter's interest in whether a sense of obligation is a consequence of a normal, everyday favor.

What of the two-condition experiment in which the two conditions are "low" and "high" rather than "something" and "nothing"? We may have experiments with mild and severe threat, low and high eye contact, highly cohesive groups and less cohesive groups, and so on. Although we gain something by having two points along the dimension representing two different quantities of the variable, we lose the zero point, or no-treatment control group, and thus in the abstract one strategy is no better than the other. In practice, however, one type of design often fits the variable more plausibly than the other kind does. The favor study is "naturally" suited to the treatment versus no-treatment format, but an independent variable such as self-esteem is often conceived of only in terms of low versus high.

The low/high format often provides an extra advantage in the realm of experimental control; thus when designing an experiment, it is a good policy to consider whether this format is appropriate for the variable to be studied. The advantage is that it is frequently possible to make the conditions more similar to each other on irrelevant dimensions when a low/high design is used than when a present/absent design is used, and thus the causal variable can be pinpointed more accurately. For example, if self-esteem is varied by giving the subject false feedback from a personality test, subjects in both the low and high conditions can get the same instructions, take the test, and come back for a second session in which the experimenter tells them their scores. Subjects in both groups go through the same experiences, except when they receive the one crucial bit of information about their test performance. In the severity-of-initiation experiment, the women in the mild and severe initiations had many of the same experiences: They all had to undergo an initiation, they all had equal attention from the experimenter, and they all read lists of words. The difference was simply in the words included on the two lists. Although it is often *possible* to hold irrelevant experiences constant in a present/absent design, it is usually easier to do so in a low/high design.

In summary, two levels of a variable are often sufficient for an initial exploratory study, although there is some risk involved when the independent variable is a continuous variable, which may have different effects at different levels and *no* effect at some levels. The two-level experiment basically tells us that a relationship exists. Usually further studies are necessary to understand the relationship fully, and these will often involve sampling a number of different levels of the independent variable, adding control groups and even adding new independent variables. The simple two-level experiment is usually only a beginning.

The Number of Independent Variables

How many variables should one look at in a single experiment? Again, there is no simple answer. It is often desirable to manipulate more than one independent variable, because certain events emerge only in interaction with others. Moreover, we become much more certain that our results are *not* merely an artifact of a specific operational definition if we can predict and demonstrate interactions. Consider a 2×2 factorial experiment by Elliot Aronson, Ben Willerman, and Joanne Floyd (1966), in which a stimulus person was either competent or incompetent and either did or did not spill coffee on himself at the close of an audiotaped interview. These authors predicted that a blunder would enhance the attractiveness of a highly competent person, because (they reasoned) the only unattractive thing about highly competent people is that they don't seem quite human. The authors decided to have the competent person spill coffee all over himself, because they felt that such a blunder would be humanizing. As predicted, this increased his attractiveness—he was rated more attractive than when he did *not* spill coffee. But these results could simply be a function of the fact that coffee spilling is not really so much a clumsy act as it is a charming act. That is, we may like people who spill coffee because coffee spilling, in and of itself, is an endearing, attractive thing to do. But in this experiment, the authors also varied the competence of the stimulus person. In addition to a highly competent person, they exposed subjects to an incompetent person who either did or did not spill coffee. They found, as predicted, that the incompetent person was seen as *less* attractive when he spilled his coffee than when he didn't. Thus the experiment demonstrated that coffee spilling, in and of itself, is no virtue; it only enhances the attractiveness of particular kinds of people, not all people. (In terms of our discussion in Chapter 1, there was no main effect for coffee spilling.)

We can see, then, that in certain situations, investigating combinations of variables—like adding levels of the same variable—contributes essential clarity to an experimental finding. It is easy to think of yet other independent variables that we might add to the Aronson, Willerman, and Floyd situation. We might try to discover whether the subject's own level of self-esteem affects liking for the butterfingered hero (cf. Helmreich, Aronson, & LeFan, 1970); whether women coffee spillers elicit different reactions than men coffee spillers; whether it is necessary that the blunder harm no one but the blunderer; whether any kind of behavior that introduces variety in the homogeneous character of the competent person produces the effect or whether the behavior must be silly or embarrassing. We could also add new *dependent variable measures,* in case our independent variable has an effect on more than one type of behavior. For example, we might want to measure the subject's willingness to take a risk in a social situation after seeing the blunder, sense of insight or understanding of the competent person, or predictions of other behavior the competent person might engage in. Why not?

Why not, indeed? Theoretically, there is no limit to the number of factors one might vary or measures one might take. It often happens, however, that adding a new variable creates an additional experience for subjects, one that may not be well integrated with the rest of the experiment and that makes the situation more complicated and less comprehensible for them. If we decide to determine the effects of the subject's self-esteem in addition to our other variables, we may have to take an extra 10 minutes to administer the self-esteem measure, and the subject may devote some attention throughout the experiment to wondering what that test is all about. Sometimes, variables can be added without complicating the subject's experience—for example, if male experimenters are compared with female experimenters, or smiling gazers with nonsmiling gazers. Even self-esteem could be added unobtrusively if self-esteem tests had been given to all members of the subject pool as part of their introductory psychology course. But when a new variable makes the experiment more intricate and less integrated for the subject, it is a good idea to ask oneself whether the extra information that might be gained is worth it. It is essential to realize that the more tests, measures, instructions, and events one hurls at the poor subjects, the more confused, bored, irritated, or resentful they are likely to become. We cannot state specific rules for how complex an experiment should be. Our own rule of thumb is that it should be only as complex as is necessary for the important relationships to emerge in a clear manner. The "why not" approach to psychological research is frequently self-defeating. Simply because Professor Smedley happens to have a measure of sex-role orientation lying around is no justification for plugging it heedlessly into every experiment done under Smedley's supervision. Such procedures often achieve nothing but a blunting of the impact of the major variables. For some questions, sex-role orientation might be predicted to interact with other independent variables in affecting the behavior to be measured; for others, it may be irrelevant.

Typically, the reason for adding a new independent variable is that one is specifically interested in that variable in relation to another independent variable. In other words, one has a *reason* for adding the variable, a reason that is well articulated and intimately related to the purpose of the particular experiment, not simply a vague notion that variable X "might be interesting." Helmreich, Aronson, and LeFan (1970) added subjects' self-esteem as a variable to the experiment in which the competent person spills coffee, because the original explanation of the findings seemed to imply that the subjects' own self-esteem was neither particularly high nor particularly low, and the investigators suspected—and found—that the results did not hold for subjects outside this range of moderate self-esteem.

Thus one reason for adding independent variables is that we predict that they will interact with other variables in influencing the subject's behavior in the particular situation we are studying. Another major reason for adding independent variables is that we hope that they will *not* have this kind of interactive influence. The investigator wants to show that the effects are *not* due to certain features of the experiment which are theoretically uninteresting, like the particular task used or the order in which the measures are administered. He or she hopes that the effects will generalize across these relatively trivial procedural details. A full demonstration of the generality of the effect cannot, of course, be provided in a single experiment; to do so the investigator would have to construct an impossibly huge and cumbersome design, varying everything that might possibly mitigate or enhance the basic effect. But the investigator may try to figure out which of the theoretically irrelevant details might be the most plausible candidates for testing, in that they are the most likely to interact with the interesting independent variable. Once having identified a variable that seems especially likely to restrict the generality of the findings, the investigator can add it as a new independent variable.

One such variable is the person who serves as the experimenter (or the confederate, especially if the confederate delivers the treatment). In social psychological experiments in which the investigator is often studying an interpersonal behavior or evaluation, the people involved (experimenter and confederate) are frequently not the neutral deliverers-of-stimuli they are supposed to be, and their idiosyncrasies can have a strong effect on the subjects' reactions.

The investigator can deal with this problem by making "experimenter" or "confederate" an independent variable. In many social psychological experiments only one experimenter is used; thus, the variable "experimenter" is *held constant,* and, as is the case with any other variable that is held constant at a given level, we can never be sure whether the results have general applicability or whether they are limited to that particular level (in this case, to a particular experimenter or confederate). For example, if we have five experimenters, each of whom runs an equal number of subjects in every cell of a 2×2 design, and if we make the assignment of an experimenter to the subject a part of the overall randomization scheme, we end up with a $2 \times 2 \times 5$ factorial design. By systematically controlling the assignment of subjects to each experimenter—that is, by treating "experimenter" as an independent variable in the design—we can find out exactly how much of the subject's behavior on our measures is a function of the particular experimenter who happened to interact with that subject. If some experimenters induce overall higher levels of responding on the dependent-variable measure than do others, regardless of condition, this will show up as a main effect for experimenters. This is not a serious problem if the *relationships* among the experimental conditions remain the same for each experimenter. If experimenters induce different responses in different conditions, this will show up as an interaction between the experimenter variable and one or both of the other variables. This means that the effect does not generalize to all the experimenters used in the study.

If the data analysis shows that the influence of a particular experimenter is negligible compared to the effects of the treatments—that is, if the treatment differences are the same for each experimenter—we will have much greater confidence in the generality of the effect than if only a single experimenter had been used. If the "experimenter" variable does produce a significant interaction, we will know that we don't fully understand how our variables operate, and we will have an opportunity to reexamine our hypotheses and procedures and make revisions. The use of several experimenters is not easy; it complicates the analysis, involves training several people instead of one, and introduces annoying scheduling problems, to point out a few of the obstacles. But, unlike the addition of some other independent variables, it does not have the drawback of introducing a new series of procedures into the experience of the subject, since each subject sees only one experimenter. Thus the use of multiple experimenters cannot threaten the internal validity of the experiment, and it can provide important information about generality—information that is often sadly lacking in reports of social psychological experiments.

Another way of ensuring that the experimental results are not specific to one particular experimenter or confederate is to allow the "experimenter" or the "confederate" variable to vary randomly and thus to become a source of random error. Instead of using one person as the confederate for all subjects or systematically varying the confederate as an independent variable and using three or four confederates, the investigator uses a different confederate for each subject. Needless to say, this procedure greatly increases the background noise of random error, since the confederates' performance is not standardized. If the treatment variables *do* have an effect which shows up above this background noise, however, the investigator is a great deal more confident that the variables are robust and generalizable than would be the case if only a single confederate had been used.

One example of the use of this procedure is an experiment by Ellsworth and Lee Ross (1975) in which the independent variable was the amount of eye contact and the dependent variable was the intimacy of the conversation. Two same-sex subjects were scheduled for each hour. Upon arriving, the first subject was taken into a room, and the experimenter explained that the experiment was designed to study encounter-group techniques for achieving intimacy. One of these techniques was to carry on a "conversation" in which one person did all the talking for five minutes and the other person simply listened. Another technique involved the amount of time the listener spent engaging in eye contact with the talker. The first subject was told to be the listener. In one condition, she or he was told to look the other subject in the eye throughout the interaction, and in another condition to look away from the other subject. (In both conditions, the listeners were told that the eye-contact techniques they used would *enhance* intimacy.) Thus the first subject/listener served as a one-session confederate who administered the eye-contact manipulation. The second subject (the talker) was given the same instructions, *except* for information about the eye-contact variable. The two subjects then engaged in an interaction, in which the second subject talked about him- or herself and the first subject responded by looking toward or away from him or her. The conversation was scored for intimacy by an observer who did not know about the eye-contact condition. At the end of the experiment, both subjects answered questions about how intimate they felt the interaction had been.

In eye-contact experiments, the person who does the looking is in an exceptionally favorable position to bias the results, and thus single-experimenter experiments are particularly dangerous unless the looker can be kept unaware of one or more of the crucial variables. The technique of using separate confederates for each subject goes a long way toward solving this problem, since none of the confederates is aware of the hypotheses or of the other conditions in the experiment. Also, any of their personal peculiarities simply contribute to random error, instead of appearing as an artifact, as they would if only a single experimenter were used.

THE ANALYSIS OF CHANGE SCORES: PROBLEMS OF PRETESTING

Central to the hypotheses of a great many experiments in social psychology is the concept of *change*. We may predict that hearing someone remark on a subject's intelligence will change the subject's liking for that person; that receiving a mild threat against playing with a toy will change a child's evaluation of the toy; or that seeing a frightening movie about lung cancer will change a smoker's attitude toward the habit and may even change the habit itself.

Many of the variables studied in research on change are considered to be relatively enduring states. Attitudes are perhaps the most frequently studied example. We do not usually conceive of a subject as making a decision about an attitude at the very moment we ask "What do you think about capital punishment?" (although the subject may make a decision about what to *tell* us his or her attitude is). Instead, we assume the existence of an enduring attitude, and we postulate that our independent variable will shift that attitude from point X to point Y. A child in the Aronson-Carlsmith (1962) study about the forbidden toy, for example, liked the toy well enough to rank it second best at the beginning of the experiment. We assume that after the mild threat, while waiting in the room for the experimenter and playing with other toys, the child's liking for the forbidden toy dwindled, moving down the scale, so that when the experimenter returned and asked again how much the child liked the toys, he ranked the forbidden toy lower than he had before. At no time during the experiment was the child without *any* attitude toward the toy.

In such social psychological experiments, involving changes in attitudes or liking, a *pretest* seems a useful procedure. If we assume that subjects have *some* attitude toward capital punishment before they come to the experiment, a pretest of this attitude serves as a baseline against which we can assess the amount of change induced by the attitude-change treatment.

In Chapter 1 we briefly described the use of pretests of employee morale before the introduction of an intervention in a corporation. In this quasi-experiment, the pretest served two functions: (1) to assess the degree to which the experimental and control groups were similar in morale *before* the treatment was administered and (2) to assess the amount of change in morale in both groups *after* the intervention was introduced to the experimental group. In the present discussion, we deal with the use of pretests in *experimental* designs—that is, those in which subjects are assigned at random to the experimental or the control group. For purposes of simplicity, we consider only designs in which one level of an independent variable is compared with a no-treatment control group. However, the basic principles can readily be extended to designs involving more than one level or more than one independent variable.

For example, suppose that Aronson and Carlsmith did not have access to a nursery school for their study on mild and severe threats and therefore had to devise a version in which they could use college students. Under the guise of doing an attitude survey about various mass media publications, they bring each male college-age subject into a room in which five magazines are laid out on a table: *Fortune, Good Housekeeping, The National Review, The Journal of Personality and Social Psychology,* and *Dental Health.* The subjects are asked to rate how enjoyable they find each of these magazines. Then a confederate comes in and calls the experimenter out of the room to deal with some emergency. Before leaving, the experimenter explains that the subject will be asked to rate a list of other types of media, apologizes for leaving, and says, "You can read a magazine while you wait. I'd appreciate if you didn't touch the [second-ranked magazine title], though, since it's new and it doesn't belong to me." (For reasons of simplicity, we will consider only the mild-threat condition. A severe-threat condition might consist of threatening to refuse payment or credit for the experiment if the subject touches the magazine.) In the control group, the experimenter simply picks up the second-rank magazine and takes it along. If the subject has no opportunity to read it, he will not be responsible for making a decision not to read it and thus should experience no dissonance.

After half an hour the experimenter returns, confesses that he left the subject's ratings in another building, and asks the subject to rerate the five magazines before going on to the list of other media, so that the experimenter can have all of the subject's data on one sheet. The design (without the severe-threat condition) is as follows:

Group 1:   Pretest → Mild threat (dissonance) → Posttest
Group 2:   Pretest → No treatment   → Posttest

The dependent variable is the change in subjects' ratings from pretest to posttest. It is important that both the treatment group and the control group be pretested; otherwise we would have no way of knowing whether the final differences in their evaluation of the magazines were due to the mild threat or to the pretest. This design has a high degree of internal validity. Since both groups were pretested, we know, first, that differences between them are not a function of prior testing. Second, we are also reasonably sure that extraneous events which occurred between the pretest and the posttest are not responsible for the difference, since it is difficult to conceive of an extraneous event that would happen repeatedly to the subjects who had been threatened but never to those who had not been threatened. Random assignment of subjects, coupled with the practice of running subjects in individual sessions, makes this an unlikely possibility. (Note that if we had run the subjects in two large *groups*—one threatened and one not threatened—we would have opened the door to the "extraneous event" possibility, since any event that happened in only one condition would happen to *all* the subjects in that condition and thus would serve as an additional variable differentiating between experimental group and the control group.) In terms of other potential threats to internal validity (see Chapter 5) listed by Donald Campbell and Julian Stanley (1966)—

for example, differential maturation of the two groups, changes in the measuring instrument over time, statistical regression, and prior inequality of groups—this design is also a good one.

The main problem with the pretest-posttest control-group design is external validity. Note that all the subjects in this design are pretested. Thus we have no evidence that the threat would have any effect on subjects who were not pretested. We know that the observed difference between the two groups was not due solely to pretesting, since the control group got the pretest too, but we cannot be sure that the effect was due solely to the threat, either. It is possible that the two events—pretest and threat—taken together, had an effect that neither would have alone. In other words, the *interaction* between the pretest and the threat might be responsible for the subject's devaluation of the magazine. This problem is often referred to as **pretest sensitization.** In the present instance, we can imagine that the pretest inclines subjects to think about the experimenter's casual suggestion that they spend time reading the magazines and to take special note of the threat to keep their hands off one of the magazines. The threat may serve as a reminder of the subjects' initial rankings (the pretest) and may induce them to think more about how they really feel about the magazines and why the experimenter might have wanted them to refrain from reading one of them. By the time the posttest questions are asked, this *combination* of events—pretest and warning—might arouse suspicion in subjects so that they wonder whether the threat was designed to change their opinions. Even if subjects did not become suspicious, however, the contrast between their pretest evaluation and their behavior during the experiment (avoiding one of the magazines they like best) might heighten the dissonance, so that the subjects' evaluation of the magazine would decrease more than that of a comparable subject who had not been pretested.

Campbell and Stanley (1966, p. 18) offer the following example of a situation in which such an interaction might arise. Films and other propaganda designed to reduce prejudice are often tried out on test audiences before being circulated to the target populations. Often, the test audience is given a set of attitude items designed to measure prejudice before seeing the film and is then retested after seeing the film. Thus the experience of the test audience differs from that of the target population, because people in the former group are given an occasion to think about their attitudes before they see the film, whereas the target audience only sees the film. It is possible that: (1) the pretest makes people concerned about their attitudes, so the film's message has greater impact; (2) the pretest makes people defensive about their attitudes, so the film has reduced impact; (3) the pretest makes the meaning of the film more obvious to the subjects, since their attention has already been directed to the issue of prejudice; (4) the pretest followed by the film causes people to realize that they are part of an experiment designed to change their attitudes. In all these cases, as well as others one can think of, the test subjects' behavior is caused by the combination of pretest and film, and we have no way of knowing whether the film alone would have the same effects.

Research on pretest sensitization indicates that its usual effect is to reduce the power of the independent variable to create change, so that investigators may erroneously conclude that their variable has no effect. In a new situation, however, it is impossible to tell how the pretest will affect the response to the independent variable, and the generalizability of the effect to unpretested subjects is open to question.

There is an easy solution to the problem of pretest sensitization, namely, to eliminate the pretest and to carry out the following "posttest-only control-group design" (Campbell & Stanley, 1966, p. 25):

Group 1:   Mild threat (dissonance)   →   Posttest
Group 2:   No treatment   →   Posttest

If we are conducting an *experiment*—that is, if we assign the two groups to conditions at random—we can assume that they were equivalent before the experimental treatment. We do not have to measure them before the treatment to check on their equivalence, since randomization ensures that there are no factors which systematically differentiate them. No matter which magazine the subjects are told not to read—so long as it is the same magazine for all subjects—the experimenter can expect the threat to result in a devaluation of the magazine and can be quite sure that the average rating of that magazine would have been approximately the same in the two groups if a pretest has been administered. (Note that we could not have used subjects' second-ranked magazine, whatever it might have been, because we have no pretest ratings.)

But this design has its own difficulties. For some subjects, the magazine might already have been the lowest-ranked. If so, obviously the subject could not lower its rank. This would not cause systematic error, since randomization ensures that the number of subjects who dislike that magazine will be about the same in the two groups. It may, however, weaken the effect, since not all the subjects would be able to devalue the magazine. One solution to this problem would be to make the target magazine one with a strong probability of being ranked high by most of the subjects. For example, the experimenter could expose undergraduate male subjects to *Fortune, Good Housekeeping, The Journal of Personality and Social Psychology, Dental Health,* and *Playboy* and ask them not to touch the *Playboy*. In this way the experimenter can be reasonably sure that relative to the other magazines, *Playboy* has no place to go but down. This is the technique used by Freedman in his replication (1965) of the original Aronson-Carlsmith study. Instead of asking the subjects to rank-order the toys, Freedman gave them four rather junky little toys and a fantastic robot that flashed lights, made remarkable noises, and moved on the command of a remote-control button. Freedman's study, then, was a posttest-only replication of Aronson and Carlsmith's original pretest-posttest design.

The posttest-only control-group design has all the same qualities of internal validity as the pretest-posttest control group design, plus the important advantage of external validity described above. However, there are occasions when the experimenter *wants* to have pretest data, and then, of course, the posttest-only design is no help. For example, the experimenter may want to know whether the experimental treatment has different effects on people with different initial opinions. The effect of the mild threat may be strongest when the subject is forbidden access to his or her most-preferred choice, becoming less strong as the forbidden object falls lower in the subject's hierarchy of alternatives. In order to perform the internal analysis necessary to obtain information relevant to this question, the experimenter will need pretest data. Or, the experimenter may want to *know* whether an interaction between pretesting and the treatment occurs. The posttest-only design ensures that such an interaction is not responsible for the specific differences found in the experiment, but it does *not* provide any information about the possibility of such an interaction. Just as the pretest-posttest design leaves unanswered the question of how unpretested subjects would be affected, the posttest-only design leaves unanswered questions about how *pretested* subjects would be affected. For variables such as school performance, which are measured in an environment in which repeated testing is the normal state of affairs, the "natural" state of subjects may be the pretested state.

If the experimenter wants either to study the interaction between pretesting and the treatment or to be able to generalize to both pretested and unpretested populations, neither the pretest-posttest design nor the posttest-only design is sufficient. Instead, the experimenter needs a combination of these two designs, one referred to by Campbell and Stanley (1966, p. 24) as the **"Solomon four-group design"**:

Group 1:   Pretest →   Mild threat (dissonance)   →   Postest
Group 2:   Pretest →   No treatment   ↪   Posttest
Group 3:   Mild threat (dissonance)   →   Posttest
Group 4:   No treatment   →   Posttest

Posttest ratings made by subjects in group 1 reflect a combination of pretest effects, extraneous influences of the passage of time, the experimental treatment, and the interaction between pretest and treatment. Posttest ratings made by group 2 reflect pretest effects and extraneous influences, but not the treatment or its interaction. Differences between groups 1 and 2 thus must be due to the combination of the treatment and any pretest-treatment interaction that may exist. Posttest ratings made by subjects in group 3 reflect the effects of the treatment plus the influence of the passage of time. "Subtracting" groups 2 and 3 from group 1 gives us an indication of the size of the pretest-treatment interaction. Group 4 reflects only the extraneous influences of the passage of time; by subtracting group 4 and group 3, we get an assessment of the effect of the treatment alone. If groups 1 and 3 are the same and if groups 2 and 4 are the same, we can conclude that neither the pretest nor the pretest-treatment interaction affects the subjects' behavior.

The excellent, highly informative Solomon four-group design can extend our knowledge of the generality of a finding by providing more than one replication of the effect of the basic treatment. This design is more complicated and time-consuming than the posttest-only design and does not add anything to the internal validity—the basic question of whether the treatment had an effect—of that design. If the experimenter is *not* interested in generalizing to pretested subjects or in studying the possible pretest-treatment interaction, little is gained by the use of this more complicated design.

WITHIN-SUBJECTS VERSUS BETWEEN-SUBJECTS DESIGNS

One basic decision that the experimenter must make in designing an experiment is whether to use a **within-subjects design** or a **between-subjects design.** Almost all the experiments we have discussed in this book have been characterized by between-subjects designs, that is, each subject is exposed to one and only one of the experimental treatments, so that each condition of the experiment is made up of a different group of individuals. A particular subject is exposed to *either* a severe threat *or* a mild threat, *either* a negative personality evaluation *or* a positive personality evaluation, *either* a person who stares *or* a person who looks away. Therefore, the observed differences between conditions on the dependent variable also represent differences *between* (groups of) *subjects*.

In a within-subjects design, each subject is exposed to *all* experimental treatments, so that each condition of the experiment is made up of the *same* group of individuals. The Hovland and Weiss (1951) experiment on communicator credibility (see Chapter 2) is one example of a within-subjects design. Hovland and Weiss were interested in whether statements attributed to trustworthy sources produced more attitude change in subjects than did statements attributed to untrustworthy sources. The authors also wanted to find out if it made a difference whether the statement itself was positive or negative on the attitude issue. In a between-subjects design, each subject would have read one statement (for example, a positive statement by a trustworthy source), and any attitude change would be compared to that of a subject who had read a different kind of statement (for example, a positive statement by an untrustworthy source). Each subject would have contributed data to only one of the experimental conditions. In the within-subjects design used by Hovland and Weiss, however, subjects were given booklets containing statements about four different issues and attributed to four different sources. Each subject read: (1) a positive statement by a trustworthy source; (2) a positive statement by an untrustworthy source; (3) a negative statement by a trustworthy source; and (4) a negative statement by an untrustworthy source. The subjects then answered an attitude questionnaire that included questions about all four topics in their booklets. Thus each subject participated in all four experimental conditions, and—in a sense—each subject served as his own control.

By using a within-subjects design, the experimenter can eliminate the random error due to individual differences among the subjects making up the experimental groups. A particular subject who is exceedingly skeptical of any perceived influence attempt, for example, may change very little compared to a more persuasible subject. In a between-subjects design, the skeptic would get only one communication, and this subject's general unwillingness to change might lead the investigators to believe that the *communication* was less persuasive than it really was. This subject's peculiarity would not be a source of *systematic* error, because random assignment of subjects to conditions ensures that there will be an approximately equal number of small changers in every group. It would, however, contribute to random error, because there would be no way of analyzing the results so as to separate individual peculiarities from the background error. With a within-subjects design, this subject's low baseline for change would not be a source of error, because what we are interested in is the *difference* in attitude change shown from one communication to the next. Thus a subject whose attitude changes one point for an untrustworthy communicator and three points for a trustworthy communicator provides data that exactly match those of a subject whose attitude changes six points for an untrustworthy communicator and eight points for a trustworthy one. Since each subject serves in all the conditions, the analysis allows us to assess the difference between individual subjects (in this case five points) separately from the difference between the experimental treatments.

In social psychological experiments that involve high-impact manipulations, within-subjects designs are rare. This is because in such research situations there is a strong probability that participation in one condition will influence—or "contaminate"—a subject's response to the second condition. If we give subjects highly positive feedback from a personality test one day and observe their reaction, we cannot plausibly ask them back the next day and tell them that tests indicate that they are extremely neurotic. The subjects may decide that personality tests are totally unreliable and therefore not be too upset by the negative feedback, or they may suspect the motives of the experimenter and figure out that the feedback is simply a technique for assessing their reactions. Such a process is technically known as a **carryover** effect. Unless the experimenter is specifically interested in the effect of prior positive feedback on the response to subsequent negative feedback or vice versa, a within-subjects design is inappropriate whenever a carryover effect is suspected.

Within-subjects designs are often used in studies in which subjects are asked to make judgments about hypothetical events or people. Subjects generally receive a series of short descriptions or "vignettes" and are asked to evaluate them in some way. For example, subjects may read a series of episodes in which one person causes harm to another. In some cases, the harm was unforeseeable, in some cases the harm was foreseeable, and in some cases it was intentional. For each vignette, the subject rates the blameworthiness of the harmdoer (McGraw, 1987). Or the subject is given a series of vignettes about a divorce case, in which some factor—such as the age of the children—is varied, and is asked to say whether the mother or the father should receive custody. Or the subject may be given a series of problems designed to reveal judgmental biases. These designs are attractive because they make it very easy to collect a large amount of data in a very short time.

The problem of carryover effects in these paper-and-pencil studies is less salient than it is in a study in which something actually happens to the subject. Consider the case of subjects who are induced to perform a harmful act that could have been foreseen and are then asked how sorry they feel. The subjects are apt to respond quite differently compared to subjects who are *first* induced to perform an unforeseeable harmful act, followed by a second episode in which they are induced to perform the same foreseeable harmful act. If subjects are just reading about the harmful acts of other people these carryover effects are less obvious. But they still may exist. The subject who evaluates several harmdoers may judge them *in relation to each other,* so that Jenny's transgression, for example, is seen as less blameworthy because it is not so bad as George's. Subjects who do not know about George may evaluate Jenny differently. If we are interested in studying comparative judgments or context effects, a within-subjects design is perfectly appropriate. But if we are interested in how subjects respond to a given stimulus or person or event in isolation, within-subjects designs are not trustworthy, and researchers must take a number of precautions to ensure that these experiments produce valid results (see Greenwald, 1976). It is to these precautions to which we now turn.

Counterbalancing

Although a within-subjects design can eliminate subject variables as a source of error, it introduces the possibility of a dangerous artifact—the order of conditions. Suppose that in the Hovland and Weiss experiment each subject's booklet presented the communications in the exact same order: (1) positive statement, trustworthy source; (2) negative statement, trustworthy source; (3) positive statement, untrustworthy source; (4) negative statement, untrustworthy source. In this design, each condition is perfectly confounded with its *order* in the series. Thus it is possible that the untrustworthy sources would induce less attitude change *not* because they are untrustworthy but because they come last in the series. One can think of a variety of reasons for this occurrence. Perhaps by the time the subjects get to them, they have begun to find the task tiresome and are no longer reading very carefully. Or, it is possible that the sudden exposure to an untrustworthy source on trial 3, after two highly credible sources, produces a **contrast effect,** so that the subjects become even more extreme in their original attitudes. By trial 4, untrustworthy sources are no longer a surprise, and therefore the contrast effect is mitigated. Such a response on the part of the subjects, determined by the order of conditions, would be indistinguishable from a true differential effect between the persuasiveness of untrustworthy sources making positive statements and the persuasiveness of untrustworthy sources making negative statements. In this case, the attempt to rule out subject variables by using each subject in each condition is doomed, because the subject who reads the third communication is not exactly the "same" subject who read the first communication; change can occur from reading two communications by highly trustworthy sources. To return to the concept of *error*, (nonartifactual) random error generated by providing a number of different orders of the stimulus materials would be replaced by (artifactual) systematic error caused by carryover effects. And this could threaten the internal validity of the experiment.

The solution to this problem is to make sure that the subjects do not all get the same communications in the same order. One way of doing this is to **counterbalance** the treatments, so that different groups of subjects get the communications in different order—for example, as follows:

Group	First communication	Second communication	Third communication	Fourth communication
1	Positive, trustworthy	Positive, untrustworthy	Negative, trustworthy	Negative, untrustworthy
2	Positive, untrustworthy	Negative, untrustworthy	Positive, trustworthy	Negative, trustworthy
3	Negative, trustworthy	Positive, trustworthy	Negative, untrustworthy	Positive, untrustworthy
4	Negative, untrustworthy	Negative, trustworthy	Positive, untrustworthy	Positive trustworthy

In this design (a **Latin-square design**), each group receives the four communications in a different order. In addition, each treatment appears in each position, so that if there are any special effects that result from being the first (or last) communication, they will be spread evenly across all the different treatments and thus will not be confounded with any particular treatment. It is important, of course, that subjects be assigned to groups (orders) at random, in order to rule out the possibility that the apparent treatment effects are really due to complex interactions between groups and order. (This problem is too complex to analyze here; a more detailed explanation appears in Campbell & Stanley, 1966, p. 52, and Lindquist, 1953, pp. 258–264.)

Note that the counterbalanced design presented here does not include all possible orders of the communications. An alternative solution to the order problem would be to assign each subject at random to one of the 24 possible orders of the four communications. This would be equivalent to taking the systematic error introduced by order in the single-order design and changing it to random error. For an experiment like that of Hovland and Weiss, in which changing the order of conditions was simply a matter of stapling the booklets together in different ways, such a procedure would be relatively easy to follow. In other experiments it may be much more difficult, and a Latin-square design, or even a between-subject design, might be the only feasible solution.

Combination Designs

There is no rule for determining whether a between-subjects design or a within-subjects design is more desirable. Occasionally, it is possible to use both techniques in the same experiment. For example, in the forbidden-toy study, Aronson and Carlsmith (1963) had each child participate in the mild-threat and the severe-threat conditions. Half of the children received the mild threat in the first experimental session; half, the severe threat in the first experimental session. Forty-five days later, in the second session, each child received the other experimental treatment. The experimenters hoped that the 45-day interval would allow any carryover effects to dissipate. This design actually allowed the experimenters to see how realistic their hopes were, since they could compare the response to mild threat of children who received the mild threat *first* with those who received the mild threat *second*. If this comparison had revealed a carryover effect, the experimenters could still have analyzed the responses from only the first session, comparing the children who received the mild threat with the children who received the severe threat in a between-subjects design. Fortunately, there were no carryover effects, and the data could therefore be analyzed by the more powerful technique of a within-subjects design, comparing each child's response to the mild threat and to the severe threat.

Another example, of combining a between-subjects design and a within-subjects design in the same experiment is a study by Ellsworth and Carlsmith (1973). They were interested in whether a person expresses more aggression against a victim who maintains eye contact or against one who looks away. As a between-subjects design, this required having some subject-aggressors faced with victims who invariably looked at them, and having other subjects faced with victims who invariably looked away. Such consistent behavior may lead subjects to interpret the looking as a personality trait of the victim; the subjects' behavior in this situation might be determined by a decision that the victim was a challenging person or a submissive person. This design would provide evidence about the kinds of inferences subjects make on the basis of people's habitual modes of eye contact. It does not, however, answer the question of whether each specific instance of eye contact or gaze aversion has an enhancing or inhibitory effect on the amount of aggression expressed at that moment, since each instance of eye contact would be seen as confirming an overall impression. In order to assess these effects of eye contact, a within-subjects design is necessary in which the victim sometimes meets the aggressor's gaze and sometimes looks away.

Ellsworth and Carlsmith recognized that the between-subjects design and the within-subjects design address slightly different questions, but they felt that both questions were interesting and that both shed light on different aspects of the overall problem of the effects of the victim's visual behavior on the amount of aggression expressed. Therefore, they incorporated both a within-subjects design and a between-subjects design into one experiment, assigning subjects at random to the "victim always looks," "victim never looks," and "victim sometimes looks" (within-subjects design) conditions. The investigators could have run two experiments, one with a between-subjects design and one with a within-subjects design, but by incorporating them into one design they ensured that no changes in the subject population or other temporally related changes that might occur between the two experiments could distort the results. Although this combination design is not quite orthodox, it was appropriate to the authors' interests. We might note parenthetically that researchers will often need to combine and modify the standard designs discussed here to suit the unique requirements of a particular question.

Matching

Although random assignment of subjects makes it highly unlikely that there will be any systematic differences between subjects in the experimental and control groups, it lacks the sensitivity, or precision, of a within-subjects design. As we have noted, the within-subjects design allows us to study the effects of our treatments, unclouded by differences among subjects. When each subject receives treatment, we can look at treatment differences "within subjects." When an experimenter expects the independent variable to have an influence that is small (although perhaps important) compared to the differences that naturally occur among subjects, a within-subjects design is very tempting. However, as we have pointed out, many social psychological experiments do not easily fit into a within-subjects format, because we do not expect the subjects to "recover" from the first treatment in such a way that they will be able to experience the second as a totally new stimulus situation. The technique of **matching** provides some of the advantages of each design. It is a between-subjects design in that different subjects are used in experimental and control conditions, but it is like a within-subjects design in that special steps are taken to make the subjects in the two groups more similar, thereby reducing variability due to individual differences.

In a matched-subject design, the experimenter finds pairs of subjects who are "matched"—that is, very similar to each other—and then places one of the subjects in the experimental group and the other in the control group. Such matching will be most useful when the dimensions on which the subjects are similar are closely related to the dependent variable. IQ is an example of a variable on which subjects are often matched, as it has a strong effect on behavior in a wide variety of situations. Suppose, for example, that in an experiment on communicator credibility and attitude change, the ten people in the experimenter's seminar were to be used as subjects, with five subjects in each group. Suppose also that the experimenter had good reason to believe that people with very high IQs would be only minimally affected by the persuasive communication. If there are two people in the seminar with IQs over 150, there is a chance that both will be in the same group. If they are in the high-credibility group, their failure to change their attitudes will lower the group average substantially, so that the experimental results might not show any effect for communicator credibility. However, if both geniuses end up in the control group, the effect of credibility would be falsely exaggerated. Either way, the results of the experiment will be misleading. The experimenter would like to make sure that one high-IQ student gets assigned to the experimental group and the other to the control group. In order to achieve this end, the experimenter might first rank-order all the students in the seminar according to IQ and then take the top two students (the two with IQs over 150) and *randomly* assign one of them to the experimental group and one to the control group. The experimenter then considers the students ranked 3 and 4 and randomly assigns one of *that pair* to the experimental and one to the control group, and so on until the members of all five *matched pairs* have been randomly assigned to groups. This is a simple form of matching, and it ensures that there will be no major chance differences between the two groups on the variable the experimenter is interested in controlling.

IQ is only one example of a variable the social psychologist might want to control by matching. Indeed, it is possible to match subjects on more than one characteristic, so that for each subject in the experimental group with an IQ of 125 and self-esteem score of 3, there would be a control subject with an IQ of 125 and self-esteem score of 3. Matching on several different characteristics becomes difficult, however, since with the addition of more and more characteristics, it becomes harder and harder to find two subjects who are exactly the same on all the relevant measures.

A very common example of matching on a large number of variables is the use of identical twins. Since identical twins share a common genetic heritage, they are very similar on a large number of dimensions. A famous example of the advantages to be gained by matching comes from the Lanarkshire milk trials (described by McNemar, 1962). In this experiment, 5000 children were given pasteurized milk for four months. Another 5000 children were given raw milk. Each child's height and weight were measured at the beginning and end of the experiment. The experiment suffered from a variety of difficulties, but the interesting point for us is the claim by "Student" (1931) that 50 pairs of identical twins would have yielded the same amount of information for 2 percent of the cost of the original experiment. Here, we see a good example of a situation in which differences between subjects (weight gain in four months) are large compared to the effect of our independent variable. Matching allows us to see treatment differences which are very small, since the weight gains of our matched pairs would be very similar in the absence of any experimental treatments.

Finally, it should be stressed that after matching, the subject *must* be assigned to the two (or more) conditions at random. Matching is not a substitute for random assignment but rather an additional procedure that can increase the sensitivity of our measurements. Occasionally, experimenters have assumed that they could take two naturally occurring groups, construct two new groups by matching individuals from the two original groups, and call the derived subset of one naturally occurring group the "experimental" group and the subset of the other group the "control" group. The matching in this case is not a substitute for randomization. The groups still differ on an unknown number of variables besides the one in which the experimenter may be interested. If the group originally differed on the variable for which subjects were selected and matched, extremely serious problems involving regression artifacts can arise. These are discussed more fully by Campbell and Stanley (1966). Both Underwood (1957, pp. 98–99) and Campbell and Stanley (1966, pp. 70–71) find that matching without randomization is an unacceptable procedure, even for quasi-experimental designs.

Subject Loss

A serious potential source of error in between-subjects designs (including matched-subjects designs) is differential loss of subjects from the various conditions of the experiment. It often happens in social psychological research that not all the subjects make it though all stages of an experiment. In experiments using a design with a delayed posttest, for example, some of the subjects who were present for the pretest and the treatment may fail to return for the posttest. In experiments in which subjects are asked to support a position they don't believe in, or to administer electric shocks to another person, or to perform some other behavior which they consider arduous or immoral, subjects may withdraw from the experiment before it is over. Indeed, the experimenter has an obligation to make clear to subjects that they are free to do so. In experiments involving deception, subjects may guess the true purpose of the experiment, and if that happens their data must be discarded from the analysis.

In an experiment with a within-subjects design, loss of subjects can jeopardize external validity, since the loss of many subjects may suggest that the results hold for only a certain type of person: the type of person who makes it through the whole experiment. Since each subject lost is lost from *all* conditions, however, subject "mortality" in a within-subjects design does not affect internal validity. In a between-subjects design the problem is more serious. If more subjects are lost from one condition than from another, systematic bias is introduced into the design. Any differences in the behavior of subjects in the two (or more) conditions of the experiment *could* now be due to differences in the kinds of subjects who make up the groups. If some subjects in the treatment group become suspicious and have to be dropped from the experiment and replaced by new subjects, while all the original subjects assigned to the control group are run without any problems, we may legitimately ask whether differences between the two groups are due to the treatment or to the fact that the final group of subjects run in the experimental group—those who experienced the treatment without suspicion—were inherently different from the control subjects (for example, less intelligent or more trusting).

Whenever subjects are dropped from an experiment, the experimenter should consider whether subject variables potentially associated with the loss seem to provide a "plausible rival hypothesis" (Webb, Campbell, Schwartz, & Sechrest, 1966) for the results. A good example of subject loss which could affect the outcome of an experiment is provided by Charles Kiesler, Barry Collins, and Norman Miller (1969, pp. 60–61) in discussing forced-compliance research. When subjects are asked to do or say something that supports a position antithetical to their own beliefs, they occasionally refuse. In experiments in which some subjects are offered large payments for performing the counterattitudinal behavior and other subjects are offered small payments for performing the same behavior, it can happen that more subjects in the low-incentive condition refuse to perform the behavior than do so in the high-incentive condition. Now the basic prediction in these studies is that subjects in the low-incentive condition will change their attitudes farther in the direction of the formerly antithetical position than will subjects in the high-incentive condition. In order to see how differential subject loss provides a plausible rival hypothesis predicting this same pattern of results, we must consider the characteristics of the subjects who refuse to argue this position. It is quite possible that they are the subjects who most disagree with this position to begin with. We assume that due to random assignment, the general distribution of attitudes is the same in the two groups at the beginning of the experiment, but once all the people with the attitudes most strongly against the position to be advocated have dropped out of the low-incentive group, the two groups are no longer equal in terms of their predicted positions on the dependent-variable measure. We might well expect the remaining low-incentive subjects to be more positive toward the counterattitudinal position before they even undergo the treatment, since all the really negative people in that group have dropped out. The resulting difference in attitudes between the two groups would thus be due to the differential rate of subject loss, not to the experimental treatment. Several investigators have suggested that the people who drop out of the low-incentive condition are in fact the people with the most negative attitudes to begin with (Kelman, 1953; Kiesler, Collins, & Miller, 1969).

The best method for dealing with this problem is to design the procedure so that no subjects will be lost. In Chapter 7 we will discuss the value of pilot testing as one procedure that can be used to reduce subject attrition by ensuring that the mild threat, or the severe initiation, or the low incentive is just sufficient to keep all subjects in the experiment behaving as the experimenter asks them to but still set at a level easily distinguished from the severe threat, the mild initiation, or the high incentive. One important function of pilot testing is to ensure that the procedure will not lead to subject loss. Subject loss is a problem that should be faced at the beginning of the research, before any actual subjects are run, rather than at the data-analysis stage.

Even with the best of precautions, a few subjects are likely to be lost. In such a case, the experimenter examines the pattern of subject loss to see if the failures to complete the experiment are equally distributed across conditions. If they are, the experimenter becomes more confident that the data have not been biased by subject loss. The experimenter may also want to study the individual subjects who dropped out, especially if there is a preponderance in one condition, in order to find out whether they all had similar reasons for leaving and whether their reasons suggest a plausible alternative explanation for the results. If, for example, the experiment is measuring persistence of attitude change over a fairly long period, it may be that the subjects who fail to complete the experiment do so because they (or their families) have moved away from the area. It is unlikely that the decision to move was influenced by the treatment, and so we gain confidence that the internal validity of the study was probably not endangered. Even here, however, there may be some concern about external validity. Our treatment differences may be valid only for people who show a more stable residence pattern. It is important, then, to gather as much information as possible about the reasons for subject loss. Even though the experimenter may be in no mood to have a personal chat with the subject who is jeopardizing the validity of the findings by refusing to continue, there are good reasons for doing so. The information gained can provide important data about the plausibility of alternative explanations. Before running any subjects, the experimenter might sit down, think of the ways in which differential subject loss might bias the results, and draw up a set of questions relevant to these hypotheses. Then when a subject does drop out, the experimenter will know what to ask and can salvage important information from an otherwise unfortunate situation. (This type of discussion is also important for the subject's sake, since refusing to continue an experiment can be a difficult and embarrassing thing to do, and the subject may need reassurance that it was all right.)

Likewise, an experimenter who decides to drop a subject on account of suspicion should find out when the subject became suspicious and how this suspicion affected his or her behavior. If two or three suspicious subjects are found, and if they agree on the causes and effects of their suspicion, it is a good idea to examine the data of the experiment, asking whether the pattern of results could be caused by suspicious subjects who were not discovered or by a preponderance of trusting subjects in one group.

Occasionally, an experimenter will report that subjects were lost because they failed to understand the instructions or did not answer all the questions on the dependent-variable questionnaire. As appealing as the control ensured by written or tape-recorded instructions and stimulus materials is, there is no substitute for the presence of a living, breathing experimenter. The experimenter has the ability to make sure that no subjects are lost for this sort of trivial reason. To make sure that the subjects understand the instructions, the live experimenter can ask if they have any questions and check to make sure that they understand. Likewise, when picking up the subjects' questionnaires at the end of the experiment, the experimenter can look them over and, if questions have not been answered, can hand them back to the subjects and ask them to fill in the missing items.

Kiesler, Collins, and Miller (1969, p. 61) also point out that subject loss can produce bias only if subjects are lost after they have been randomly assigned to conditions. Subjects who fail to show up, who become suspicious of the cover story before they have been assigned to treatment conditions, who refuse to fill out the pretest questionnaire, or who leave the experiment for any other reason before they are randomly assigned to conditions may constitute a threat to external validity, but they do not introduce systematic bias into the experiment (i.e., they are not a threat to internal validity). This is one additional reason for keeping experimenters blind to the subject's condition until just before the treatment is introduced and for making the random assignment as late as possible in the experiment (see Chapter 9).

A FEW WORDS ABOUT DATA ANALYSIS

Statistical analysis of data is not a method for making the results of an experiment interpretable. Rather, the interpretability of results is a function of the design of the experiment: The better the design, the more unequivocally the experimenter will be able to evaluate the effects of the variables. Although statistics can sometimes salvage useful data from an experiment that has gone awry, they cannot unconfound variables, reduce random error, or add conditions necessary for an understanding of the results. The basic purpose of statistical tests is to assess whether differences in the behavior of subjects in the various conditions of the experiment are greater than differences that might result from chance had the independent variables exerted no effect.

The best time to begin thinking about data analysis is *before* conducting the experiment. The perpetual plaint of statisticians whose aid is sought by psychologists and other social scientists is that they are not consulted until after the experiment has been completed, until *after* it is too late to make sure that the appropriate data will be collected. Thus it is a good idea to sit down before the experiment and to think about the kinds of numbers that will be available after the subjects have been run. What will be done with these numbers? What can they show? Are there other data which can be collected which could aid in understanding the phenomenon? If the experimenter is unsure about the possibilities of data analysis at this point, now is the time to consult a statistician, not after the damage has been done.

Running Subjects in Groups

When the experimental instructions are easily administered and the treatment does not involve personal interaction with the individual subjects, the experimenter may be tempted to save time by running the subjects in groups. But in these situations, the subjects' responses are not independent. Any peculiar events that happen during a particular session happen to several subjects, not just one, and thus become potential variables affecting the behavior of that subset of subjects. This is most dangerous when a whole group is in a single condition—for example, when they all see an antiprejudice movie or hear a speaker trying to change their attitudes. Since all the extraneous error-producing factors happen to all subjects in this group, they cannot be considered independent observations; instead, the whole group should be treated as *one subject* for purposes of data analysis.

If, however, each group consists of an equal number of subjects in every experimental condition (for example, if the independent variable is delivered by printed instructions, so that no one knows the other treatments exist), the solution is somewhat different. "Groups" now becomes a factor in the design, and its effects are analyzed like those of any other factor. Suppose that an attitude-change experiment had a 2×2 design with high-versus-low credibility of source and rational-versus-emotional communication. Now, if ten groups of eight people each were run, two people in each condition in each group, the experimenter would analyze the data as a $2 \times 2 \times 10$ factorial design, so as to be able to assess the influence of membership in a certain group independently of the influence of other variables. This is essentially the same procedure that is used when several different experimenters are used in one experiment.

Getting a Feel for the Data

Finally, getting the most out of data analysis, and thus getting the most out of an experiment, involves "getting a feel" for the data. Many people find it useful, before beginning the actual analysis, to spend some time looking at the data in order to get some idea of the possible relationships that might occur. Tables of means, indications of consistency or inconsistency (within-condition variances), and graphs can provide information and hunches and new hypotheses that do not show up in a simple significance level. Data analysis is not simply a means of hypothesis testing; it can also be a means of generating new hypotheses. After performing the main tests relevant to the hypothesis, it is often useful to "play with the data" by dividing them up in different ways and performing a variety of internal analyses. Although it is, of course, impossible to infer cause-and-effect relationships between variables that were not manipulated, there is often a wealth of material that can suggest other possible relationships and provide detailed hypotheses about the exact meaning and applicability of the major findings.

IF AT FIRST YOU DON'T SUCCEED

What does the experimenter do when the experiment does not work? Is the necessary conclusion that the hypothesis was incorrect? Is it not that simple. As implied throughout this book, there are literally dozens of reasons for the failure of a given experiment to support a hypothesis, only one of which is that the hypothesis is wrong. In an area such as social psychology, with few standardized procedures for manipulating the independent variable, where ethics and good taste confine us to weak empirical operations, where our measuring instruments are rather insensitive, and where the phenomena under study are frequently delicate and transient, it seems almost miraculous that any "true" hypotheses are supported experimentally. Consequently, it would be somewhat arrogant of the experimenter to conclude, after one failure, that the hypothesis was incorrect: arrogant because this conclusion implies that the experimental operations were perfect. No experimental design, successful or unsuccessful, is complete in itself. In Chapter 2 we stressed the value of a *se-*

ries of experiments, some of which may be successful and some unsuccessful, as a method for fully understanding a phenomenon. Each experiment suggests new questions that lead to the next.

Moreover, the running of an experiment—even a successful one—is almost always methodologically instructive. An experimenter can usually see weaknesses in the experiment; a few changes can frequently strengthen the design or procedure and increase the probability of meaningful results. Consequently, following an unsuccessful experiment, the experimenter can pick up the pieces, return to the drawing board, and attempt to improve the design or procedure.

But how many times should this be done? It should be clear that by testing the same hypothesis on several occasions, the experimenter begins capitalizing on chance factors. We would not have much confidence in a finding (significant at the .05 level) if we know that the experimenter had failed on 19 previous occasions to verify the same hypothesis. Clearly, 19 failures are unnecessary to make us question the real (as opposed to the statistical) significance of a given positive finding; any number will do (McNemar, 1962).

An experimenter can decrease the probability of failure by pretesting each aspect of the experimental procedure, strengthening the independent variable, refining the dependent variable, setting the stage in a more interesting and impactful manner, adding conditions to rule out artifacts, and so on. For example, one might run the experiment only up to the point at which the independent variable had been introduced, terminate the procedure, and attempt to determine how successful that induction had been—not by observing effects on the dependent variable, but by direct checks on the manipulation. Thus, when running the final experiment, the experimenter is fairly well convinced that the procedures are as good as they can be. This renders failure more meaningful and, hence, more conclusive. This is not to say that one should never rework an unsuccessful experiment. But pilot testing can trim this to a minimum. (Of course, pilot testing the whole experiment until it works raises the same statistical problems as unsuccessful first attempts. Whether complete run-throughs of the experiment are called "pilot tests," "pretests," or "experiments" is immaterial.)

We cannot overemphasize the importance of pilot testing and of thinking carefully about the experiment in advance so as to anticipate and eliminate potential weaknesses and sources of error. A great deal of time and effort can ultimately be saved if the experimenter carefully hones the manipulations and measures before beginning the experiment proper. In subsequent chapters, we will discuss some concrete strategies for doing just that.

As a careful reading of this book should indicate, experimentation in social psychology presents a multitude of formidable problems. However, we must hasten to add that it is the challenge presented by these problems that makes this area so exciting. Throughout this book readers are provided with descriptions of the myriad difficulties encountered in doing good experimental work in social psychology. But we will have failed miserably if we do not also manage to convey the excitement inherent in overcoming these difficulties. The *hard* parts are the *interesting* parts. As a form for asking a question of nature, the experiment is characterized by important advantages, as well as by some disadvantages. Unthinking application of a ready-made design to one's question, like pulling a computer program off the shelf, may accentuate the disadvantages while diminishing the advantages. But using an experimental design creatively, modifying it to enhance its virtues and minimize its flaws, is an absorbing and exhilarating experience, beneficial to the field and personally rewarding to the experimenter.

ALTERNATIVES TO THE CONTROLLED EXPERIMENT

The focus of the preceding four chapters—indeed, of the majority of this text—is on the controlled experiment. Throughout, we do not hesitate to state our conviction that the experiment is the single best method for explicating cause-effect relationships. Because the experiment is the only method that allows us to make valid and unequivocal causal assumptions—if it's done right—it is the standard against which the value of other methods is assessed. Indeed, the closer any method comes to approximating an experiment, the more confidence we have in causal inferences based on its results.

Having said all of that, we hasten to add that proficiency in the use of hammers does not make every object a nail. As valuable as experiments are, some situations preclude their use on ethical or practical grounds. It would be immoral to use random assignment to place one community in a tornado condition and another in a control condition to study the effects of a disaster, even if we could. The effects of some variables—natural disasters, parenting practices, divorce, mental illness—are so powerful that it is unconscionable to test them using experiments. And sometimes, even with relatively innocuous (or even beneficial) treatments, random assignment is impossible for practical reasons. Further, not all interesting questions are *causal* questions. Some simply involve describing regularities in human behavior. Do people overestimate the proportion of other people who share their beliefs? Does the same facial expression signal anger in different cultures? Do children progress through predictable stages of cognitive development? Some questions involve subject variables such as social class, race, gender, or personality variables for which it is impossible to create meaningful experimental analogs in the laboratory or the field. In all those situations, it is necessary to find an alternative to the controlled experiment.

For demonstrating cause-effect relationships, the controlled experiment possesses certain advantages unequaled by other research methods, but no one method is best in an absolute sense. One's choice of method should be dictated by both the nature of the research question and the phenomenon under investigation. Moreover, to the extent that results obtained using numerous and varied methods—experimental, quasi-experimental, correlational—all converge, our faith in the validity of our inferences about social behavior is enhanced.

WHEN NONEXPERIMENTAL METHODS ARE DESIRABLE

Despite the advantages of experiments in enabling researchers to make unequivocal causal inferences, other considerations sometimes dictate forgoing the controlled experiment in favor of alternatives. First, as we mentioned above, some variables cannot be experimentally varied. Even though they are not amenable to experimental investigation, these variables may be profoundly important in helping us to predict and understand human behavior and might interact with other variables in which the researcher is interested. For example, in a recent review of research, Alice Eagly and Valerie Steffen (1986) found evidence for a small but consistent relationship between gender and aggression—overall, men tend to be slightly more aggressive than women. However, the influence of gender depends on the context within which aggression occurs. To cite but one example, although men are somewhat more aggressive than women in general, the difference is more pronounced in the case of physical aggression than verbal aggression. Of course, because subject gender cannot be manipulated in the laboratory, one cannot justifiably say that gender *per se* causes some people to behave more aggressively than others. Nonetheless, social psychologists who have questions about variables that predict aggression or other social phenomena need not—and should not—abandon research because some of those variables cannot be experimentally manipulated. Instead, for *some* questions, these researchers must use alternatives to the controlled experiment.

Other variables are out of bounds to social psychological researchers for ethical reasons. An experimenter cannot ethically manipulate love or hate, alcoholism, psychosis, or any of a large number of other things that are believed to be extremely important in motivating human social behavior. However, the researcher may believe that some of these variables are related to problems so pressing that they require immediate attention and that it is important to gather relevant information, even though it will not be possible to use experimental techniques that permit causal inferences.

Some processes operate over a longer time than is typically available to a laboratory researcher. Examples are the process of psychotherapy, the development of language in children, and the dynamics of a group that has predicted the end of the world a year from today. Researchers may be interested in these natural processes for their own sake or as instances of the operation of theoretically interesting variables. In either case, they would be unlikely to have much confidence in the results of an experimental analog that lasted only an hour or two.

Sometimes social psychologists adopt alternatives in studies conducted in the real world to reduce the chances that their subjects will feel like "guinea pigs" and therefore behave differently than they would in their normal interactions. In laboratory studies, it is often possible to disguise the true purpose of the experiment from the subjects, but they almost always know that they are in an experiment. Some kinds of behavior—particularly unflattering behavior—though common enough in other situations, may be very hard to elicit in the laboratory. Subjects are motivated not to show signs of stupidity, pettiness, recalcitrance, or aggression when they know that the experimenter is observing them. In a natural setting, subjects may be quite unaware that they are being studied at all, and so it is possible to rule out the hypothesis that a certain behavior is laboratory-specific. Of course, these natural settings do not always allow the researcher to conduct a true experiment.

Finally, many researchers use alternative methods as a means of suggesting, clarifying, refining, or extending experimental research findings. Often a broad correlational study will suggest hypotheses that can be tested and variables that later can be manipulated experimentally. Thus, *before* an experiment is run, correlational research can generate many ideas that can be further explored in more controlled conditions. *After* an experiment has been run, the researcher may want to return to the field to test out some implication of the findings in a natural setting. At this stage, a carefully conducted study may indicate other variables that mitigate the effects of variables isolated in the lab and thereby provide some information—often of a cautionary nature—about the generality of the results of the experiment.

An excellent example of the alternation between lab and field as a fruitful research technique is provided by a series of classic studies of group cohesiveness conducted by Leon Festinger and his colleagues at M.I.T. In the laboratory, cohesiveness was varied by appropriate descriptions of the experimental groups as highly attractive (Back, 1951) or highly cohesive (Schachter, 1951). Outside the laboratory, the researchers studied an M.I.T. housing project (Festinger, Schachter, & Back, 1950). One part of the project, called Westgate, had existed for some time, and within each court there was a great deal of communication among members and an overall liking for the group as a whole; the researchers defined these courts as cohesive units. The other part of the project—Westgate West—was newer, and the members seemed to act more as individuals than as group members; thus, the Westgate West living units were defined as low in cohesiveness. The research group asked the same kinds of questions in both the laboratory and the housing project and developed their theories on the basis of both types of research. In both situations the cohesive groups imposed greater pressure toward uniformity and tended to shun members who failed to go along with the group norms.

Sometimes, nonexperimental information is collected *during* an experiment. Even in the laboratory, the richness and complexity of the events that take place in social interaction are often so great that many potentially important variables cannot be controlled. But if they are identified and measured, their relationships with the main variables of interest can be studied, and these relationships may suggest new possibilities for further experimentation. If the experimental prediction is not confirmed, the nonexperimental data may help the investigator to figure out whether the independent variables were misinterpreted or weak, the measure was inadequate, some extraneous variable interfered, or the original conceptualization failed to take into consideration some important aspect of the phenomenon. Such an analysis, called an **internal analysis**, cannot prove a causal relationship—it is still a correlational analysis, even if it takes place in the context of an experiment—but it can be extremely useful as a source of information for guiding future experimentation.

Even when an experimental prediction is confirmed, an internal analysis can provide useful information. For example, it may increase the experimenter's confidence that the independent variable resembles its real-world counterpart. In an experiment designed to find out whether people with low self-esteem or high self-esteem were more likely to cheat, Elliot Aronson and David Mettee (1968) not only *manipulated* self-esteem, assigning subjects to high, medium, or low self-esteem conditions at random, but also gave subjects a test that *measured* their preexisting, or "real," levels of self-esteem. The test was administered before the subjects were given the false personality-test information that constituted the experimental manipulation of self-esteem, so that their test scores could not be affected by anything the experimenter told them. The correlation between the real self-esteem scores and the amount of cheating tended to support the authors' results obtained on the basis of the experimental manipulation of self-esteem; either way, the people with low self-esteem cheated more that the self-confident subjects did. The highest percentage of cheaters was found in the group of subjects who were given negative personality feedback (manipulated self-esteem) *and* who had unfavorable self-concepts to begin with (measured self-esteem). The lowest percentage was found in the opposite group: the subjects who were given positive personality feedback and who had favorable self-concepts to begin with. The finding that low baseline levels of self-esteem tended to influence subjects in the same direction as the negative personality feedback they were given—in both cases, the subjects were more likely to cheat—strengthened the experimenters' confidence that giving subjects unfavorable feedback from personality tests was in fact affecting their level of self-esteem.

A corollary function of an internal analysis performed within the context of a successful experiment is to provide data that may have a bearing on the plausibility of an alternative explanation for the main results. For example, one alternative explanation of the results in the Aronson and Mettee experiment was that receiving a low score on the personality test made the subjects angry and that they cheated on the test or order to get revenge, perhaps intending to invalidate the results of the experiment. According to this explanation, the increased level of cheating was due not to low self-esteem but to anger. The data from the measurement of chronic self-esteem levels do not support this alternative explanation, however; the fact that subjects with "chronic" low self-esteem behaved in the same way as subjects whose self-esteem had been lowered by unfavorable personality test feedback suggests that self-esteem was in fact the important factor differentiating cheaters from noncheaters.

So far in our discussion of alternative methods, we have discussed them in general terms—as if they are all pretty much alike. In one sense, they *are* similar: Unlike the controlled experiment, none of them can provide unequivocal answers to questions about causal relationships, because only in an experiment can we control and systematically vary the independent variable and assign subjects at random. However, as we noted in Chapter 1, alternative methods vary tremendously in terms of how closely they approximate a true experiment. Some correlational studies tell us *nothing* about causal relationships between variables. But there are some quasi-experimental designs that afford researchers considerable control over experimental conditions and differ from experiments only in that individual subjects are not assigned to experimental or control conditions in a truly random fashion. Thoughtful and thorough statistical analyses of data generated in these quasi-experiments can allow researchers to make *tentative* statements about cause and effect.

CORRELATIONAL STUDIES

In Chapter 1 we discussed a number of research methods—experiments, quasi-experiments, correlational studies—that might have been used to discover whether people who undergo a severe initiation to join a group will be more attracted to the group than people who undergo a mild initiation or no initiation at all. And we noted a fundamental limitation of a correlational study: the inadequacy of such an approach in establishing a causal connection between severity of initiation and liking for the group. That is, Aronson and Mills (1959) might have chosen to study existing fraternities, and rated initiations for severity. Later, they might have returned to interview new members of the different fraternities and had the members rate how attractive they found their respective fraternities. Such an approach would have yielded an index (a correlation coefficient) of the strength of the relationship between the two variables but would have failed miserably in determining the exact nature of that relationship. For example, severe initiations might cause new members to rate their fraternities as more attractive. However, fraternities that are highly attractive to begin with might have to resort to severe initiations to limit membership to only the most desirable of pledges; that is, the fraternities' attractiveness might cause severe initiations. This is an example of the direction of causality problem inherent in many kinds of correlational research. No less problematic is the possibility that some third variable—such as pledges' initial motivation to join *any* fraternity as opposed to *a certain* fraternity—might be responsible for the observed relationship between severity of initiation and liking for the group. Thus, the major disadvantage of the correlational study described above is that it does not allow researchers to make definitive statements about just what causes what.

This does not mean that all correlational studies are useless in enabling researchers to make tentative causal inferences. Indeed, some correlational designs offer a *partial* solution to the directionality problem we described above. One such design, labeled by Donald Campbell and Julian Stanley (1966) the **cross-lagged panel technique**, provides just such a partial solution. Predicated on the notion that "causes" precede "effects," the cross-lagged panel design involves collecting correlational data on at least two separate occasions. That is, two variables assumed to be related are observed at time 1 and again at time 2.

For example, Monroe Lefkowitz and his colleagues (Lefkowitz, Eron, Walder, & Huesmann, 1972) were interested in the relationship between the amount of violence children watch on television and their tendency to behave aggressively. Rather than conduct a laboratory experiment, they chose to study behaviors in the real world using a correlational investigation. Initially, these researchers measured the relationship between the violence contained in third-grade children's favorite television shows and their aggressiveness in the classroom. And they *did* find a relationship between expert ratings of violence in the children's preferred television shows and peer ratings of classroom aggression. Had Lefkowitz and his colleagues terminated their research at this point, it would not have been informative with regard to the *causal* relationship between watching television violence and behaving aggressively. As we noted in Chapter 1, it is possible that children who are aggressive to begin with are more likely than other children to prefer violent television programs; that is, initially high levels of aggression might cause children to prefer violent TV fare. Alternatively, a steady diet of TV violence might cause children to behave aggressively. Therein lies at least one source of ambiguity in a simple one-shot correlational study.

Aware of that problem, Lefkowitz and his colleagues did not stop there. Ten years later, they were able to contact about half of their initial subjects—quite a feat, given the passage of a decade. Once again, the researchers obtained ratings of the violence content of subjects' preferred television shows and peer ratings of their aggressiveness, and they were able to calculate the strength of the relationship between those two variables. Armed with data from two sets of observations separated by a 10-year lag, the researchers could calculate additional correlation coefficients: (1) between TV violence ratings at time 1 and time 2; (2) between aggression ratings at time 1 and time 2; (3) between TV violence ratings at time 1 and aggression ratings at time 2; and (4) between aggression ratings at time 1 and TV violence ratings at time 2. Figure 5-1 provides a summary of those correlations for male subjects.

The correlation coefficients of interest are those on the diagonals: (1) the correlation between TV violence ratings at time 1 and aggression ratings at time 2, and (2) the correlation between aggression ratings at time 1 and TV violence ratings at time 2. The usefulness of these two correlation coefficients is based on the assumption that what comes sooner *might* cause what comes later, but that the reverse is impossible: What comes later cannot possibly cause what came before it. Thus, if TV violence in third-graders is cor-

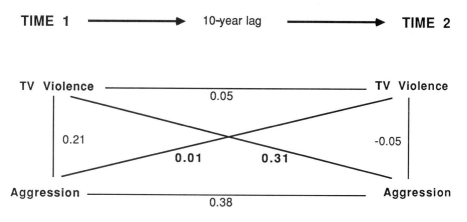

FIGURE 5-1
Correlations between television violence and aggressive behavior in boys. [From J. M. Neale and R. M. Liebert (1986). *Science and behavior: An introduction to methods of research* (3rd ed.), Englewood Cliffs, NJ: Prentice-Hall. (*Used by permission.*)]

related with aggression 10 years later, one might assume a causal relationship between those two variables. Similarly, if aggression in third grade is correlated with TV violence preferences 10 years later, one might assume a causal relationship between *those* two variables. To determine which of the two assumptions is accurate (watching violent TV in third grade leads to aggression 10 years later, or being aggressive in third grade leads to watching violent TV programs 10 years later), the researchers pit these two correlations against one another. Lefkowitz and his colleagues found that the correlation between TV violence ratings at time 1 and aggression ratings 10 years later ($r = .31$) was significantly higher than the correlation between aggression ratings at time 1 and TV violence ratings 10 years later ($r = .01$). Thus, they felt fairly safe in assuming that watching television violence causes aggression rather than the other way around.[1]

---

[1] As we've noted, the cross-lagged panel design is only a *partial* solution for problems inherent in making causal inferences based on correlational data. First, it does not rule out the possibility that some third variable is responsible for an observed correlation. Second, before they can make even tentative assumptions about which of two correlated variables causes the other, researchers must be confident that they have obtained reliable measures, and that they have chosen an appropriate time interval between observations. Finally, a number of researchers have questioned the use of correlation coefficients as appropriate indices of association and have recommended more sophisticated statistical techniques (for example, see Neale & Liebert, 1986; Rogosa, 1980). Nonetheless, most researchers are in agreement about the validity of the underlying logic: Indices of association can be used to make tentative assumptions about causal links when the relationship between two variables is measured at more than one point in time. Furthermore, laboratory and field experiments, and subsequent correlational studies employing more sophisticated statistical techniques (e.g., Eron & Huesmann, 1980; Eron & Huesmann, 1986; Huesmann et al., 1984) have supported the initial conclusion of Lefkowitz and his colleagues.

Sometimes researchers are interested in being able to make at least tentative causal inferences based on correlational data. When that's the case, the cross-lagged panel technique is preferred over correlational studies in which observations are made at only one point in time. But not *all* research is aimed at establishing a causal relationship between two variables, and even the "simplest" of correlational studies can be valuable in formulating and evaluating theory. Theories specify certain relationships between phenomena. *One* way to evaluate the adequacy of a theory is to observe whether predicted relationships between these phenomena do indeed exist, by carefully examining variables of interest and determining if they are associated in ways predicted by the theory. Especially in the early stages of theory development and refinement, it is the task of researchers to discover whether there is a relationship between variable X and variable Y, period. Is there a relationship between birth order and achievement motivation? Is there a relationship between self-esteem and liking for others? Is there a relationship between frustration and aggression? Correlational studies are well suited to answering these kinds of questions. Once it has been established that theoretical predictions about the relationships between variables are accurate, other methods—such as the controlled experiment—can be used to test more specific causal assumptions. In essence, correlational studies are good first, but tentative, steps in evaluating theory.

Finally, there is one important thing correlational data can tell us about causality, and that is that *no* simple causal relationship exists. Although correlational data cannot prove causality, they can disprove it. If none of their correlations between television violence and aggression had differed significantly from zero, Lefkowitz and his colleagues would have had good reason to doubt that violent television has much of an effect on aggression. Sometimes complex combinations of other variables can mask a real correlation between the two the investigator cares about—perhaps even masking a true causal relationship—but even in these cases, the experimenter has to recognize that any causal relationship is more complicated than expected.

PSEUDOEXPERIMENTAL (PREEXPERIMENTAL) DESIGNS

As we have noted, nonexperimental designs vary in terms of how closely they approximate a controlled experiment.[2] Purely correlational studies, whether based on one observation or a series of observations, differ from experiments in a number of ways. One important way is that researchers who conduct correlational studies do not administer a treatment. Whatever the assumed "independent variable" (e.g., the amount of violence children watch on televi-

---

[2] The following discussion of various types of pseudoexperimental design is based on Donald Campbell and Julian Stanley's (1966) monograph, *Experimental and Quasi-Experimental Designs for Research*, Chicago: Rand-McNally.

sion), it is beyond their control. The researchers do not create the variables of interest but rather find a setting in which they occur naturally.

In this section, we will discuss a number of designs that are closer approximations of the controlled experiment. These methods *do* involve an independent variable administered by the researcher. After subjects are exposed to this variable, its effects are assessed by measuring some dependent variable. However, these designs differ from experiments in that they do not contain appropriate standards of comparison (control groups or control observations) against which to measure the effects of the independent variable. Because of the lack of control inherent in these designs, numerous variables—in addition to the independent variable—might have produced an observed effect. Therefore, like correlational designs, these pseudoexperimental designs do not permit completely valid causal inferences about the effect of the independent variable on the dependent variable.

The One-Shot Case Study (Posttest-Only Design)

Suppose that you are interested in the effects of alcohol. Probably the simplest thing to do would be to invite a group of people in, give them all the dry white wine they wanted, and observe their actions. You might write down that they seemed very relaxed and contented, that they touched one another a great deal, and that they said they were feeling more relaxed and less inhibited than usual. What would you learn from your study? Much less than you might think.

We present this kind of study—in which one group is observed during or after an event that interests the researchers—merely as a point of departure. The most fundamental weakness of such a study is that it provides no basis for comparison, and comparison is essential to science. Without a basis for comparison, we have no information about similarities and differences. For example, suppose that a man goes from the city to visit his friend in the country and that while he is out walking, he sees an owl. He has seen pictures of owls before, but he has never seen a live one. When he gets back to the house, he tells his friend, who asks, "Was it a big one?" This question is unanswerable. Since the man has seen only one owl, he has no idea what's big for an owl; that is, he has no basis for comparison. He might say, "It was bigger than a pigeon," and this might enable the friend—who knows the size range of owls in the vicinity—to decide whether it was a "big" one. Similarly, if the friend from the country were to visit the city, she would be unable to say whether the subway made good time on her first ride.

One might object that this is a far-fetched example, since in the alcohol study the researcher was measuring how happy people were, how much they touched one another, and so on. It is not as though this were the researcher's first experience with happiness, or physical contact, or inhibitions; he or she has a sort of feeling for how groups of people usually behave when they come over—a whole storehouse of thoughts, sensations, and memories about past parties. But a "sort of feeling" is really a very vague and nebulous basis for comparison, subject to all kinds of distortion from forgetfulness, personal bias, expectations about the results of the experiment, and so forth. A researcher who wants to compare two sets of measurements should make both sets of observations in the same way, with the same care. Even the most thoughtful conjecture about what the data would look like without the independent variable is no substitute for a standard of comparison.

The alcohol example is an obvious one, so transparently inadequate that you may well be grumbling that there is no point in wasting so much exposition on a design so stupid that nobody would ever think of using it to conduct research. Campbell and Stanley (1966, p. 6) call this type of design—in which a single group is observed on a single occasion—a **one-shot case study**, and surprisingly enough, it is not uncommon. One-shot case studies are not always easy to detect, because they are sometimes used when a vast amount of complex information about some person or group is collected and tabulated and analyzed and compiled into a presentation so erudite and detailed that the reader may lose sight of the fact that no other person or group was studied. An entire team of researchers, interested in how parental divorce affects child development, might study a sample of 500 or even 5000 children whose parents were divorced, measuring school performance, general psychological adjustment, number of friends, incidence of delinquent acts, bed-wetting, and a hundred other variables, and interviewing each child and each parent in depth. The task of collecting, tabulating, and organizing the data is immense, and the reader of the resulting 600-page book may find it difficult to remember that all this care and precision is misplaced because no comparison has been made. Conducting such a study is analogous to building a castle on quicksand. It is impossible to tell whether the children are different from the average for their social group on any of the variables. It is impossible to tell where they stood on all the measures before the divorce; maybe nothing has changed.

Is there ever any point to using this technique? Certainly, if nothing else is possible. Occasionally, one may happen on a once-in-a-lifetime situation, such as the Chernobyl disaster or the loss of the space shuttle *Challenger*, when there is no choice but to study it then and there as it occurs or to let it slip away into oblivion. When the choice is between letting an interesting phenomenon go by and studying it, even though the study may be an isolated analysis, it would be foolish to pass up the opportunity because no better methods are available. Our criticisms of various designs are meant not to discourage research but to *improve* it. In the hypothetical study of the effects of divorce, there was no apparent reason that the study could not have used a sample of 250 or 2500 children of divorced parents and an equal sample of children whose parents were not divorced, and this would have been a far better study. Sometimes, however, one is exposed to a special case: a patient with a well-differentiated case of multiple personality, a group of people who firmly believe that the world will end on a particular date in the near future, a cultural group (such as the kibbutz) that has drastically curtailed the role of the nuclear family. Anthropology is based on the in-depth study of individual cultures. A special case that does not conform to common behavior patterns in our society can provide valuable information about the range of human behavior.

Given the constraints of a one-shot case study, there are more or less adequate ways of carrying it out. If one is interviewing a person or a group of people after a disaster, one can ask them about their behavior in other situations; although this is not a good basis for comparison, it is better than nothing. In addition, if the researcher has a choice between situations that offer differing amounts of control over the variable whose effects are being studied, the researcher should generally choose the situation that can be more closely controlled. Thus, in the alcohol study, the fact that you, the investigator, handed out the wine makes this study somewhat superior to a correlational study in which you simply observed people who were already drinking when you walked in, since you had *some* control over the occurrence of the treatment. But if you have this much control, you can usually conduct an even better study.

One-Group Pretest-Posttest Design

To return to the alcohol study, suppose that you invited the group over at 8 P.M. and simply observed them from 8 until 10 (the *pretest* observations), handed round glasses of wine, waited an hour to be sure it had begun to take effect, and then conducted a second set of observations from 11 P.M. until 1 A.M. (the *posttest*). Now you have something to compare: the pre–10 P.M. observations with the post–11 P.M. observations. If you find that people are happier, more relaxed, and so on after drinking the wine, you know one thing that you couldn't know in the first study: It wasn't just that those people were in that state all along, even when they first walked in the door.

But this technique still leaves a good deal to be desired. First, you can't say that the increase in happiness and relaxation would not have occurred anyway, even if you hadn't served drinks. There are other things that could have caused the increase. Any number of things might have caused your subjects to change their behaviors between 10 P.M. and 1 A.M., and these other possibilities threaten your ability to make a valid causal inference about the effects of alcohol consumption on social behavior. Campbell and Stanley (1966) refer to these variables that are beyond the control of the researcher as **threats to internal validity**. They prevent the researcher from concluding that the independent variable was the sole cause of the outcome. Although this **one-group pretest-posttest design** (Campbell & Stanley, 1966, p. 7) is an improvement over the one-shot case study, a number of these threats to internal validity still exist:

1 Perhaps something else happened between the pretest and the posttest that caused changes in behavior. Perhaps just sitting around and talking with the group for a while would have resulted in greater relaxation and a lowering of inhibitions; conversation can most certainly loosen people up. Or perhaps someone told a joke, and the whole group cheered up and relaxed. These uncontrolled events that occur between the pretest and posttest might well be the cause of a change in behavior revealed in the posttest. These threats to a valid causal inference are called **history** effects and are a source of rival explanations for the apparent effects of the independent variable.

2 Or perhaps the guests acted relaxed because it was late and they were getting tired. **Maturation** refers to changes that unfold within subjects as a function of the passage of time between the pretest and the posttest, independent of any external events. Maturation can refer to any number of internal biological or psychological processes—growing older, growing tired, growing bored, growing hungry, or whatever—that provide a rival explanation for the effects of the treatment.

3 Perhaps your subjects saw you writing things down and didn't want to look uptight; or perhaps they guessed that you wanted to see if they acted inebriated after drinking the wine. When people are the objects of investigation, the very fact of being observed—and not the treatment—can be the cause of a change in their behavior between the pretest and the posttest. This threat to internal validity is called **testing**.

4 You observed and recorded people's behaviors over the course of a five-hour period. Perhaps you yourself were tired and relaxed from 11 P.M. to 1 A.M., knowing that the study would soon be over, and you wrote down your observations more casually or failed to notice small indications of tension in the room. Perhaps you'd indulged in a little of the independent variable yourself. Measuring instruments themselves—hardware or human observers—can change between pretest and posttest. Mechanical measuring instruments can malfunction or deteriorate. Human observers can become more experienced or more fatigued between the pretest and the posttest; their observations may become more accurate and reliable or more haphazard with the passage of time. Thus, differences between subjects' pretest scores and posttest scores might be due to changes in the **instrumentation** itself rather than the effects of the treatment.

5 Perhaps after drinking the alcohol, a number of subjects left the room unnoticed before you began your observations at 11 P.M. Of course, the subjects who left the room may not have differed from those who remained, but you can't be sure. Perhaps unlike those whom you observed growing more relaxed and convivial from 11 P.M. until 1 A.M., these subjects grew anxious or depressed after consuming alcohol and left to go recover; or perhaps the alcohol had no effect on them at all and they left because your party bored them. If the subjects who left the party differ systematically from those who remain, you can't be sure if differences between pretest and posttest scores are due to effects of treatment, or due to the fact that subjects who remain in the study are somehow different from the initial sample. This threat to internal validity is rather gruesomely known as **mortality**, because some subjects fall by the wayside.

All the above extraneous variables—specific interfering events, the passage of time, the presence of the tester, changes in the tester over time, or subject attrition—are confounded with the treatment and give us reservations about a too-confident belief in the effects of alcohol. It impossible to disentangle the effects of alcohol from the effects of anything else that might have changed between the first and second sets of measurements.

Again, it should be pointed out that this kind of design is not uncommon and that complicated and extensive observations often mask the simplicity and inadequacy of the basic design. The case study of a patient undergoing therapy is typically an example of this type of design. A schizophrenic's pretreatment behavior may be outlined in detail, with long historical accounts of the patient's childhood and of the parents' personalities. Then, the schizophrenic may be examined for years, during the course of a novel and complex therapeutic method (the treatment); the final write-up may contain fascinating interview transcripts, careful charts of day-to-day variations in a large number of the patient's behaviors, dramatic accounts of how the patient appeared to be sliding back into the abyss, and finally the excruciating step-by-step improvement that eventually culminated in the patient's triumphant release from the hospital. But all we know is that the patient got better. We don't know *why*; maybe the therapy had something to do with it, maybe not.

Once again, we should emphasize that when no more sophisticated design is feasible, it is often better to conduct research according to this simple one-group pretest-posttest design than to neglect an opportunity to collect interesting information. Leon Festinger, Harry Riecken, and Stanley Schachter (1956) used a design of this sort to study a group whose members had predicted the end of the world, and the general theory the researchers used to interpret their findings was subsequently supported by an extensive program of laboratory research. Taken in conjunction with the experimental studies, the study of the doomsday group provided important evidence of the applicability of the findings to real-life situations, as well as a great deal of suggestive data on the detailed dynamics of the process of dealing with an event that disconfirms one's most important expectation.

The Static-Group Comparison Design

In the first pseudoexperimental design, the one-shot case study, we pointed out that the only kind of comparison that the researcher could make was between the treatment group and remembered impressions of other groups or assumptions of what the group under study might have been like without the treatment. In the second design, the one-group pretest-posttest design, a comparison was afforded by measuring the same group before and after they had drunk alcohol. But this comparison was confounded with many changes that could have occurred as the night wore on: in the subjects (maturation), in the experimenter (instrumentation), and in the environment (history, testing, and mortality).

There is a second alternative in the choice of a standard of comparison: **a static-group comparison design.** Suppose that on the night you ran the original one-shot case study of the effects of alcohol, someone else in your building was having a party at which no alcohol was served. Knowing that your original study suffered from the lack of a comparison group, you might decide to run down the hall and make a few observations at the other party, where no one was drinking wine. The trouble with this plan is that you have no way of knowing that the alcohol had anything to do with differences you might find between your party and the other person's. Maybe your friends were livelier to begin with. That is, perhaps differences in the behavior of people at the two parties were not because alcohol was consumed at one party and not at the other, but because people at each of the two parties were different from one another at the outset. Campbell and Stanley (1966, p. 5) refer to this threat to internal validity as **selection**. Any time two or more comparison groups are used, and subjects are not assigned to those groups at random, selection poses a threat to valid causal inference.

Different kinds of guests might have attended the two different parties. Furthermore, the parties might have differed on other dimensions: Maybe the other person's furniture was less comfortable than yours, maybe the other person has a stomach ache and is sorry that people are coming over that night. There are many factors besides the alcohol that could create differences between the other person's party and yours. And selection may have *interacted* with these other factors to produce differences that would be erroneously attributed to the alcohol treatment. For example, maybe guests at your party react differently to being observed than guests at the other party because you're their friend, and they don't expect it of you (selection × testing interaction); maybe guests at your party got up later than guests at the other party, and don't tire as easily during the course of the evening (selection × maturation interaction); maybe people at your party are less likely than guests at the other party to leave before you make your observations (selection × mortality interaction). Because you can't know whether the guests at the two parties would have behaved identically if you hadn't distributed alcohol, you can't conclude that the differences you observe have anything to do with drinking. Thus, such a comparison group is not very useful, as it doesn't really "control" for very much.

Still, the fact that this is not the best type of control group should not prevent you from going down the hall and making observations at the other party. If it is the best control group you can find, it is better than nothing and should be used.

QUASI-EXPERIMENTAL DESIGNS

Some nonexperimental designs provide the researcher with more control than is afforded by the pseudoexperimental designs discussed above.[3] In these

---

[3] Once again, we have relied heavily on the excellent discussion provided by Campbell and Stanley (1966). Space limitations preclude a detailed discussion of *all* of the quasi-experimental designs discussed in their monograph. Interested readers are encouraged to consult their classic for further information.

quasi-experimental designs (Campbell & Stanley, 1966, p. 34), the researcher is able to control the administration of a treatment—for example, when it is administered, and to whom—and the collection of dependent variable data. The major difference between quasi-experiments and true experiments is that in the former, subjects are not assigned at random to experimental groups. As a result, quasi-experiments have one advantage over controlled experiments: They are more feasible research techniques when researchers move beyond the laboratory to applied or field settings in which random assignment of individuals to conditions is impossible. However, there is a trade-off, for the lack of random assignment robs the quasi-experimental researcher of the power to make unequivocal statements about cause and effect—statements that *can* be made when a true experiment is used. Even so, quasi-experiments are valuable research tools, for depending on the patterns of results obtained in these kinds of studies, researchers are able to make *relatively straightforward* causal interpretations.

There are two general kinds of quasi-experiments: In **interrupted time series designs**, the effect of the independent variable is assessed by comparing multiple observations of the same group of individuals, either before and after administration of one level of the treatment, or after the administration of different levels of a treatment. In essence, these quasi-experiments make use of a *within-subjects* design (see Chapter 4). In **nonequivalent control group designs**, the effect of the independent variable is assessed by comparing two or more groups of subjects—subjects who are not assigned at random to their respective groups. These quasi-experiments make use of a *between-subjects* design (see Chapter 4).

Time-Series Experiment (Simple Time Series Design)

Remember our one-group pretest-posttest design. In that pseudoexperiment, the experimenter would have preferred to make the observations from 8 to 10 P M., then go back in time to 8 P.M., erasing everyone's memory of the intervening events, and start over. This, of course, is impossible, but a slight improvement in this direction can be made if the experimenter can observe the same group of people regularly—every day or once a week—at 8 P.M. No longer does the investigator have to conduct the pretest, introduce the treatment, and conduct the posttest all on the same night. Whenever the group comes over, the experimenter can observe people's behavior. After several nights of this, the experimenter will give the group alcohol and continue with the observations. The next few times they come, the researcher will continue to observe the group's behavior, again without handing out alcohol. The experimenter now has what Campbell and Stanley (1966, p. 37) call a **time-series experiment**.

Why not just invite the group twice, once giving them alcohol and once not? This procedure would eliminate such factors as the group members' fatigue over the course of the evening, but most of the problems of the pretest-

TABLE 5-1

Alcohol served	Day	Number of touches
No	Monday	4
No	Tuesday	3
No	Wednesday	5
Yes	Thursday	15
No	Friday	7
No	Saturday	4
No	Sunday	5

posttest design would still remain. For example, the group members might be more relaxed the second evening, because the situation is more familiar to them. We are more confident about drawing conclusions from a time-series study, because this type of study allows us to see how distinctive the alcohol night is, compared to a number of similar occasions without the alcohol.

A specific example will allow us to explain this advantage more clearly. Suppose that one of the measures is the number of times people touch one another. Table 5-1 shows what the data might look like. We now know that something distinctive happened on Thursday night and that on all the other nights there was roughly the same amount of touching. Would we know this if we had observed the group just on Wednesday and Thursday? No.

Suppose that the familiarity hypothesis were correct; the data might then look like those shown in Table 5-2. Since we have a whole series of observations, we are not likely to make the mistake of attributing the Wednesday-Thursday difference to the effects of alcohol.

Or suppose that the range of variability in touching is greater than we would have imagined and that the data looked like those shown in Table 5-3. In this case we would have to conclude that the amount of touching was controlled by extraneous variables. In all three sets of data, people touched one another 5 times on Wednesday and 15 times on Thursday; if we had measured only on Wednesday and Thursday, we would have no clue as to the role of alcohol in this change. By examining these data samples, however, it is evident that only

TABLE 5-2

Alcohol served	Day	Number of touches
No	Monday	0
No	Tuesday	1
No	Wednesday	5
Yes	Thursday	15
No	Friday	25
No	Saturday	40
No	Sunday	60

TABLE 5-3

Alcohol served	Day	Number of touches
No	Monday	8
No	Tuesday	21
No	Wednesday	5
Yes	Thursday	15
No	Friday	9
No	Saturday	2
No	Sunday	13

in the first case does our hypothesis about the effects of alcohol receive any support; thus, the advantages of the time-series design over the one-group pretest-posttest are apparent. Of course, we hasten to add that the time-series design does not automatically eliminate all the threats to internal validity inherent in the latter design. *History* is still a major threat to internal validity. That is, anything else that happened Thursday, before or during the group meeting, might have been responsible for the increase in touching. There might have been an article in the newspaper that day on the importance of expressing positive feelings; or Thursday might have been the only sunny day of the week. This problem, the investigator's inability to control adventitious events, is the primary disadvantage of this design. However, depending on patterns revealed in the data, multiple observations before and after the treatment enable researchers to use logic to rule out many of the other threats to internal validity.

Equivalent Time-Samples Design

Above we noted that history was the most serious threat to the internal validity of the time-series design when a single administration of a treatment is imbedded within a series of observations. We noted that it was possible that an event unrelated to the treatment could conceivably occur, resulting in an erroneous causal inference about the impact of the treatment. There is a partial solution to this problem. If the independent variable being studied is assumed not to have permanent effects on the behavior being observed, a slight modification of the previous design can add a large measure of control over undesirable influences from outside events. Instead of presenting the treatment once during the series of observations, we present it several times. Such a design—called an **equivalent time-samples design** (Campbell & Stanley, 1966, p. 43)—involves careful observations during a period in which the treatment is absent (a baseline or control period), followed by observations during a period in which the treatment is present (an experimental period), followed by another control period, another experimental period, and so on.

This modification is applicable to the alcohol study, since we expect the incidence of touching to return to a normal, baseline level after the influence of the wine has worn off. Applying this modification to the alcohol study, we would assign the treatment (alcohol) to days of the week, at random if possible. Thus, we might end up with the schedule shown in Table 5-4. If the hypothesis is confirmed, the data may look something like Table 5-5.

If the experiment is continued over a few weeks and treatments can be assigned to days at random, we can conclude that extraneous events are not causing the increase in touching. Even if we cannot assign treatments at random, we still have a great deal more confidence in the effect than we did when the treatment was administered only once. Any extraneous events that increased touching would have had to "just happen" to occur on the same days that we gave the group alcohol; therefore, the more days on which we conduct

TABLE 5-4

Day	Alcohol served
Monday	No
Tuesday	No
Wednesday	Yes
Thursday	No
Friday	Yes
Saturday	No
Sunday	Yes

TABLE 5-5

Day	Alcohol served	Number of touches
Monday	No	3
Tuesday	No	4
Wednesday	Yes	16
Thursday	No	3
Friday	Yes	12
Saturday	No	6
Sunday	Yes	15

the study, the less likely this alternative hypothesis (history effects) becomes. It should be noted that this design is not feasible if the effects of the independent variable are not temporary. Moreover, even when treatment effects are not permanent, care should be exercised in choosing the interval between observations; enough time must elapse to enable subjects to return to their pretreatment states before control observations are made. On the whole, however—provided that proper precautions are taken to control potential sources of systematic error, such as the effects of testing, experimenter bias, and so on (see Chapters 8 and 9)—this is not a bad design, even though it lacks a separate control group.

Nonequivalent Control-Group Design

In previous sections we discussed two basic methodological attempts to gain a measure of control in a nonexperimental situation. The first method involves measuring the same group before and after the experimental treatment. This technique was the basic source of control in the one-group pretest-posttest design and in the two time-series designs. One of the major difficulties with this technique is that it fails to control for extraneous events; other incidents or changes between the pretest and the posttest may have affected the posttest observations. Of course, the equivalent time-samples design makes these other interpretations less plausible, but it can be used only with treatments that will "wear off" between sessions. The second type of control, used in the static-group comparison design, involves giving the treatment to one group and measuring two groups: the one that received the treatment and another group. The main problem with this design is that there is no way of telling whether the two groups were the same at the outset.

By combining these two types of design, we can create a study that substantially reduces both of these sources of error. Campbell and Stanley (1966, p. 47) call the combination design a **nonequivalent control-group design**. From the pretest-posttest design, we take the control provided by pretesting; from the static-group comparison design, we take the control provided by using two groups. Both groups are pretested, one group is given the treatment, and then both groups are posttested. We choose groups that are as similar as possible and try to make our pretreatment measures simultaneous.

If you were to use this combination design in the alcohol study, you might arrange in advance for a friend to have a party on the same night as yours, to play the same sort of music, to invite the guests to come at the same time, to engage in approximately the same sort of activities, and so on. On the night of the party, you would conduct your observations (at both parties) as usual from 8 to 10 P.M.. Then, you would serve the wine to the guests at your own party only. From 11 P.M. to 1 A.M. you would continue your observations, again alternating between the two parties. Suppose the data on the number of touches at two different parties at two different times were as in Table 5-6.

This pattern of results tells us a good deal. First, since it is apparent that the groups were the same before you handed out the alcohol at your party, you have obtained the evidence of the baseline similarity that you wanted. Second, it tells us that the people at your party touched one another more after you handed out the alcohol: more than they had before, and more than the people at the other party did during the same period.

Many of the problems of the pseudoexperimental one-group pretest-posttest design (see pages 167–168) are now brought under control; if fatigue, familiarity with the group, or other temporal factors are causing changes in the guests' behavior, you will expect these effects to show up at both parties, and your data will be able to show this difference (see Table 5-7).

In the one-group pretest-posttest design you would have had only the data from the ''your party'' column and might have mistakenly attributed the effect to the alcohol. With the data on both parties before you, you would not be likely to make this error, since you can see that the same increase in touching occurred even without the alcohol. Likewise, though you cannot control the equivalence of the two groups before the introduction of the alcohol, you at least have the data from your pretest observations to help you decide whether it is reasonable to assume equivalence. If the groups are behaving differently between 8 P.M. and 10 P.M., your data will also show this difference (see Table 5-8).

In the static-group comparison design, your only data would be the post–11 P.M. observations, and you might decide that alcohol was making a difference. With the pretest and posttest data from both parties before you, you will not draw the false conclusion that the alcohol created the differences between the

TABLE 5-6		
Observation times	Your party	Other party
8 P.M. to 10 P.M.	5 (alcohol)	5
11 P.M. to 1 A.M.	15	5

TABLE 5-7		
Observation times	Your party	Other party
8 P.M. to 10 P.M.	5 (alcohol)	5
11 P.M. to 1 A.M.	15	15

TABLE 5-8

Observation times	Your party	Other party
8 P.M. to 10 P.M.	5 (alcohol)	0
11 P.M. to 1 A.M.	15	10

groups; you can see that the size of the differences (five touches per time period) was the same both before and after the alcohol.

The remaining serious source of error is the problem of other specific events that occurred at one party but not at the other. Any such event might be responsible for the posttest differences between the groups, and the investigator using this design must be continually alert to such alternative explanations.

Multiple-Group Time-Series Designs

By extension, it is readily apparent that increased control may be achieved by adding a second (or third) group to the time-series designs discussed above, especially to the time-series experiment (simple time-series design). Thus, if two groups met every day for a week, but only one group received alcohol on any given night, even the "special events" interpretation mentioned above would become less plausible, because it would be unlikely for some extraneous event to occur only on nights when one group was administered alcohol, and always to that particular group. You also gain a great deal of confidence in the results when you are able to give alcohol to one group on some nights and to the *other* group on other nights, because you can show that the results are not specific to your friends. If you can make the assignment of treatment random, you are within an ace of having an experimental study; the only thing that stands in your way is the random assignment of individuals to one or another group. Of course, in this example, the idea of getting the same group of people to come to seven parties at the same place in the same week may seem a little implausible; but there are many natural settings, such as classrooms and workplaces, in which regular group meetings are standard operating procedure. These kinds of situations are tailor-made for quasi-experiments such as **multiple-group time-series designs**. Not only does the researcher sacrifice relatively little of the control extant in a true experiment, but the question of generalizability of results to a real-world setting is moot.

GENERAL TECHNIQUES FOR IMPROVING NONEXPERIMENTAL DESIGNS

In following the alcohol study through its various developments, we have seen that the adequacy of the comparison group is one of the major design features that determines our confidence in the results of a nonexperimental study. The other most important defense against error and uninterpretable results is the investigator's ability to introduce the treatment. For the sake of simplicity, we did not raise this as a central issue in the alcohol series; in all cases, we assumed that the experimenter was free to decide when and if to serve drinks to the group. The pitfall for an investigator who cannot control the occurrence of the treatment is readily apparent. The researcher does not know what causes a particular group to be exposed to the treatment (in this case, to drink alcohol); a group that is naturally exposed to a treatment may differ in a variety of treatment-related ways from one not exposed to the treatment. Any of the environmental or personality variables that result in a group's imbibing alcohol may also cause it to behave differently from a group that does not drink; any of these potential "third variables" can cause differences in our observations.

Each of the nonexperimental designs we presented can be conceptualized as having a relatively strong form and a relatively weak from, depending on whether the experimenter can *control the occurrence* of the variable under study. If this is not possible, the study is purely correlational. If it is possible, the researcher's study falls somewhere in between a correlational study and an experimental study. And, of course, if the investigator can assign the treatment to individual subjects at random, the study is an experiment.

To sum up, in designing a nonexperimental study, the investigator should concentrate first on trying to devise a situation in which the variables under study can be manipulated. In some cases this will be patently impossible; for example, social class, age, sex, IQ, and a large number of other variables cannot be manipulated. Other variables—such as teaching methods, working conditions, or advertising campaigns—can be manipulated, but cannot always be assigned to subjects at random. The second step is to determine, if possible, who will get the treatment, when it will be introduced, and what other group(s) will be observed. In all nonexperimental studies, even when variables cannot be manipulated, the investigator may improve the study by carefully considering whose behavior will be measured and when. Our confidence in the possibility of causation in the relationship grows in direct proportion to these improvements in the design.

The Importance of Reliable and Valid Measurement

Once the design has been chosen, a number of techniques can be employed during the actual running of the study to add to the experimenter's confidence that the relationship observed is a true one; most of these techniques involve procedures for making the observations themselves. Even a straight correlational study can be greatly improved—in terms of its ability to suggest specific hypotheses and variables worth following up—by careful attention to measurement.

Since correlational designs usually consist of nothing more than two sets of observations (measurements), the more specific and controlled the observations are, the clearer the results will be. In formulating a research question or hypothesis, it is always a good idea for the researcher to think ahead to antic-ipate the possibilities for error. The investigator can control some of these by choosing one of the more "advanced" nonexperimental designs, by carefully selecting appropriate control groups, by finding a concrete, easily measurable behavior to represent a global conceptual variable, and by introducing other specific techniques to increase measurement standardization and decrease bias (see Chapters 8 and 9). Even if some types of error—such as possible third-variable correlations—cannot be controlled, the "informed" researcher is still in a much better position than the one who is ignorant of such potentially dis-ruptive factors. Of course, it is best to have control of as many aspects of the situation as possible, but when this is impossible, awareness of exactly *which* aspects are uncontrolled is extremely important. The researcher can use this knowledge in a variety of valuable ways. First, awareness of other variables that may affect the behavior under observation may allow the researcher to measure these variables and analyze the data to determine whether any of them were confounded with the primary variable of interest.

For example, a researcher may hypothesize that people who talk a great deal are more likely to be perceived as leaders than are quiet people, but may also realize that many other variables—such as IQ, past leadership experience, and social class—can affect whether a person is perceived as a leader. There-fore, in addition to asking subjects to rate how good a leader a given person is and measuring the amount of time that person spends talking, the researcher may also give the "leader" an IQ test, ask the person (and others) about his or her leadership experience, and determine that person's social class. If people who are perceived as leaders talk more but are no different from nonleaders on the dimensions of IQ, experience, and class, the researcher has more confi-dence in the hypothesis; a certain amount of "control" has been achieved by *measurement* of possible third variables.

Anticipation of such third variables can also guide the investigator to the choice of a subject sample in which the effects of an extraneous variable are relatively improbable. For example, it has often been hypothesized that boys whose fathers were away from home during the child's first few years of life will turn out to be less "masculine" than boys whose fathers were present all along. However, since father absence is much more common in the lower classes than in the middle classes, the results of most studies are indissolubly confounded with the effects of social class. Aware of this problem, Kuckenberg (1963) tested the hypothesis in a sample of doctors' sons. Thus, the multitudinous extraneous variables associated with social class and occu-pation were ruled out as alternative interpretations of the results.

Many of the specific techniques discussed in the rest of this book as im-provements for experimental studies can also be applied to nonexperimental studies. The fact that a situation does not allow an experimental study does not mean that rigorous methods should be abandoned. Techniques for eliminating bias, measuring the dependent variables, and avoiding problems common to social psychology experiments can all be exercised outside the laboratory. In many ways, a nonexperimental study demands greater creativity, since the obstacles to the achievement of meaningful results often increase as the researcher relinquishes control, but this should certainly not discourage the researcher from venturing outside the lab.

From the Field to the Laboratory to the Field (and Back)

In pointing out the need for creativity, we raise the possibility of going beyond existing techniques. The list of nonexperimental designs presented in this chapter is certainly not exhaustive; the designs are simply examples, and you may be able to think of better ones. Social psychology has been dominated by laboratory experiments for some 30 years, and there is a great need for innovative and informative nonexperimental research. Any given problem can be investigated in a variety of ways: as a laboratory experiment, as a field experiment, or as a nonexperimental study in either the lab or the field. By choosing any technique, the researcher invariably sacrifices the ability to collect clear data on some aspect of the problem, often because such a sacrifice is necessary to collect data on some *other* aspect. To choose a situation that best fits the problem, the investigator must decide what exactly is to be studied and what can be sacrificed for the sake of this information.

To cover a problem thoroughly, the investigator may decide on a series of different kinds of studies, so that the strengths of one sort of study compensate for the weaknesses of others, and vice versa. For example, early nonexperimental studies conducted in the field can provide ideas, hypotheses, and suggestions that might never occur to the experimenter sitting in an office and meditating over the question. These ideas and hypotheses can be refined, modified, and improved by careful follow-up studies (experimental and/or nonexperimental), and the effects of the basic variables suggested can be subjected to the rigorous test afforded by the experimental method.

On the basis of laboratory experimentation, cause-and-effect relationships can be sorted out. Some variables may be discarded as irrelevant; some may appear to be more powerful than they had previously. Various smaller aspects of the larger, real-world problems can be tested and confirmed or disconfirmed. New variables and hypotheses that seem more basic than the old ones may be discovered and tested. At this point, armed with these new refined hypotheses, the experimenter may do well to return to the field to see how the variables fare when they are thrown into the pot with other variables in a natural setting.

An excellent example of the value of moving from the laboratory to the field comes from the literature on the effects of mood on altruism. Techniques for inducing a positive or negative mood have been developed in laboratory settings. These mood inductions typically involve having subjects read affectively positive or affectively negative passages (e.g., Aderman, 1972) or having them reminisce about happy or sad experiences in their own past (e.g., Moore, Underwood, & Rosenhan, 1973). In the typical laboratory experiment, after subjects have experienced the mood induction, they are given the opportunity to exercise their generosity by donating money for a good cause or by helping a confederate of the experimenter. Although results are mixed, studies employing this technique generally show that a positive mood increases helping. Despite many replications of this effect—across time, across laboratories, across investigators—the validity of these experiments has been questioned by some. Specifically, some critics challenge the artificiality of the setting in which helping behaviors are solicited and performed; others point to potential demand characteristics associated with the rather unusual mood-induction experience.

To counter these criticisms, researchers in the area have used field settings. Movie theaters are excellent settings for "natural" mood-induction treatments. That is, thousands of people attend movies: comedies that make them happy, or tragedies that make them sad. Benton Underwood and his colleagues (1977) took advantage of the emotional impact of motion pictures in a study of the effects of mood on helping. After careful pilot research, these investigators chose a double feature of *Lady Sings the Blues* and *The Sterile Cuckoo* as a (negative mood) treatment condition and chose two other double features to serve as neutral control conditions. The dependent variable (helping) was measured using a commonly occurring event: solicitation of donations to a nationally known charity, with collection boxes placed outside the movie theater lobby.

Of course, a major design problem encountered by Underwood and his colleagues (1977) was the fact that people do not assign themselves to movies at random. That is, *selection* was a potential threat to the internal validity of their study. If these researchers found that people who attend sad movies donated significantly less, they could not be sure whether it was something about *people who choose to attend sad movies*—and not the movies themselves— that accounted for the difference in helping. Although random assignment of movie goers to conditions was a logical possibility, there were drawbacks. For example, it would have been logistically difficult. And more important, problems of artificiality and reactivity—the very problems the use of field settings can prevent—would have been reintroduced. Therefore, the researchers decided to live with the selection threat and to alter the design to take it into account. To eliminate selection as a plausible rival hypothesis, they randomly alternated the timing of solicitation across different nights. That is, on some (randomly determined) nights, the opportunity to donate to the charity was available to people as they were entering the theater, *before* they had seen the double feature. On other (randomly determined) nights people had the opportunity to donate as they were leaving, *after* they had seen the double feature. Donations collected as people entered the theaters served as a check on the comparability of the groups before the treatment, that is, before they had seen a sad or neutral double feature. Fortunately for the investigators, the groups did not differ in their initial donation rates as a function of the movie they chose to attend. This pattern of results preserved the logic of random assignment—initial equivalence between experimental and control conditions—despite the procedural deviation from that ideal. Moreover, people who had viewed sad movies contributed significantly less on their way out of the theater than did people who had seen neutral movies. Thus, the results also supported conclusions based on "artificial" laboratory experiments.

We'd like to make two points related to this example. First, this study conducted in the field was not and could not be simply a "transplanted" replication of laboratory procedures. Major alterations were necessary to take advantage of the field setting. The researchers had considerably less control in the theater settings. They could not control administration of the treatment; neither could they control extraneous sources of variation. On any one night, a host of irrelevant events may have occurred during the course of the movies; projectors might have broken down or a disturbance might have erupted in the audience, and these extraneous events could have been confounded with the mood-induction treatment. The researchers not only were helpless to prevent such events but would not even have been aware of them had they occurred. In addition, as we've already mentioned, the experimenters were unable to assign subjects at random to conditions; in essence, they had to rely on "luck" to establish the initial equivalence among the groups.

Second, results of this quasi-experiment *as a single isolated study* would have been difficult to interpret without the context of conceptually similar laboratory experiments. This difficulty is partly due to the ambiguities introduced by altering the design of laboratory experiments and partly due to constraints inherent in a field setting where some degree of control is often sacrificed and where manipulation checks and random assignment, for example, are not always possible. The convergence of results across methods and across settings greatly enhances our confidence in both sets of findings. However, had the field study *failed* to replicate the laboratory results, numerous alternative explanations would have rendered interpretation very difficult.

Field studies—experimental and nonexperimental—are valuable in delimiting the parameters of the applicability of laboratory research. The researcher may find that the generality of some of the hypothesized causal laws are questionable, since in the real world other variables are always present to modify the effects isolated in the lab. Once these other variables are identified, the researcher may then return to experimental research, this time varying more variables at a time, testing new combinations and relationships among variables, refining hypotheses, building a theory. Natural settings can provide the evidence necessary to determine the generality of the results and to suggest new variables that must be brought under control if the research is to have widespread applicability, and experimental studies can be used to test causal relationships.

In summary, the right question is not: Are nonexperimental methods valuable? Every nonexperimental research method—correlational studies, pseudo-experiments, and quasi-experiments—has its place in the social psychologist's array of research tools. When conducted with ingenuity, careful thought and planning, and attention to measurement concerns, nonexperimental studies can serve as inspiration for theorizing *and* as means to evaluate and refine theory derived from experimental results. Thus, a far better question to ask is: Given my goals, given my research question, given methodological demands of the setting in which I choose to answer that question, which is the tool that best suits the requirements of the task?

FINDING AND CREATING SETTINGS

In a typical sequence of events, the experimenter first has a general idea—a hypothesis, a notion of a relationship between two variables, or just curiosity—about the effects of one variable on another. Then, the experimenter must determine how to translate that idea into a social situation. The problem is not unique to social psychology, but many issues are more salient here than in other disciplines, because there are few standard procedures in experimental social psychology. Once experimenters have decided on the *form* the research question will take (i.e., the specific design to be employed), the next step is to decide on the *content* of the question (i.e., What setting will be used? What specific rationale will be provided to subjects? How will the independent variable be operationalized? What will constitute the dependent-variable measures?). There are no hard and fast rules about how this is done, and choosing and creating settings demands much in the way of imagination, ingenuity, and critical thought.

The experimenter starts with an idea or question about a causal relationship between two conceptual variables: Does lowered self-confidence make one more susceptible to the temptation to cheat? When someone asks a favor, is a person who is feeling guilty more likely to comply? Is aggression inhibited when the victim looks into the attacker's eyes? Whatever the question, the experimenter must create a workable set of procedures that address it fairly. This task demands not only the invention of a procedure for delivering the independent variable and measuring its effect on the subject's behavior but also the construction of a contextual framework, a *setting* in which the treatments make sense and have impact, the measurements are sensitive and accurate, and all elements of the experiment are plausible. In practice, these three problems of designing and conducting an experiment (treatment, measure, and setting) overlap; a decision about one usually has implications for the others. The experimenter considers them all together, trying out various combinations, tinkering with one or another until coming up with a situation in which the treatments and measures are plausible and appropriately salient, and in which the subjects feel that each aspect of the procedure is meaningful in terms of the purpose of the experiment as they perceive it.

The experimenter must consider whether treatments and measurements adequately represent the underlying conceptual variables and appear reasonable to the subject. If everything appears natural, the subject will not stop to wonder about the situation, and a major source of error variance, the ideas and interpretations of the curious subject, is removed. Increases in the plausibility of the treatments and measures do not necessarily improve the correspondence between the conceptual variables and their empirical representations. Sometimes, the most plausible manipulations may be conceptually ambiguous. In many social psychological experiments, the goal of creating a plausible setting is not perfectly compatible with the goal of constructing clear and straightforward representations of the variables. Embedding the variables in a meaningful drama can often add to their complexity and increase the number of possible alternative explanations. Thus in many situations, there is some conflict between the goal of plausibility and the goal of conceptual clarity, and the experiment often represents a compromise.

For example, the situation created in the Aronson-Mills (1959) study of severity of initiation was convincing, and the experimental treatment struck the subjects as a natural and necessary aspect of the proceedings: If they were to join a group organized to discuss sex, of course they should be screened to see if they were capable of discussing sex comfortably, and reading a list of words referring to sexual topics appeared to be a most appropriate test. But the high degree of plausibility and impact created by this treatment was achieved at the expense of the conceptual clarity of the empirical realization of the independent variable: unpleasant effort. As the treatment is elaborated to increase its plausibility, the results become more subject to alternative explanations. As we mentioned in Chapter 2, one alternative explanation of the Aronson-Mills experiment was that the subject was sexually aroused by reading the words. In a subsequent conceptual replication of this experiment, Gerard and Mathewson (1966) used an electric shock instead of the list of dirty words: an initiation that was rationalized as a test of "emotionality." Although less plausibly interpolated into the experimental context, this treatment was also a less ambiguous representation of the conception "negative effort." In constructing treatments and measures, then, the experimenter must always be cognizant of two sets of constraints: those imposed by the perceptions of the subject (plausibility and impact) and those imposed by the conceptual definition of the variables (veridical representation and freedom from alternative interpretations).

Since the treatments and measures are often born of a compromise between the conflicting demands of plausibility and veridicality, in preparing a situational context the experimenter can concentrate primarily on the overall impact and credibility of the experiment. By the experimenter's choice and composition of the setting, treatments and measures can often be integrated into a meaningful whole.

EFFECTIVE RESEARCH SETTINGS

What are the characteristics of an effective setting? The setting an investigator creates—indeed, whether the investigator *creates* one as opposed to *seeking one out*—depends on the nature of the research question. Although there are exceptions, researchers typically start with an idea about how abstract constructs are related. To test specific causal hypotheses, the experimenter must find or create empirical realizations of conceptual variables, and the more abstract and general the constructs are, the greater the number of concrete realizations from which to choose. These choices often involve deciding upon a particular setting in which to conduct an experiment, for example, in the confines of the social psychological laboratory versus the world outside. Each setting has its own advantages and disadvantages, and often the advantages of one setting are solutions to the disadvantages of the other. For example: (1) behaviors that cannot be convincingly induced in the laboratory can often be successfully induced in the field; (2) given the complexity of the real world, experimental effects demonstrated there are often more convincing than the same effects obtained in the well-controlled sterility of the laboratory; and (3) the control afforded by laboratory experiments allows investigators to make more unequivocal statements of cause and effect and enables them to detect subtle or elusive effects that would be obscured by the "noise" of random error variance in the field. Given these trade-offs, the question remains: the laboratory or the field? Again, one's choice should be determined by the nature of the research question. For example, if you are interested in investigating the factors that influence the outcome of jury deliberations *per se*, then the courtroom is the preferred setting, because in the laboratory decisions made by mock jurors seldom have significant ramifications. Thus, it is appropriate in this case to study *juries*. However, if you are interested in studying the independent and interactive effects of independent variables (e.g., information vividness, source credibility) on the ways people make decisions in general—the kinds of decision making of which jury deliberations are but one example—then simulation studies conducted in the laboratory are usually preferable.

Regardless of one's choice of research setting—the laboratory versus the field, for example—as we shall see, the characteristics of a good choice of *laboratory* setting are often the characteristics of a good choice of a *field* setting as well. Of course, the problems inherent in creating an effective laboratory setting are not the same problems inherent in finding an effective field setting. Before turning to the latter concerns, we will begin our discussion by describing characteristics of a good laboratory setting.

Effective Laboratory Settings

What is an effective laboratory setting like? First, it is *coherent*. The subject perceives all the events that happen as integral elements of the central purpose of the experiment. The experimenter introduces tests and treatments without referring to extraneous interests ("Oh, by the way, we're also interested in how this relates to X") or providing a different rationale for each new event. Rather, the experimenter relates each event to the same general purpose as the other aspects of the experiment. The relationship of each event to the common theme appears clear and logical. The subject is not simply told that the event is related to the purpose of the experiment; once it has been explained, the connection appears self-evident. Long, convoluted explanations are usually ineffective for this purpose, leading to confusion or suspicion on the part of the subject.

An exception to this principle is the introduction of treatments or measurements which the subject believes have no relation whatsoever to the experiment, as in the case of the "accident" technique of producing the independent variable, for example, having smoke pour into a room in which subjects complete questionnaires (Latané & Darley, 1968) or having a woman "fall from a chair" in a nearby room (Latané & Rodin, 1969). These "wholly extraneous events" should stand out against a background which *does* appear sensible. That is, the rationale and procedures employed in an experiment in which an accident is embedded should make sense to subjects, independent of the accident itself. If from the subjects' point of view the "real experiment" doesn't make sense, they are likely to react to even the most convincing of "accidents" with skepticism.

The second attribute of an effective setting is *simplicity*. There is no point in concocting a long, involved tour-de-force of an explanation which achieves coherence only by virtue of a series of complex and ingenious chains of reasoning. An investigator does not need a complicated script or a cast of thousands to conduct a valid, meaningful experiment, however enjoyable and challenging to the imagination it may be to design and conduct such an experiment; the subject is *not* an actor in a Cecil B. DeMille epic. Instead, having less interest and less time to make sense of the script, the subject is likely to respond to such an experiment with confusion, suspicion, or boredom. A useful check is to pretest the experimental rationale and procedure on one's friends; if they react with blank stares, it is unlikely that a subject will be able to follow it, and some revision is in order.

Third, an effective experimental context is *involving*. If the subjects lose interest in the experiment, their attention will wander. If deception is involved, this inattention may provide the opportunity for questions and hypotheses to come into the subjects' thoughts, and they may see through the deception. If no deception is involved, subjects' motivation will still be diminished, other hypotheses may still be generated, and the possibilities for error will increase. In addition to making the overall experiment involving, the experimenter places the emphases where they are needed. Often, several events are occurring at the same time, and the experimenter's plan calls for a major portion of the subject's attention to be devoted to one of the events. The experimenter attempts to engineer the situation so that this event is made salient. For example, if the experimenter wants to arouse aggression in a subject by having an obnoxious confederate deliver an inordinate amount of stressful distracting stimulation while the subject is working on a task, the task is not made so exciting and absorbing that the subject will be able to disregard the noxious stimuli.

Finally, an effective context contributes to the *creation of the same baseline state* in all subjects. In the next chapter, we will elaborate upon the desirability of this procedure and will point out that diverse methods may be necessary to bring about the same internal state in different subjects. For now, let us say that it is important to make subjects as similar as possible before introducing the independent variable. This can be facilitated by using the context to provide a uniform frame of reference in which all the subjects have the same understandings, perceptions, and motivations with regard to the experimental situation. Insofar as all subjects can be brought to the same psychological state before the independent variable is introduced, the experimenter will be able to administer a standard version of the experimental treatment with more confidence that it will affect the subjects in a similar way. In many ways that is preferable to varying the treatment itself to achieve the closest approximation to the desired internal state for each subject. Making the subjects similar before any treatments are introduced can limit the generality of the results to subjects who are in that particular state but cannot affect the internal validity of the experiment by allowing bias in the independent variable or by obscuring the conceptual definition of the independent variable. The setting of the Aronson and Mills (1959) experiment, discussed in Chapters 1 and 2, illustrates how various aspects of the situation can reduce the diversity of the subjects' perceptions of the independent variable by providing them with an integrated conceptual framework in which to view the standardized experimental treatment.

Pilot testing can be useful in creating a situation that elicits relatively uniform baseline responses from the subjects. The experimenter can ask the pilot subjects how they feel (about the confederate, the task, or whatever the independent variable is supposed to affect) before the treatment is introduced. We hasten to add that this check on baseline levels is often an unwise procedure during the *actual experiment*, as it may sensitize the subjects to those aspects of their behavior which the experimenter is trying to affect and thus distort the influence of the treatment. During pilot testing, however, the experimenter can use some of the subjects for the sole purpose of providing this kind of information about consistency of response, without worrying that the final data will be uninterpretable. If there is a wide variability in response, the experimenter can change the experimental situation until stability is achieved.

The experimenter may attempt to not only achieve a consistency of response to the situation but also set this response at a particular level. When the response is one that will ultimately be measured by the dependent variable, the experimenter wants the subjects' behavior to be maximally free to vary with differences in the independent variable. Thus, the experimenter often wants a situation in which the baseline level of the behavior is intermediate, so that it can either increase or decrease in response to the treatment. This is especially true when the experimenter posits a *curvilinear* relationship between the levels of a treatment and some outcome measure, such as the inverted U-curve that maps the relationship between arousal and performance. For example, if the effects of fear on obedience are being studied, the experimenter wants to start out by finding a situation in which about half of the subjects obey and half disobey, before introducing the treatment. That way, when the treatment is introduced, the behavior will have "room to change" in either direction.[1] If the basic situation is one in which virtually all subjects disobey, observing changes due to the independent variable will be very difficult. The point may seem obvious, but is often violated: There are many published studies that report no effects, experiments in which the baseline level of responding was so high that improvements could not possibly have been detected.

In other cases, an experimenter will *not* want an intermediate level. If the treatment itself involves the performance of a certain behavior, the experimenter will want all the subjects in the experimental condition to perform that behavior. For example, in their classic experiment, Jonathan Freedman and Scott Fraser (1966) were interested in testing the hypothesis that people who agree to perform a small favor will subsequently be more willing to comply with a request for a much larger favor than will people who were never asked to perform the small favor. In order to investigate this hypothesis, the experimenters had to find a small request with which almost everyone would comply. In this experiment, all subjects in the "small favor" condition agreed to perform the small favor, which was to put a small sticker advocating safe driving on the windows of their homes. Because nearly all the subjects in the "small request" group complied, Freedman and Fraser were able to study the effects of initial compliance with requests for a small favor on subsequent compliance with requests for a very large favor.

Effective Field Settings

The experimenter who moves outside the laboratory is no longer in a position to *manufacture* a setting that is coherent, simple, involving, and so on but instead must *choose* an existing setting which is appropriate for the problem. In

---

[1] More specifically, if subjects score "low" on a given variable prior to treatment, even the most impactful manipulation may not succeed in lowering their scores further, even though there is otherwise good reason to believe it will; this phenomenon is called the **floor effect**. However, if subjects for whatever reasons score unusually "high" on some variable, even the most impactful treatment may not succeed in raising their scores further, as predicted; this phenomenon is known as a **ceiling effect**.

so doing, the experimenter tries to seek out natural situations possessing the characteristics of effective settings, namely, coherence, simplicity, impact, and the ability to bring subjects to a similar baseline state.

These qualities of a good experimental setting are important whether the research is conducted in the field or in the laboratory. However, there are differences in the problems to be solved and the decisions to be made in setting the stage, depending on whether the research is to be carried out in the laboratory or in a more natural setting. In the field, the experimenter must choose a setting that contains the elements thought to be important and that contains a minimum of elements *not* deemed to be important. Such "extras" only serve to make events more complex, and results directly related to the causal hypothesis are therefore less easily interpretable. Furthermore, the experimenter seldom has much opportunity to modify the setting, and in some field experiments no verbal explanation at all can be provided.

Above and beyond the criteria for effective experimental settings in general, what are additional characteristics of an effective field setting? Again, there is no general answer, for the desirability of any given real-world setting is a function of the experimenters' goals, that is, the specific hypotheses they set out to test. An appropriate setting to test one hypothesis may be highly inappropriate for testing a different hypothesis. These differences aside, effective field settings are ones in which events are meaningful and impactful to subjects and in which the experimenter has the *power to intervene* in a systematic way in ongoing events. For example, New York City subways provided an excellent field setting for the experimental study of bystander interventions in emergencies (e.g., Piliavin, Dovidio, Gaertner, & Clark, 1981; Piliavin & Piliavin, 1972; Piliavin, Piliavin & Rodin, 1975; Piliavin, Rodin & Piliavin, 1969). In these and similar studies, experimenters were able to systematically vary "victim" characteristics and other characteristics of the emergency setting. Note that if a field experimental setting does not enable researchers to intervene experimentally—that is, to assign subjects at random to one or another treatment or control condition—the study is no longer a true experiment, and causal inferences about the effects of an independent variable become tentative at best.

An effective field setting also affords investigators the opportunity to study behaviors that for ethical or practical reasons are not easily elicited in the laboratory. For example, when laboratory subjects are aware that they are being observed by the experimenter, they may be loathe to behave in ways that make them appear aggressive, stingy, cowardly, greedy, compliant, gullible, and so on. A good field setting is one in which subjects are not motivated to appear socially desirable, as is the case when they find themselves under the watchful scrutiny of an experimenter in the laboratory. Consider a field experiment conducted by Dennis Regan, Margo Williams, and Sondra Sparling (1972) on the effects of guilt on altruistic behaviors. The experiment was conducted at a shopping mall, and subjects in the experimental group were induced to believe that while taking a confederate's picture, they broke his expensive camera; subjects in the control condition were informed that the malfunctioning camera was not their fault—that it frequently failed to work. Soon thereafter, a second confederate crossed the subject's path, carrying a torn grocery bag from which candy spilled onto the ground. The dependent variables of interest included the number of subjects in each condition who informed the second confederate that the bag was torn, and the number in each condition who stopped to help her pick up the candy. The subjects were not aware that their responses were being recorded. Indeed, they were unaware that they were subjects in a social psychological experiment. It is possible that were a similar experiment conducted in the laboratory, differences between the experimental and control groups would have been attenuated by a motivation on the part of *all* subjects to appear considerate and altruistic under the watchful gaze of a visible experimenter.

FIELD STUDIES: CHOOSING A SETTING

We have noted that whether one creates a setting or finds one, an effective experimental setting is among other things coherent, simple, and impactful. However, what constitutes "coherent," "simple," and "impactful" is not necessarily the same in a field setting as in a laboratory setting. Furthermore, different means must be used to achieve these qualities.

A real-world setting is *coherent* if it is bounded in time or space and if it encompasses a single major event. For example, let's consider a field experiment by Ellen Langer, Arthur Blank, and Benzion Chanowitz (1978). These experimenters tested the hypothesis that people sometimes automatically and mindlessly comply with a request, no matter how senseless *reasons* for the request might appear upon closer inspection. In one study, subjects using a photocopy machine at the City University of New York were approached by a male or female experimenter and asked to interrupt their work to allow the experimenter to make copies. In this 2×3 factorial experiment, subjects were randomly assigned to one of two request magnitude conditions and to one of three explanation conditions. Requests were either small or large (to allow the experimenter to make either 5 or 20 photocopies); and they were accompanied by no explanation ("May I use the Xerox machine?"), by a placebic (uninformative) explanation ("May I use the Xerox machine, because I have to make copies?), or by an informative explanation ("May I use the Xerox machine, because I'm in a rush?"). The dependent variable in the experiment was whether subjects in each of the six experimental groups interrupted their work to allow the experimenter to go first. Langer and her colleagues predicted that when the request was small, subjects would comply equally with informative and uninformative explanations, but that when the request was large, subjects would comply more with informative explanations than with uninformative explanations. Their hypothesis was confirmed. When compliance was not costly, there was no difference in the number of subjects who complied with informative versus uninformative explanations; in the face of the small request, they evidently did not pause to consider the *reason* for the request. However, when compliance was effortful, fewer subjects engaged in "pseudothinking" behaviors; in the face of a more costly request, fewer subjects allowed the experimenter to make copies when he or she provided an uninformative explanation for the request to usurp the photocopier. This setting was coherent, in that it took place at a particular spot, and in that clear temporal boundaries to the event were set by the subjects' arrival at the photocopy machine and by their immediate responses to the experimenter's request.

Simplicity is difficult to achieve outside of the laboratory. Control over extraneous events is greatly reduced, and many real-world situations are intrinsically characterized by a multiplicity of activities. To some extent, simplicity can be achieved by choosing a very small event or one that lasts for a short time, but often such events do not reflect the kind of important variables that may have led the experimenter to abandon the laboratory in the first place. One way to maximize the likelihood of simplicity and coherence is to choose a situation that is focused on a single main event, such as a public meeting or a local emergency. For example, Albert Hastorf and Hadley Cantril (1954) chose a Dartmouth-Princeton football game as the attention-focusing event in a study of how attitudes affect people's perceptions. The subjects were spectators at the game, and their perception of what happened greatly depended on whether they were Dartmouth fans or Princeton fans. More recently, Robert Cialdini and his colleagues (1976) conducted a series of field experiments to study the effects of football wins and losses on college students' tendency to "bask in reflected glory" when their teams were victorious. After victories, students were more likely to wear apparel that bore school names, emblems, or insignia, and were more likely to use the word "we" in referring to the victory than they were when their teams lost. Both experiments demonstrate that if the participants' attention is focused on a single major event (or series of events), the researcher can achieve some of the benefits of simplicity without sacrificing importance or involvement.

The investigator can often provide the focusing event by introducing one or more treatments into a natural situation. This procedure also gives a measure of control over the emphasis of the situation, allowing the experimenter to introduce the independent variable in such a way that it will have impact for the subjects without so violating the situational norms that it stands out as peculiar. An excellent example of the plausible introduction of an experimental treatment into a nonlaboratory context is an experiment conducted by Howard Leventhal and Patricia Niles (1964). These investigators were interested in the effects of fear-arousing communications on attitude change, and the particular frightening issue they used to explore this relationship was the correlation between smoking and lung cancer. They chose a large health exposition held in the New York Coliseum as their setting and introduced their experimental treatments, movies about lung cancer, as an exhibit in the exposition. After listening to a brief introductory lecture, a third of the subjects saw movies that were extremely frightening, a third saw a milder version, and the rest did not see a movie. At the end of each session, the audience's attention was directed to a nearby booth where free chest X-rays were being offered. One of the measures was the number of people in each condition (high, medium, and low fear) who subsequently stopped in at the chest X-ray booth. The treatment was salient and involving; the measure was clear-cut and meaningful in terms of the underlying conceptual variables. At the same time, both aspects of the experiment seemed perfectly natural in the broader context of the health exposition.

By controlling which of the films the subjects saw, Leventhal and Niles were also able to ensure that the subjects who saw the two films were comparable with one another and with the subjects who saw no film, thus solving one of the major problems of field research, that of self-selection. Subjects in the various experimental conditions were also more similar to one another than would be the case in many laboratory experiments. All had chosen not only to come to the health exposition in the first place but also to attend the exhibit on lung cancer. Variability was presumably greatly reduced, since subjects in the three conditions were similarly motivated and involved at the time they were exposed to the communications. However, because we do not know what makes a person go to a health exposition and decide to look at an exhibit on lung cancer, we do not know what characteristics define the population to which we can generalize. Perhaps the results apply only to medical personnel; perhaps only to hypochondriacs. Nonetheless, internal validity will not be threatened if we can ensure that the subjects in the groups to be compared are equivalent prior to the introduction of the independent variable. The best way to ensure equivalence, of course, is to assign subjects from the same sample to conditions at random. When this is not possible, the choice of a comparison group becomes extremely important.

When it is impossible to introduce treatments or to assign subjects to conditions at random, field research can be conducted by taking advantage of "natural experiments," situations in which major changes involving a variable of interest to the experimenter are planned in advance by an outside agency. Consider, for example, the 1983 airing of the ABC television program, *The Day After*, a movie that graphically depicted the aftermath of a nuclear attack on the United States. Well in advance of its showing, *The Day After* was the subject of numerous cover stories in national news magazines, and movie stars, politicians, learned physicists, educators, and even members of the Reagan administration aired their views on the program and its potential impact on viewers, especially children. Of course, the extent to which the program would have powerful and longlasting effects on attitudes and public opinion here and elsewhere in the world was an empirical question: one that this natural experiment afforded researchers the opportunity to study. The enforcement of desegregation in a specific school or other institution is an example of a more protracted planned change. The investigator may have a chance to examine the situation in advance, to find out what kinds of information will be readily available when the time comes, and to gain an understanding of the prechange setting that can be an aid in selecting an appropriate comparison setting.

Often, the field researcher will have to choose not just one, but two settings, one to serve as a control for the other. If desegregation is to be enforced in one school by busing, the researcher will be better able to understand the effects by also observing another, not-yet-desegregated school. Here, the primary consideration is comparability. Although it is impossible to guarantee equivalence of groups without random assignment, the researcher who is careful about choosing settings can often guard against the most important sources of noncomparability. In selecting contextual situations for the study, the researcher first tries to think of the most plausible extraneous factors that could mimic the effects of the independent variable and produce the predicted differences and then attempts to find pairs of settings that do not differ in terms of these extraneous factors. For example, in a study designed to determine whether arbitration clauses in employment contracts actually reduce the amount of strife between workers and management, it is necessary to compare corporations that have such clauses with those that do not. The researcher attempts to find two corporations that are as similar as possible on other important dimensions—for example, two telephone companies (holding industry constant) in northern Virginia (holding region constant) with comparable numbers of employees (holding size constant), one that provides for arbitration and one that does not. In order to check on the comparability of the two companies the researcher may take measures of aspects of company life not expected to be affected by the arbitration clause and may also look into the companies' records to see whether they had similar levels of employer-employee strife before one company introduced the arbitration provision. If differences do not show up on any of these measures, the researcher may be quite confident (although never entirely certain) that the two settings are equivalent.

An additional measure to ensure that differences are due to the independent variable and not to settings is to choose several pairs of settings, settings as different as possible from the other pairs. Thus in the example on arbitration, the researcher may study not only the two Virginia telephone companies, but also two lumber companies in Oregon—one with an arbitration clause and one without. If the effects of the arbitration clause appear to be similar in both pairs of companies, the researcher becomes even more confident that extraneous differences in setting are not responsible for the results, since these extraneous factors may be expected to differ greatly in the two different work settings.[2] The details of these issues go beyond the scope of our discussion here; Thomas Cook and his colleagues provide a more complete discussion of these topics (Cook & Campbell, 1979; Cook, Leviton, & Shadish, 1985).

In selecting a setting for field research it is important to understand the question precisely. What exactly is being sought? Although experimental control is typically reduced in the field, it is unwise for the experimenter to as-

---

[2] We are indebted to Professor William Gould of the Stanford Law School for this example.

sume that since perfect control is unattainable, one setting is as good as another or (as too frequently happens) that the question might as well be correspondingly vague. By making a specific formulation of the research problem, the experimenter is in a better position to choose a setting and to get the most out of it. The experimenter will have some idea of the kinds of factors that might interfere with the collection of information relevant to the question and can examine potential settings with an eye to minimizing these factors. The experimenter will also avoid the problem of collecting too much data on a wide variety of vaguely specified questions and later finding that the information needed to answer any one of them adequately is not available. When faced with the richness and complexity of the real world, there is often a strong temptation to leave no stone unturned, but the illumination gained from such an approach is often so widely dispersed that no single object is clearly visible in the overall obscurity.

LABORATORY EXPERIMENTS: CREATING A SETTING

In choosing a context outside of the laboratory, the experimenter looks for situations that are coherent and contained and then embeds the stimuli and/or measures in the situational background. In a sense the experimenter tries to choose a situation that tells its own story, and the main task is to make the elements added to the setting consistent with this story and to set them at the appropriate level of salience. In a laboratory experiment, the experimenter must create a context in which the experimental operations seem reasonable. Sometimes, events in the laboratory can also tell their own story, as in the classic "lady in distress" experiment conducted by Bibb Latané and Judith Rodin (1969). In their experiment, subjects were left alone by a female confederate who was later heard to fall from a chair in her office as she climbed up to retrieve some papers. Via a tape recording, subjects heard a crash as the woman and her chair collapsed to the floor, and they heard her exclaim, "Oh, my God, my foot....I...I can't move it...Oh...my ankle...I...can't get this . . . thing . . . off me." Thus, with some ingenuity, the experimenter *can* create a setting similar to emergency situations that occur outside the laboratory. More often, however, the experimenter must provide the "story" by introducing a rationale for the research that ties together all the experimental operations and elements into a coherent whole.

Providing a rationale is usually necessary to prevent the subjects from attempting to decipher the reasons for the experiment. If they are given no explanation of the proceedings, the subjects are likely to try to figure out the reasons behind the experimental events. At best, this will result in an increase in random error, due to variation in the subjects' interpretations of the experiment. A more serious consequence is the possibility that systematic error will be introduced, due to uniformity in the subjects' interpretations. A rationale is designed to provide subjects with a ready-made explanation to distract them from attempts to interpret the experimental events for themselves.

A good rationale accounts, in a plausible manner, for all the necessary aspects of the experiment to prevent the subjects from speculating about what the experimenter really has in mind. The rationale should capture the subjects' attention so that they remain awake and responsive to the experimental treatment. This is not meant facetiously; if the rationale for an experiment strikes subjects as trivial or silly, they may simply tune out. For example, if the experimenter professed interest in the effects of small temperature changes on people's ability to concentrate on abstruse technical prose, the subjects might stop listening to the instructions and might not put much effort into reading the article. If subjects are not paying attention to the independent variable, it is certain to have little impact on them. If the experimental treatment in the example above were a message embedded in the technical article, many subjects might miss it entirely.

The setting may be relatively simple, or it may involve an elaborate scenario, depending on the demands of the situation. Obviously, the experimenter should set the stage as simply as the requirements of the experiment permit. If a simple setting succeeds in providing a plausible rationale and in capturing the subjects' attention, there is no need for greater elaboration. Sometimes, however, the simplest situation may provide such meager stimulation that the subjects' interest is not secured. For example, suppose that one wants to make the subjects fearful. One might achieve this simply by telling them that they will receive a strong electric shock. But one is more confident of arousing strong fear if one has set the stage with a trifle more embellishment. This can be done by providing a medical atmosphere, inventing a medical rationale for the experiment, having the experimenter appear in a white laboratory coat, and allowing the subjects to view a formidable electrical apparatus, as in Stanley Schachter's (1959) experiments. One might go even further by providing the subjects with a mild sample shock, implying that the actual shocks will be much stronger.

Such elaborations as these, designed to make a single coherent event appear vivid and forceful, are unlikely to interfere with the underlying simplicity of the situation as perceived by the subject. They are not confusing, because their purpose is simply to enhance the salience and impact of the same basic event. Surface elaborations, introduced to set the tone and to provide orchestration for the basic theme carried by the basic rationale, do not violate the canon of simplicity, provided that they are all consistent with the basic facts of the situation presented to the subject.

A problem arises when the experimenter wishes to introduce an instruction or measure that cannot be brought into close harmony with the overall situation conveyed by the cover story. If the new event is to make sense to the subject, a new and independent rationale must be devised. This kind of elaboration *does* pose a threat to simplicity and coherence. The subject may become confused or suspicious or distracted from the main theme. Therefore, the experimenter should be extremely cautious about introducing new and different explanations for events that do not "fit" the basic rationale. In some cases it is better to go back and try to devise a cover story that does include all the experimental events or to modify the procedure so that the events can be brought into line with the original story.

When the overall situation has high impact, the experimenter is sometimes better off simply omitting extraneous explanations. If the experiment is sufficiently involving, and if events unfold relatively rapidly, events regarded by the detached, dispassionate experimenter as potentially inconsistent or unexplained in terms of the cover story may not be at all puzzling to the subject. The experimenter, attempting to look at the experiment from the subjects' point of view, may have examined and reexamined the procedure, unearthed a number of discrepancies or unexplained aspects of the experiment, and may feel that the subject should be given some sort of explanation for these troublesome spots, even at the risk of introducing factors extraneous to the basic theme of the rationale. Now it may very well happen that the subject, caught up in the flow of events, does not pause to reflect on the petty mysteries revealed by intensive study of the script and in fact may be completely oblivious to their existence. By interrupting the flow of events with a superfluous explanation for an unnoticed inconsistency, the experimenter may succeed in focusing the subject's attention on the inconsistency, thereby raising suspicion instead of laying it to rest. There can be danger in "protesting too much"; sometimes it is better to keep quiet about small details, even when an explanation has been devised. Pilot testing provides an excellent opportunity to assess both the necessity of introducing new information and the effectiveness of explanations already included.

It is perhaps already clear that what we have called "setting the stage" not only leads into the independent variable but is often a part of it. That is, in the example of the Schachter experiments, the electrical paraphernalia, the medical cover story, the white coat, and the electric shock constitute both the experimental treatment and the setting. The fear-arousing stimulus (fear of electric shock) is part and parcel of the whole situation and derives some of its threatening properties from the forbidding machinery and medical "precautions." Indeed, in many experiments that are highly coherent from the point of view of the subject, the background flows into the experimental treatment, resulting in a reduction in the clarity of the conceptual independent variable. The white coat and the medical rationale may have introduced an aura of authority into the Schachter experiment, for example, so that the subjects were motivated to "look good" for the high-status experimenter, which increased their motivation to obey. Instead of simply feeling fear, subjects may have experienced a complicated blend of emotions. This problem is not unique to the Schachter experiment but is to some extent characteristic of most of the experiments described in this book. As we mentioned at the beginning of this chapter, the coherence and plausibility provided by the mutual interdependence of the independent variable and the setting may be gained at the expense of conceptual clarity, in that the situational trimmings may carry with them increased possibilities for alternative explanations.

How should the experimenter deal with this problem? Needless to say, when a clean, straightforward treatment which is high in plausibility and impact and low in extraneous embellishments can be found, it is to be preferred over a more elaborate experimental setting. The experimenter's purpose in introducing embellishments is not aesthetic but functional. Often, the clean, straightforward treatment is also transparent, confusing, or weak. Thus, despite its theoretical clarity, it introduces possibilities of very obvious alternative explanations of its own, such as suspicion and conformity with experimental demand characteristics. In effect, the experimenter creates an involving situation for the purpose of avoiding the obvious sources of error, even though to do so entails the risk of introducing nonobvious confounding variables. In order to minimize this risk, the experimenter should examine the situation thoroughly for possible alternative influences and should attempt to rule them out or at least measure their effects. One of the primary values of systematic replication— that is, holding the conceptual variable constant and changing its empirical realizations—is that the alternative explanations for any one experiment are not likely to apply in the settings employed in the others (see Chapter 2).

Just as the independent variable may blend into the background situation, the measurement of the dependent variable follows naturally from the context, if the stage has been properly set. The behavior asked for in the cover story may in fact be the actual dependent variable. For example, in the Asch conformity experiment (1951), the subjects were told that the experiment dealt with their perceptual judgments of lines. At the same time, their stated judgments of the lines were the crucial data; they were the dependent variable in both the perception experiment described to the subjects and the actual conformity experiment. Similarly, in Milgram's (1973) study, the dependent variable was the point at which the subject ceased administering electric shocks, the same electric shocks that were an integral part of the cover experiment.

The integration of the dependent-variable measure with the experiment as a whole increases the coherence of the situation and should be attempted whenever possible. Unfortunately, this technique is not always feasible. Often, the dependent variable is not the behavior asked for in the cover story but some other behavior. For example, in Festinger and Carlsmith's (1959) experiment on forced compliance, the crucial datum was the subject's evaluation of a recently performed boring task. The evaluations were not collected until the experiment had been completed, and they were not collected by the experimenter but by a person the subject had not seen before, whose purpose apparently had nothing to do with the experiment. A similar technique was used in the experiment by Aronson and Mills (1959), in which subjects were asked—seemingly as an appendage to the main experiment—to evaluate the group they had joined. Although the data collection may not be integral to the rationale, it is important that it not appear to be tacked on; if an experimenter casually tosses yet another questionnaire at subjects, the subjects are unlikely to take their task any more seriously than the experimenter's lackadaisical manner implies. The task must make sense and seem important in terms of the general setting.

In some cases a completely separate but plausible stage can be created for the measurement of the dependent variable. Thus, Festinger and Carlsmith arranged that all Introductory Psychology subjects were told that some subjects in experiments would be interviewed about their reactions to the experiments in which they participated. Before the particular subjects in the experiment were told that they were to be interviewed, they were reminded that such an interview was part of the general Introductory Psychology course structure and that they had been selected to take part.

FACTORS THAT MAY AFFECT THE VALIDITY OF DECEPTION EXPERIMENTS

The astute reader may have noticed the deception implied by the words "rationale," "story," and "scenario" in our discussion of setting the stage in laboratory experiments. In essence, we were addressing ways to successfully deceive subjects about the true purpose of our investigations. In Chapter 3, we discussed some of the ethical questions raised by the use of deceptive cover stories. And we briefly noted that ethical concerns are not the *only* kinds of questions that have been raised about experiments employing deceptive techniques. Some critics have also pointed out possible methodological problems inherent in conducting deception experiments. We shall conclude this chapter by examining these methodological criticisms.

Generalized Suspicion

One practical objection to the use of deception that was of great concern in the 1960s and 1970s is that continued reliance on deceptive techniques creates in the minds of potential subjects an image of social psychologists as untrustworthy people (see, for example, Kelman, 1968). From a methodological point of view, this objection suggests that as social psychologists' reputation for double-dealing becomes more widely known, subjects will be increasingly likely to enter an experiment prepared to suspect any and all communications from the experimenter and determined to guess the true purpose of the experiment. How will this suspicion affect the subjects' behavior in the experiment? This question has been a matter of much speculation. Some have suggested that subjects who think that they have guessed the experimenter's hypothesis may try to modify their behavior in order to support the hypothesis. Others have suggested that suspicious subjects will do the exact opposite, making responses that they think will disconfirm the hypothesis. Alternatively, subjects may be motivated to present themselves as rational, healthy, and likeable people, regardless of their intuitions about the experimenter's hypotheses. Finally, it has been suggested that all these and other factors are operating, so that the net effect of a heightened level of suspicion among experimental subjects will simply be an increase in the amount of extraneous variation and hence in the amount of random error. It should be noted that these more or less distressing effects would *not* be restricted to deception experiments. If subjects are generally suspicious of psychology experiments, and if suspicious subjects do behave differently from unsuspicious subjects, they will behave that way in all experiments, whether or not deception is actually employed.

Projecting this situation into the future is probably unrealistic. There is some evidence (Stricker, 1967; Stricker, Messick, & Jackson, 1969) that suspicion has been fairly widespread for some time. Subjects drawn from psychology classes have often heard or read about deception experiments, and certain paradigms (such as that of the Asch experiment) are so well known that trying to use them is probably not sensible with such populations. Subjects' prior experience in other deception experiments may also create a suspicious set. During the 1960s and 1970s, when deception experiments were more widely questioned by researchers, Martin Orne (1962) and Kenneth Ring (1967) suggested that a general mistrust of the cover stories in social psychological experiments may be the norm in student populations. However, Robert Edelman (1970) found no such evidence of a "generalized" suspicion among college students. His deception involved false feedback of scores on an IQ test, and subjects became suspicious when deception was present but were not suspicious when a deception-free version of the same paradigm was used. Edelman also found that suspicion was not related to the magnitude of the deception, that is, to the size of the discrepancy between the subject's true score and the false feedback. Thus, it cannot be stated that because college students are generally mistrustful, deception cannot and does not work; were that the case, many experimenters would have been out of business long ago. Not all subjects are inherently mistrustful of experimenters. Moreover, whether a given deceptive technique is effective depends on the specific nature of the deception, on how artfully and convincingly a cover story is presented, and on a host of factors yet to be systematically investigated.

Although the effects of suspicion on subjects' behavior in experiments have not been fully explored, some research indicates the kind of differences that might exist between suspicious and unsuspicious subjects. Both Herbert Kelman (1968) and Lawrence Stricker and his colleagues (1969) conclude that the only definite result of generalized subject suspicion is an increase in extraneous variability. However, in a study of the effects of prior experience in a deception experiment on behavior in a future experiment, Irwin Silverman, Arthur Shulman, and David Wiesenthal (1970) found that the major effect of previous deception was to increase the subjects' desire to present themselves in a favorable light in the second experiment. Subjects responded to their deception experience by "increasing evaluation apprehension and their tendencies to present themselves as psychologically strong and stable" (1970, p. 208). In addition, the previously deceived subjects complied less with experimental demands than did subjects who had never participated in a deception experiment. Whether the subjects' experience was with an ego-supporting or an ego-threatening deception made no difference in their behavior in the second experiment. These results suggest that previous experience in deception experiments has some systematic effects on subjects' behavior in future experiments. (See also Greenberg & Folger, 1988.)

Suspicion of the True Purpose of a Specific Experiment

A different problem for the social psychologist involves the subjects' fore-knowledge or accurate guessing of the true purpose of a specific study. Here the evidence is somewhat more encouraging. Evidence for accurate guessing of the purpose of a given study has been found only when the deception was in some sense "obvious" (Brock & Becker, 1966; Fillenbaum, 1966; Stricker, Messick, & Jackson, 1969). For example, if the design of a very well known experiment such as the Asch experiment is used, high rates of accurate guessing are likely to be observed among college student subjects. Likewise, when subjects have previously participated in a deception study with a specific type of manipulation, they are likely to recognize a similar manipulation in a subsequent study. Finally, subjects are likely to be suspicious when the information they are asked to believe is extremely discrepant from their expectations, as in the Edelman (1970) study, in which subjects who completed 40 items on an IQ subtest were told that the national average for college students was 110 or 180 items.

It has also been suggested that subjects may find out about the deception involved in an experiment from other subjects who have already participated in the experiment and learned its true purpose during the debriefing session. Aronson (1969) has shown, however, that when the postexperimental interview is conducted in the manner suggested in Chapter 4, and further elaborated in Chapter 10, subjects comply with the experimenter's request and refuse to reveal the nature of the experiment to their friends who are scheduled to participate in the same experiment. This evidence is persuasive: The "future subjects" were confederates of the experimenter and had been explicitly instructed to try their best to wheedle the relevant information out of the former subjects.

Although Aronson's experiment indicates that subjects can be persuaded not to tell others about the deception involved in an experiment, the study by Edelman (1970) indicates that even when subjects are told, the information has little effect on their behavior. In the Edelman study a confederate posing as the subject who had just finished the experiment approached the real subject in the waiting room and said, "You'd better be on guard. There's something phony about that experiment." This information had no effect on the subject's suspicion, however; as we have mentioned above, the suspicion level was already high due to the implausibility of the treatment. Incidentally, it should be pointed out that the suspicious subjects in the Edelman experiment did not really guess the true purpose of the experiment, which was to assess the variables that affect suspicion.

Measures to Reduce Suspicion

The possible effects of suspicion are explored in much greater detail by Arie Kruglanski (1975), who concludes that subjects do not generally form hypotheses which are systematically related to the experimental treatments. He also finds minimal evidence of the biasing effect of specific subject motivations, such as cooperativeness, negativism, "faithfulness," evaluation apprehension, or the use of volunteer subjects. Still, the fact that the effects do not seem to be systematic is no justification for assuming that suspicion will be nonexistent or irrelevant in a specific experiment. Precautions designed to minimize suspicion are the better part of discretion.

It should be immediately apparent that the use of a subject population characterized by an attitude of generalized suspicion toward psychological experiments makes the use of procedures high in experimental realism not only desirable, but imperative. If subjects are deeply involved in the experimental situation—or interested in it for its own sake—they will be less likely to turn their attention to other things, such as conjectures about the experimenter's intentions. The subjects should care more about the apparent nature of their immediate experience than about their ability to assess its true nature. If the situation has a great impact on them, if it is absorbing, if it demands attention and alertness and leaves them no time for speculative lapses, the deception is more likely to be effective. We consider the use of procedures high in experimental realism to be the best technique for counteracting suspicion.

Taking additional precautions may further enhance the effectiveness of the deception. Stricker, Samuel Messick and Douglas Jackson (1969) propose several possible measures to ward off suspicion. They suggest that the experimenter attempt to use subjects who have not previously participated in deception experiments. Where feasible, this is a generally good plan, though it should definitely be considered a supplement to, not a substitute for, the use of experimental realism. Many experimenters recruit subjects from academic classes other than Introductory Psychology, and experiments in real-world settings or experiments using children as subjects are even more effective defenses against the problem of subjects' experimental sophistication. Probably the least desirable type of subject is the student whose spare cash is earned entirely by participating in psychological experiments and who therefore signs up for every available study. In certain experiments the use of an experimentally naive student population becomes more important. For example, if two experimenters are using highly similar experimental treatments, they would be ill-advised to use the same subject pool. Likewise, an investigator whose design includes a replication of a well-known study should make an extra effort to find subjects who are not likely to have heard of it. If the study to be replicated is an experiment that was described during the first week of the course in Introductory Psychology, needless to say, the experimenter should not use students from the class.

These remarks may seem obvious when stated in this fashion, but our experience suggests that they are often forgotten in practice. We recommend that the experimenter both *consider* the adequacy of the usual sources of subjects in relation to the particular experiment to be conducted and *look carefully* for any exceptional features of the experiment that might limit the range of appropriate subjects. Beyond this general recommendation, a modicum of common sense is probably a better guide to choosing a subject population than is any list of specific criteria.

It has also been suggested (Kelman, 1968; Stricker, Messick & Jackson, 1969) that the greater the number of deceptions used in an experiment, the greater the probability that subjects will detect some aspect of the deception. There is no research on this specific question, so far as we know, although the laws of probability would seem to indicate its plausibility. We tend to agree with this position when several *independent* deceptions are to be introduced into a single experiment. In planning research, the experimenter should search for alternative techniques for *each* use of deception in an experiment and not simply make a decision about whether the experiment as a whole requires deception. If the probabilistic model of deception detection is apt, the search for nondeceptive methods probably has practical advantages. However, in many studies employing multiple deceptions, these deceptions are not discrete but are interdependent contributions to the realism of the situation as a whole. In many experiments it is difficult to determine if they include multiple deceptions or if they consist of a single major deception which has implications for several different events in the experimental situation. As we've noted previously in this chapter, in any experiment it is important that the subject regard the situation as a whole as coherent and meaningful. If it is necessary to elaborate the experiment to make all events consistent with the cover story, the gains in experimental realism may far outweigh the potential danger from increased opportunity for suspicion. In short, if the subject accepts the general situation presented in the cover story and if all aspects of the experiment make sense in terms of this overall conception, the likelihood of suspicion about difficult aspects of the deception will be less than it will be in a less coherent situation, even though there may be "fewer" deceptions involved.

As an example, let us take another look at the Aronson-Mills (1959) experiment described in Chapter 2. Superficially, it appears that this experiment involved a great many deceptions: a story about group processes, a prerecorded tape supposedly representing an ongoing discussion, another story about subjects' unfortunate embarrassment in discussing sex, a fake "screening device," and others. On closer scrutiny, however, it is apparent that these deceptions were interdependent elements in a single, consistent story. Each deceptive aspect of the setting enhanced the impact and/or plausibility of the independent and dependent variables and contributed to the coherence of the experiment.

The major problem presented by the hypothesis was that of justifying an initiation for admission to a group. This was solved by (1) the format of a sex discussion and (2) the cover story that the experimenters were interested in studying the dynamics of the discussion process. Combining these two aspects of the setting, one could (3) mention the fact that reticence about sex distorts the discussion process, so that (4) it is necessary to eliminate those people who are shy about sexual matters by (5) presenting the subjects with an embarrassment test.

All aspects of the setting led directly to the manipulation of the independent variable in a manner that made good sense to the subjects, thereby allaying any suspicion, while placing the emphasis of the study where it belonged: on the initiation. Moreover, this setting allowed the experimenter to use a tape-recorded group discussion (for the sake of control) while maintaining the fiction that it was an ongoing group discussion (for the sake of impact). The experimenter simply informed the subjects that some participants still found it difficult to talk about sex freely because the presence of others staring at them made them self-conscious. Therefore, to make it easier on the participants, they sat in separate cubicles and communicated through microphones and earphones.

The fiction of an already formed group served a dual function. Besides increasing the overall impact of the experiment, it allowed the experimenter to explain to the subjects that the members had been recruited before the initiation was made a requirement for admission. Conveying this information to the subjects eliminated a possible confounding variable, namely, that subjects might like the group better in the severe-initiation condition because of the feeling that they had all gone through the same harrowing experience.

Finally, because of the manner in which the cover story had been developed, the dependent variable—the evaluation of the group—seemed a very reasonable request. In many experimental contexts, obtaining a rating of attractiveness is difficult because it arouses suspicion. In this context, however, it was not jarring to a subject to be told that each member stated her opinion of each discussion session, and therefore it did not surprise the subject when she was asked for her frank evaluation of the proceedings of the meeting. Ultimately, the success of a general deception used to integrate various aspects of the experiment is an empirical question: Do the subjects find it plausible? In the Aronson-Mills experiment only one of the 64 subjects voiced any suspicion.

Another technique that has been suggested for increasing the effectiveness of an experimental deception is to delay debriefing until all subjects have participated in the experiment. There are several ethical objections to this procedure, and in general we do not feel that the risk to the well-being of the subjects is worth the potential gain in effectiveness. Moreover, the difference in effectiveness of the two techniques may be minimal, provided that the postexperimental debriefing is sensitive and thorough, so that the subject is aware of the gravity of the consequences of telling future subjects about the nature and details of the experiment (Aronson, 1966).

Besides taking these precautions to increase the probability that the deceptions used will be successful, the experimenter should also attempt to find out whether this goal was achieved in each instance. A good experimenter observes the subjects carefully during the session, looking for signs of skepticism, and during the postexperimental interview makes every effort to persuade them to voice any doubts about the veracity of any part of the procedure, and if they had any, what they thought was really going on. An alarming number of subjects may voice suspicion when strongly encouraged to do so, but if the deception has been successful, their descriptions of the nature of the deception and the true purpose of the experiment typically lapse into vague generalities. Once satisfied that the subjects have not actually seen through the specific deceptions used in this particular experiment, the experimenter can help the subjects save face by guiding them gradually toward the discovery of these deceptions and the purpose of the experiment.

SUMMARY

Throughout this chapter, we have sounded a simple yet important theme, one that is true for all varieties of psychological experimentation, but that is often ignored in other fields of psychology. Although important for all areas of psychology, it reaches its maximum salience for research in social psychology. That theme really just recognizes that the typical subject in psychological research is a thinking, problem-solving organism and that it is important that the subject is attending to the same problem (responding to a communication, learning a list of nonsense syllables, deciding whether X is an example of Y) that you are interested in studying. A "stage," or more generally an experimental setting and (sometimes deceptive) procedure, that does not ensure that the subject is concentrating on the same set of issues the experimenter is concerned about is doomed to failure.

CHAPTER 7

THE INDEPENDENT VARIABLE

In the preceding chapter we wrote of the problems and concerns addressed by experimenters as they attempt to find or create settings for conducting experiments. Once a suitable setting has been chosen or created, it is the task of the experimenter to translate the abstract causal construct in his or her hypothesis into a concrete set of operations—to administer the independent variable to subjects. In this chapter, we discuss the "nuts and bolts" of just how that is accomplished.

TYPES OF INDEPENDENT VARIABLES IN
SOCIAL PSYCHOLOGICAL EXPERIMENTS

A waitress in her mid-20's moved from table to table in a restaurant in a small southern town. At each table, she took orders, brought food and drinks to the patrons, left the bill and returned change to the customers after they had paid for their meals. When she returned to deliver change, the waitress approached the paying customer from the side or from slightly behind, leaned forward, and without making eye contact, said in a friendly yet firm tone, "Here's your change." She then left a blank survey that patrons were to complete and leave in an envelope on the table before they left the restaurant. Finally, once the customers had left, she returned to the table, secured the restaurant rating questionnaire, and collected her tip.

In fact, the waitress was a carefully trained and rehearsed confederate of April Crusco and Christopher Wetzel (1984), two experimenters interested in the effects of being touched. Throughout this field experiment, waitress-confederates served customers as they normally would. However, just prior to returning change, they randomly assigned customers to one of three experimental conditions: a no-touch control condition; a brief hand-touch condition; or a longer shoulder-touch condition. Because customers were randomly assigned to conditions at the *close* of their interactions with the waitress-confederates—blind to subjects' experimental condition until that point—only the touch manipulation differentiated customers from one another. Thus, the independent variable in this experiment was the nature of physical contact initiated by the waitress-confederates. Levels of the independent variable defined the conditions of the experiment. In this case, there were three: not touching the customer; touching only fleetingly on the hand; or touching on the shoulder.

We often begin by thinking of the independent variable at a more abstract conceptual level. There are several different types of relationships that can exist between the experiment's conceptual independent variable and the events that actually happen to a subject in the experiment. At the simplest level, as in the experiment on touching, the experimenter may be interested in a particular concrete variable for its own sake. The independent variable, the touch, was not a representation of some more abstract conceptual variable; instead, the concept and the event were so closely linked as to be almost identical. The study on touching may be viewed as the investigation of a simple stimulus-response relationship. The purpose of the experiment was to determine the effects of an external stimulus (touching) on subjects' responses (questionnaire service ratings and tipping). The studies of bystander intervention discussed earlier (Latané & Darley, 1968; Latané & Rodin, 1969) also exemplify this type of research. Here, the independent variable was the mere presence of other people in a situation in which the subject was faced with an emergency. There are relatively few difficulties involved in translating the idea of "presence of others" into an experiment treatment.

In the majority of social psychological experiments, the situation is more complicated. Consider the Asch (1951) experiment, in which the subject was faced with a unanimous majority who disagreed with him. Asch was not *specifically* interested in unanimous majorities of seven or eight people. Rather, he was interested in the broader, more abstract conceptual variable "group pressure," and the unanimous majority was the particular concrete event he chose as his empirical realization (Chapter 1) of the concept of group pressure. The particular event is taken as *representative* of the broad class of events that are included in the concept of group pressure. Other experimenters may use different, equally valid empirical realizations of the same conceptual variable. In Chapter 2 we discussed the relationship between conceptual variables and their empirical realizations in detail and noted that the experimenter's concerns are not solely with the specific realization of the independent variable being used in any particular experiment. Instead, the experimenter's interest may extend beyond the specific events contained in the particular empirical realization to include the whole class of events subsumed within the abstract category. Again, the experimenter is interested in a stimulus-response relationship, but the real "stimulus" of interest is much broader than the specific situation set up for the relationship, as shown in Figure 7-1.

The situation becomes still more complex when the investigator's hypothesis involves an internal stimulus variable that cannot be manipulated directly. For example, several researchers have been interested in studying the effects of guilt. Recall the field experiment of Regan, Williams, and Sparling (1972) described in Chapter 6, in which subjects were asked to take a confederate's picture at a shopping mall. Some subjects were induced to believe that they had broken his very expensive camera, and others were informed that the camera malfunctioned all the time and that they were not responsible. The subjects who believed they had broken the camera—the guilty subjects—subsequently helped a second confederate more than did the nonguilty control subjects.

The conceptual independent variable in this study was a feeling of guilt. That is to say, the experimenters were interested in comparing the behavior of subjects who felt guilty with the behavior of subjects who did not. Since it is impossible to vary the subject's internal state directly, the experimenter must use the indirect method of creating an external stimulus designed to bring about that state. Regan, Williams, and Sparling created a situation in which subjects were induced to take a photograph, and thus to break an expensive camera. They expected that subjects would react to this transgression with a feeling of guilt. The feeling of guilt was then expected to lead to differences in the subject's willingness to help another person.

As in the case of all studies involving a broad conceptual variable, the conceptual independent variable and its realization are not the same, and investigators are not particularly interested in the specific events involved in the stimulus situation, for example, as in the case above, destruction of a camera. In studies in which the conceptual variable is an abstract category of external stimulus events, such as "group pressure," the experimenter is interested in the particular events used only insofar as they are representative of the broad category. In studies in which the conceptual variable is an internal state

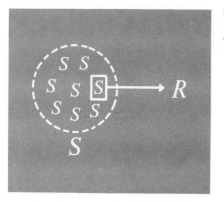

FIGURE 7-1
Independent variable as representative of
a class of variables.

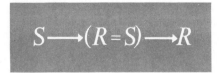

FIGURE 7-2
Conceptual independent variable as
an internal state.

such as guilt, the experimenter is not interested in the particular events except in terms of their success in arousing the internal state whose effects are to be studied. Theoretically, the external event produces the independent variable (internal event), and the independent variable produces the behavior.[1] Thus, there are two stimulus-response relationships involved: (1) The internal state (conceptual variable) is a *response* to the particular experimental situation, and (2) at the same time it is a *stimulus* for the dependent variable. These relationships are shown in Figure 7-2.

When internal states are of concern, the investigator is primarily interested in the *second* of these stimulus-response relationships; the first is merely a means of producing the stimulus for the second. Thus, in other studies designed to test the effects of guilt, a wide variety of methods for producing guilt has been used. Subjects have been induced to break an expensive piece of laboratory equipment (Wallace & Sadalla, 1966); to upset a graduate student's carefully ordered pile of index cards (Freedman, Wallington, & Bless, 1967); to give electric shocks to another subject (Carlsmith & Gross, 1969); to lie (Freedman, Wallington, & Bless, 1967); and to succeed on an experimental task because they had been tipped off to a trick for solving it (Carlsmith, Ellsworth, & Whiteside, 1968). None of these situations was particularly interesting to the experimenter for its own sake, but only as a means of inducing guilt. The conceptual variable guilt is the unifying factor tying these events to the experimental results.

In experiments involving the effects of an abstract conceptual variable, the investigator must face the difficult and complicated task of constructing an empirical realization that will represent the general concept or that will produce the desired state of mind in the subject. How can this be done? Unfortunately, there are few standard techniques. In social psychology, few experimental manipulations of the same conceptual variable are identical. The researcher must usually construct an experimental situation appropriate for the particular question or hypothesis, borrowing only bits and pieces from previous work. A situation that is appropriate for studying the effects of negative effort on liking for a group—as in the Aronson-Mills (1959) experiment—might not work if the experiment later wants to investigate the effects on liking for a color (Aronson, 1961) or liking for the whole experiment. As the experiment is modified to cre-

---

[1] Technically, the term "independent variable" refers only to the concrete manipulations or empirical realization involved. We use the term loosely, however, to include the conceptual independent variable and hope that the meaning will be clear in context.

ate a plausible situation in which to study these other questions, the experimental treatments will usually have to be modified to fit the new situations, as in the variety of guilt studies described above. Likewise, social psychological experiments depend so heavily on the special nature of the subculture under study that even those relatively standard procedures that *do* exist must often be altered drastically so that they make sense to the particular sample with which the experimenter is working.

The fact that subject populations differ across places and that populations change over time has been a source of criticism of experimental work in social psychology. For example, Kenneth Gergen (1973) contends that cultural groups differ from one another in terms of values, norms, and patterns of social behavior, making it impossible to make valid generalizations based on one or a few studies. He adds that the capriciousness of social phenomena—that is, temporal changes in the values, norms, and ways of behaving which characterize any given culture—also make the kind of broad, sweeping regularities sought by psychologists impossible to discover. Naturally, social phenomena vary across populations. For example, subjects far removed from academia might not appreciate the importance of knocking over an ordered pile of index cards. Similarly, a low score on an IQ test might not be a blow to their self-esteem. Subject populations can change over time, as well. If Aronson and Mills tried to replicate their severity-of-initiation study today using a new population of sophisticated, sexually liberated students, they might find that reading a passage from *Lady Chatterley's Lover* would not be embarrassing for their subjects and thus would no longer constitute a "severe" initiation; what is deemed a severe initiation or unpleasant at one point in time—say, by college women in the 1950s—might hardly raise an eyebrow in the 1990s.

However, the abstract conceptual variables (e.g. "severe" initiation or "unpleasant effort") change only in the sense that experimenters might need to consider alternative *specific empirical realizations* of a construct as social phenomena differ across populations, or as they change with the passage of time. Although concrete *manifestations* of abstract constructs may vary as a function of time or locale, relationships between or among the constructs *themselves* may be far less variable. From a broad perspective, it is trivial that concrete manifestations of such concepts as "cohesiveness," "guilt," "aggression," "altruism," "self-esteem," "conformity pressure," or whatever might vary as a function of different subject populations or of temporal changes. But because these manifestations frequently *do* change, it is of *practical* importance to the experimenter and makes it of little use to outline *specific* techniques for experimentally varying such abstract concepts: There is no "Top 10" list for producing a good mood, for example. Of course, in the short run treatments that have been successful can often be reused, and when circumstances permit the use of a situation and subject population similar to those used in other experiments, it is a good idea to try using the same procedure, rather than thinking up a whole new idiosyncratic treatment. When an established technique can be used, it is much easier to integrate the experimental findings with those of other experiments in the same area. When a new method is introduced, it is sometimes difficult to assess the extent to which the results are a function of procedural changes rather than of the real conceptual differences the experimenter has in mind. In designing an experiment, the investigator should read other people's research on the same topic and use the same or similar techniques when appropriate. Often, however, the investigator will not find a good method that fits the problem. What we hope to be able to do in this chapter is to provide some general guidelines, some rules of thumb, some intuitions, and some recommendations which may serve to direct an experimenter toward a sensible and effective empirical realization of the independent variable.

Our discussion of the ways in which independent variables may be realized rests heavily on the use of deception. In Chapters 3 and 6 we discussed many of the ethical and methodological issues involved in the use of deception. The focus on such techniques in this chapter should not be construed as an indication of a preference for deceptive techniques. Rather, it will become apparent that procedural difficulties are often compounded when deception is used, and thus it becomes necessary to devote considerable discussion to those difficulties and some ways around them. Conversely, a lengthy discussion is hardly in order to describe how to experimentally vary the size of a group between two and eight, for example.

THE BASIC REQUIREMENT: RANDOMIZED ASSIGNMENT

The first and most important guideline has already been suggested in our discussion of the nature of an experiment in Chapter 1. If we are to carry out an experiment that allows for causal inferences, we must determine which treatment each subject gets by the principle of randomization. If chance determines who gets which treatment, we know that any differences we observe are due to differences in the treatments, not to preexisting differences between or among subjects who were assigned to the various conditions.

In most laboratory experiments, random assignment of subjects to conditions is relatively easy to achieve by flipping a coin, rolling dice, or more commonly, consulting a table of random numbers. And in some field experiments, it is likewise relatively easy to assign subjects to conditions at random, to determine, for example, whether to touch a specific customer in a restaurant or whether to stare at a specific driver.

In some rare situations field researchers may safely forgo random assignment and rely instead on the haphazard distribution of naturally occurring events to serve as real-life analogs of controlled experimental designs. For example, Stanley Parker, Marilynn Brewer, and Janie Spencer (1980) conducted a study on the effects of a natural disaster, a devastating brush fire that swept through a Southern California community, on the premise that the hit-or-miss pattern of destruction caused by the fire was essentially the product of a "natural randomization" process. Among the homes in close proximity at the height of the fire, only chance factors—changes in wind direction and velocity, location of the fire-fighting equipment, traffic congestion, and so on—determined which homes were burned to the ground and which were intact when the fire was finally brought under control. Thus, homeowners who were victims of the fire were essentially equivalent to those who were more fortunate, and any group differences in attitudes and perceptions following the fire could safely be attributed to the differential experience of the "natural" administration of the independent variable. Of course, in such "experiments," the burden of proof is on the investigator to make a convincing case that subjects were unlikely to differ systematically on relevant variables *prior* to the event. For example, if stone houses survived the fire and wooden houses burned down, we could not be so sure that differences between the victims and the nonvictims were due to the fire; as with the Three Little Pigs, people who choose to live in stone houses may be more practical, safety-conscious, or perhaps neurotic than their happy-go-lucky neighbors in wooden houses.

Whatever the setting of an experiment, the randomization requirement may seem obvious, but in practice any one of a number of considerations can lure the experimenter into forgetting about it, thereby defeating the purpose of doing an *experimental* study in the first place. It is to these considerations to which we now turn.

Individual Differences as "Independent Variables"

The most common pitfall occurs when the independent variable is something that we feel is already a characteristic of the person (a "subject variable"), and so we do not try to vary it experimentally. Instead, we measure it and then look at differences between people with widely separated scores on our measure. For example, if we are concerned with differences in performance between subjects with high self-confidence and those with low self-confidence, we might measure self-confidence in a sample of people and then compare the performance of the high-scoring subjects with that of the low-scoring subjects. This of course is a correlational study, even though it may be conducted in the laboratory with a high degree of control over the subsequent measures. As a correlational study, it suffers from the indigenous weakness already mentioned: One cannot know whether differences in the subjects' behavior are *caused* by differences in self-confidence. Self-confident subjects differ from self-doubting subjects in many ways, any one of which might cause the observed differences in their behavior (see Chapter 1).

We are not suggesting that individual differences do not exist; anyone who has ever tried to persuade an "introverted" friend to attend a large, raucous party is confronted with the difference between someone who is introverted and someone who is extraverted. Neither are we suggesting that such differences are unimportant in a scientific sense. Many investigators are interested in exactly these kinds of differences.[2] Our purpose here is just to make clear once again the distinction between experiments in which the table of random numbers decides which subject gets which treatment and studies in which something or somebody else makes that decision: studies in which individual differences are manipulated versus studies in which they are taken "as is."

Often, variables such as test scores, sex, age, and class are included in a study in which the main focus is an experimentally controlled independent variable. When used in conjunction with random assignment, evidence about individual differences can add to the precision of the experiment. Here, the purpose is not to look at the *effects* of these subject variables but simply to measure them to determine the *generality* of the effects of the true independent variable *or* to decrease the unexplained (error) variability in the experiment. For example, recall from Chapter 4 that Helmreich, Aronson, and LeFan (1970) conducted an experiment designed to explore the generality of the finding that very competent people are liked better when they commit some kind of "humanizing" blunder or pratfall (Aronson, Willerman, & Floyd, 1966). As in the original experiment, the investigators *manipulated* the competence of the stimulus person by showing a videotape recording of an interview in which the stimulus person's answers to questions showed him to be either a top student with many honors and a wide variety of successes, or a dull student with no honors and a wide variety of failures. They also manipulated the stimulus person's experience of a pratfall, by showing half the subjects in each condition a sequence in which the person accidentally spilled a cup of hot coffee all over himself. In addition to the two manipulated variables, the experimenters *measured* the subjects' self-esteem. They found that the pratfall increased liking for the competent stimulus person only when the subjects had average levels of self-esteem. Subjects with very high or very low self-esteem liked the competent person better when his perfection was unmarred by a blunder. Thus, the authors learned that the generality of the original finding was limited to subjects of average self-confidence, and this refinement in their knowledge about the applicability of the "pratfall effect" led to new and interesting hypotheses about the phenomenon. In this experiment, of course, we would not claim that low (or high) self-esteem *caused* the subjects to reject the blundering hero; we can make no inferences about self-esteem as a causal variable. Statements about causality can be made only when the independent variable consists of treatments that are randomly assigned to subjects.

But what if we are interested in the effects of some subject variable? Do we have to resort to a nonexperimental method and give up the chance to make causal statements? In many cases it is possible to effect a temporary change,

[2] For example, the extensive literature on sex differences and research in this area is important and interesting. However, the problems of drawing causal inferences from such research have been reemphasized by the women's movement: Observed "sex differences" may be due to differences in upbringing, education, social pressures, the relationship between the experimenter and the subject, or any other number of experiential factors.

even in relatively important personality characteristics, through the judicious use of an experimental treatment. Ordinarily, one can influence such habitual modes of responding for only a short period of time and in only one small area, but that may be enough for the purposes of testing the hypothesis involved.

For example, Aronson and David Mettee (1968) varied subjects' self-concept experimentally, so that they could assign subjects at random to "high," "medium," and "low," self-esteem conditions. They did this by giving the subjects a set of personality tests at the first session of an experiment and giving them false feedback about their personality at the beginning of the second session. When they arrived at the second session, the subjects read evaluations of their total personality, supposedly based on the tests they had taken. Some received very positive assessments, some very negative assessments, and some were told that their tests had not yet been evaluated. Thus, subjects entered the real experiment (the second session) with temporarily induced high, "unaltered," or low self-esteem, based on personality-test feedback. They were then subjected to a situation where it was worth their while to cheat in a game of cards. Since the levels of self-esteem were under the control of the experimenters and were randomly assigned, the experimenters were able to conclude that the differences in self-esteem *caused* differences in the subjects' cheating behavior. Thus, when it turned out that subjects in the low self-esteem condition were more likely to cheat at a card game than were subjects in the high or medium self-esteem conditions, the experimenters could conclude that the low self-esteem treatment caused cheating. Had they relied on a personality measure, it could easily have been the case that unknown factors that *produce* low self-esteem *also produce* cheating.

Performing an Internal Analysis

Nonrandom assignment of subjects to experimental conditions is not confined to the use of personality measures in lieu of experimental treatments. It often takes place in more subtle ways, one of the most common occurring when the experimenter is forced to perform an **internal analysis** in order to make sense out of the data. Such a situation arises when the experiment apparently did not "work." The experimenter has assigned subjects randomly to treatments, but finds that when the dependent variable is measured, subjects in the two conditions do not behave differently as predicted. But suppose that besides measuring the dependent variable, the experimenter has had the foresight to provide a separate measure designed to find out whether the experimental treatment succeeded in producing the internal state that constituted the conceptual variable. This measure, often called a **manipulation check**, provides the experimenter with important information.

For example, suppose that the experimenter wants to study the effects of anxiety on ability to concentrate. In the design, the experimenter might want the treatment in one condition to make the subjects anxious and that in the other condition to keep them calm. In addition to measuring the subjects' ability to concentrate (the dependent variable), the experimenter includes a measure of anxiety to determine the success of the procedure. Now, suppose that in conducting the experiment, the experimenter finds that subjects in the "anxious" condition and those in the "nonanxious" condition exhibit no differences in ability to concentrate. The experimenter can return to the measure of anxiety and find out whether the anxiety-producing procedure was successful, that is, whether the subjects in the anxious condition show more anxiety than do those in the nonanxious condition on this measure. If there are no differences in anxiety (as measured by the manipulation check), the experimenter concludes that the anxiety-producing procedure was unsuccessful. Because no differences in anxiety were produced, the experimenter can hardly expect the dependent variable to show differences. That is, no differences in ability to concentrate can be expected between the subjects who were supposedly made anxious and those who were not.

In such a case, experimenters often reanalyze their data, using the subjects' responses on the manipulation check as a substitute for the independent variable. That is, subjects who appear to have been made anxious in the experiment (regardless of whether the experimenter tried to *make* them so) are considered to belong to one condition (high anxiety); those who did not become anxious, to the other (low anxiety). The experimenter *now* predicts that the dependent variable measure will differ significantly between these two reconstituted groups of subjects. This is an internal analysis.

Let us pursue this example. The experimenter attempts to vary the extent of anxiety experienced by the subjects and then measures their ability to concentrate on some test. The measure of concentration is the number of problems the subject finishes on a concentration test composed of 10 problems. The data are shown in Table 7-1.

Clearly, there are no differences between the two conditions in ability to concentrate as measured by the number of problems subjects successfully completed. But suppose that the experimenter has conducted a manipulation check, asking the subjects to rate how anxious they felt on a scale from 0 (no

TABLE 7-1
NUMBER OF PROBLEMS COMPLETED BY SUBJECTS RANDOMLY
ASSIGNED TO HIGH-ANXIOUS AND LOW-ANXIOUS CONDITIONS

Subject	High-anxiety condition	Subject	Low-anxiety condition
1	5	6	2
2	10	7	2
3	2	8	8
4	3	9	9
5	10	10	9
Total completed	30		30
Average	6		6

TABLE 7-2
RESULTS OF MANIPULATION CHECK, BASED ON
SUBJECTS' SELF-REPORTED ANXIETY RATING

Subject	High-anxiety condition	Subject	Low-anxiety condition
1	3	6	3
2	1	7	2
3	2	8	0
4	3	9	0
5	0	10	1

anxiety) to 3 (very high anxiety). The results of the manipulation check are given in Table 7-2.

It is apparent that the treatment designed to produce anxiety was not very effective. Although the overall level of anxiety in the high-anxiety condition is higher than it is in the low-anxiety condition, some subjects who were given the treatment designed to keep them calm (low-anxiety condition) are actually more anxious than some who were given the high-anxiety treatment. The experimenter reasons, in effect, "Well, my treatments didn't work very well, but my *hypothesis* about anxiety and concentration may still be true." So the experimenter now divides the subjects into two new groups, placing those who scored high (anxiety rating of 2 or 3) on the manipulation check in one group and those who scored low (0 or 1) in another group, and performs the internal analysis shown in Table 7-3.

When one looks at the results of the internal analysis of these data, anxiety *does* seem to be related to ability to concentrate. Such data can be useful and provocative, but statements about causality should be approached cautiously. Indeed, since the effect was not due to the experimental variable, no causal statement can be made. Some of the "highly anxious" subjects may have been made so by the anxiety manipulation, but clearly others were anxious for other

TABLE 7-3
INTERNAL ANALYSIS TO TEST HYPOTHESIS ABOUT ANXIETY AND CONCENTRATION

Subjects with high scores on anxiety test			Subjects with low scores on anxiety test		
Subject	Problems completed	Anxiety rating	Subject	Problems completed	Anxiety rating
1	5	3	2	10	1
3	2	2	5	10	0
4	3	3	8	8	0
6	2	3	9	9	1
7	2	2	10	9	0
Total	14			46	
Average	2.8			9.2	

reasons. Since people who become anxious easily may be different from people who do not, we are dealing with a set of unknown variables. We don't know what made the subject check a 0 or 1 instead of a 2 or a 3 on the anxiety scale (it certainly wasn't the anxiety manipulation), and thus we don't know what was responsible for the subject's performance on the test. If the manipulation check was given at the end of the experiment, it is possible that subjects who realized that they weren't getting many of the problems done *became* anxious about being so slow. In this case, the direction of causality would be the reverse of that proposed by the experimenter; instead of anxiety causing poor performance, poor performance is causing anxiety. We have no way of knowing. The fact that the experimenter *once* assigned subjects to treatments at random is irrelevant: The current analysis is not based on that assignment, but rather on a *measured* subject variable, and thus it is a *correlational study*. The experimenter may find that the results of this internal analysis are encouraging enough to warrant a new experiment on the relationship between anxiety and concentration, this time using a more forceful manipulation of anxiety. The internal analysis is useful, since it provides such suggestive information. Until the second experiment has actually been conducted and the predicted results obtained, however, the experimenter is not justified in making causal claims about the effect of anxiety on concentration.

It should be noted that the useful function performed by an internal analysis—suggesting new hypotheses and interpretations of the data—is not limited to experiments in which the manipulation is a failure. In a successful experiment the results of an internal analysis may lead to qualifications of the main results, suggestions about the principles of operation of the variables involved, hypotheses for further experiments, or even assurance that some potentially confounding variable is irrelevant. A provocative discussion of these phenomena is given by Lee Cronbach (1975). In some cases an internal analysis can indicate how likely it is that a manipulated personality variable duplicates the effects of the corresponding "real" personality variable. For example, in the Aronson-Mettee (1968) study, the experimenters manipulated self-esteem through false feedback from personality tests and found that low self-esteem led to more cheating. In addition to manipulating self-esteem, however, the authors had a *measure* of self-esteem from one of the personality tests that the subjects had taken during the first session. They found that subjects whose personality test scores actually *did* indicate low self-esteem tended to behave like subjects who were placed in the "low" condition on the basis of false feedback. Similarly, subjects with high "chronic" self-esteem tended to behave like subjects with high "manipulated" self-esteem. Thus, by performing an internal analysis, the experimenters gained additional information which increased their confidence that it was really self-esteem that was being affected by the personality-feedback treatments. This illustrates another function for internal correlations using a measured subject variable: providing support for the experimenter's conceptual definition of a manipulated variable.

Allowing Subjects to Choose Their Own Conditions

Another situation in which treatments are assigned nonrandomly occurs when subjects assign themselves to the experimental condition: **self-selection**. In certain experimental situations the subject is given a choice about what to do. The experimenter then compares the subsequent behavior of subjects who choose one alternative with that of subjects who choose the other. For example, in an experiment designed to study how moral attitudes change after people have been exposed to a temptation to cheat, Judson Mills (1958) gave sixth-grade subjects a test as part of a "contest" in a situation in which it was either very easy or very difficult to cheat. It turned out that there were honest subjects and cheaters in all the conditions and that their attitudes about cheating differed after the contest was over. Since the subjects had not been assigned to conditions by the experimenter but rather decided for themselves whether or not to cheat, it is impossible to say that cheating *caused* differences in their attitude change. If this had been all there was to the experiment, the results would not have been very useful; there may in fact be important differences between those who choose to cheat and those who do not. In relinquishing control of the situation to the subjects, the experimenter is left with a nonexperimental study.

Curiously, the problem of choice is a particularly sticky one, since several interesting questions in social psychology involve hypotheses about the effects of making a decision. To study these questions, it is obviously important to give the subjects a perception of free choice, for if they think that their decisions are made for them by the experimenter, their behavior will not be relevant to the basic question. Yet the perception of choice must remain nothing more than a perception, for as soon as the subjects take advantage of it, we are beset by the problem of nonrandom assignment.

In some experimental situations this problem can be solved by using *instructions* that create a perception of choice, although little choice is actually present. For example, one might wait to present some of the drawbacks of a choice until after the subject has made an irrevocable decision. In presenting the negative aspects of the chosen alternative, the experimenter can often create a strong impression that any reasonably intelligent person would have been aware of these drawbacks and that, in fact, hardly any other subjects chose that alternative.

A different solution to this problem is to explore the situation and to pilot-test until finding a level of a variable just sufficient to inhibit subjects from actually choosing a "wrong" behavior. For example, in the experiment by Aronson and Carlsmith (1963) in which children were given either a mild threat or a severe threat to prevent them from playing with a desirable toy, it was important that the threat be strong enough, even in the mild condition, so that no children actually played with the forbidden toy. However, the threat could not be too strong, since the experimental hypothesis hinged on the child's not having a terribly good reason for leaving the toy alone. The situation had to be such that although making a choice about whether to play, the child would always end up choosing not to play and would be bothered by the lack of a good reason for this choice. It is sometimes possible to find such a level by careful pretesting.

Such pretesting can also be used to create situations that will reliably elicit any kind of behavior the experimenter wishes to study; it is not limited to studies in which choice is the independent variable in the experiment. Carlsmith, Ellsworth, and Jane Whiteside (1968) conducted an experiment in which subjects who were about to take an experimental test were "tipped off" by a confederate; that is, the confederate told them how to do well on the test. The independent variable was confession; the experimenters were interested in whether subjects who confessed to having heard about the experiment would still show the compliance effect reported in other studies of guilt. Thus, the experimenters wanted subjects in one condition to confess that they knew the trick and subjects in the other condition not to confess. After extensive pretesting, the experimenters found a situation which invariably induced confessions. Since they were interested in the effects of confession itself rather than in the *decision* to confess, it was easy to arrange a no-confession condition: The experimenters simply left the room before the subject had a chance to confess. Coarse tactics (like leaving the room) are often useful when the independent variable involves some interpersonal behavior which the experimenter wants to elicit in one condition and to prevent in another condition. The experimenter simply removes the opportunity.

CREATING AN EMPIRICAL REALIZATION OF THE INDEPENDENT VARIABLE

An experimenter has three major questions when trying to construct an empirical realization of the independent variable. First, what specific event should be used for the treatment in the experiment? Second, how should this event be presented so as to have maximum impact on the subject, and how does the experimenter know whether the intended impact has been achieved? Third, if the predicted results are such that they could be spuriously achieved by "cooperating" subjects (or distorted by uncooperative subjects), how does the experimenter keep the subjects from guessing what effect the independent variable is supposed to have on their behavior?

There are two general classes of experimental treatments; the empirical realization can consist of (1) a set of instructions to the subject or (2) an "event" to which the subject is exposed. In practice, these two techniques are not always separable; they usually blend into each other. Most "event" manipulations contain verbal instructions to the subject, at least as a means of setting the stage. In experiments in which the independent variable is manipulated by means of instructions, the instruction often consists of a description of events that might happen to the subject. Nevertheless, it is useful to separate the two techniques conceptually. A good illustration of the manipulation of an independent variable primarily through the use of instructions is to be found in well-known "group cohesiveness" experiments conducted by Leon Festinger and his colleagues (for example, Back, 1951; Festinger & Thibaut, 1951; Schachter, 1951). In these experiments the cohesiveness of a group was varied by informing the subject that the group members were especially selected so that they would like one another (high cohesiveness) or that, despite repeated attempts, the experimenter was unable to accomplish this feat (low cohesiveness).

In contrast, were such an experiment to be carried out by an experimenter who wished to avoid instructions and instead present the subject with a vivid "event," we would expect minimal verbal description. Instead, a group of confederates would agree with any opinion voiced by the subject, approve any actions, and express effusive positive regard at every turn. Another subject, of course, would be disagreed with, disapproved of, and disliked by a set of confederates well trained in this unpleasant task.

Theoretically, the difference between the two techniques is intimately tied up with the issue of control versus impact. Typically, when things happen to a subject, we have much less control over them and much less confidence in how to interpret the subject's reactions than we do when we read instructions. However, it is almost always the case that events that happen during the course of an experiment will have a far greater impact on a subject than will a mere set of instructions. The crux of the problem is illustrated by the following example: Stating that a person and the other members of a group will like each other is almost certain to have less impact than presenting the person with real people doing likeable things. But can we be sure that our subjects will interpret these behaviors as likeable? Will they assume that the others like them? Once again, we find that the choice between two approaches is neither absolute nor easy. Both techniques have advantages, and the experimenter must choose the one that better fits the particular problem. Finally, the experimenter's choice is likely to be a combination of both. Below we try to accentuate the distinction and point to important considerations for each technique.

Instructions

The investigator who chooses to use instructions must attempt to make them interesting and forceful, since instructions are usually weak in impact. *First*, the experimenter must make sure that the instructions command the subject's attention; the subject whose mind is on other things may never even attend to the manipulation. The experimenter should speak clearly and emphatically, maintain eye contact with the subject, and pause to let the important points sink in.

Second, the experimenter should ask questions to make sure that the subject has understood the essential features of the manipulation. If deception is involved, this may be a delicate task, since the experimenter must ask the questions and get the relevant information without revealing the purpose of the experiment.

Third, it is a good idea, when possible, to set up a situation in which the subject *must* understand the instructions in order to know what to do in the rest of the experiment. That way, the subject will be motivated to understand the instructions, and the behavior of one who doesn't comprehend instructions will reveal the misunderstanding to the experimenter in the rest of the experiment. The importance of motivating subjects to attend to and understand task instructions cannot be overestimated, especially in judgment studies in which instructions are often designed to direct subjects' attention to the relevant dimensions of the stimuli presented to them. Unless subjects are alert and attentive, and motivated to stay that way, all the care and effort devoted to systematic control over stimulus conditions will have been wasted.

Fourth, instructions should be kept simple. Complicated instructions are more likely to lead to variability in the subjects' interpretations and may also make it more difficult for the experimenter to know what aspects of the instructions constitute the effective stimulus. The experimenter who is manipulating several independent variables in the same experiment should try to avoid putting more than one manipulation into the instructions; instructions containing several manipulations are almost certain to be more complicated and difficult to absorb than those containing only a single manipulation. Instructions, like other types of treatment, can be pretested and revised in order to increase their clarity and impact and reduce the variability of the subjects' interpretations.

Sometimes the impact of an instructional manipulation can be increased by preparing the subject for it beforehand. For example, in the group-cohesiveness experiments mentioned above, the subjects were told upon recruitment about the experimenters' effort to create highly cohesive groups and were asked to answer some questions which would enable the experimenters to place them in a group whose other members had similar interests. The answers to the questions were not used, but presumably this advance information served to pique a subject's interest in the composition of his or her particular group and to render more plausible the instructional treatment that took place during the actual experiment.

Another way to make sure that the subject is attending to a verbal treatment is to put the manipulation in the form of false feedback about an event that he or she has already experienced in the course of the experiment. Individual subjects can be told that they have scored high or low on a test they have taken, that opinions they have already expressed agree with those of another subject, and so on. Groups can be given false results of secret balloting or can be told that their interaction has been high or low on some dimension (cooperation, quality of performance on a group task, inhibition, etc.). Here, an event is used to get the subjects involved, so that a verbal treatment (presumably based on the event) will have greater impact.

An experimental treatment of this sort falls somewhere on the continuum between simple verbal instructions and the construction of an "event." The main drawback of this technique is that the report may not be plausible to the subject, who may have had different experiences with the event. A subject who cannot solve more than one or two of the questions on a test is unlikely to believe she received a high score; similarly, a subject who sits frowning and taciturn on the fringe of a group is not likely to believe a vote indicating that she is the most popular member of the group. The experimenter should try to make the event ambiguous enough so that the subject is deprived of information that could contradict the false feedback.

For example, in one experiment Lee Ross, Mark Lepper, and Michael Hubbard (1975) gave subjects the task of discriminating between fake suicide notes and notes actually written by people who had attempted suicide. Because the subjects had little experience with similar tasks and no clear definition of the requisite skills, and because there was no way of telling whether one's guesses were correct or incorrect, it was easy to convince the subjects that they succeeded or failed at the task, much easier than it would have been if the experimenter had tried to give false feedback based on a more objective or familiar test, such as an IQ test.

Events

We used the term "events" in connection with the independent variable as if events are all more or less alike. This is not the case. Sometimes an event is something that *happens to* subjects: A confederate attacks subjects' philosophy of life; subjects inadvertently break a camera or blow up an expensive piece of equipment; they are stared at or touched; their perceptions are called into question by a unanimous majority; they are threatened with an electric shock; and so on. Other times, events are far less personally involving and far more benign: Subjects read newspaper headlines; they watch a videotape in which someone spills coffee on himself; they see another person's answers to an attitude survey; they look at cartoons and rate how funny they are; and so on.

One dimension on which these events can be ordered is that of impact on one end and control on the other. Of course, one characteristic of a "dimension" is that events can fall anywhere along a continuum. For example, at what point does group pressure cease to matter much to subjects? When members of a unanimous majority disagree with subjects' judgments and berate them for their stupidity face-to-face? When subjects hear the voices of the majority over an intercom? When a series of flashing lights communicates the majority's disagreement? When subjects are handed a note summarizing discrepant judgments of the unanimous majority? At what point will these stimuli fail to capture and hold subjects' attention?

In current social psychological research, particularly the "judgment" studies carried out by psychologists interested in attribution and social cognition, subjects frequently make judgments about written descriptions of hypothetical people or events, rather than events they experience directly. Control is high, impact is low, and researchers are faced with a troublesome problem: The way people reason about hypothetical events may differ from the way they reason about real ones.

Not all social cognition research uses simple verbal stimuli and paper-and-pencil measures. Throughout the history of social psychology, research styles have ranged from highly controlled, relatively unrealistic "pure" techniques to noisy, involving techniques high in experimental realism. The Hovland attitude change group relied heavily on written communication and paper-and-pencil measures; La Piere studied attitudes by traveling around the country with a Chinese couple and attempting to register at hotels. Likewise, although many judgment studies rely on vignettes, it is possible and often preferable to study social cognition using high-impact events.

Lee Ross, David Greene, and Pamela House (1977), for example, asked subjects to read descriptions of hypothetical situations and to indicate which of two responses they would make. They found that people see whichever choice they make as relatively common. The authors termed this the "false consensus" effect. People also believe that making the other choice reveals quite a bit about a person's personality, while their own choice (the "normal" choice) is not particularly revealing of personal disposition.

So far, the study was like many social cognition studies, a paper-and-pencil study of responses to hypothetical situations. The subjects never really had to choose between two alternatives. In a follow-up study, the experimenter told subjects that he was interested in attitude change and "communication techniques," and asked them to exit the building wearing a large sandwich-board sign with the painted message "Eat at Joe's" and to observe people's reactions. Some subjects agreed to do it; others did not. The results replicated those of the first study: Subjects who agreed to wear the sign thought that 62 percent of those who were asked would agree; subjects who refused thought that 67 percent would refuse. Those who agreed made inferences about the kind of person (up-tight, humorless) who would refuse; those who refused made inferences about the kind of person (attention-grabbing, frivolous) who would agree. The realistic second study convincingly demonstrates that the false consensus effect is not unique to paper-and-pencil games, but occurs when people really commit themselves to decisions. As Lee Ross argues, "[The] cost of procedures that simultaneously eliminate both realism and noise are ... formidable. One loses the capacity to produce theories and empirical generalizations that are not merely 'correct,' but also powerful relative to competing processes, i.e., theories and generalizations likely to be useful in the goals of understanding, predicting, and controlling behavior in real social contexts"(Ross, 1987, p. 143).

In recent years, experimenters have made increasing use of interactive microcomputers. Such microcomputers are frequently used to present stimuli to subjects and to record their responses. Not only does such technology improve the precision with which the stimuli can be varied and with which subjects' responses can be recorded, but it also makes for a more interesting, vivid and engaging task for subjects.

Throughout the remainder of this section, we devote out attention to experimental events which fall toward the impact end of the continuum. This is *not* to say that experiments in which "events" are verbal stimuli are not valuable and important tools for understanding social behavior. It *is* to say that because impactful events or "strong" manipulations that happen to subjects are often complex and more difficult to "pull off" successfully, there are more problems and methodological concerns associated with their use. That being the case, it seems prudent to provide a more extensive discussion of ways in which these events can be implemented, always with an eye toward enabling experimenters to infer valid causal relationships between empirical realizations of the independent variable and some effect of those realizations.

Often, we favor the use of an event rather than a set of instructions, despite the problems posed by the difficulty of interpretation. The meaning of an event can often be ascertained through the process of systematic replication, whereby different events with overlapping meanings can be used to test the same hypothesis in different experiments. In addition, it is often possible to increase the likelihood that a subject will arrive at the intended interpretation of the event. Sometimes this can be accomplished through the skillful combination of events and instructions. An example is an experiment by David Landy and Aronson (1968) in which the investigators wanted to find out if people react more strongly to personal evaluations if they regard the evaluator as a "discerning" person. The authors predicted that subjects who are evaluated positively by a discerning confederate should like the confederate better than if he were not discerning. However, subjects who are evaluated negatively by a discerning confederate should dislike the confederate more than if he were not discerning. In other words, they were predicting an interaction between type of feedback (positive versus negative) and the confederate's power of discernment (discerning versus not discerning). How does one vary the subjects' perception of the confederate's discernment? One could do it by instructions; that is, one could simply say to the subject, "Say, by the way, this fellow is really a discerning person; I thought you might be interested." But for reasons of credibility, the investigators felt that it would be better to allow the subject to arrive at this judgment independently. They therefore started out by having the confederate perform a task in the presence of the subject; the task was such that by varying the confederate's behavior, the subject might easily be induced to regard the confederate as either discerning or not discerning.

The word "might" epitomizes the problem of manipulating events. The subject *might* interpret this behavior in a multitude of ways. In order to maximize the likelihood that the subject would consider this behavior relevant to discernment and nothing else, the investigators: (1) asked the subject to observe the confederate's behavior on a task (in the context of an experiment on social judgment); (2) told the subject that "degree of discernment" was an aspect of the confederate's behavior that was of particular interest to them; (3)

asked the subject to rate the confederate's discernment; (4) informed the subject exactly how the confederate's behavior might reflect either high or low discernment; (5) had the confederate behave either one way or the other; (6) had a handy and meaningful check on the manipulation, in the form of the subject's actual rating. It can readily be seen that this technique is a compromise. It may lack the impact of obscene words or electric shock, but it has more impact than does a set of instructions. At the same time, it capitalizes on the easy interpretability of verbal instructions by focusing the subject's attention on the variable (discernment) that the experimenter wants to manipulate. In effect, Landy and Aronson told the subjects in advance what the event would mean and then created the event, giving it the clarity of a set of verbal instructions, but without sacrificing the impact characteristic of event manipulations.

One advantage of events over instructions is apparent when we consider the problem of subjects' becoming aware of our hypothesis and allowing this awareness to influence their behavior. For many experiments in social psychology, the ideal empirical realization of an independent variable is an event that the subject does not connect with the experiment at all. This is the best way to guarantee that the subject has no hypothesis of concern to the experimenter. Frequently, it is also the best way to guarantee that the manipulation has an impact on the subject. For example, a subject told that a particular communication was written by T. S. Eliot (Aronson, Turner, & Carlsmith, 1963) may yawn and ignore this information or, even more important, may have the detachment to sit back, look at the ceiling, and begin to hypothesize that the experimenter is concerned with the effect of a high-prestige communicator. For this reason, the manipulation is a relatively weak one. But consider a subject faced with a person to whom he has been delivering electric shocks who is now screaming, beating on the walls, and begging to be let out of the room (Milgram, 1973); consider a subject who has a dozen wires attaching him to an apparatus that has suddenly short-circuited, so that it looks as though he may be in danger of being electrocuted (Ax, 1953); consider a subject who has just broken someone else's expensive camera (Regan, Williams, & Sparling, 1972); consider a subject who, to his dismay, discovers that a group of normal-looking people all judge the length of a line differently than he does (Asch, 1951). These subjects are very unlikely to yawn or to start playing intellectual games; they have a problem of their own—for example, what to do about this poor fellow who is screaming in the next room.

Several classes of techniques have been used successfully to present the independent variable as an event unrelated to the experiment, so as to have a maximum impact on the subject. Not perceiving them as part of the experiment, the subject will not speculate about their purpose or their relationship to the experimenter's hypothesis. Many experiments have actually used a combination of several of these techniques.

The Accident   Perhaps the most effective of these techniques, but one of the most difficult to set up, is the "accident." An experiment by Albert Ax (1953), designed to compare the physiological reactions characteristic of fear and anger, provides one of the best examples of this procedure. The subjects believed that the experiment was designed to study metabolic differences between hypertensives and normals and that all they had to do was lie on a mattress and listen to music while their physiological responses were being measured. In the fear condition, while the subject was lying there with leads from the recording apparatus attached to his ear, leg, chest, abdomen, face, and fingers, one of the finger electrodes "accidentally" began to emit shocks that gradually became stronger. When the subject spoke to the experimenter about the shocks the experimenter expressed alarm and acted as though the situation was out of control, pushing a lever which caused sparks to fly from the apparatus near the subject and exclaiming in confusion that there appeared to be a dangerous short-circuit in the system. This procedure enabled the experimenter to produce fear without its being blunted by the subject's knowledge of being in a protected environment. From the subject's point of view, the "accident" occurred outside of the context of the preplanned experiment and thus retained the impact and unpredictability of a real-world event.

Another ingenious example of the accident technique comes from the experiment by John Wallace and Edward Sadalla (1966), in which the subjects worked on a task that involved a large, expensive looking machine. During the course of the experiment, a confederate induced the subject to push a forbidden button labeled "Do Not Touch" on the experimental apparatus, whereupon the machine exploded and appeared to be totally destroyed. Festinger and Carlsmith (1959) used a similar technique when they told the subject that due to an accident, the regular confederate had not shown up and then asked the subject to play the role of the confederate. Indeed, the "accident" procedure has been used so frequently and so successfully that it might be said that part of being a good experimental social psychologist involves learning how to say "whoops" convincingly.

The Confederate   A variation on the accident procedure is to use a confederate who introduces the manipulation of the independent variable. Once the confederate has been carefully trained to produce a convincing performance, this procedure may be easier to carry out than the accident technique. Like the accident technique, however, the introduction of the independent variable by confederates may arouse suspicion in some cases. In one experiment by Aronson and Darwyn Linder (1965), the subject heard herself being evaluated by the confederate in the context of a verbal-reinforcement experiment. This was described to the subjects as a standard part of the procedure. Although it succeeded for most subjects, a few found it odd that such personal material would be used to measure the effects of reinforcement on verbal behavior. Thus, impact and credibility are not automatically achieved by the simple introduction of a confederate into the procedure.

Often, it can be made to appear that the manipulation is not a regular part of the procedure but is something which the "other subject" (really a confederate) just happened to do on this occasion. For example, Schachter and Singer (1962) attempted to manipulate euphoria by having a confederate waltz around the room, shooting rubber bands, playing with hula hoops, and practicing hook shots into a wastebasket with crumpled balls of paper. Presumably, the subject interpreted this behavior as a unique event unrelated to the experimental procedure. Similarly, Jack Brehm and Ann Cole (1966) attempted to manipulate their subjects' feeling of obligation toward another person. They accomplished this by having the confederate go out to buy a soft drink from the vending machine and "thoughtfully" bring one back for the subject too. This "unique" event, although it appeared to be unrelated to the experiment, succeeded in making the subject feel somewhat uncomfortable toward the confederate. John Darley and Bibb Latané (1968) used a confederate very effectively in an experiment designed to discover the factors that affect people's willingness to help others in an emergency. Subjects believed that they were members of a group discussion that took place over an intercom system (in order to protect the privacy of the other members, since they were supposed to discuss personal problems). The confederate (posing as another subject) hesitantly revealed that one of his worst personal problems was that he was prone to nervous seizures. Later on, when it was the confederate's turn to talk again, he began to stutter and gasp, and his voice grew louder and more incoherent as he stammered out that he was on the verge of a seizure and begged for help. Clearly, the subjects perceived the event as exceptional, something completely beyond the bounds of the experiment; as one subject said to herself, "It's just my kind of luck, something has to happen to me" (1968, p. 381).

The Whole Experiment as a Treatment A third method of having the empirical realization of the independent variable perceived as separate from the experiment is to use the whole experiment (as perceived by the subject) as the treatment, measuring the dependent variable at some later time. This technique is rather difficult in practice, since subjects may think that some of the experimental events are intended to affect them; when the procedure is carried out well, however, they are unlikely to perceive the whole experience as the treatment. For example, Carlsmith and Gross (1969) performed an experiment designed to investigate the effects of hurting someone on subsequent compliance. In their experiment they induced the subject to administer electric shocks to a confederate. The entire procedure was presented as a learning experiment, with the subject playing the part of the teacher and administering shocks whenever the confederate made an incorrect response. After performing this task, the subject was given an "explanation" of the experiment and was told that it was over. Shortly thereafter, the confederate asked a favor of the subject, who responded to this request without realizing that it was part of the experiment.

THE ISSUE OF STANDARDIZATION

Ideally, the empirical realization of an independent variable is forceful enough to have maximum impact and clear enough to generate the intended interpretation in all subjects. There is no list of specific techniques for achieving this ideal. However, some important general guidelines can be established. At the heart of the question is one crucial, yet frequently misunderstood, point: It is extremely important for all subjects to be in the same psychological state as a result of the manipulation of the independent variable. This does not necessarily mean that all subjects should be exposed to the identical independent variable. This *does* mean that the experimenter's skill and wisdom should be used to make sure that all subjects arrive at a similar understanding of the instructions (or the implications of the "event" manipulation). To achieve this goal, the experimenter should take considerable latitude in delivering the instructions. This is a tricky issue and is one that may raise doubts in the minds of many investigators. Our point is this: In their zeal for standardization, many experimenters make an effort to have all instructions to the subjects tape-recorded, printed, or computerized, attempting to make sure that all subjects are exposed to identical stimuli. Such an effort is admirable, but in practice it ignores the fact that people are different, and as a consequence, the same instructions do not mean the same thing to all subjects. More prosaic, yet more important, subjects differ greatly in their ability to understand instructions. For example, one of the most common mistakes the novice experimenter makes is to present the instructions too succinctly; consequently, a large percentage of the subjects fail to understand some of the important points. To ensure that all subjects understand what is going on in an experiment (especially one as complicated as most social psychological experiments are), a good deal of *redundancy* is necessary.

More important than simply providing redundancy, however, is ensuring that each subject *fully understand* all the instructions and events that occur in the experiment. The first thing the experimenter should try to do is to make these instructions and events as simple as possible without making them uninteresting. If the experimental situation is still complex, as is usually the case, the experimenter should make sure that the subject is not missing or misinterpreting anything. The experimenter can do this only by a combination of clear instructions, questions, pauses, and probes and by repeating or paraphrasing key parts of the instructions until satisfied that the subject is completely clear about all of them. The point seems self-evident, but is has been our experience that many experiments have failed precisely because the instructions were never made clear and redundant enough to get through to all the subjects.

An example may point up the difficulties. In an experimental investigation of compliance (Carlsmith & Gross, 1969), the experimenters were interested in finding out whether compliance with a request is more likely shortly after a person has hurt someone, and if so, whether the person is more likely to comply with a request made by the individual who has been hurt or with one made by a bystander who witnessed the event. As the experiment was set up, there were three participants: a teacher (in some conditions the subject, in others a confederate), a learner (always a confederate), and a witness (in some conditions the subject, in others a confederate). It was important that the subject know which of the two confederates was the learner and which played the other role. However, the learner-confederate could only be kept blind to what condition the subject was in by being kept ignorant of whether the subject in any given session was the teacher or the witness. Accordingly, the three participants were separated by partitions so that they could not see one another; the subject was brought into the experimental room alone and was given an explanation of the experiment, with heavy emphasis on which person (sitting in which seat) would be learner and which would play the other role. Despite strong attempts to make these instructions redundant, 12 of the first 15 subjects missed enough of the information so that they did not know which confederate was in which role. Luckily, postexperimental probing revealed this weakness in the procedure, which would have vitiated the whole experiment had it not been discovered, since the subject would not know whether the person making the request had been hurt or not. The identity of the two confederates was a key fact of the experiment, so in order to pound that fact into the subjects' heads, the experimenters revised the procedure to make the distinction between the confederates so blatant that no one could mistake them. The confederates' clothing differed greatly; the subject was introduced to only one of them before the experiment began; and the instructions were made "overly" redundant, so that finally the identities of the two confederates were impressed on the subjects' minds. The point of this is not that subjects are thick-headed, but that experimenters are often so familiar with their own procedures that they are unable to put themselves in the position of someone who is hearing the experiment described for the first time.

There should be little argument about the merits of using simple and redundant instructions to ensure that the subject understands the experiment. What we are suggesting goes beyond that, however. First, although instructions should be clear and repetitious, it is unwise to make them too repetitious, or the bright subjects may become bored or annoyed. However, some subjects are bound to miss the point, even when the instructions are exceptionally clear and repetitious. Thus, the same set of instructions may bore some subjects and baffle others. How can this be avoided? It does not take much expertise to pick out the subject who cannot grasp the meaning of the instructions. Often, such a subject would like to ask for more information but is too timid to interrupt, and so sends out a variety of obtrusive nonverbal cues signaling perplexity. Usually, the experimenter will notice these cues; in fact, in most cases it may be difficult *not* to notice them. But some experimenters may feel that they should ignore this information and should instead continue to follow their standardized scripts, so as not to introduce extra variability into the experimental situation. We feel that when situations of this sort arise, the experimenter should not try to maintain a mechanical "standardized" format. If, in the course of delivering the instructions, the experimenter sees a vacant or uncomprehending expression on the subject's face, efforts to get through to the subject should be increased, even at the expense of departing from a standard set of instructions. Certainly, if the subject did manage to overcome timidity and make a verbal request for clarification, few experimenters would refuse to give it. We are simply suggesting that the same procedure be followed when the subject's uncertainty is obvious, albeit unspoken. Otherwise, one advantage of the use of standardized instructions, reduced random error variance, will be offset by an increase in that same error variance caused by some subjects' failure to comprehend task instructions.

The situation is analogous to teaching, in that the experimenter has a certain quantum of information to get across. Few teachers would continue to read a prepared lecture after all the students had dropped their pens and were staring with blank faces; instead, they would go back and try to find out where the difficulties lay, in an effort to attain their original goal of communicating the information. The experimental situation is similar: There is no reason for an instructor to disregard feedback from the person being instructed, just because their relationship is one of experimenter to subject. Of course, the experimenter should keep a record of exactly what was said to each subject, in the interests of replicability and a fuller understanding of the behavior of any subjects who deviate markedly from the rest.

Again, we anticipate that many experimenters will disagree with us, suggesting that standardization is the hallmark of an experiment. We agree, but exactly what is it that should be standardized? What the experimenter says, or what the subject understands? We feel that the more variability there is in the subjects' comprehension of the experimental operations, the more likely it will be that the changes caused by the independent variable will be obscured. Of course, by allowing the experimenter to depart from a standardized script, one may increase the possibility of introducing a systematic bias. But if proper techniques are employed to eliminate bias, this ceases to be a problem. (Some of these techniques are discussed in Chapter 9.) In particular, if the experimenter who is giving the instructions is unaware of the subject's experimental condition, there is no way in which variations in the presentation can systematically bias the results. Similarly, in many cases the attempt to make sure the subject fully understands the situation takes place before the introduction of the specific experimental treatment and thus cannot bias the results. Clearly, we do not advocate any sort of flexible presentation in contexts in which such variations could introduce systematic error.

With the issue of standardization, as with many of the other issues we have discussed, we are faced with a tension between two important desiderata: On the one hand, it is critical for the experimenter, when writing up the research, to describe accurately the nature of the treatment. On the other hand, it is important that all subjects be in the same psychological state as a result of the experimental treatment. The problem may be easy to solve when the treatment is clear and simple, for example, when the treatment consists of an experimenter staring at some subjects and looking away from others, or touching some subjects and not touching others. But when the treatment calls for, say, sexual arousal of the subject, the situation is more complex.

We may take the case of sexual arousal as a polarizing example, one that moves beyond the presentation of instructions and into procedures that might entail the presentation of dramatically different stimuli to different subjects. Suppose that we want to study the effects of sexual arousal on liking. Our independent variable calls for sexually arousing the subjects in one condition. We could pick a selection of salacious passages from pornographic novels, collect them into a booklet, and have all the subjects in the sexual arousal condition read the booklet from cover to cover. In this case each subject is getting the same version of the independent variable. The effectiveness of the treatment depends on whether the particular selection of passages we have chosen has a widely generalized eroticism that will succeed in "turning on" all the subjects in the arousal condition. As an alternative, we could accumulate a large variety of potentially arousing material—books, pictures, movies, and so on—in which the themes as well as the media were diversified, and try to find the stimulus that was most arousing for each subject. Subjects' tastes might differ widely, and if we used this sort of procedure, not all subjects would be exposed to exactly the same stimulus. But presumably, if we were successful in our "something for everybody" strategy, all subjects *would* become sexually aroused. The first procedure certainly is superior on the dimension of "stimulus standardization." Although that is desirable when feasible, it may be more important to see to it that all subjects are in the state required by our conceptual independent variable, even though different amounts or even kinds of stimulation are required to produce this state. In other words, often our conceptual independent variable is really some sort of response, like sexual arousal, which we believe will act as an internal stimulus for subsequent behavior. In cases like this it may be more important to strive for standardization of this response, our real independent variable, than for standardization of the external stimulus intended to produce that response.

Consider the analogous situation in animal research. If we want to study the effects of arousal on some performance and we decide to manipulate arousal by administering an appropriate drug, we do not give the same amount to each subject. Typically, the variation comes about because we correct for some individual difference factor, such as the animal's weight. Thus, although we are administering different dosages to each animal, we are in fact administering a standard amount per kilogram of body weight. But at other times the level of the external stimulus might be set according to some aspect of the animal's performance. For example, we might introduce just enough rewarding brain stimulation to bring the animal to a threshold level of bar pressing so that the subject presses a bar on 50 percent of the occasions that the stimulation is received. Animals in one condition are at threshold, and in another condition they are not; the independent variable is the level of bar pressing, and it is the same for all animals in a given condition. The brain stimulation is the external stimulus that is designed to bring the animals to the appropriate level of the independent-variable dimension, and it is not necessarily the same for all animals. It may take different amounts of brain stimulation to bring different animals to threshold.

Some of the resistance to such flexible administration of the independent variable in social psychology stems from the fact that at the present state of development of our techniques, we lack accurate procedures (such as rate of bar pressing) for deciding when a subject has reached a standardized level on one of our complicated variables; therefore, we often have no clear criterion for deciding how the manipulation may need to be altered in order to bring any given subject to the intended level. Daniel Katz, for example, objected to these suggestions primarily on the grounds that our means of assessing the presence of the intended internal state are subjective and that by using such techniques, experimenters "no longer rely upon the variables created and manipulated but upon the psychological equivalence of effects produced" (1971, p. 277). Assessing the effectiveness of the treatment for individual subjects is not *necessarily* a matter of the experimenter's subjective impressions, however. For example, in order to determine amount of sexual arousal, we might attach a (male) subject to a phalloplathismograph, give him some arousing material to read or look at, measure his response, and if necessary, give him another installment, continuing to show him arousing stimuli until some criterion response has been measured. Of course, such a manipulation check may be difficult to justify within the context of some social psychological experiments.

The technique preferred will depend to some extent on the precise nature of the conclusion the experimenter wishes to draw. If interested solely in discussing the effects of reading a particular salacious short story (as an editor of *Playboy* or *Penthouse* might be), the experimenter would prefer the standardized stimulus presentation. If, however, the experimenter wishes to make inferences about sexual arousal per se, a group of sexually aroused experimental subjects is needed. Of course, most people would agree that an erection is better evidence for sexual arousal than the presentation of a standard set of stimulus materials. Presumably, if we could find as clear physiological evidence for criterion levels of other psychological states as we can for sexual arousal, there would be little resistance to the idea of varying the stimulus presentation in order to achieve these levels in all subjects.

Physiological responses are not the only type of response that can be used to indicate the effectiveness of the manipulation of the independent variable, however. The goal is to bring subjects to a given state, and as long as that state is specifiable in terms of some other measurable response such as verbal reports, overt behavior, or nonverbal cues, we see no reason to insist on using a standard stimulus presentation, rather than a standard response, as the criterion. Any measure that can be used as a manipulation check can be used as a criterion; the difference is simply that we are suggesting that the experimenter use the information as soon as it is available, rather than wait and find out that the manipulation was ineffective when it is too late to do anything about it.

As an example, consider the internal state of guilt, for which there is no known physiological measure. In the Carlsmith and Gross experiment (1969), guilt was operationalized by having the subject administer painful shocks to another person in the context of a teacher-learner experiment. The stimulus situation was relatively standardized; the teacher-learner interaction consisted of 15 trials, on exactly 9 of which the learner made a mistake, and the subject was required to administer a standard shock. The subject believed that each of the shocks was of the same voltage. The authors might instead have used a situation similar to the Milgram (1973) situation, in which the voltage of each shock delivered as punishment was higher than the last, and their empirical realization of the conceptual variable "guilt" might have been delivery of a shock of 300 volts or some other specific number. In this case, differing degrees of pressure might be necessary to bring different subjects to this level, but the level itself would be taken as the indication that the desired amount of guilt had been aroused. Whenever the subject reached that level, the induction could be terminated and the dependent variable measure introduced.

Katz also stated that "if one could assess clearly and accurately the psychological states of individuals, and if we knew how to produce them, then we would have no need for all the previous language about experimentation" (1971, p. 277). In the first place, the fact that we may be able to find a way to assess a given a state in a given context does not imply that we can "assess clearly and accurately the psychological states of individuals" in general. The techniques suggested in this section are not intended to be used in every experiment, but only in situations in which some means of assessment is available. We do not insist that this criterion measure have guaranteed accuracy. Indeed, the issue of "accurate" assessment of psychological constructs raises issues that are much more general than the specific recommendations we are making (see, for example, Schneider, Hastorf, & Ellsworth, 1979); we do feel, however, that some form of criterion assessment is often better than no assessment, and for this reason we do not insist that our measures be perfect.

Second, in most experiments social psychologists have to make some assumptions about their abilities to produce and assess psychological states: not only in experiments in which an effort is made to standardize responses to the independent variable, but also in experiments in which response standardization is less important. The creation of any independent variable treatment designed to create a given state is an attempt to produce that state, and in a way it seems more ambitious for the social psychologist to presume to have found a technique so effective that it will work for everyone than it is to aim for such a technique but to realize that it might fall short in some cases. Likewise, the problem of assessment is not limited to assessing the success of the manipulation, but rather occurs in all social psychological experiments when the dependent-variable measure is taken.

The great difficulty with using the subject's response as a criterion, of course, is that we cannot always specify exactly what we did. But sometimes we can. To return to our example on sexual arousal, we might have a standard series of literary selections that we present one at a time until the subject is aroused, stopping at different places for each subject when a certain level of arousal is reached. Obviously, it is desirable to be able to specify in exact detail just what was done with a subject. Further, as techniques become better and we become more and more certain how to manipulate variables, we may also expect to develop measures that will give a clear indication of whether the independent variable has influenced the subject in the manner intended.

Until that time comes, we should assume that there will be variability in the subject's understanding of the treatment, whether the treatment consists of a tape recording, a printed set of instructions, or an interaction with the experimenter. We are certainly not recommending that the experimenter *seek* to present variable instructions. The experimenter should start out by attempting to construct a standard operating procedure. Pretests should be conducted, and if the subjects show little consistency in their interpretations, the experimenter should modify the treatment until finding a standard procedure that does produce consistent responses. But even with all this careful preparation, not all subjects will see the stimulus in a way that conforms to the experimenter's expectations. Our recommendation is that the experimenter recognize that variability exists in the subjects' understanding of the instructions and that on some occasions a standardized manipulation may not fit. On these occasions, experimenters would do well to increase stimulus variability deliberately in order to decrease the variability in the subjects' understanding of the stimulus situation. Of course, these variations must be describable when the experimental procedure is written up and cannot be used unless adequate techniques for eliminating experimenter bias are employed.

Pilot Testing the Independent Variable

How can we be sure that we have a good empirical realization of our independent variable? How do we know if subjects are attending to the features of the situation we expect they will? How do we know that the complex series of events encountered by the subject really is arousing what we think or hope it is? We have discussed some of the answers to this question at an abstract theoretical level; here, we attempt to give some practical advice on how to determine whether a treatment is producing the intended conceptual variable. The most general technique for finding out just what a treatment is doing to people is to run some **pilot tests**. Pilot tests are not necessarily formal rehearsals of the experiment; one need not run pilot subjects through the entire experimental procedure from start to finish. The purpose of these "trial runs" is to check out the experimental paradigm for the existence of unforeseen technical problems—to get the bugs out of the procedure—and any technique that is useful for discovering these rough spots can be a suitable "pretest."

The discoveries made during pretesting and the consequent adjustments and modifications of the procedure represent one of the most important sequences of events in constructing an experiment. Informative as they are, these discoveries and revisions seldom, if ever, appear in the final, published version of an experiment. Thus, in this section we will rely even more heavily than usual on our own research and experiences.

During pretesting the experimenter can conduct long, probing interviews with the subject. Often, the subject is capable of providing valuable hints as to where the weaknesses in the treatment occurred, what parts of it were misunderstood, and where it evoked reactions different from those the experimenter intended. For example, in one study (Aronson & Carlsmith, 1962), the experimental treatment was designed to give the subject an expectation of success or failure on a test. Since the experimenters wanted the test to refer to an ability that was vague enough so that they could give the subjects convincing false feedback about their performance, they decided to call it a test of "social sensitivity." On each trial of the "test," the subject was to look at photographs of three men and pick out which one was Jewish. But when they tried the test out, pilot subjects became upset, arguing that it was impossible to recognize Jews on the basis of appearance. Those who did try it failed to build up any expectations about their future performance, even when they had attained consistently high (or low) scores on four blocks of 20 trials each. Because the subjects believed that judging a Jew from appearance was entirely a matter of chance, their perceptions of how they would do on the next series of trials was unaffected by the feedback about how they had done on the last series. On the basis of the information gained from these pilot subjects, the experimenters changed the test so that the subjects were asked to pick out schizophrenics rather than Jews, and from then on the experiment ran smoothly. Apparently, subjects are less threatened by the implications of picking the faces of schizophrenics than of Jews, and they readily accepted the level of ability that was experimentally communicated to them.

If deception is used, the pretest subject is the best source of information about the effectiveness and credibility of the cover story. Such interviews can, of course, be conducted while the experiment is actually being run, but it is usually during pilot testing that the most valuable information is obtained, since the experimenter still has the opportunity to make extensive alterations in the procedure without invalidating the experiment.

If one is particularly interested in the adequacy of the empirical realization of an independent variable which corresponds to some internal state, it is a good idea to interview the pilot subject right after the treatment, without continuing the whole experiment. If one waits until the experiment is over and then attempts to question the subject about the dependent variable as well, the subject may find it difficult or impossible to describe the effects of the experimental treatment. Studies of cognitive dissonance offer a good case in point. The general hypothesis in all dissonance studies is that subjects will do whatever they can to reduce the dissonance. Suppose that the experimenter is running pretests in order to find out if the manipulation really did produce dissonance. If subjects are not questioned until the end of the experiment, those who have succeeded in reducing all the dissonance might well report that the manipulation of the independent variable aroused no dissonance or discomfort whatever. Take, for example, the study by Festinger and Carlsmith (1959). In this study, subjects in the dissonance condition spent an hour working on a tiresome, apparently purposeless task and then were paid $1 to tell another subject that the task was fun and exciting. The treatment designed to produce the dissonance was the payment of an inadequate sum for the false description of the task. According to the prediction, the subjects would reduce this dissonance by changing their opinion of the task in a favorable direction. If subjects were not questioned until the end of the experiment—when they had already changed their attitudes so as to reduce most of the dissonance which had been created—they might well report that they felt no discomfort about saying that the experiment was interesting, in return for payment of $1. If, however, they were interviewed immediately after agreeing to give the false description, they might be able to report more accurately on whether the treatment had caused the expected reaction.

The dissonance example provides an illustration of the major difficulty with the use of introspective reports: Too often, subjects are unable or unwilling to explain just what the effects of some treatment have been. Following an experiment, it is not at all uncommon for subjects to deny any feelings of the kind the experimenter expected to arouse, although their behavior throughout the experiment was just what would be anticipated if they had experienced precisely those feelings. This basic fact, of course, is the reason why psychologists have turned from introspection to behavioral research. For example, in the study on severity of initiation, the women who had undergone a severe initiation expressed favorable opinions of the boring group, as the theory predicted. When the experimenter explained his hypothesis to these women, many of them made such comments as: "Gee, that's a fascinating experiment, and I'm sure severe initiations really work that way on some people, but I loved that group because they said such good things."

As Timothy Wilson (1985) points out, the mental processes that *guide* our behaviors are different from the mental processes we employ when we consciously attempt to *understand* or *explain* our behaviors. When subjects attempt to reconstruct their inner experiences rationally, and tell the experimenter about them, they may fail to capture the elusive thoughts or feelings that gave rise to their original behaviors. Subjects' retrospective self-reports may thus at best be an imperfect approximation of their perceptions and feelings at the time an event occurred. As a consequence, even when subjects are asked to report their feelings immediately after the administration of the independent variable, they may not be able to give accurate descriptions. People are not always able to articulate subtle psychological states, and often they come up with plausible but inaccurate accounts of the influences on their behavior (Nisbett & Wilson, 1977). In addition, in some situations, subjects may feel inhibited about revealing their feelings, even if they can formulate them accurately. Some subjects may feel that an interview with a psychologist is an opportunity that should not be wasted on reports of their immediate responses to the experimental situation. In a variety of situations, introspective reports—even if taken immediately—may not be a trustworthy means of assessing the effectiveness of the independent variable.

A more difficult but far better technique for checking whether the experimental technique is producing the desired internal state is to run a number of pilot subjects in a separate experimental paradigm, in which the dependent variable is some behavior presumed to be a direct indication that the intended subjective state has been aroused. In other words, instead of manipulating one variable and measuring its effect on some other variable, we temporarily ignore the relationship between the independent variable and other variables and instead concentrate on the relationship between the treatment and some measure of the state or response that would logically seem to indicate the presence of our intended independent variable. Returning to the discussion with which we opened this chapter, our eventual prediction is that there is a relationship between a certain kind of internal stimulus and some kind of behavior. In the final experiment we will administer a treatment designed to elicit the internal state, assume that it has been produced, and measure to see if it in turn produces the predicted behavior. What we are suggesting as a means of checking on the appropriateness of the treatment is that we carry out a pilot experiment with the same manipulation and see if the internal state has been elicited. In other words, we perform a simple, one-stage experiment, using as our dependent variable some behavior that we believe is a direct indication of the internal state.

Consider again the experiment by Aronson and Carlsmith (1963), in which children were asked not to play with an attractive toy. In one condition the admonition was put in the form of a mild threat; in the other, in the form of a severe threat. Although intuitively the two threats seemed to differ along a dimension of severity, it would have been desirable to substantiate that intuition by providing independent evidence of this difference. One way of doing this would be simply to ask the child how severe the threat was, but the children were so young that they probably would not have given useful answers to such an abstract question. A better technique would be to run other subjects in a pilot test in which the forbidden toy was made more desirable, so that a number of children would in fact disobey that admonition. With the toys actually used in the Aronson-Carlsmith experiment, even the mild threat was severe enough so that no child went against it. If the toys were made so desirable that some children played with the forbidden toy in spite of the threat, and if this disobedience was more common when the threat was mild than when it was severe, we would be confident that the severe threat was really more severe than the mild threat.

It should be obvious by now that pretesting does not consist of a set of formal procedures. The pretesting stage of an experiment provides an opportunity to become familiar with the situation and even to allow one's intuitions their say: about ways of testing the hypothesis that will "fit" the situation, about procedural changes that will make the experiment coherent and meaningful, about the kinds of variables that are likely to influence the subjects in the particular subculture from which they are to be drawn. For example, if one wants subjects to engage in some counterattitudinal behavior, pretesting provides an opportunity to find out what the subject's attitudes are and therefore what is counterattitudinal. If one wants to expose nursery school children to mild and severe threats, the pretest stage is the time to get to know the children and find out what kinds of things are threatening to them. It is a time to observe the experiment from the subject's point of view, to develop an intuition of what the situation "feels like," and to tinker with it until it "feels right." Part of the knack of being a good experimenter is an ability to seek out relevant information in the pretest stage and an openness to hunches and intuitions gained in the process of watching one's own experiment develop.

The Advantages of a Live Experimenter

In an attempt to avoid bias and gain a kind of control over the stimuli presented to the subjects, many experimenters have turned to the use of "canned" operations in the form of tape recordings, printed instructions, and computer-presented instructions. There are many situations in which the use of these techniques is justified and even essential. There are situations in which such methods can have a great deal of impact, such as the Darley-Latané (1968) experiment, in which the confederate's "nervous seizure" was really a tape recording. However, we should not lose sight of the fact that a live experimenter is not simply a bias-producing machine but instead frequently is a necessary ingredient in the experimental process. In this chapter and elsewhere (see Chapter 4) we have already discussed the important role an experimenter can play in making sure all subjects understand the instructions. In addition, the live experimenter can often succeed in "selling" a cover story to a degree that cannot be matched by canned instructions. Many times, when we read about the experimental procedure of a deception experiment as reported in a journal article, we are struck by the simplicity and transparency of the subterfuge and are amazed that it was successful. But the success of a cover story in disguising the true purpose of an experiment cannot be judged solely by looking at the words spoken by the experimenter. The manner of delivery makes a crucial difference. An explanation is often made more plausible by the physical presence of the experimenter who, through earnest demeanor and maintenance of eye contact, can frequently succeed in convincing the subject that the "experimental problem" described in the cover story is not only a legitimate object of scientific inquiry but is even an interesting and exciting area of investigation.

Moreover, the live experimenter can detect not only the fact that the subject is not understanding a set of instructions or is becoming inattentive but also that a subject is beginning to appear incredulous. Thus, the experimenter may repeat, answer questions, and deviate slightly from the prepared script in order to allay any doubts that may occasionally creep into the mind of a subject. Just as some subjects are, by nature or experience, brighter or more wide-awake than others, some subjects are more suspicious than others. For this reason, it would be absurd for the experimenter to stick blindly to the prepared script when a slight change in wording or emphasis might allay the subject's suspicions. Again, what we are advocating is not the abandonment of control but rather the attainment of a richer kind of control through an attempt to have all subjects in approximately the same state of mind when the independent variable is introduced. Let us reemphasize the fact that the use of a live experimenter often raises the possibility of bias in an experiment. We are well aware of this, and we believe that an experimenter should keep a careful record of any deviations from the script and should start all over again with a better manipulation if these deviations (especially those designed to allay suspicion) become frequent. But there are many ways of avoiding bias that do not sacrifice the advantages of the "personal touch" of the human experimenter who, in our opinion, should not become another victim of automation. (The problem of bias and techniques for avoiding it are discussed in Chapter 9.)

Parenthetically, it should be pointed out that "facing up" to a subject has other advantages as well. Most important of all, it lets the experimenter see what is going on. By shutting the subject up in a room with a tape recorder, a booklet, or a microcomputer, the experimenter too is shut off from information that could be of the utmost importance in interpreting the outcome of the experiment. For example, in attempting to convey a set of instructions to a subject in a face-to-face interaction, the experimenter may come to realize that these instructions are not viable; there is nothing quite like a yawn in the face to convince the experimenter that the instructions are dull and unmotivating. If the instructions are presented on a tape recording, the experimenter might never see the yawn and might run the whole experiment without realizing that the subjects are totally indifferent to the treatment. Similarly, if deception is used, there is nothing like the skeptical yet pitying look of an incredulous subject to convince us that we had best go back to the drawing board. As mentioned above, a talented experimenter can occasionally "sell" a rather incredible cover story. At the same time, there are some experimental situations which are inherently so transparent that a very sophisticated and elaborate cover story is required. In dealing with our own research assistants, we have found that we can waste a great deal of time and energy trying to convince a novice experimenter that his or her cover story is inadequate. A pilot trial on one subject is far more convincing.

Thus, the live, two-way exchange between subject and experimenter is an important learning experience. Few things are as unnerving (and therefore as educational) as being stuck for an hour with a subject who doesn't believe a word you're saying and couldn't care less. One way of avoiding such experiences is to build better and more convincing experiments. A good social psychology experiment never bores a subject, unless boredom is the conceptual variable.

Who's Running This Experiment, Anyway?

We have placed great emphasis on the experimenter's ability to interact with the subject. Our suggestion is that in the course of presenting the instructions to the subject, the experimenter should be certain that the intended information is being communicated and that the subject understands the instructions. This inevitably involves asking whether the subject understands or has any questions. There is a danger inherent in this strategy. If given the opportunity, some subjects attempt to wrest control of the session away from an unwary experimenter. When the experimenter asks if they understood, such subjects may take the floor and begin to ask questions which have nothing to do with the experiment, discuss previous experiments they have been in, and ask questions pertinent to aspects of the procedure which are yet to come. If this occurs, the experimenter stands in danger of either invalidating the experiment by engaging in long and friendly conversation with the subjects or offending and angering them by cutting them off too short. Thus, although we advocate a flexible procedure, this flexibility should operate within a limited range. In most experiments wide variation in the experimenter-subject rapport will increase the error due to variability among subjects' perceptions of the experiment; at worst, it could conceivably interact with experimental treatments in a manner which would make significant results meaningless, due to systematic error.

A good general rule in such a situation is for the experimenter to answer only those questions that clarify aspects of the procedure already covered but never to indulge the subject's ramblings and never to allow a subject to reorganize the sequence of instructions merely by asking a question pertaining to material that would have been covered a few minutes further along in the presentation. While setting the stage (see Chapter 6), the experimenter often has a chance to forestall future inappropriate comments from the subject; the best way to do this is by means of a short prelude to the main instructions, in which the experimenter explains the importance of control and uniformity in experimental situations and requests the subject to ask questions only for clarification. The experimenter should also state willingness to chat with the subject after the experiment, when these constraints will no longer apply. Most subjects can understand this and are not offended. In spite of this preface, occasionally a subject will deviate. If this occurs, the best way to field irrelevant chatter or anticipatory questions in the course of the experiment is to repeat, politely but firmly, that it is necessary to achieve a high degree of experimental uniformity and that, consequently (1) it would be preferable to shelve this discussion until after the experiment, or (2) the question raised will be answered in a few moments.

THE DEPENDENT VARIABLE

The term "dependent variable" refers to the phenomenon—be it belief, sentiment, or behavior—that we attempt to influence with our treatments and that we measure at the end of the experiment. The results of an experiment consist of differences in measures of the subjects' behavior; in devising a dependent variable, the experimenter seeks to find a measure that will reflect the differences caused by the independent variable. In this chapter we will discuss the alternatives open to an experimenter and the considerations to be weighed in choosing among them.

We think of an experiment as successful when the experimental treatments are responsible for variation in the subjects' behavior (as measured by the dependent variable). The experimenter may want to measure liking, for example, to see if people who have undergone a severe initiation will like the group better than will people who have had a mild initiation. Or, the experimenter may want to measure aggression, to see if people who have recently experienced frustration are more aggressive than are people who have not. If the independent variable is an effective one, the dependent-variable measure will show large differences among the subjects in different conditions and small differences among the subjects in the same condition; for example, subjects in the severe-initiation condition will like the group much more than will subjects in the mild-initiation condition, and all subjects in the severe-initiation condition will like the group about the same amount. Likewise, in the experiment on aggression, all subjects in the frustration condition should express a great deal of aggression, and all subjects in the other condition should express little aggression. How a subject behaves *depends* on the treatment given, hence the term "dependent variable."

Like the independent variable, the dependent variable can consist of behavior in which the experimenter is interested for his own sake, or behavior that the investigator considers a manifestation of some conceptual variable, such as an internal state or a general class of behavior (see Chapter 7). As an example of the first type of research, consider the experiments by Darley and Latané and their colleagues on bystander intervention. Through reading newspaper accounts about city dwellers standing by apathetically while a woman was stabbed to death, these investigators became curious about the factors that determine when people will help others in an emergency. The behavior they were interested in was, quite simply, helping: not as an indication of some internal state or some general category of behavior (such as "altruism"), but for its own sake. In order to study this behavior, they conducted a number of experiments in a variety of situations involving a person in trouble. For example, they set up a situation in which the subject heard a woman in the next room fall down and cry for help (Latané & Rodin, 1969) or in which a confederate appeared to be on the verge of having a serious nervous seizure (Darley & Latané, 1968). In all their experiments, the dependent measure was straightforward and easily measurable: whether the subject helped the person in distress.

More often, the aim of the social psychologist is to discover laws that are more general or more abstract. Rather than predicting one particular behavior, the social psychologist makes a prediction that may be reflected in a large variety of responses, all following from an understanding of the central process. The conceptual dependent variable is an abstract category, such as "aggression" or "conformity," or an internal state, such as "affection." The investigator who studies aggression, for example, may want to draw conclusions that apply to a range of phenotypically different behaviors, including physical attack, verbal criticism, refusal to respond, backbiting, and hostile fantasies.

In terms of the stimulus-response model discussed at the beginning of Chapter 7, it should now be apparent that there are many situations in which neither the independent nor the dependent variable is directly observable. If both are conceptual variables, as in the hypothesis that frustration leads to aggression, the stimulus-response chain consists of four elements:

experimental treatment → frustration → aggression → measured behavior

The investigator devises a treatment designed to serve as a stimulus for the internal state, frustration, which constitutes the conceptual independent variable. The hypothesis is that frustration is a stimulus for another state (or class of behaviors) that the experimenter calls aggression; this second stimulus-response relationship, which is the crux of the hypothesis, follows its course entirely "inside" of the subject, and the psychologist has no direct access to it. Finally, the aggression is hypothesized to be a stimulus for a particular overt behavioral response that can be measured, such as delivering a large number of electric shocks to the person who has provoked the aggression. All the dissonance experiments we have discussed in this book are of this type. The experimenter creates a situation designed to arouse dissonance in a subject, and the theory predicts that the subject's response to the dissonance will be an unobservable motivation to reduce it. The experimenter then provides the subject with an opportunity to behave in a way that will satisfy this motivation and then measures the behavior.

For example, in the Festinger and Carlsmith study (1959), the experimenter paid the subjects in the experimental group $1 to say that a long and tedious task was really fun and exciting. This manipulation was designed to produce a state of dissonance between the subjects' cognition that the task was unpleasant and the cognition that they had nonetheless described it as interesting. The subjects were motivated to reduce the dissonance by reevaluating the task and deciding that it wasn't really offensive or boring but was quite interesting and enjoyable. Finally the experimenter asked the subjects to indicate on a rating scale how much they liked the task. This rating scale was the operational measurement of the conceptual dependent variable. The authors tried to arrange the setting so that the internal response of interest, in this case a positive reevaluation of the boring task, would be reflected in the subjects' external, measured response to the question.

In such an experiment, there are two crucial inference links which demand the investigator's skill: the initial link between the external stimulus conditions and the conceptual independent variable, and the final link between the conceptual dependent variable and the observable behavior. Often, one of these requires very little translation from theory to practice. The experiment on the effects of touching (Crusco & Wetzel, 1984) is an instance of a study in which the independent variable was relatively direct and obvious. The experimenters were interested in how people respond to being touched. The state had to be operationally defined in that the length and the location of the touch were circumscribed beforehand, but it was not an empirical realization of a more abstract independent variable.

A study by Aronson and David Landy (1967) illustrates the use of a relatively straightforward dependent variable. The authors wanted to test the hypothesis underlying Parkinson's law, that is, people "need" more time to accomplish a task when they were previously allowed an excessive amount of time to complete a similar task. The dependent variable was simply the amount of time the subject spent on the task. In the rare cases where neither the independent variable nor the dependent variable requires an inferential leap from external event to internal state, the experimenter's task is greatly simplified, although a plausible context for the manipulation and measurement of the variables (see Chapter 6) may still be needed. Frequently, the investigator deals with situations in which both inferential links are necessary. We have examined the problems and procedures for dealing with the first of these links: the creation of the independent variable. In this chapter we deal with the second: how the social psychologist chooses a measure that will reflect the property to be observed.

The problems of measuring a dependent variable are conceptually parallel to those for the independent variable:

1 What specific thing (verbal statement, behavior, physiological response, or whatever) does the experimenter want to select and record in order to achieve the most direct representation of the conceptual variable?

2 Paralleling the problem of impact for the independent variable, how does the experimenter make sure that the subject is taking the measurement seriously?

3 How can the experimenter prevent the subjects from "cooperating" by consciously responding in the manner which they feel will be most useful to the experimenter rather than the manner which honestly reflects their responses to the experimental treatment?

One of the first decisions facing the experimenter is the choice between a behavioral measure and a verbal measure. Actually, this distinction is not so simple, for it is possible to recognize a continuum ranging from behaviors of great importance and consequence for the subject to trivial paper-and-pencil measures of minimal concern to the subject. At one extreme the experimenter could measure the amount of tedious labor a subject actually performs for a fellow student (as a reflection of, say, liking for that student, which has been experimentally influenced). At the other extreme one could get the subject to circle a number on a scale in response to the printed question "How much did you like that other student who participated in the experiment?" Close to the behavioral end of the continuum would be a measure of the subject's commitment to perform a particular piece of behavior without actually performing it.

Within the broad category of verbal measures, there are two main varieties: the questionnaire and the interview. The behavioral end of the continuum has few broad subcategories, since typically the behavior measured is specific to the particular dependent variable the experimenter has in mind—delivering shocks as a measure of aggression, choosing another person for a partner as a measure of liking, and so on—whereas an interview or a questionnaire can vary in content to cover a wide range of dependent variables. Each of these methods of measurement—the questionnaire, the interview, and the behavioral measure—presents characteristic problems, and to some extent each has had characteristic applications in social psychological research. The assessment of attitude change—one of social psychology's greatest contributions—has been almost entirely dominated by the questionnaire. Some issues are more important for the two types of verbal measure than for behavioral measures; still others are common to all three. We shall begin by discussing the advantages and disadvantages of verbal measures in general, proceed to specific consideration of questionnaires, rating scales, and interviews, and summarize the problems involved in the use of verbal measures. We will then move to a discussion of the advantages and disadvantages of behavioral measures. Finally, we will discuss the broad general issues to be taken into account in choosing one of these types of measures.

VERBAL MEASURES

Advantages of Verbal Measures

One of the main advantages of verbal measures is that they are easy to use. Instead of training observers to record momentary actions or devising an elaborate situation to elicit a particular behavioral response, the experimenter simply hands the subject a questionnaire or sits down with the person and asks for the necessary information. As we shall see, this simplicity may sometimes be deceptive, but it is one important reason for the prevalence of verbal measures in social psychological research.

Second, verbal measures have a certain face validity. If we could put complete faith in the subjects' answers, we would be in the advantageous position of having direct access to the exact information we wanted. A behavioral measure appears to be a less direct method of finding out about a subject's internal state. For example, suppose that the experimenters in the severity-of-initiation study had assessed liking for the group by asking subjects whether they would become permanent members and come in to participate in the group discussion once a week for the entire school year. The experimenters would like to infer that joining the group was a reflection of liking, but there are other possibilities. The severe-initiation subjects might join because they felt more obligated, for example, feeling that it would be very difficult for the experimenter to find another person who could pass the severe initiation. Using a verbal measure, the experimenter can ask directly: "How much did you like the group?" Again, we shall raise the questions about this face validity in certain situations, but in principle it is a valuable asset.

Third, an interview or a questionnaire allows the experimenter to ask many *more* questions, thereby giving the subject more than one opportunity to react to the independent variable. With a behavioral measure, by contrast, the experimenter has only one chance: The subject either does or does not perform the behavior; if the latter, the experimenter is often left without any other source of information about whether the independent variable had an effect or about what went wrong. The subject in the severe initiation might refuse to join the group, apparently disconfirming the hypothesis. But suppose that she had come to admire the group so much that she thought it was "too good for her" and so refused to join because she didn't think she could perform at that high level. The severe initiation would have had a profound effect, fully supporting the hypothesis, but the behavioral measure would miss it. With a verbal measure, the experimenter can ask many different questions, all designed to find out whether the subject felt positively toward the group: "Do you like the group?" "Do you admire the group?" "Do you think it would be fun to be a member?" "Do you think the discussion was valuable?" If in fact the subject has come to feel positively toward the group, it is unlikely that this favorable feeling would go undetected, whatever form it took.

In a verbal measure, the experimenter can also include questions which are not intended as a direct assessment of the dependent variable but which might be useful later on in an internal analysis (see Chapter 7). The experimenter might ask, for example, how many of the obscene words the subject typically used in her everyday conversation. Presumably, the initiation would be more severe for a subject who had never before uttered any of the words than for a subject whose everyday language was more colorful, and thus the information gained from this question might be useful in interpreting weak or inconsistent results.

Finally, verbal measures provide a simple means of assessing small changes in the subject's feelings. Behavioral measures often (though not necessarily) allow a very limited number of options, sometimes only performance versus nonperformance of the behavior. For example, in the severity-of-initiation study, many subjects who might not agree to become permanent members of the discussion group might check a 6 instead of a 5 on a 10-point rating scale, indicating that their feelings toward the group were slightly more favorable than neutral. Although it is certainly possible to design a behavioral measure that will allow for subtle distinctions of this sort, it is not always easy; interpreting and classifying complex behaviors can be a cumbersome task. As an alternative, the rating scale provides a ready-made method for assessing fine gradations of feelings or attitudes.

Questionnaires

Any measurement technique has inherent limitations, and within these limits a technique can be used well or badly. The psychologist must first choose the general technique most appropriate for the particular problem and must then work within its limitations to tailor the measurement device to the property to be measured in the specific context created in the experiment.

In social psychological experiments, and especially in the measurement of attitudes, beliefs, perceptions, and expectations, the questionnaire is the most common measurement instrument, despite a long history of criticism and controversy about its use. Compared to most other types of measurement, including the interview, paper-and-pencil measures are relatively simple and convenient to use. For this reason it is easy to fall into the trap of using a questionnaire measure simply because it is convenient and not because it is particularly suitable for understanding the variable in which the experimenter is interested. No measure should be chosen on this basis, and much of the criticism of questionnaires is really criticism of their indiscriminate use.

The questionnaire is most appropriate when the investigator is specifically interested in the subject's *verbal responses* and knows in advance exactly what questions he or she wants the subject to answer. Since the subject usually fills it out without help, use of the questionnaire should be restricted to situations in which the instructions and the questions are clear and easy to understand. If these conditions are met, the questionnaire has the advantage of being the simplest and often the least expensive measurement device. If the conditions are not met, the experimenter may discover too late that the questionnaire has failed to elicit the information desired. Worse yet, the experimenter may *not* discover it. Subjects may have misunderstood or misinterpreted important questions without the experimenter's knowledge. Before conducting an experiment with a questionnaire as the dependent-variable measure, the experimenter should give the questionnaire to a few pilot subjects to make sure that their interpretation of the questions is the same as the experimenter's.

Most of the advantages of the questionnaire over the interview pertain to standardization; the instructions, the wording, and the order of the questions can more easily be kept constant across subjects, and often the form of the subject's answer is similarly constrained. As we pointed out in Chapter 7, administering the identical taped or printed stimulus materials to all subjects does not guarantee uniformity of interpretation, and the same is true when the "stimulus" is a response measure such as a questionnaire.[1] However, if during the pilot testing of the measure the questions have been found to be straightforward and easily understood, so that the experimenter can be reasonably sure that they will mean the same thing to most of the subjects, standardization confers several important benefits.

First, the administration of a questionnaire requires minimal participation from the experimenter, who can simply hand the questionnaire to the subject and leave the room. Thus, this procedure is often less susceptible to bias than is an interview or direct behavioral observation. If it is impossible to keep the person who measures the dependent variable unaware of which condition each subject is in, the questionnaire is one of the safest alternatives. Likewise, if the people who administer the measures are inexperienced experimenters, the questionnaire is a relatively safe technique, since it requires less skill and training than are needed for an interview or many types of behavioral observation. Since the direct personal participation of the experimenter is unnecessary, questionnaires are uniquely appropriate for administration to large groups of subjects in a single sitting. Although not common in the context of an experiment, the collection of individuals into a large group for measurement is sometimes valuable, for example, when the experimenter wants to get pretest or baseline measures on the sample from which the subjects are to be drawn or wishes to take a follow-up measure after the experiment itself has been completed.

---

[1] The classic example is the so-called double-barreled question in which two subjects may give identical responses to the same item, even though they are really responding to two different questions. For example, consider the following statements: "Criminals are getting out of hand in this country, and we need capital punishment to show them that we really mean business about wiping out crime." "Abortion is a sin against nature and ignores the rights of the unborn child." "The draft guards against a professional army which may pose a threat to our civilian government, and constitutes a duty which every citizen must perform." In each case, two subjects may disagree with the statement, but for *different reasons*: for example, because one subject does not believe that a professional army will pose a threat, and because another subject does not believe that it is the duty of every citizen to serve in the armed forces.

The questionnaire can also provide anonymity. In social psychological experiments the subject can immediately be assigned a code number that serves thereafter as the sole identification of that person's data. The ethical advantages of this procedure are obvious, especially if the questions are personal or allow for answers that could conceivably be used against the subject. From a methodological point of view, the assurance of anonymity may increase the likelihood of honest reporting on the part of the subject. If convinced that no one will ever be able to trace questionnaire responses back to their source, subjects will be less tempted to edit answers in the direction of the normal or desirable response.

Finally, the presentation of a questionnaire can create a setting in which the subject feels reasonably comfortable about expressing personal beliefs, values, or experiences in a standardized and therefore easily scorable form. If the experimenter is interested in simple "agree-disagree" responses, scalar responses, or easily accessible factual material, the imposed standardization of the questionnaire makes it an appropriate tool. Likewise, the questionnaire is often the best instrument for presenting any kind of forced-choice question, since it minimizes argument. Needless to say, the use of closed questions does not automatically force subjects' experience into closed categories, and it may result in spurious results if the subject has great difficulty in organizing personal beliefs in that manner. Pilot testing can usually solve this problem or at least reveal whether the questions are amenable to a closed-answer format, if the investigator concentrates on the suitability of the question form as well as on the meaningfulness of the content. In any case, the questionnaire is the most appropriate vehicle for a dependent variable that consists of a set of rating scales, and many questionnaires consist entirely of scales. Many of the advantages and disadvantages of questionnaire measures are exemplified by the advantages and disadvantages of rating scales.

Rating Scales

Rating scales, on which the subject reports a perception or evaluation of some person or thing referred to or included in the experiment, are one of the most common means of measuring the dependent variable in social psychology. In order to reflect differences caused by the independent variables, a dependent variable must be quantifiable in some respect. The experimenter wants to know if a severe initiation will produce *more* liking for the group than a mild one will, if a communicator with higher prestige will produce *more* attitude change, if a person who has had little contact with blacks is *more* prejudiced against them than is someone who has had a great deal of contact. One way of achieving this quantification is to ask subjects a simple yes-or-no question, *count* the people in each group who say yes, and express this figure as a percentage. For example, Freedman and Fraser (1966) wanted to find out whether complying with a trivial request makes people more likely to comply with a large request later on. Their experimental treatment divided the subjects into two groups: those who had been asked to perform the small favor and those who had not yet been approached with any request. All subjects were then solicited with the large request, and the dependent variable was the percentage of people in each group who complied with this request.

Since in many social psychological studies, however, we want to make finer distinctions, subjects are not usually restricted to a simple yes-or-no answer but are given a range of choices from strong agreement through mild agreement through a neutral position and so on all the way to strong disagreement. This is done in part because the experimental treatments that are feasible in the laboratory are often relatively weak and may have only a minor effect on the subject, particularly if we are interested in affecting a strongly held attitude. For example, if we want to test the hypothesis that our independent variable will make people more favorable toward unilateral disarmament, it would be foolish to use a questionnaire that simply asked, "Are you for or against unilateral disarmament?" because it is unlikely that any independent variable we could create in the laboratory would be strong enough to turn many people from hawks to doves (or conversely). Our independent variable could actually be quite effective, and we would never know it, because our measure does not allow us to observe anything less than total effectiveness. A rating scale allows us to measure smaller or more subtle changes in the subject's expressed opinion.

Rating scales are a measure suitable for the conditions described above. The subjects are limited to a choice among a restricted number of well-defined answers, often with standard wordings ("Agree slightly," "Agree very much," etc.). In addition, when the subjects are asked to rate how much they enjoyed the experiment or some part of it, how much they liked another subject or the experimenter, or where they place themselves on some very personal dimension, they may prefer to answer anonymously.

Most of the types of scales discussed below were originally devised for the purpose of measuring enduring attitudes about important issues: attitudes toward the United States, minority groups, current events, child-rearing practices, divorce, political figures, and so on. A great deal of protesting and reliability checking went into the construction of each particular scale (e.g., a scale of U.S. patriotism) within any one of the general categories. In social psychological experiments, the "attitudes" measured are usually much more limited responses to certain aspects of the experiment, although experiments designed specifically to study attitude change have occasionally used fairly important issues. As a result, experimenters have often used scales modeled after the ones discussed below, without comparable care and concern about psychometric properties. Some of the reasons for this apparent carelessness will be discussed below. For the time being, we remind you that experimental social psychologists often use the form of a certain type of scale without conforming to the underlying assumptions or suggested procedures for constructing that scale.

The Thurstone Scale   L. L. Thurstone devised an attitude scale based on the assumption that the underlying dimension of an attitude could be represented by an ordered series of opinion statements about a given object or issue, ranging from extremely unfavorable to extremely favorable, and that the attitude of any person would be represented by the small number of such statements he or she would endorse which fell close to each other on the scale. In addition, Thurstone attempted to create scales so that the difference in favorability of attitude between any two contiguous points would be the same as that between any other two contiguous points (an "interval" scale; see Selltiz, Jahoda, Deutsch, & Cook, 1963, pp. 193–194). A successful scale of this sort can measure how much more favorable one person is than another and, in attitude-change experiments, how much more one person's attitude has changed than another's, regardless of their initial attitude positions, because in theory a change from 5 to 7 represents the same amount of change as that from 1 to 3.

In the first stage of constructing a Thurstone scale, judges classify a large number of opinion statements according to their degree of favorability. The most common method (though probably not the best; see Scott, 1968) is the method of *equal-appearing intervals*. A large number of judges are independently asked to sort all the opinion statements into 11 piles, with the most favorable statements at one end, the neutral statements in the middle, and the most favorable statements at the other end. Thurstone recommended that "several hundred" judges be used (Thurstone & Chave, 1929, p. 17); more recent writers have suggested the use of 50 to 300 judges (Selltiz, Jahoda, Deutsch, & Cook, 1963, p. 380). The judges are supposed to try to equalize the size of increments in favorability between one pile and the next. Then, the scale value of each opinion statement is calculated, most simply by taking the mean of the pile numbers assigned to it by all the judges. If the judges disagree about a given statement, thus making its classification inconsistent, it is discarded as ambiguous. Finally, the attitude scale itself is constructed by choosing about 20 items that cover the entire range of the attitude dimension, from most unfavorable to most favorable. The exact degree of favorability of each item is already known, because it has been calculated on the basis of the judges' sorting of the statements. The scale is now ready to be given to the subjects whose attitudes are to be measured. An example of a Thurstone scale constructed and used by C.K.A. Wang and Louis Thurstone (1931) is given in Table 8-1.

The scale values are the average values assigned to the statements by the judges; these values are not shown to the subjects, and the statements are presented to the subjects in scrambled order. The subject's task is simply to check each statement with which she or he agrees; the subject's *attitude score* is the mean or median scale value of the items checked. Ideally, each subject will check only items that are adjacent in their original scale values. The investigator aims for a scale having a wide range of mean attitude scores across sub-

TABLE 8-1
ATTITUDE TOWARD BIRTH CONTROL

Scale value	Statement
0.0	**1** The practice of birth control is equivalent to murder.
0.9	**2** Birth control should be absolutely prohibited.
1.1	**3** Birth control is race suicide.
1.7	**4** Birth control reduces the marital relation to the level of vice.
2.3	**5** Decency forbids the use of birth control.
2.8	**6** The practice of birth control evades man's duty to propagate the race.
3.3	**7** The practice of birth control may be injurious physically, mentally, or morally.
3.6	**8** Birth control is morally wrong in spite of its possible benefits.
4.5	**9** The slight benefits of birth control hardly justify it.
5.4	**10** Birth control has both advantages and disadvantages.
5.8	**11** People should be free to do whatever they wish about birth control.
6.6	**12** Birth control has nothing to do with morality.
7.4	**13** Birth control is necessary for women who must help earn a living.
7.6	**14** Birth control is a legitimate health measure.
8.0	**15** Birth control increases the happiness of married life.
8.3	**16** Birth control information should be available to everybody.
9.2	**17** Uncontrolled reproduction leads to overpopulation, social unrest, and war.
9.6	**18** Birth control is the only solution to many of our social problems.
9.8	**19** Only a fool can oppose birth control.
10.5	**20** We simply must have birth control.

Source: L. L. Thurstone (Ed.), (1931) *The measurement of social attitude*. Chicago: University of Chicago Press. Reprinted by permission.

jects, but on which each individual subject endorses only a narrow range of items. Failure to achieve this end may indicate that several different dimensions are represented by the scale; for example, a subject's attitude about birth control might involve considerations of both morality and social welfare. Thus in the example presented here, a subject who checked items 3, 6, and 12, with the rather widely scattered scale values of 1.1, 2.8, and 6.6, respectively, might believe that the population is dwindling dangerously, that there are no other world issues involved in birth control, and that it is a pure and simple practical matter of preserving the species.

One criticism of the Thurstone scale has been that the same mean attitude score may be given to two individuals whose pattern of beliefs with reference to the attitude may be quite different. For example, the delusional subject mentioned above, who believes that the human race is dying out and that birth control has nothing to do with morality (item 12) because it is a matter of dire *necessity*, attains a mean score of 3.5. This attitude score is almost identical with that of a regretful Catholic who believes that birth control is morally wrong in spite of its possible benefits (item 8, scale value = 3.6).

Although investigators should try to create scales which will not result in a wide scatter of responses, the fact that identical scores can be reached in different ways is not necessarily a catastrophe. The two subjects may still *be* the same in terms of overall favorability, in terms of any implications the attitude may have for endorsing governmental or church policy statements or other behavior the experimenter may wish to predict, despite the difference in their rationales for their attitudes. Both, for example, might be expected to oppose the use of public funds for the dissemination of birth-control literature. Whether this is a serious drawback for the investigator depends on the question, that is, on the purpose for which the attitude scale is being used.

A more technical criticism of the Thurstone scale is that the attitudes of the *judges* may affect their initial sorting of opinion statements. The statement "People should be free to do whatever they wish about birth control," which has an approximately neutral scale value, might be regarded as sanctioning murder and therefore as extremely unfavorable by a judge who believes that controlling overpopulation by birth control is equivalent to mass murder. Research has shown that judges with different attitudes *do* tend to assign different scale values to the same items (Dawes & Smith, 1985; Hovland & Sherif, 1952); however, the rank order of items tends to be the same. What this means in practice is that the judges may not be able to construct a scale whose values are absolute or whose intervals are equal, but they can agree in their ordering of the items from least to most favorable. This removes one of the hoped-for advantages of the Thurstone method, but it does not put it at a disadvantage compared to other methods, since no one has yet achieved a completely successful interval scale for attitudes.

The Likert Scale In a Thurstone scale, the opinion statements represent a graded series of points on a continuum, and the subject makes one of two responses (agree-disagree). In the Likert scale the situation is reversed: The opinion statements represent the two general categories "favorable" or "unfavorable," and the subject indicates the extent of agreement by checking one of a graded series of five points ranging from "strongly approve" to "strongly disapprove."

A Likert scale is constructed by collecting a large number of opinion statements concerning an issue and asking a sample of subjects to indicate the *extent* of their own agreement with each statement. The most unfavorable response to each item is scored 1, and the most favorable response is scored 5 (or vice versa). Thus, each person has a score from 1 to 5 on each item, and a person's total score, representative of an overall attitude on the topic studied, is simply the sum of the item scores. After administering the scale to the preliminary sample, the scale maker then examines each item to see how well it discriminates between the people with the most favorable overall attitudes (top 25 percent) and those with the least favorable attitudes (bottom 25 percent). If the high scorers and the low scorers both respond to a given opinion statement in the same way, that item is discarded, on the assumption that it does not tap the same attitude as the scale as a whole. The final scale is constructed from the items that consistently elicit strong agreement from the most favorable pretest subjects and vice versa. A sample of such a final scale is given in Table 8-2.

The numbers in parentheses in the table show how each response is scored and are not included on the questionnaire given to the subject. The subject's task is to underline the response that indicates his or her position with regard to the opinion statement, and the overall favorability of the subject's attitude is represented by the sum (or average) of the numbers corresponding to the response. In the racism scale in Table 8-2, the lower the score the more racist the person's attitude.

The most common criticism of the Likert scale is that many combinations of responses can result in the same score. For example, suppose that a certain subject's prejudice takes the form of a strict separate-but-equal doctrine. That person will check "Strongly approve" to both items 10 and 11 and might mildly agree with items 12 and 14, since they do not require any black-white contact. If this subject is uncertain as to how to apply the "separate-

TABLE 8-2
EXCERPT FROM A SCALE ON WHITE RACISM

9 Negroes belong in one class and should be treated in about the same way.				
Strongly approve	Approve	Undecided	Disapprove	Strongly disapprove
(1)	(2)	(3)	(4)	(5)

10 Negro homes should be segregated from those of white people.				
Strongly approve	Approve	Undecided	Disapprove	Strongly disapprove
(1)	(2)	(3)	(4)	(5)

11 Where there is segregation, the Negro section should have the same equipment in paving, water, and electric light facilities as are found in the white district.				
Strongly approve	Approve	Undecided	Disapprove	Strongly disapprove
(5)	(4)	(3)	(2)	(1)

12 If the same preparation is required, the Negro teacher should receive the same salary as the white.				
Strongly approve	Approve	Undecided	Disapprove	Strongly disapprove
(5)	(4)	(3)	(2)	(1)

13 Practically all American hotels should refuse to admit Negroes.				
Strongly approve	Approve	Undecided	Disapprove	Strongly disapprove
(1)	(2)	(3)	(4)	(5)

14 No Negro should be deprived of the franchise except for reasons which would also disenfranchise the white man.				
Strongly approve	Approve	Undecided	Disapprove	Strongly disapprove
(5)	(4)	(3)	(2)	(1)

Source: R. A. Likert (1932). A technique for the measurement of attitudes. *Archives of Psychology, 22,* 5–55.

but-equal'' philosophy to the other two questions, the total score will be $3 + 1 + 5 + 4 + 3 + 4 = 20$, the same score as that of an extremely wishy-washy person who only knows that the Fifteenth Amendment gives the vote to blacks and who supports the Constitution $(3 + 3 + 3 + 3 + 3 + 5 = 20)$. As we have pointed out, this problem is not unique to the Likert scale; its seriousness depends on the question the investigator poses and on the behavior being studied.

The Guttman Scale The Guttman scale is based on the assumption that opinion statements can be ranked in favorability so that agreement with any given statement implies agreement with all less strongly favorable items. According to Louis Guttman (1944), any scale that fitted this model perfectly was perfectly *unidimensional*. Unlike the Likert and Thurstone methods, whereby a person's total attitude score might reflect any one of a variety of patterns of response, a given attitude score on a Guttman scale can, theoretically, be reached in only one way. If we know an individual's score, we know how that person responded to every single question on the questionnaire.

In constructing a Guttman scale, a number of items are administered as an attitude test to a sample of subjects, and their responses are analyzed to determine how closely they fit the ideal model. Thus, if there are three ($N = 3$) items, of which A is the most favorable and C the least, there are four ($N + 1$) acceptable response patterns (scale types) in terms of the following model:

Score	Agrees with item:			Disagrees with item:		
	A	B	C	A	B	C
3	X	X	X			
2		X	X	X		
1			X	X	X	
0				X	X	X

Adapted from Selltiz, Jahoda, Deutsch, & Cook, 1963, p. 374.

Any other pattern of responses—for example, agreeing with A and C but disagreeing with B, is considered erroneous. If in fact A is more favorable and C is least favorable, it would make no sense to agree with A and disagree with B or C. Of course, this will be so only when we can truly order the items. The proportion of pretest scores which actually conform to one of the ideal patterns is taken as an index of the adequacy, or *reproducibility*, of the scale. Guttman considered a reproducibility coefficient of .90 the criterion for an adequate (''scalable'') set of items. If this figure is not reached in the analysis of the scores of the pretest subject, the items assumed to be responsible for the most ''errors'' are dropped, and the scale is retested on new samples of subjects until the criterion has been achieved. The final set of items constitutes the

TABLE 8-3

SOME ITEMS DESIGNED TO MEASURE ATTITUDES TOWARD PREMARITAL SEX

1 I approve of petting at any time before marriage.
2 I approve of coitus when a couple is in love and finally engaged to be married.
3 I approve of coitus when a couple is in love or going steady.
4 I approve of coitus on random or casual dates.
5 I approve of coitus at any time before marriage.
6 I would prefer not to marry a virgin.

Source: Adapted and excerpted from H. T. Christensen and G. R. Carpenter (1962). Value-behavior discrepancies regarding premarital coitus in three Western cultures. *American Sociological Review, 27,* 66–74. Reprinted by permission. Also in Shaw & Wright, 1967, p. 104.

attitude test which is administered to the subjects. An example of a group of items from a Guttman-type scale is given in Table 8-3.

The items are usually presented in scrambled order, and the subject's task is simply to check the ones with which she or he agrees. The score is that of the applicable scale type. If the subject has not responded according to one of the scale types, the minimum number of changes necessary to make the responses conform to a scale type are performed, and the subject is given the score corresponding to the resulting type.

The use of a successful unidimensional scale avoids the problem of different attitude patterns in the same score, as in the case of the regretful Catholic and the subject who fears that the human race is heading for extinction (the hypothetical subjects in our discussion of the Thurstone scale). But one might legitimately ask whether we have gained anything by devising an attitude scale on which these two subjects *do* answer all the same questions in the same way, or else receive different attitude scores. If a set of beliefs is truly multidimensional (so that two people can have very different beliefs which nonetheless lead to similar actions), little is gained by forcing them into a unidimensional measuring device which obscures the differences. If we devise a scale on which two subjects with different beliefs check all the same answers, we do not know anything more about the subjects' attitudes than we did with the Thurstone (or Likert) scale; in fact, we know *less*, since we have no way of discovering that they base their positions on very different beliefs. The items of a scale that fails to differentiate between these two at any level will probably be vague and general, like the items above on premarital sex, in order to avoid tapping into specific areas of disagreement between the two subjects. However, if we devise a Guttman scale which deals with a single dimension on the attitude—say, fear of the extinction of the human race—one of our two subjects will get a very high score and the other a very low score, yet this differentiation may be misleading if we want to know how the two subjects will vote on a bill to make free birth-control pills available to everyone. In other words, people may have a general tendency to behave one way or another with regard to a given issue, and this tendency may be the result not of a unidimensional force, but rather of a variety of factors. In considering the Guttman scale (or any scale, in fact) the most important step is to decide what you want to learn from the scale and/or what kind of behavior you want to predict.

A related problem with the Guttman scale is that a set of items producing scalable responses (i.e., unidimensional) for one population may not work for another population. The scale items may be ordered differently, or they may not fall into any consistent order. Thus, the scale must be pretested on a sample of subjects similar to those to be used in the final study.

In summary, the major drawbacks of the Guttman scale are the ambiguity and dubious validity of assigning the subject a score corresponding to the nearest scale type, the questionable utility of "unidimensional" items, and the likelihood that the scale will simply end up with items that are widely spread in popularity (though not necessarily unidimensional), resulting in ineffectiveness in detecting differences among the subjects. William Scott, in a review of attitude measures (1968, p. 224) concludes that these deficiencies may be sufficient cause for avoiding use of the Guttman scale for attitude measurement.

The Semantic Differential The semantic differential was devised by Charles Osgood, George Suci, and Percey Tannenbaum (1957) as a means of assessing the *connotative meaning* of a concept for a given subject or group of subjects. The connotative meaning of a concept includes all of its suggestive or implicit significance, as distinct from its *denotative meaning*, or dictionary definition. For example, the primary denotative meaning of the English word "mother" is "a woman who has borne a child" (*Webster's New Universal Unabridged Dictionary*, 2d Edition, N.Y.: Dorset & Baber, 1983, p. 1173), but most people attach a good deal more significance to the concept than is contained in this definition. Moreover, this additional significance varies widely across individuals and across cultural, age, class, and ethnic groups. For some people the word "mother" might conjure up an image of a frail, sweet little old lady sitting in a rocking chair and crocheting doilies; others might immediately think of a large and strident harridan grabbing and shoving people at a bargain counter. These extra meanings attached to the concept "mother" are connotative meanings, and Osgood, Suci, and Tannenbaum assumed that an individual's attitude toward a concept is included in the connotative meaning he or she attaches to that concept.

Because the semantic differential is applicable to *any* concept, no set of opinion statements is necessary. Instead, the name of the concept—"mother," "birth control," "integration," "premarital sex," or whatever—is presented to the subject, who is asked to rate it on a series of 7-point bipolar scales in the following format:

Kind _____ _____ _____ _____ _____ _____ _____ Cruel

For example, a subject whose idea of "mother" involves extreme kindness and generosity will check the blank closest to the "Kind" end of the scale. If the term "mother" connotes extreme cruelty and meanness, the subject will check the blank nearest to the "Cruel" end of the scale. The closer to the end point the check is placed, the more strongly the subject feels that the adjective at that end represents his or her idea of the rated concept. The subject who is neutral or perfectly ambivalent checks the middle blank.

Osgood, Suci, and Tannenbaum (1957) found that the connotative meaning of most concepts could be almost entirely accounted for by three underlying dimensions: evaluation (good-bad), potency (strong-weak), and activity (active-passive). For example, the connotative meaning of the rocking chair image of the concept "mother" might be summarized as very good, very weak, and very passive, whereas the harridan image might be characterized as fairly bad, very strong, and very active. By giving the subject a number of scales representing each of the three dimensions, the authors hoped to obtain an accurate picture of the personal connotative meaning the concept held for each subject. The evaluative component was seen as measuring the direction and intensity of the subject's "attitude," although other workers have also included the potency and activity dimensions in their conceptualizations of attitude.

The semantic differential instrument which is given to subjects usually consists of the adjective pairs with the highest "loadings" (a technical term which need not concern us here) on the three dimensions. For the *evaluative* dimension, these scales are: good-bad, beautiful-ugly, sweet-sour, clean-dirty, tasty-distasteful, valuable-worthless, kind-cruel, pleasant-unpleasant, happy-sad, sacred-profane, nice-awful, fragrant-foul, honest-dishonest, and fair-unfair. For the *potency* dimension, they are: strong-weak, large-small, and heavy-light. And for the *activity* dimension, they are: active-passive, fast-slow, and hot-cold. For example, the subject whose concept of mother is of the frail, rocking chair type might check the ends of the scales corresponding to the following adjectives on each of the three dimensions:

Evaluative dimension		Potency dimension	Activity dimension
Good	Beautiful	Weak	Passive
Sweet	Clean	Small	Slow
Tasty	Valuable	Light	Cold
Kind	Pleasant		
Happy	Sacred		
Nice	Fragrant		
Honest	Fair		

Of course, there may be exceptions; perhaps the subject sees the concept "mother" as sad instead of happy, but on the whole the "good, weak, and passive" would be expected to emerge in the subject's ratings.

Because it is so vague and open-ended, the semantic differential may be a better measure of general affective states than is a questionnaire with more specific items. For example, in a study of the effects of early separation from the father on later sex-role attitudes, Lyn Carlsmith (1973) found that on the semantic differential, boys whose fathers had been absent had similar ratings for the concepts "ideal self" and "mother"; boys whose fathers had always been present rated "ideal self" closer to the concept of "father."

In social psychology, the subject's responses on the semantic differential can provide the data for a simple attitude measure. In measuring attitudes the experimenter simply assigns a number to each blank of the evaluative scales from Good = 7, to Neutral = 4, to Bad = 1, or vice versa and takes the mean ratings across all the evaluation scales as the subject's attitude score. (The experimenter may repeat this process for the other two dimensions.) Often, some of the scales are omitted, or adjective pairs that seem to be evaluative and more appropriate to the issue at hand are substituted. Since literal-minded subjects may sometimes balk at some of the scales, such as fragrant-foul and sacred-profane, in giving instructions it is important to stress the necessity of filling in all the scales and to mention that the subjects may have to use their imagination in some cases.

One problem with the semantic differential is that not all the evaluative adjectives elicit differences in attitude on all concepts. Pretesting should be carried out to determine whether the adjectives chosen "work" (i.e., correlate highly with each other) for the particular attitude objects to be studied in the experiment at hand. Often, it turns out to be more useful to use only a few adjective pairs.

Scales and Questionnaires: General Considerations

Rarely does a social psychological experiment make use of any of these methods according to the strict criteria for scale construction and pretesting listed above. Usually, the experimenter's test resembles the format of one of these types of scales, but the items are seldom pretested on separate samples of subjects. Although the elaborate procedures of scale construction may be superfluous, since many simply constructed scales such as the semantic differential correlate very highly with the more complex ones (Shaw & Wright, 1967), pretesting is always a useful means of ensuring that subjects' responses to the questionnaire used are a function of the particular *experimental situation* the investigator has devised and *not* to superfluous contextual factors such as characteristics of the questionnaire or rating scale itself.

Recent experiments by social cognition researchers have revealed that there is nothing "uncomplicated" about completing even the simplest of questionnaires or rating scales. Fritz Strack and Leonard Martin (1987), for example, note that the provision of even a simple discrete response—such as rating a discussion group by circling numbers from 1 to 15 as did subjects in the Aronson-Mills severity-of-initiation experiment—is the result of a long and complex series of intrapsychic events. (Figure 8-1 provides their model of these processes.) Respondents must first *interpret* the question or statement correctly, and the meaning assigned to the item is often a function of factors other than the wording of the item; for example, previous questions can serve as cues for the interpretation of a subsequent ambiguous question.

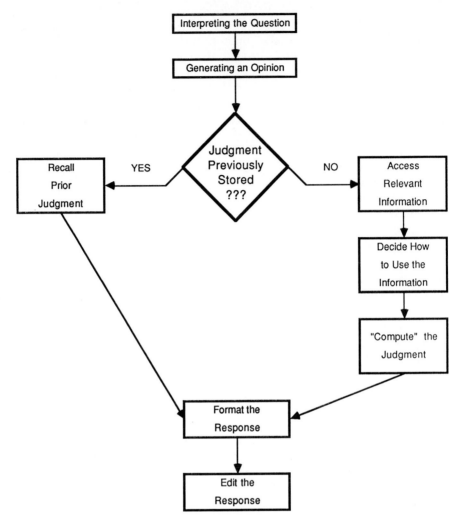

FIGURE 8-1
Model of information processing in a survey situation. [*Strack & Martin (1987)*.]

According to Strack and Martin, once subjects have (correctly or incorrectly) interpreted the question, they must *generate a response* to it. If the judgment is not one subjects have made before, they must generate one on the spot, and again, a multitude of factors influence their responses. To provide a valid judgment, the subject must be able to recall relevant information. For example, in the Aronson-Mills experiment, when asked to rate how intelligent the discussants were, subjects had to remember the specific content of the discussion. In addition to recalling the specifics of the discussion group they were rating in the experiment, subjects may have also recalled other discussion groups they had overheard, or in which they were participants, and those recollections may have also influenced their ratings of the boring discussion group. Memories of *their own* past behaviors relevant to the question might also have influenced subjects' ratings. For example, if in past sex-related discussions, subjects remained quiet and passive and wished they had talked more, even the most inane of discussants' contributions in the severity-of-initiation study might have been rated as "interesting." The process of generating a meaningful response to a rating scale is further complicated by virtue of the fact that a fixed format (e.g., "Circle a number from 1 to 15"), often employed in the interest of control, may not use categories or anchors that we normally use. How often, for example, in our day-to-day lives do we indicate our opinions by circling a number from 1 to 15? Thus, to provide a valid measure of the dependent variable, subjects must *format their responses* to fit the options provided by the experimenter.

Finally, once subjects have interpreted a question, reached a judgment, and formulated that judgment in the context of the format of the question, they must decide whether to indicate their "true" and "honest" response. Although the anonymity often afforded subjects is an advantage of questionnaires or rating scales, there is no guarantee that subjects will not *edit their responses* to be "kind" to the experimenter or to present themselves in the most desirable light.

This discussion is not intended as an indictment of the use of questionnaires and rating scales. When used correctly and with an awareness of their limitations they are valuable tools for experimental researchers. Neither is it intended as a critique of the internal validity of the Aronson-Mills experiment. That is, even though any number of contextual factors (aside from the independent variable) may have influenced subjects' ratings, because subjects were randomly assigned to experimental conditions, the influence of these extraneous factors contributed to random error variance, but were *not* a source of systematic error. We simply want to make the point that completing a questionnaire or rating scale is a complicated enterprise. Because this is so, experimenters as well as survey researchers need to be constantly aware of the important influence of subtle "irrelevant" contextual factors on subjects' responses. For, as Strack and Martin (1987, p. 123) point out, "Asking, and consequently answering questions . . . never occurs in a vacuum."

Lest readers throw up their hands and toss their questionnaires out the window in the face of the previous discussion, we hasten to add that there are a few general precautionary measures that can increase the reliability or validity of a questionnaire measure. First, the more questions asked or scales used to answer the same underlying question, the more reliable and the less affected by random error the subject's answers will be—up to a point (Scott, 1968, p. 239). If only a single question is used, a minor feature of the wording, such as "How much do you like . . .?" versus "How much do you approve of . . .?" may cause a subject with a favorable attitude to hesitate in endorsing it and perhaps to choose a neutral answer that does not represent his or her general feelings. If several questions are asked on the same topic, the subject with a favorable attitude should choose the positive answer to most of them and thus would be "correctly" classified when the data were tabulated. Of course, too many versions of the same question may begin to appear so redundant that the subject stops paying attention or wonders what the experimenter is *really* trying to get at.

Second, questions should be worded so that a given direction of response (e.g., a "positive" attitude) is indicated by answering "yes" (or "true" or "agree") to some questions and "no" (or "false" or "disagree") to other questions, since some subjects tend to check more "yes" answers than "no" answers regardless of the content of the questions. Similarly, some subjects tend to check extremes on the scale; others, perhaps more cautious types, cling to the middle. There are many other technical details that can affect the validity of a questionnaire measure, and a thorough presentation of the difficulties that can arise in questionnaire construction, and some possible ways to avoid them, is given in Scott (1968) and in a chapter by Robyn Dawes and Tom Smith (1985). These precautions should be taken in the construction and pretesting stages, since methods for eliminating response biases after the data have been collected are not very satisfactory (Dawes & Smith, 1985; Schuman & Kalton, 1985; Scott, 1968).

We have stated that one of the advantages of questionnaire measures is that the subjects seldom need help in filling them out, which confers the benefit of anonymity and avoids some of the dangers of bias. This advantage goes hand in hand with a problem, however. If the subjects do not understand how to express their answers in terms of the rating scales, their response may be meaningless, and the experimenter may discover this too late or not at all. This problem becomes especially acute when one moves beyond the traditional college sophomore population to samples in which subjects may have difficulty understanding questionnaires produced by a highly verbal graduate student. The point seems obvious, but it may be overlooked by an experimenter who simply gives out the questionnaire and hands the responses to a data analyst.

One solution to this problem is to teach the subjects how to use the rating scales. However, this technique may overemphasize the experimenter's concern with the questionnaire, so that subjects guess that it is the crucial dependent-variable measure. But this approach need not be heavy-handed. A more subtle method is to teach the subjects about scales *in a different context*, so that by the time they have to fill out the questionnaire, they will already have learned how to express their responses. For example, in one experiment (Carlsmith, Collins, & Helmreich, 1966), the subjects believed that they were participating in a marketing-research survey conducted to find out what kind of music appealed to high school students. The subjects were asked to listen to a "practice" record and to rate it on an 11-point scale. In this context, the experimenter had an opportunity to explain in depth the mechanics of the scale. Subsequently, all subjects filled out a series of scales rating several different records, giving the experimenter ample opportunity to be sure they understood the scales. After these ratings were completed, the experimenter mentioned that the kind of mood the subjects were in and their recent experiences might affect their ratings of the records and asked them to fill out a few rating scales about the "tests" they had been working on right before they came into the room where the record survey was being conducted. These ratings were the dependent-variable measure in the experiment. Since the subjects had just been instructed in the use of the scales, there was no danger of losing data due to the subjects' inability to understand the measure.

Another major problem with questionnaires is that they are more likely to be treated casually by the subject than is almost any other type of measure. The experimental hour may be almost over, and the subject may simply fill out the questionnaire as fast as possible, in order to move on to the next activity. If the subjects simply race through the pages of questions, checking scales without giving them much thought, unconcerned about the exact wording of the questions, the data collected will inevitably be highly affected by random error, and thus the results of the whole experiment may be distorted or obscured. The key problem is inducing the subjects to take the questionnaire seriously. To some extent this problem can be diminished by making the questions interesting and by instructing the subjects to respond carefully, insofar as this is possible without overemphasizing the fact that the questionnaire contains the important measure. The problem is inherent in the use of the questionnaire, however, and in this respect the interview is a superior technique.

Interviews

The great advantage of an interview over a questionnaire is that the interviewer, merely by being present, can succeed in inducing the subject to pay heed, and therefore stands a better chance of getting a serious, honest response. In addition to increasing the subject's motivation to respond carefully and honestly, the interviewer also makes it possible to ensure that the subject interprets the questions correctly and responds in the desired amount of depth and detail. In an interview, the precise meaning of the question can be emphasized, the subject can be exhorted repeatedly to think carefully before answering, and the experimenter can repeat sections which are unclear to the subject. This procedure requires more time than a questionnaire does, but it is time well spent. The interview is often shunned because of the possibility of inducing bias, but if the experimenter has been kept blind to the condition the subject is in, or if the interviewer is someone other than the experimenter who is blind to the condition, it can be used effectively.

If the interview helps the subject to understand the questions, it may also help the experimenter to understand the answers. If a subject responds ambiguously to a questionnaire item, the experimenter usually does not discover it until it is too late to find out what the subject meant. In a interview, however, the experimenter can follow up an incomprehensible or contradictory response with a probe for further clarification or a question which redirects the subject's attention to the information the experimenter is looking for. The interview is better suited than the questionnaire to situations in which the experimenter wants to use open-ended questions to ascertain the subject's overall reaction to the experiment or some part of it, frame of reference, interpretation of events, and the underlying perceptions which led to this interpretation. It is therefore especially useful for pilot testing, to determine how the treatment affected the subject and how it might be improved; for postexperimental information-gathering, to assess suspicion and the subject's general reaction to the experiment; and for situations in which the subject is suddenly asked to focus attention on some aspect of the experiment which has not previously been made salient. If the experimenter is skilled and sensitive, the interview may be preferable even to an anonymous questionnaire when the questions are personal or emotionally laden, as in the situation in which subjects believe that they have hurt another subject and the experimenter wants to know how they respond to their own unkind behavior.

The advantages of the interview depend on a good interviewer; an inept or insensitive interviewer can easily turn them into serious disadvantages. In this sense the interview is a more risky technique than the questionnaire. There are a few precautions that the experimenter can take to reduce that risk. First, the questions should be worded so that the subjects can understand and answer them and so that they do not threaten the subjects' self-esteem by making them appear incompetent, inconsistent, or immoral. It is a good idea to develop the wording of the questions in advance, revising it during pilot testing; this both increases the probability of achieving comprehensible and nonthreatening questions and decreases the amount of error variance. The flexibility of the interview technique is not sacrificed by the use of questions with standardized wording, since the interviewer can always tailor the situation to the individual subject by repetitions and follow-up questions. Although it is important to remain unaware of which condition each subject is in, the interviewer should know the intent of each question and the kind of information it is meant to elicit, in order to evaluate whether the subject's answers are adequate. The interviewer may also ask one or more closed questions (with a limited number of response alternatives) in order to collect scorable data, unless there is a previously devised objective scheme for coding open-ended responses. The transaction from the preparatory stage of relatively free and easy conversation to a forced-choice question may require special tact and practice. In general, however, it is to be preferred to the subsequent categorization of responses by coders, which introduces a further inferential step into the proceedings, thereby jeopardizing reliability. Of course, if all the questions are of the closed-answer format, one may simply take the measure by means of a questionnaire.

A detailed discussion of specific techniques of interviewing is beyond the scope of this book. However, the work of Cannell and Kahn (1968) and Schuman and Kalton (1985) provides suggestions and guidance. Interested readers might also find a chapter on interviewing by William Crano and Marilynn Brewer (1986, Chapter 12) a useful introduction to the topic.

Some General Problems with Verbal Measures

All the measures we have discussed so far are verbal or *self-report* measures. In using them, we rely on the subjects to tell us how they were affected by the independent variable, although they are not always aware that the question has these implications. If the experimenter is primarily interested in the subjects' verbal behavior—that is, what people will say after exposure to the independent variable—verbal measures are appropriate. But often, the experimenter wants to find out how the subjects feel, what they expect or believe, or how they will behave as a result of the experimental treatments. Their verbal reports are thus an *indirect* measure of the dependent variable that interests the experimenter. It may be the most direct measure the experimenter can think of, but still there is no *necessary* correspondence between what the subjects feel, expect, believe, or do, and what they say.

A subject's response to a question may be determined by many factors besides the variable that the experimenter has in mind. We have already pointed out the necessity for making the questions understandable so that subjects are *able* to provide an answer which they believe to be true and which falls into the experimenter's frame of reference. Whether the subject does provide this answer depends on a variety of *motivational* factors. The subject may be motivated to gain the experimenter's approval by making a favorable impression, and the answer a person believes is most likely to achieve this end may not be the same as the one the person believes to be true. In other words, the subject may give an answer which is socially desirable or likely to be rewarded by the experimenter, especially if the "truth" might be construed as unflattering or humiliating. In order to avoid this source of error, experimenters often stress that there are no right or wrong or better or worse answers to the questions. Other techniques designed to minimize the subject's motivation to "look good" are emphasizing the anonymity of the responses and refraining from expressing approval or disapproval in interviews.

In some situations, subjects may also be motivated to provide data that will confirm (or disconfirm) the experimenter's hypothesis, and so they will try to "psych out" the experiment and answer the questions accordingly (Orne, 1962). As we pointed out in Chapter 7, one way to reduce the likelihood of this kind of response is to make the experiment so involving that the subject has no time to puzzle over the experimenter's intent. Other techniques will be discussed in Chapter 9.

In attempting to make sure that the subject is able to answer the questions, it is important to make the questions not only understandable but also specific enough so that the subject can answer them with confidence. Since in social psychological experiments the questions are often aimed at determining the subjects' response to some concrete aspect of the experimental situation, the criterion of specificity is often automatically satisfied. Sometimes, however, the investigator asks a question that is extremely vague or abstract, in the hope of measuring a generalized attitude or overall personality impression or as an attempt to prevent the subjects from remembering their earlier responses to a similar question.

There are drawbacks in this technique. First, it may be unwise to assume that the subject's conception or attitude is so vague or general that it is independent of specific circumstances. Second, there is a good deal of evidence to show that people's inferences about complex traits in themselves or others have little relation to their actual behavior; much more valid results are obtained by asking the subject about the behavior directly (Mischel, 1968). Selltiz and colleagues make this same general point with regard to rating scales: "If the concept of what is being measured is vague, as it is in some rating scales, it is unlikely that the ratings will be clear in meaning. When the concept of what is being measured is ambiguous, the ordering of individuals may actually be quite arbitrary, and even distinctions of greater or less become meaningless" (1963, p. 356).

In attempting to ensure that the subject is *motivated* to tell the truth as he or she sees it, the experimenter can arrange the situational contingencies so that it is clear that the subject will not be punished for telling the truth and by making sure that no responses provoke a negative reaction. Unfortunately, it is impossible to reward the subject for honest responses, since if the experimenter knew what the "honest response" was, there would be no need to question the subject in the first place. The experimenter can, however, attempt to get the subject motivated to conduct a valid, bias-free experiment and to therefore provide valid, bias-free answers. Stephen Weber and Thomas Cook (1972) provide some evidence that, in some situations, subjects can be motivated to provide honest answers. One excellent technique for doing so is to enlist the subject's aid as an experimenter. We will discuss some of the other advantages of this strategy later in this chapter, in the section on disguising the measure. The technique is especially well-adapted to studies of person perception; for example, the subject might be told to take on the role of an experimenter, without being told that the dependent variable is the "experimenter's" perception of the other subject (or confederate). The Aronson-Linder (1965) study, described in greater detail in Chapter 9, is an example of this procedure.

Even if the subject understands the question perfectly and is highly motivated to give an honest answer, it may be impossible to do so. When asked a question for which there is one response that "looks better" than another, or when there are other subtle pressures toward distortion, it is very easy for the subject to give that response, really believing in its veracity. The problem is that it is often much easier to say something commendable than it is to do something commendable. The costs of doing something, expending time and effort, and coping with special problems that arise may not be at all salient to the subject whose only task is to answer a question. It is easier to say that one wishes to save the redwoods than it is to call 50 people and solicit funds in support of this cause; it is easier to check ''7—I like him very much'' than it is to take someone on as a roommate for a year.

The *salience* of a verbal measure raises additional problems. In questioning the subject (describing the questionnaire or actually asking the questions in an interview), how much should the experimenter emphasize the importance of the subject's answers? If the measure is to have impact so that the subject is involved and takes the questions seriously, the importance of the answers should be stressed. However, the experimenter often wants to conceal the true purpose of the questions. The subject who believes that the questions are extremely important may have a greater motivation to look good and may therefore be more likely to give the socially desirable response. The subject who figures out that the questions are the dependent-variable measure may rethink what happened in the experiment and thus figure out the experimenter's hypothesis. For example, if the subjects in the study on severity of initiation had surmised that the experimenter was primarily interested in how much they liked the group, they might have thought back and begun to wonder whether the initiation was supposed to have anything to do with their reactions.

In order to prevent the subject from recognizing the hypothesis, the experimenter is often tempted to administer the dependent-variable measure in a casual manner, almost as an afterthought. A common device is the ''Oh, by the way'' technique. ''Oh, by the way,'' the experimenter might remark, ''the psychology department is interested in how subjects feel about experiments.'' Engaging in a haphazard search, the experimenter finds a dog-eared questionnaire lying around, hands it to the subject, and leaves the room. By thus deemphasizing an interest in the questionnaire, the experimenter stands a good chance of masking its essential importance. The problem is that the experimenter may succeed too well; the subject may treat the questionnaire as casually as the experimenter appeared to treat it and may, accordingly, check off responses almost at random. The interview is an improvement over the questionnaire in this respect; when used judiciously, it can be more powerful than a questionnaire without arousing suspicion. For example, Aronson and Linder (1965) reported an experiment which failed when the dependent variable was measured by a questionnaire but succeeded when the subjects were interviewed. The experimenters found that subjects who were given the questionnaire thought that it was an unimportant part of the experiment and did not answer the questions very carefully. This resulted in a large amount of random error, and therefore the results did not reach an acceptable level of statistical significance. However, the interviewer, who was introduced as the experimenter's ''research supervisor'' and who had high status and an earnest demeanor, induced the subjects to take the interview seriously and to think carefully about their answers. Since the interviewer was ignorant of what condition the subject had been in, the superior results achieved with this technique could not have been due to bias in the interview.

To summarize, there are three main problems with verbal measures. First, they are measures of what the subjects *say* about themselves. What a person says about the variable which interests the experimenter may not correspond to a more direct measure of that variable. Many psychologists have pointed out that the day-to-day rewards and punishments for verbal endorsements of a certain type of behavior are very different from the rewards and punishments contingent on the actual performance of the behavior (Bandura & Walters, 1963; Kaufman, 1970; Mischel, 1968). Subjects in psychology experiments, like most other people, have a history of often saying one thing and thinking, feeling, believing, or doing another. For one thing, it is usually easier to make a verbal statement about doing something than it is to do it. Thus, verbal measures become less useful and less valid the more the experimenter is concerned with behavior and the more accustomed the subject is to receiving differential rewards for performing that behavior and for saying positive things about it. Of course, there may be inferential links involved in the use of behavioral measures, too, but behavioral measures are often unobtrusive, so that the subject is not aware of the necessity of vigilance in self-presentation.

This brings us to the second problem common to the use of verbal measures: The subjects almost always *know* that something about themselves is being measured at that moment. They have a form to fill out or questions to answer. They may not know that it is the measure of major concern to the experimenter, and sometimes they may not know that it is related to the experiment at all, but they know that they are providing data for someone, and they may alter their responses in the light of that knowledge.

Finally, as we mentioned earlier, the verbal measure is less involving. The subjects are not totally wrapped up in what they are doing, and they have time for the sort of rumination that might lead to distortion of answers. Alternatively, if the measure is completely uninvolving, subjects may not consider their answers at all. The essential dilemma of verbal measures is that a measure which concerns the subjects enough so that they answer carefully may concern them enough so that they censor their answers.

BEHAVIORAL MEASURES

Despite their shortcomings, verbal measures continue to far outnumber behavioral measures in social psychology, and this very prevalence is perhaps the most important reason for turning to behavioral methods. As Eugene Webb and his coauthors put it, "the principle objection [to interviews and questionnaires] is that they are used alone. No research method is without bias. Interviews and questionnaires must be supplemented by methods testing the same social science variables but having *different* methodological weaknesses"(Webb, Campbell, Schwartz, & Sechrest, 1966, p. 1). It has often been argued that verbal measures are the only effective means of getting at some sorts of information—for example, a person's "perceptions, beliefs, feelings, motivations, anticipations, or future plans" (Selltiz, Jahoda, Deutsch, &

Cook, 1963, p. 236)—and the only *possible* means of attaining information about certain variables—for example, "past behavior or private behavior, such as sexual behavior or dreaming, which are, by their very nature, either unfeasible or impossible to observe" (Selltiz, Jahoda, Deutsch, & Cook, 1963, p. 236). Since 1963, when these statements were written, our knowledge about both dreaming (Dement, 1972) and sexual behavior (Masters & Johnson, 1966) has been greatly extended through research involving direct behavioral measurement. These investigations should serve as cautionary examples to the social psychologist who believes that it is impossible to use a behavioral measure for the phenomenon under study.

Measures of Overt Behaviors

One of the most important advantages of behavioral measures over verbal measures is that they are often less reactive. The concept of **reactivity**—defined and discussed at some length by Cook and Campbell (1979), Cook, Laura Leviton and William Shadish, Jr. (1985), and Karl Weick (1985)—refers to the observation that often the mere measurement of the dependent variable interacts with the independent variable or other events in the laboratory so that effects are found that would not be seen otherwise. Suppose, for example, that subjects are shown a movie designed to reduce prejudice.[2] Later on, they are given a questionnaire that is supposed to assess prejudice. A control group of subjects who have not seen the movie are also given the questionnaire, and the experimenter discovers that the responses of subjects who saw the movie are less prejudiced than those of the control group. The experimenter concludes that the movie was effective in reducing prejudice.

But there are other possibilities. The subjects might have been completely unaffected by the movie *until* they saw the questionnaire, which clearly dealt with prejudice. As a result of seeing the questionnaire, the subjects might have suddenly remembered the movie and realized for the first time that it, too, was about prejudice. The questionnaire might have induced them to think about the movie, and this combination of events might have been the crucial variable influencing their attitudes. In effect, the dependent-variable measure was necessary to "activate" the independent variable, which might have had no effect if no measure was taken.

Note that this problem is conceptually different from the problems of demand characteristics, discussed in Chapter 9. We are not postulating that the subjects change their prejudiced attitudes because the experimenter wants them to, but only that no change would have taken place without the intrusion of a very obvious device for measuring the dependent variable; this device is *reactive* in that it cues changes that otherwise would not have happened.

---

[2] This example is based on one used by Benton Underwood (1957) in a slightly different context.

With a behavioral measure, it is often possible to make the measurement without the subject's awareness. If the subject is unaware of the measure, the problem of reactivity is eliminated.

A second advantage of behavioral measures is that doing something is typically more absorbing and engrossing than answering questions about it retrospectively, so that even when the subjects know that their behavior might be being measured, their concern with the measurement may be so peripheral to the main focus of their attention that it is unlikely to interfere very much with their behavior. In the Milgram (1973) experiments, in which the dependent variable was the amount of shock subjects were willing to deliver to their "student" in a learning task, subjects had all the information necessary to realize that their behavior could have been measured, but it is not likely that they spent much time speculating about this possibility, with their victim begging them for release and the experimenter coldly requesting them to increase the shock level. If the behavior assessed by the dependent-variable measure has important consequences or implications for the subject, the experimenter's evaluation or expectations are less likely to be influential factors. A subject may check a different point on a liking scale to go along with the experimenter, but she is less likely to choose a steady "boyfriend" just because she thinks the experimenter wants her to.

One criticism of behavioral measures is that they are more subject to random error, either because the behaviors are multiply determined or because of the unreliability of measurement. For example, in an experiment with child subjects in which the amount of time spent "being nice to" another child was taken as a measure of liking, it could be argued that a child might be nice to someone for many reasons, some of which were irrelevant to liking: The child might want to get possession of something the other child had, might be afraid of the other child, or might be obeying mother's orders. Second, it might be difficult to get a reliable measure of when the child was or was not "being nice." Some observers might classify casual conversations as "niceness," with others reserving the label "nice" for more definite acts of generosity.

In part, these criticisms reflect the traditional uses of observational measurement in *nonexperimental* settings. Although it is certainly true that a behavior may be affected by more than one variable, it is at least equally true of verbal measures. Moreover, when an overt behavior is the dependent variable in an *experiment*, the fact that it may be multiply determined is less serious, since it is in the nature of an experiment to hold constant extraneous variables (see Chapter 1) so that differences in the behavior of the experimental groups and the control group can be attributed to manipulations of the independent variable.

The concern with unreliability also reflects the more traditional use of behavioral measures, whereby observers often had to watch an extremely complex and unstructured interaction and code the subjects' behavior into abstract categories such as "tension release," "ego strength," or "regressive behavior." The unreliability was probably in large part a result of the observers' task, which required them to observe all behavior and to record complex *inferences* from the behavior rather than simply to take note of the behavior itself. The advantages of obtaining a direct behavioral measure, especially in studies aimed at predicting behavior, are largely dissipated by coding the behavior into broad inferential categories when it occurs. If we want to predict what subjects will do, their "ego strength" score, though based on actual behavior, may be at least as useless as a questionnaire response.

What we are advocating is a direct measure of the behavior selected. The simplest use of a behavioral measure is to provide an opportunity for the subject to engage in a particular activity and record whether the subject does so. Ideally, the "activity" should be a *specific* behavior that is unmistakable and requires little inference; "hitting," for example, is more specific than "showing aggression" as a category. For instance, Aronson and Mettee (1968) conducted an experiment in which the dependent variable was whether or not the subject cheated. Three subjects at a time played a series of blackjack games in which the "dealer," a rather fallible machine, often erred by giving the subject two cards at once. It always happened that the top card, the one the subject was supposed to keep, caused her to lose the game by going over 21 points and the bottom card, which she was supposed to return to the machine, virtually guaranteed a winning hand. The subject could easily cheat by returning the wrong card, and the dependent variable was simply the number of subjects in each condition (high self-esteem versus low self-esteem) who cheated.

It is also sometimes possible to get for each subject a behavioral measure which is more precise than a simple, all-or-none measure of performance versus nonperformance of a given response. A subject's behavior may be quantifiable in terms of its *frequency, rate, speed, duration, latency, extent, intensity*, and perhaps other dimensions as well. An example of *frequency measure* is provided by a study by Ellsworth and Carlsmith (1973). A subject was placed in a situation whereby shocks could be administered to a victim. The victim either looked the subject in the eye or gazed elsewhere. During the five-minute interaction, the subject could give as many shocks as desired. The number of shocks administered was the dependent variable. By looking at the number of shocks per minute, the experimenters could translate this measure into a measure of rate.

A study of staring by Ellsworth, Carlsmith, and Henson (1972) illustrates the use of *speed* as a dependent variable. Subjects moved away from the experimenter faster when she stared at them than when she didn't. Aronson and Landy (1967) also used speed as a dependent variable, in this case speed as related to task completion, in their study of Parkinson's law. They found that subjects who had been given little time to complete an initial task finished a subsequent task with no time restrictions faster than subjects who had been given a long time to complete the first task.

The use of *duration* as a dependent variable is illustrated by an experiment conducted by Mark Lepper, David Greene, and Richard Nisbett (1973). These researchers used percentage of free-choice time children chose to spend drawing pictures with magic markers as a measure of their intrinsic interest in that activity. Similarly, in Freedman's (1965) study of severity of threat, the dependent variable—relative liking for toys—was originally assessed by measuring how much time the child spent playing with each toy.[3]

Walter Mischel, Ebbe Ebbesen, and Antonette Zeiss used *latency* as a dependent variable in studying delay of gratification (1972). Children were given a choice between two snacks (pretzels and animals crackers) and were told that they could have the one they wanted if they waited until the experimenter returned. At any time during the 15-minute waiting period, however, the child could signal for the experimenter to return, but by doing so would forfeit the snack preferred and would have to settle for the other one. The dependent variable was the amount of time the child waited before signaling the experimenter.

An ingenious method for measuring the *extent* or *amount* of behavior, in this case, the general activity level of children, was devised by Jerome Schulman and John Reisman (1959) and has been used in several subsequent studies (e.g., Maccoby, Dowley, Hagen, & Degerman, 1965). The measurement device, termed an "actometer," was a self-winding calendar watch adjusted so that instead of winding the watch, the subject's activity moved the hands; thus, the number of "hours" of actometer time elapsed at the end of the experiment served as a measure of the subject's activity level.

Intensity was used as a dependent variable by Gordon Allport and Philip Vernon (1933). They asked their subjects to describe a frustrating event and gave them a piece of paper which was really a set of blank sheets alternating with sheets of carbon paper. The experimenters simply counted the number of sheets of paper on which writing was visible. More recently, James Kulik and Roger Brown (1979) used an intensity measure to assess the effects of frustration on subjects' aggression. Briefly, subjects called (confederate) donors to solicit charitable contributions. Subjects who were led to expect that potential donors would contribute generously responded more intensely in the face of frustration than subjects who expected minimal success. When confederates refused to contribute, subjects in the former group responded more intensely, speaking more harshly and slamming the telephone receivers down with more force.

These examples provide illustrations of behavioral measures of cheating, aggression, avoidance, work time, dissonance reduction, interest, delay of gratification, hyperactivity, and forcefulness, and none of them involved panels of expensively trained judges making complex inferential attributions. Webb and his colleagues (1966) also suggest a large variety of **unobtrusive measures** that can be used in field settings: the rate of replacement of tiles in front of various museum exhibits as an index of their popularity (the exhibit of hatching chicks was by far the most popular at one museum); the number of trip-insurance policies taken out at an airport as an index of anxiety about flying; and the clustering of blacks and whites in classrooms where seating is vol-

---

[3] Experiments don't always go as researchers intend: The timer Freedman used broke in mid-study. Thus, he was forced to forgo this continuous duration measure, and resorted instead to a head count of the number of children in each experimental condition who played with the toy.

untary as an index of racial attitudes. We assume that if behavioral measures can be found for this range of variables, they can be found for many others as well. The excuse that a variable does not lend itself to behavioral measurements seems increasingly feeble in the light of these developments.

In addition to the techniques of behavioral measurement we have indicated, there is a realm of behavior that has been subject to intensive research but has not often been used as a dependent variable in social psychological experiments more generally. The behaviors studied are expressive movements and nonverbal cues. So far, most of the research in this area has been aimed at associating various nonverbal cues with the kinds of psychological variables that often occur as conceptual intervening or dependent variables in other social psychological studies, such as anxiety, liking, and hostility (Weick, 1968). The advantage of measuring these behaviors as dependent variables is that they are much less likely than verbal behaviors to be edited by the subject who wishes to convey a good impression or one that confirms the experimenter's hypothesis. Some of these measures, such as the use of voice frequency to measure anxiety (Mahl, 1964), may be extremely difficult to control, even when the subject is making a conscious effort to do so. A variety of other stress or anxiety measures based on tone, tempo, and disturbances of speech have been suggested by George Mahl and Gaynelle Schultze (1964). Interaction distance has been successfully used as a measure of liking (Feldman & Kleck, 1970) and may also be useful in a variety of other contexts (Sommer, 1969). Eye contact may also serve as a measure of liking within the normal range of neutral to positive experimental contexts (Exline, 1971). Of course, it would be wrong to assume that any nonverbal cue which has been the subject of a published report is necessarily a valid indicator of a particular psychological variable, and before plugging a nonverbal measure into an experiment, the experimenter should examine the literature on the specific cue being considered, in order to judge whether its discoverer's claims are justified. Excellent reviews of research on nonverbal cues have been published by Klaus Scherer and Paul Ekman (1977) and Ross Buck (1984). Karl Weick (1968) includes a section on their use as dependent-variable measures in his chapter on observational methods in the *Handbook of Social Psychology*.

Behavioroid Measures

In many experimental settings in which a direct behavioral measure is inconvenient, an approximation of a behavioral measure may be achieved by measuring the subjects' *commitment* to perform the behavior, without actually making them carry it out. We call this a **behavioroid** measure. An example of a behavioroid measure is supplied by Aronson and Vernon Cope (1968), who assessed the degree of the subjects' liking for the experimenter by having the departmental secretary ask them to volunteer to make telephone calls to prospective subjects on behalf of the experimenter. The measure was quantitative; the number of phone calls the subject agreed to make was assumed to indicate the degree of liking for the experimenter. The subject did not actually make the phone calls, for the experiment was terminated immediately after the subject volunteered.

Similarly, David Marlowe, Robert Frager, and Ronald Nuttall (1965) wanted to determine the extent to which a subject became *more* committed to liberal beliefs when holding these beliefs resulted in the loss of an opportunity to make money. The major dependent variable was a statement by the subject indicating degree of willingness to spend a great deal of time escorting some visiting black students around the campus. As in the Aronson-Cope experiment, the procedure did not actually require the subject to perform the behavior, only to make a commitment to do so. But even though the data in both of these studies are merely verbal statements, they have far different implications from such simple statements as "I like the experimenter" or "I think blacks are grand." The crucial difference between a simple questionnaire item and a behavioroid measure is that the latter has consequences. From the subjects' point of view, they cannot just check a scale and forget it, they are committing themselves to future behavior. Presumably, most subjects who volunteer to make phone calls or to escort black students do so with the firm intention of following through, though of course we cannot be certain on this point until experimental evidence is provided indicating that the size of the verbal commitment is in fact highly correlated with the amount of the relevant behavior the subject actually performs.

Physiological Measures

Physiological measures such as heart rate, blood pressure, pupil dilation, or electrodermal activity are valuable measures of internal states because most of the processes monitored are *not* under the subject's conscious control. There are some practical and conceptual drawbacks to the use of these measures, however. First, monitoring equipment can be costly. Second, the measurement process restricts the subjects' movement and may also intimidate them. Third, such measures are more reliable indicators of subjects' general *level* of arousal than they are of different *kinds* of arousal. Finally, one of the biggest liabilities of the use of the physiological measures is that they often do not reflect the kinds of responses in which social psychologists are interested.

There are, however, exceptions. Recall from our earlier discussions of dissonance experiments that one assumption underlying early experimenters' hypotheses is that cognitive dissonance, however generated, is characterized by an aversive state of *arousal*.[4] Subjects are motivated to reduce this arousal by

[4] There is recent experimental evidence, however, that dissonance is not necessarily an *unpleasant* state of arousal. Like the subjects in Schachter and Singer's (1962) classic experiment, subjects in whom dissonance is aroused may be influenced by situational cues in making inferences about the label to attach to their arousal. Thus, some experimenters have suggested that dissonance is a more *malleable* state of arousal than was first postulated (see, for example, Cooper & Fazio, 1984; Cooper, Fazio, & Rhodewalt, 1978; Rhodewalt & Comer, 1979).

changing their attitudes or behaviors in order to bring them into line with other cognitions; hence the differences in dependent-variable measures when dissonance is aroused in some subjects but not in others. Surprisingly, it took almost 20 years after the original formulation of cognitive dissonance theory (Festinger, 1957) before social psychologists incorporated physiological measures into traditional experimental paradigms to determine whether subjects believed to be experiencing dissonance were actually physiologically aroused.

An experiment by Robert Croyle and Joel Cooper (1983) provides an excellent example of the usefulness of physiological measures in this research tradition. In one experiment, subjects were randomly assigned to one of three experimental conditions. Some subjects were induced to choose to write an essay advocating a university policy with which they had previously disagreed (banning alcohol consumption on the university campus); other subjects were induced to choose to write an essay consonant with their previous attitudes; the third group was given no choice in writing an essay advocating the policy with which they had previously disagreed. As in similar ''counterattitudinal essay'' dissonance experiments, after the manipulation of the independent variable (high choice/counterattitudinal essay versus high choice/consonant essay versus no choice/counterattitudinal essay), Croyle and Cooper collected the traditional dependent-variable measure: a second measure of subjects' attitudes toward banning alcohol. In *addition*, however, the experimenters also collected physiological measures: subjects' heart rate and the electrical activity of their skin (electrodermal activity).

As predicted, subjects in the dissonance-arousing condition were significantly more aroused after writing their essays than were subjects in the other two (low-dissonance) conditions. Surprisingly, however, subjects in the high-dissonance condition exhibited no more attitude change than did subjects in the two no-dissonance groups; that is, they were no more likely to show more favorable attitudes toward banning alcohol on campus than were subjects in the low-dissonance conditions. The authors speculate that subjects in the first group failed to change their attitudes because they misattributed their arousal to being monitored by the physiological measurement devices. Perhaps like the subjects in Schachter and Singer's experiment, they attributed their arousal to the presence of the recording equipment. Having misattributed their arousal to the equipment—as opposed to the consequences of freely choosing to write an essay advocating a position with which they disagreed—they were not motivated to change their attitudes to bring them in line with their behaviors. This speculation is intriguing, and suggests a possible drawback of physiological measures. Nevertheless, the fact remains that physiological measures *were* useful in establishing the presence of arousal that was believed to accompany cognitive dissonance. Thus, physiological measures *can* be valuable tools for testing the assumptions that underlie social psychological theories related to arousal and motivation.

Indirect Measures

Of course, in the strictest sense, *all* measures of psychological variables are indirect; we have no ready access to the thoughts, perceptions, or feelings of another person. However, some measures are *conceptually* more indirect than others. By the term **indirect measures** we mean those measures for which the link to the variable of interest involves some kind of hypothetical intervening process. For example, in an interesting study of the "illusion of control," Ellen Langer (1975) sold subjects lottery tickets costing $.50 under two randomly assigned conditions. Some buyers were arbitrarily handed a ticket by the salesman; other buyers were allowed to choose their own tickets from the array. Langer was interested in the effects of illusory "control" (presumed to be higher in the condition in which subjects chose their own tickets) on subjects' confidence that theirs was the winning ticket. Rather than asking subjects how confident they felt, Langer opted instead to use a more indirect measure. After completing the purchase, subjects were approached by a confederate and were asked for how much they would be willing to sell their own tickets. The reasoning behind this procedure was that the subjects' asking price would reflect the *subjective utility* of the ticket, which in turn would reflect the subject's estimates of the *probability* that they had just purchased the winning ticket. As predicted, subjects who had chosen their own ticket asked for significantly more money before they were willing to sell than were subjects who had been denied the opportunity to choose their own.

What makes the use of this indirect measure particularly ingenious is that subjects would have probably been embarrassed to report on their *subjective* confidence had they been asked directly whether they thought they had a winning ticket. After all, they would have known that the *objective* view was that the probability was really quite low and would be influenced by purely chance factors. Assuming that this indirect measure was closely related to true subjective self-confidence, it may have enabled Langer to detect an effect that would not have been revealed by use of a direct self-report measure.

Another example of an indirect measure of a dependent variable can be found in an experiment by Michael Pallak and Thane Pittman (1972). Rather than measure the arousing effects of dissonance directly, as did Croyle and Cooper (1983), these experimenters used predictions based on traditional learning theory to devise an indirect measure of the state. Specifically, learning theorists had established that arousal facilitates performance on relatively simple cognitive tasks but impedes performance on more complex tasks. If dissonance *is* an arousing state, then these patterns of results should obtain when dissonance is the source of the arousal, and Pallak and Pittman set out to test this proposition. Prior to performance of either a simple or complex cognitive task, some subjects were induced to choose to complete a rather long and boring exercise in which for 30 minutes they were to read aloud one of three words flashed on a screen before them; other subjects were led to believe that they had no choice but to complete the boring exercise. The experimenters assumed that *choosing* to perform a boring and repetitious pronunciation exercise would arouse more dissonance than would being told one was "obligated" to do so. Furthermore, they predicted that subjects in the former group would experience the arousing effects of dissonance, which would enhance their performance on a subsequent easy cognitive task and interfere with their performance on a difficult task. Their predictions were confirmed: Compared to subjects who were given no choice but to complete the initial long and boring pronunciation task, subjects who freely "chose" to complete it subsequently made more errors in a complex cognitive task and fewer errors on a simple cognitive task. Thus, when dissonance was the postulated source of arousal, performance on a cognitive task totally unrelated to the experimental manipulation revealed results consistent with learning theory predictions. Although an indirect measure of the motivational effects of dissonance, results of this experiment augment those in which dependent measures are attitude statements, overt behaviors, or physiological responses. Moreover, this indirect measure has two advantages over more direct measures: First, as we noted in Chapter 2, one limitation of self-reports is that by intervening to assess an intrapsychic process, experimenters might inadvertently *alter* the process itself. Second, as we noted above in our description of the Croyle-Cooper (1983) experiment, even monitoring physiological responses may interfere with the phenomenon under investigation.

Indirect measures are becoming increasingly common in judgment experiments, for social cognition researchers have borrowed many useful measurement techniques from traditional cognitive psychology. Attitude researchers have long regarded differential or biased attention to and memory for pro versus con attitudinal statements as valid measures of individuals' own attitudinal positions. Recently, more sophisticated measures of recognition, reaction time, and accuracy of recall of stimulus materials have been applied to other aspects of social perception as well. As is the case with physiological measures, if subjects exert less conscious control over memory than they do over self-report measures collected via questionnaires, rating scales, or interviews, indirect measures may reveal biases that otherwise would go undetected.

For example, it is probably no longer socially acceptable for white subjects to admit that they think blacks are violent, dangerous, and prone to criminal behavior. Thus, a direct measure of these attitudes might fail to reveal such biased or prejudiced expectations even if they *did* exist in subjects' minds. Suppose instead the experimenter exposed subjects to a picture of people in a subway car. Further, suppose that in the picture a black man and a white man are apparently in the midst of an argument, and that the white man holds a straight razor in his left hand.[5] This picture and others might be presented to subjects as part of an experiment on short-term memory, and they might be asked after viewing the series to write down everything they can recall about

---

[5] This example is taken from a classic study by Gordon Allport and Leo Postman (1947), who were interested in rumor transmission. These researchers showed the picture to subjects, had them describe it to a second person, who described it to a third person, and so on. After no more than six tellings, the razor usually shifted from the white man's hand to the black man's.

the contents. If subjects erroneously recall that the black man held the razor, these *memory distortions* may be viewed as a manifestation of subjects' stereotypes, negative stereotypes they would be loathe to express in more direct measures of racial attitudes.

Or consider a clever indirect measure of subjects' gender-related stereotypes used by Natalie Porter and Florence Geis (1981). Subjects were shown a picture of either a group of men or a group of women seated around a table. The picture was described as a group of graduate students working on a research project, and subjects were asked to guess which member contributed most to the group. In both cases, their strong tendency was to choose the person seated at the head of the table. In other conditions, subjects were shown a mixed-gender group consisting of two men and three women. When a man was seated at the head of the table, he was overwhelmingly named as the greatest contributor; when a woman was seated at the head of the table, she was hardly chosen at all. Indeed, both men in the picture received more "nominations" than all three women combined. Moreover, results were similar for men and women subjects, and women targets were underchosen by self-avowed feminists and nonfeminists alike. Thus, like memories, *interpretations* can be powerful indirect manifestations of underlying attitudes that may not be revealed via more direct measurement techniques.

Reaction time measures are another useful means of measuring a dependent variable indirectly and are often used as an index of the efficiency or depth of information processing. For example, Christine and Ranald Hansen (1988) set out to test the hypothesis that facial information will be processed much more efficiently and therefore much more rapidly when facial expressions signal a potential threat. Specifically, they predicted that it would be easier for subjects to detect a lone "angry" face in a crowd of "happy" faces that it would be to detect a "happy" face amid a crowd of attention-grabbing "angry" faces. In one experiment, a tachistiscope (an apparatus that projects transient images onto a screen) was used to present subjects with pictures of crowds, and subjects were asked to respond as quickly as possible to indicate whether a "discrepant" face was hidden among the others. In some cases, all faces displayed the same emotional expression; in others, an angry or neutral face was embedded in a crowd of happy faces; and in others, a happy or neutral face was embedded in a crowd of angry faces.

Dependent-variable measures included the number of incorrect decisions made by subjects and their reaction times (measured to within a millisecond). Among results germane to their hypothesis, Hansen and Hansen found that subjects were quicker to identify angry faces in happy crowds than they were to identify happy faces in angry crowds, and they did so with fewer errors. According to the authors, the more rapid reaction time associated with the detection of angry discrepant faces (compared with happy discrepant faces) suggests that some kinds of social information are more automatically processed than others. Thus, the increasing use of such sensitive timing devices enables social cognition experimenters to measure, albeit indirectly, the efficiency with which we processs information about ourselves or others. Moreover, these reaction time measures are reliable, accurate, and capable of detecting very minor differences among experimental conditions.

CHOOSING A MEASURE

There is rarely a one-to-one relation between a conceptual dependent variable and a particular behavior. A specific behavior, like a specific verbal statement, can have multiple determinants. Thus, seemingly parallel behavioral observations and verbal questions may in fact measure different things. For example, consider an experiment in which a confederate (posing as a fellow subject) uses either praise or insults to imply that the subject is, respectively, brilliant or stupid. Suppose that the dependent variable of interest is the subject's liking for the confederate. We could measure this by devising a scale ranked from plus 5 to minus 5 and then ask for the subject's rating of liking for the confederate. Or we could use a behavioral measure and observe the extent to which the subject makes an effort to join a group that includes the confederate. This effortful behavior would seem to be a reflection of liking, but unfortunately it could be reflecting other things instead. For instance, the insulted subject might want to join the group in order to disprove the confederate's implication. Or the subject might want a chance to see the derogator again in order to return the insult. In neither case is it likely that the subject's behavior reflects "liking," and consequently the behavioral measures may produce results different from those produced by the questionnaire measure.

At the same time it is true that for many of the kinds of processes studied by social psychologists, the greater the commitment demanded of the subject by the dependent variable, the more confidence we can place in the experimental results. For example, we would have a great deal of confidence that an experiment *really* involves antecedents of aggression if the experimental treatment induced more subjects to punch the experimenter in the nose (or even to volunteer to "meet him or her outside") than occurred in a control condition. We would have far less confidence if the experimental treatment resulted in a higher rating of perceived feelings of aggression as measured by a questionnaire. First, a punch in the nose is probably a much closer approximation to the conceptual notion of aggression than is "plus 3: I feel somewhat angry." In other words, it is closer to the class of behaviors which the experimenter believes constitutes "aggression." In this case, it is probably an actual member of that class of behaviors. Second, a punch in the nose is a good indication that the subject is taking the situation seriously. Finally, since a questionnaire by its very nature poses a question, there is clearly a greater likelihood that the subjects will try to determine what they *should* answer in terms of their feelings about their own image and the experimenter's hypothesis. A piece of behavior, especially one that is not asked for (like the punch in the nose), is far less likely to reflect cooperation.

These points seem fairly obvious, but it is nevertheless uncommon for social psychologists to use behavioral or even behavioroid data. Instead, they rely very heavily on the questionnaire or rating scale. Occasionally, it may be impossible to get anything more, but we feel that this is seldom the case. All too often, it appears that the questionnaire is chosen because it is simpler to concoct and easier to administer. With more effort and ingenuity, experimenters could design many studies to include behavioral data, as is demonstrated by the wide variety of variables included in the small sample of studies listed in the previous section. When the behavior is carefully chosen, the problem of possible multiple determinants of that behavior can often be avoided.

There are several other problems to be considered when trying to make concrete decisions about how to measure the dependent variable. One recurring question is the extent to which one should constrain the behavior of the subject. This takes several forms. First, should one attempt to block most possible alternative behaviors so as to maximize the likelihood of observing changes in the specific variable of interest? For example, in a typical dissonance study in the area of communication and persuasion, if a very credible communicator states a position which disagrees with one's own, one experiences dissonance. There are four major ways to reduce dissonance in this situation: (1) changing one's own opinion; (2) trying to get the communicator to change; (3) seeking social support; and (4) derogating the communicator. One *can* easily devise an experiment which makes it difficult for the subject to utilize all but the first of these techniques. The appropriateness of this tactic depends on the question the experimenter is asking.

For example, in an experiment designed to examine the effects of some independent variable, the experimenter might ask, What effects does dissonance have on people's behavior? To get a good idea of all the ways in which dissonance can affect the subjects' behavior, the experimenter will want to leave as many options as possible open to the subjects. By closing off an option, the experimenter is closing off information relevant to the question: If dissonance leads people to choose that option, and if that option is made unavailable to the subjects, the experimenter will have no way of knowing if that is one of the effects of dissonance. For example, if the experimenter removes all possible sources of social support so that the subject knows that there is no one around to offer agreement, the subject will not seek social support, and the experimenter will not know whether seeking social support is something people normally do when they experience dissonance. If the experimenter's question involves general reactions to dissonance or preferred methods of dissonance reduction, the technique of blocking off all avenues but one may obscure what the subject *really* is likely to do in a situation of this sort.

However, suppose that the experimenter is interested primarily in the dependent variable. For example, the experimenter may be interested in interpersonal attraction and want to conduct an experiment to find out whether dissonance affects liking. In this case, whether it is better to leave many avenues open or to close off all but one depends on whether the experimenter's definition of the dependent variable is broad or narrow. The experimenter who is interested in all forms of interpersonal attraction, complimenting, helping, spending time with the other person, and so on, will want to leave all these options open. But the experimenter who is interested in some specific dependent variable—for example, does the dissonance make the subject more likely to *help* the other person at the next opportunity?—may want to give the subject a chance to help while closing off all other avenues.

Finally, the experimenter may be asking a very specific question about a relationship or testing a specific hypothesis. In this case, the experimenter might be asking: Is dissonance aroused in this situation, and does it get reduced? Stated as a hypothesis, this would be: Dissonance is aroused in this situation, and the subject works to reduce it. In this case, the experimenter wants to be sure to observe the whole of the subject's effort to reduce the dissonance, and therefore all the subject's effort should be channeled in one direction. By blocking most possible alternative modes of dissonance reduction, the experimenter can maximize the likelihood of observing changes in the one that has been left open, since if subjects are really trying to find a way to reduce the dissonance, they will all ultimately choose that path. For example, the experimenter might make the communicator a prestigious and powerful person (and therefore unlikely to be derogated by the subject) whose faith in the position taken is complete (so that the subject will perceive that it is useless to try to change the communicator's opinion). The experimenter might also isolate the subject (so that the subject will not be able to rally social support for a different position). By blocking off these three avenues, the experimenter maximizes the likelihood that the subject will reduce dissonance by *changing position*. The experimenter then stands a good chance of validating the hypothesis (if it is a valid hypothesis), because most of the leaks have been sealed, as it were; most of the dissonance that is aroused will be channeled in the direction of attitude change, and that's where the experimenter has set up the measuring instruments.

The same concern arises when one tries to decide whether to use open-ended questions or rigidly constrained measures, such as scales or other forced-choice questions. The more quantitative measure may increase the likelihood of observing differences between experimental treatments by reducing random error variance, but it may also obscure the subject's normal behavior. Any experimenter who has seen many subjects close at hand has experienced the feeling that a given subject is "really" showing lots of interesting effects, but that the measures are too constrained to be sensitive to them.

The best remedy for both of these concerns is to run a reasonably large number of pilot subjects, with the dependent variable measure as unconstrained as possible. Thus, in pilot research it may be most effective to present the independent variable and then, essentially, let the subjects to do or say what they want. Interviews are often particularly useful at this stage of the research, since they allow the experimenter to clarify ambiguous reactions of the subjects and to find out how they interpreted the question or variable, what aspects of the situation were confusing or difficult, and whether any other responses occurred to them besides the one performed. By these means we may get some ideas as to exactly what behaviors we can look at which are likely to reflect the processes that we believe are taking place. By observing what the subjects do and say in response to the treatments, we can select measures which may accurately reflect the responses of the subjects and can rule out certain alternative behaviors to maximize the likelihood of observing change on the variable being measured. Besides providing information useful in deciding what behavior to measure, the pretests can suggest how the behavior should be quantified, by providing information on the range of the behavior likely to be encountered. Once the pilot stage of an experiment is over, however, there are many advantages of a rigidly defined, quantitative measurement of the dependent variable.

In general, the purpose of pilot studies should be to arrive at effective measures and treatments and to deal with other technical problems, such as the ease of transition from one part of the experiment to the next. The purpose is not to collect data or to find out in advance whether the hypothesis is going to be confirmed but rather to construct an experiment that tests the hypothesis or asks the empirical question fairly. It is always possible to shape subjects to give the desired responses, but the experimental modifications necessary to achieve this goal may have nothing to do with the experimenter's original conceptual variables. Charles Kiesler, Barry Collins, and Norman Miller (1969, p. 77) demonstrated convincingly that repeated pretesting of the entire experiment—running pilot studies with data comparable to the data to be collected in the "real" experiment—introduces dangerous statistical artifacts which bias the final experiment in the direction of the experimenter's hypothesis. We have suggested that different aspects of the experiment be pretested separately. A couple of final rehearsals may be important to ensure that the entire procedure unfolds smoothly, but the data from these pretests should not be used. If satisfied that all aspects of the experiment are as they should be, the experimenter probably should not even look at the data from the final rehearsals and *certainly* should not check to see whether the data are positive and then include these successful pretest subjects in the final design.

RELIABILITY AND VALIDITY OF MEASUREMENT

Reliability

One of the problems in the pretest stage may be the **reliability** of the measuring instrument. The reliability of a measure refers to its consistency. A measure may be consistent in various ways, some of which are of little relevance to experimental studies. For example, one type of consistency is *consistency over time*, as in the case of an IQ test, which theoretically should provide roughly the same score for the same individual at widely separated intervals— or roughly the same relative position of a score when a person's score is compared to those of others. "Consistency over time," however, implies that what is being measured is a stable attribute. It is thus particularly relevant for tests that purport to measure enduring qualities, such as intelligence. Whether these variables really are stable is a separate question; the point to be made here is that experimental social psychologists rarely deal with such traits. Since the whole point of a social psychological experiment is to show how the dependent variable changes in response to the independent variable, the social psychologist certainly would not want the measure to be "reliable" in a testing prior to the treatment and in one subsequent to the treatment. Nor does the experimenter much care if the measure is "reliable" between two administrations—one immediately after the experimental treatment and one much later. The aim is not to effect "permanent" changes in the subject; in fact, the experimenter debriefs the subjects partly in order to undo any changes the experiment may have brought about.

Another type of reliability involves *agreement among observers*—often called **interobserver reliability**. When the dependent variable is a behavior, it is either recorded automatically or scored by observers. An example of an automatically recorded behavior is provided by the Ellsworth and Carlsmith study of eye contact and aggression; whenever the subject pressed the shock button, it activated an event recorder that made a mark on a moving sheet of paper. An example of a behavior recorded by observers occurs in a study by Thomas Landauer, Carlsmith, and Mark Lepper (1970). The dependent variable in this study was obedience, and one of the behavioral measures used was the number of blocks the child subject picked up when asked to. An observer (behind a one-way mirror) counted the number of blocks the child picked up, recorded the latency of the first time the child stopped picking up blocks, and noted the number of times the mother had to ask her child to return to the task. These measures were then combined into an overall "disobedience score." On several occasions two observers were used, and the correlation of the total disobedience scores based on the two sets of observations ($r = .96$) was used as an index of the interobserver reliability of the dependent-variable measures. Sometimes an automatically recorded behavior, for example, one recorded on videotape, will also be scored by observers later on. It is easier to ensure high reliability when the observers are required to record simple behaviors (e.g., number of blocks picked up; amount of time from the onset of the green light until the rear wheels of the car crossed the intersection; number of times the subject in the cheating study returned the wrong card). Interobserver reliability is not a problem when the measure is straightforward, as is indicated by the high level of agreement reached by Landauer, Carlsmith, and Lepper's observers. It may be argued that this level of achievement is not very spectacular, since the observers' task was not very hard. The point is that the observers' task should *not* be very hard; we are interested in the behavior, not the observers' inferences. If in the pilot stage observers show low reliability, maybe they are being asked to make complex inferences about abstract and ill-defined categories. Although it is possible to train observers until they reach agreement on complex judgments, often it may be more desirable to change the dependent variable to a different behavior, one that is more concrete and easier to measure. Two observers may be trained to make the same interpretation, but it is still an interpretation of the subject's behavior, not a record of that behavior. In communicating research results, it is important to specify the exact behaviors from which the interpretations were derived. If the experimenter's data are already in the form of interpretations, the behaviors cannot be specified, and other experimenters will not be able to replicate the results.

A third type of reliability is more relevant to verbal measures. It is analogous to the use of multiple observers, in that its purpose is to measure the same variable more than once by adding measurement operations of the same type. With a verbal measure, the "measurement operations" are test questions; provided that the items are highly correlated with one another (i.e., measuring the same thing), using more of them will result in higher reliability. During the pilot testing the experimenter can work on improving the **internal consistency** of the measure by adding new items and checking to see how well they correlate with the other items (or with the overall test score). Items that are not highly correlated with the test average are then eliminated, since they are likely to contribute a disproportionate amount of error variance and to lower the overall significance of the results. For more detailed discussions of reliability, see Selltiz, Jahoda, Deutsch, and Cook (1968), and Scott (1968), for reliability of verbal measures.

Of course, just because a measurement is *reliable* is no guarantee that it is measuring what the experimenter believes it will. A measure of cranial circumference may be highly reliable over time and over observers, but few contemporary psychologists would assert that such a measure is an accurate index of the underlying construct of intelligence. Thus, reliability is necessary but not sufficient for validity.

Validity

The **validity** of a measure refers to the degree to which differences indicated by the measure correspond to "real" differences in the conceptual dependent variable. For example, when the experimenter uses a questionnaire to measure an inner state or a behavioral tendency such as aggression it may be invalid for the purpose of the experiment, because differences in self-ratings of hostility may be more responsive to a different set of factors than differences in felt aggression or aggressive behavior.

Social psychologists frequently distinguish among three kinds of validity: (1) *face validity* (2) *criterion-related validity*; and (3) *construct validity*.

Face Validity   This concept simply refers to the plausibility or directness of the measure. For example, a set of arithmetic problems is supposed to have high face validity for arithmetic ability. Face validity in a measure is analogous to mundane realism in a treatment, and it suffers from many of the same problems. First, its direct correspondence to the real-world variable is always arguable, since it depends on the intuitions of the researcher. Second, the fact that it looks exactly like a real-world situation may not be relevant to its ability to reflect differences in the underlying conceptual variable. Certainly, the scores of children taking an arithmetic test in a classroom are affected by a great many factors besides arithmetic ability. Choosing a test on the basis of face validity may simply result in bringing extraneous error into the controlled laboratory situation. Finally, there are situations in which an experimenter does *not* want a measuring instrument to have high face validity. For obvious reasons, it is inadvisable to hand a subject a questionnaire entitled *Bigotry Index*, complete with instructions that read, "We're interested in how bigoted you are. Please read each of the 20 statements below and circle either the letter T if you think the statement is true or the letter F if you think the statement is false." When honest responses may reflect negatively on subjects, they may hesitate to respond truthfully if the measures are "too" face valid. For that reason, it is not uncommon for experimenters to search for a measure that does not look like what it is designed to measure: a measure that is *low* in face validity.

Criterion-Related Validity   Criterion-related validity ("concurrent" validity if the criterion is in the present; "predictive" validity if it is in the future) refers to correspondence between the score on the dependent variable measure and scores on some independent, objective measure of the variable. Self-report measures of height, for example, can be validated by using a tape measure, and on the basis of this comparison the experimenter can determine whether self-report is an adequate measure of height. Although this type of validity seems to be eminently desirable, there are several problems involved. For one thing, many of the conceptual variables studied by social psychologists, such as liking, aggression, and cooperation, do not immediately suggest a single objective criterion. The social psychologist often sees underlying variables as having implications for variety of behaviors, behaviors that in other circumstances might also be sensitive to other variables. If there happens to be a clear-cut criterion measure informing us of the subject's true position on the variable, we would be better off using it instead of going to the bother of constructing a separate measure. This is sometimes done, as in the Aronson and Landy (1967) study of Parkinson's law, and in some of the other studies mentioned in the section of this chapter dealing with behavioral measures. However, if direct measurement of the criterion variable is extremely inconvenient, unethical, or otherwise inappropriate, or if the criterion behavior is a *future* response that the social psychologist wishes to predict, an indirect measure can be used. In order to show that the indirect measure is a valid substitute, the experimenter could wait for a naturally occurring situation in which the extreme form of the behavior (the criterion behavior) takes place and see whether the proposed indirect measure is highly correlated with it. If it is, then the experimenter can feel confident in using the indirect measure in future laboratory research as a substitute for the "real thing."

Construct Validity   This concept involves a looser and more complicated validation procedure that can be used for conceptual variables (*constructs*) that do not logically imply a single type of criterion behavior. The investigator chooses a specific verbal or other behavior as the dependent variable but, in interpreting the experimental results, wants to generalize to an internal state or general category of behaviors covered by the conceptual definition. In order to do this, the investigator would like to provide some indication that the particular behavior chosen is a valid representation of the abstract category or construct represented by the conceptual variable. The problem, however, is that the conceptual variable does not include a definite standard for determining whether the particular behavior is a valid representative. The method of construct validation involves correlation of the independent variable with other theoretically relevant behaviors.

For example, suppose that an experimenter wants to use an unobtrusive measure of anger and has decided to call the subject "angry" whenever he or she frowns. If in testing the measure, frowning is found to be highly correlated with other indications of anger such as shouting insults, threatening to hit someone, slamming the door, and an increase in noradrenaline and is *not* correlated with other emotions, the experimenter gains confidence that frowning is a valid signal for anger. If all of these behaviors are highly correlated in a variety of situations, the experimenter also gains confidence that there is a broad underlying variable (anger) which is manifesting itself in a variety of ways. None of these behaviors achieves the status of a standard or criterion variable, but if they have high correlations with one another and with the one chosen as the dependent variable, the investigator becomes more confident that there is in fact a valid underlying conceptual variable of which these particular behaviors are manifestations. In effect, the use of this indirect procedure increases the investigator's confidence in both the conceptual variable *and* certain related potential dependent-variable measures at the same time.

In order to make use of the strategy of construct validation, it is necessary at some stage to compare several *different kinds* of dependent variable, all of which presumably reflect the underlying conceptual variable. There are other good reasons for employing more than one kind of dependent-variable measure. As Webb and his colleagues (1966) point out, any given method of measurement is subject to some kind of error, but different kinds of measures are often subject to different kinds of error. So long as only one type of measure is used, its particular source of error will provide a plausible alternative explanation for the results of the research. The validity of the experimenter's conceptual variable remains questionable as long as only one measure is used. For example, the authors point out that "almost everything we know about attitudes is . . . suspect because the findings are saturated with the inherent risks of self-report information" (Webb, Campbell, Schwartz, & Sechrest, 1966, p. 172). As long as only one method of measurement is used, its particular limitations can constitute a source of systematic error that covers an entire area of research. The heavy preponderance of questionnaire measures in attitude research has contributed to the current concern over the relationship between attitudes and behavior. It has been suggested that "attitudes" are simply responses to attitude questionnaires and may not be related to behavior at all. Had a wider variety of measures been used in the history of attitude research, we would now have a clearer idea of the behavioral implications of an "attitude."

Enhancing Validity

In order to provide the maximum evidence of validity from the use of different dependent-variable measures, the measures should differ from one another in all respects that are irrelevant to the basic conceptual variable (Webb, Campbell, Schwartz, & Sechrest, 1966; Campbell & Fiske, 1959). This is because similar types of measurement techniques are characterized by similar types of irrelevant error-producing factors. For example, the **acquiescence response set**, in which a subject tends to check "yes," "true," "agree," and so on, may be specific to questionnaires. By using different types of dependent-variable measures, one can rule out method-specific sources of error. Again, this reasoning leads to the recommendation that behavioral measures be used more frequently, in part because much of the existing data from social psychological experiments are based on verbal measures, and in part because the method-specific sources of error in behavior measures are likely to be much more variable than those involved in questionnaires, which almost always have the same types of response biases.

In social psychology, much of the validation of conceptual dependent variables through the use of different types of measure occurs informally through the process of systematic replication (see Chapter 1). A follow-up experiment often provides a degree of validation, in that a different measure of the conceptual dependent variable is frequently used. In the original study of the effects of threat on children's toy preferences (Aronson & Carlsmith, 1963), the experimenters threatened either mild or severe consequences for the children if they played with the forbidden toy, left them alone for a while with the toy, and then came back to find out how the threat had affected their liking for the toy. The dependent variable consisted of the children's verbal ranking of the forbidden toy among all the other toys. Aronson and Carlsmith found as predicted that when the threat was mild, the children ranked the toy lower than they had before the threat. It is possible, however, that in the mild-threat condition, the children, although much more tempted to play with the toy, feared that the experimenter might guess how close they had come to disobedience and therefore exaggerated their expressions of dislike for the forbidden toy in order to convince the experimenter (and perhaps themselves) that they had never even come close to playing with it. In the follow-up study by Freedman (1965), the conceptual dependent variable "liking for the toy" was measured in a different way. Instead of asking the children how much they liked the toy, Freedman simply removed the threat, left the children alone with the toys again, and measured how many children in each condition spent time playing with the formerly forbidden toy. Since Freedman, using a different measure, obtained the same results as those in the original study, the uncertainties stemming from Aronson and Carlsmith's verbal measure were greatly reduced, and the plausibility of "liking" as the relevant dependent variable was correspondingly increased.

Although multiple measures of social psychological variables are easy to find if we include all the experiments dealing with a particular conceptual variable, there are fewer examples of the use of more than one dependent-variable measure in the same experiment. The experiment by Crusco and Wetzel (1984) with which we began Chapter 7 is a notable exception. Recall that they collected *two kinds* of dependent-variable measures: patrons' ratings of service in the restaurant and the amount of the tips they left for the waitresses. Interestingly, patrons' restaurant ratings were unrelated to the touch condition to which they had been randomly assigned. Tips, however, *were* related; both types of touch yielded significantly larger tips than did the no-touch condition. Such discrepancies between self-report measures and overt behaviors are not uncommon. In this field experiment, it may have been that patrons were not consciously aware of the fact that they had been touched, and therefore ratings were unaffected. However, they may have been "unconsciously" aware of the touch, and this subliminal awareness may have manifested itself in larger tips.

In part, the failure of many researchers to use multiple measures may be due to the legitimate fear that responding to the first measure will distort the subject's responses to the second or will arouse suspicion. Certainly, the measures cannot be taken as independent for the purposes of statistical analyses (Kiesler, Collins, & Miller, 1969, p. 72), although some relevant statistical procedures do exist (e.g., see Bock, 1963). There are several possible solutions to this problem. The first is to have one of the measures tap a behavior that the subjects cannot control, either because they are unlikely to have learned the techniques necessary to control it, as in the case of physiological arousal, or because they are unaware that it is being measured, as in the use of concealed tape recordings or films of nonverbal cues.

A second solution is to measure the dependent variable in one fashion for half the subjects and in a different fashion for the other half. Returning to the Aronson-Carlsmith severity-of-threat example, the authors could have asked half the subjects to rank the toys and simply left the other half alone to play with them, then measured how long the children played with each one. This technique is *risky*—if the main goal of the experiment is a simple, publishable, statistically significant finding—and *difficult*, in that many experimental settings may initially suggest only one type of appropriate measure. However, it is a rich and valuable source of information about the conceptual variable and its manifestations. If successful, this technique leads to greatly increased confidence in the experimental results and their external validity.

Finally, it is sometimes possible to take several different, partially correlated measures and then *combine* them into a single index for the purposes of statistical analysis. For example, in their study of obedience in children, Landauer, Carlsmith, and Lepper (1970) measured obedience in several ways: number of blocks the child picked up; length of time before the child stopped picking up blocks; and number of times the mother had to ask the child to get back to work. These measures were combined into a total "disobedience score" for each child. High intercorrelations among the three different measures provide evidence for the general concept "obedience" as the dependent variable in the experiment; at the same time, the single measure (the disobedience score) available for each child reflects all aspects of the dependent variable.

Disguising the Measure

For reasons that are probably obvious by this time, it is often important to disguise the fact that a particular question or observation is actually the measurement of the dependent variable. If subjects feel that what is being "tested" by the measure is important to the experimenter, they may be more likely to try to make a good impression. It is possible that the knowledge that they are being tested reduces the subjects' spontaneity and that the more important they feel the test is, the less spontaneously they will behave. If they deduce that the measure is related to the major dependent variable, they may then be able to deduce the experimenter's hypothesis and adjust their responses to confirm or disconfirm it. For these reasons, experimenters often try to disguise the measurement of the dependent variable. This presents problems very similar to those involved in attempting to disguise the independent variable. Again, we can identify several different classes of solutions. Many of the solutions are similar to those discussed in Chapter 9 on guarding against demand characteristics and will be elaborated in that chapter.

The dependent variable can be disguised by measuring it in a situation *totally removed* from the rest of the experiment. An excellent example of this technique is the Marlowe, Frager, and Nuttal (1965) study. In this case, the experimenter who asked whether the subject would be willing to escort black students around campus was described as a professor who was in charge of a visiting program and who had nothing to do with the experiment. Similarly, Carlsmith, Collins, and Helmreich (1966) had the dependent variable assessed by a "Madison Avenue consumer research analyst." And researchers studying helping behaviors have developed creative methods of separating the collection of dependent-variable measures from the experiment proper: Subjects have been asked to lend their notes to confederates posing as fellow students (Barnes, Ickes, & Kidd, 1979); to conduct telephone interviews unrelated to the experiment (Cialdini, Darby, & Vincent, 1973); to call potential blood donors (Manucia, Baumann, & Cialdini, 1984); and to spend time with a homesick student (Fultz, Batson, Fortenbach, McCarthy, & Varney, 1986) to name but a few. Another common procedure for dissociating the measure from the rest of the experiment is to pretend that measures of the dependent variable are being collected for some other, unrelated study. Festinger and Carlsmith (1959), for example, presented the dependent variable as some information being collected for a study being carried out by other members of the psychology department.

Second, we may observe some behavior of interest when the subject is *not aware* of being under observation. A simple form of this type of disguise is often used in questionnaire measures; the questions designed to measure the dependent variable are embedded in a much larger questionnaire ostensibly presented for some other purpose. The subject's awareness of being measured can often be further diminished, or even eliminated entirely, if a behavioral response is used. For example, Robert Cialdini and his colleagues (1978) used as their dependent variable the subjects' presence or absence at the experiment for which they had volunteered. Presumably, the subjects were unaware that the experimenter was primarily interested in whether they showed up. Monroe Lefkowitz, Robert Blake, and Jane Mouton (1955), in a field experiment, used such measures as whether people jaywalked or disobeyed signs.

An alternative strategy involves actually telling the subject that you are interested in a particular measure, but *disguising the reasons* for your interest. Several different techniques fall into this general category. For example, instead of implying that it is the dependent variable, one may describe it as a covariate which must be measured because of its possible confounding effects. Thus, Aronson (1961) conducted an experiment to find out whether subjects perceived certain colors as more attractive if they had expended a great deal of effort to obtain objects painted those colors. The subjects had to fish for prizes with a hook and line. Some of the prizes were much harder to "catch" than others were, and these prizes were also painted a different color from the rest. Aronson wanted to find out if subjects came to prefer the color of these hard-to-catch objects. In order to disguise his reasons for asking this question, he told the subjects that he wanted them to rate the attractiveness of the colors because he suspected that it might have affected how hard they had worked.

Another common rationale used by experimenters to cover the reason for their interest in the dependent variable is an expressed interest in *"person perception"* rather than in liking, aggression, or attitude toward some particular trait characteristic of the stimulus person. Since the "person perception" questions include some evaluative items, the subjects' positive or negative feelings toward the person or trait can be assessed. The subject is led to believe that the experimenter is interested mainly in the person rated rather than in the rater. A classic experiment using this technique was carried out by Mason Haire in 1950, in a marketing study designed to assess housewives' attitudes and prejudices about instant coffee. The subjects were asked to describe the personality of another housewife on the basis of a shopping list she had made out. For half of the subjects the list read as follows:

> pound and a half of hamburger
> 2 loaves Wonder Bread
> bunch of carrots
> 1 can Rumford's baking powder
> Nescafé instant coffee
> 2 cans Del Monte peaches
> 5 lbs potatoes

The other half of the subjects received the following list:

> pound and a half of hamburger
> 2 loaves Wonder Bread
> bunch of carrots
> 1 can Rumford's baking powder
> 1 lb Maxwell House coffee (drip grind)
> 2 cans Del Monte peaches
> 5 lbs potatoes

The subjects believed that the researchers were interested in knowing what kind of housewife would be likely to draw up such a shopping list. In fact, however, the investigators were interested in the subjects' own opinions, particularly in the nature of their attitudes and prejudices about instant coffee, which was then a new product. They found that the subjects were much more likely to describe the instant-coffee housewife as a lazy person, a poor planner, a spendthrift, and a bad wife. Note the conceptual similarity of this "person perception" experiment to that conducted by Porter and Geis (1981).

The experimenter can also present the dependent variable as an *"objective test"* of reasoning, memory, judgment, or other qualities supposedly unaffected by values. Of course, the assumption is that the test responses can be affected by values or by some temporary subjective state manipulated by the independent variable and related to the content of the objective test. Thus, a "reasoning test" may ask: Which of the following conclusions can be drawn on the basis of this statement?, and the statement happens to mention student radicals, Republicans, blacks, Russia, pornography, or some other attitude object; the "conclusions" include a number of evaluative statements that may or may not follow from the original statement. For example, consider an item used by John Morgan (1945) in a test of attitudes toward the Japanese that was disguised as a test of logic. Subjects first read a pair of propositions, such as the following:

> A trustworthy man does not engage in deceitful acts.
> The bombing of Pearl Harbor by the Japanese was a deceitful act.

Then they were asked to check the "logical conclusion" from the following list:

1 All of the Japanese are trustworthy.
2 Some of the Japanese are trustworthy.
3 Only a few of the Japanese are trustworthy.
4 Some of the Japanese are not trustworthy.
5 Most of the Japanese are not trustworthy.
6 None of the Japanese are trustworthy.
7 No logical conclusion can be drawn from the given statements.

The logical conclusion to the syllogism is 4: "Some of the Japanese are not trustworthy." If a subject checked an item that was more extreme, such as 6: "None of the Japanese are trustworthy," it was taken as a sign of a possible anti-Japanese attitude. As a control for actual logical ability, Morgan included the same statements written in abstract form. For the example about the Japanese, the control item was: "No As are Bs. Some Cs are Bs," along with the parallel response choices. The difference between the subjects' answers to the abstract forms and to the items about the Japanese was taken as the measure of their attitude toward the Japanese.

We mentioned the possibility of using other ostensibly "objective" *memory tests* containing positive or negative attitude statements, pictures of minority-group members, and so on. With all such tests, the underlying assumption is that errors are indications of the subject's attitudes (or some other conceptual variable); thus the experimenter should make sure that the subject population is homogeneous with respect to intelligence and education or that the test includes control items, as Morgan did.

Investigators may also tell subjects that they are involved in the *preliminary stages* of research and need the subjects' help in constructing an attitude measure. Carl Hovland and Muzafer Sherif (1952) suggested that a task that simply involves sorting attitude statements into piles according to their degree of favorability might be used to assess subjects' attitudes. Subjects with strongly favorable attitudes should classify a larger proportion of the items as unfavorable; those with neutral attitudes should distribute the items evenly over the whole range; and those with strongly unfavorable attitudes should classify a larger proportion of the items as favorable. In a similar vein, Dawes, David Singer, and Frank Lemons (1972) asked subjects to write attitude statements that they thought would be endorsed by typical "hawks" and typical "doves." They found that hawkish subjects wrote more extreme statements to represent the dove position than did doves, and vice versa, and that on the basis of the attitude statements they wrote, the subjects could be classified as hawks or doves with relatively high accuracy (78–87%).

One can dispense with the need for disguising the dependent-variable measure by using individuals who are, by nature, unsuspicious. For example, Aronson and Carlsmith (1963) were able to use a simple and transparent method for measuring the dependent variable only because the subjects in that experiment were four-year-old children. These children were not suspicious of anything that was going on; they saw nothing peculiar about someone asking them to rate a number of toys on two occasions within a span of 20 minutes. The same procedure would not have been so effective if college sophomores had been used as subjects.

The dependent variable can be measured by a family of techniques that parallels the accident procedure for manipulating an independent variable. The most common of these is to claim that the pretest data have been lost, so that a second set of measures must be collected. A complicated variation on this theme was employed by Aronson and Carlsmith (1962). Here, the experimenter timed the subject's performance on four successive tests, but then pretended to forget to time the fifth, final test. After much pacing, breast-beating, and rumination, the experimenter asked the subject to take the test over again so that her performance could be timed. But the real purpose of this procedure was to give the subject an opportunity to change her answers. The number of answers changed was the dependent-variable measure and was presumed to reflect the subject's dissatisfaction with her original score. As we pointed out in our discussion of the independent variable, this kind of procedure (if successful) has the great advantage of appearing to be an event that happens only once, to this particular subject, and thus is extremely unlikely to be perceived as a situation of experimental concern to the investigator.

The final techniques involve measures which are *unlikely to be under the subject's conscious control*. Earlier, we mentioned the possibilities for the monitoring of such physiological responses as blood pressure, heart rate, pupil dilation, and electrodermal activity. Other nonverbal cues such as movements of the face and eyes, interaction distance, voice frequency, and speech disturbance can also be measured. Although not all nonverbal cues that have been studied have been shown to be valid indicators of subjective reactions, there is good evidence for some, and the possibility of taking the measurements without the subject's knowledge (by concealed cameras or tape recorders) is an additional advantage of measures of nonverbal behavior.

Although the use of concealed cameras or tape recorders is an important technique for providing useful data, it again raises difficult ethical issues that the experimenter must face squarely. Whenever possible, the subject should be informed in advance of the presence of cameras or tape recorders. Often their presence can be easily accounted for, and the subject is likely to ignore them when the critical measures are taken. When the experimenter considers that the experiment would be vitiated if the presence of the recording devices were known, it is imperative that the subject be informed of their presence during the debriefing session. Further, additional informed consent is necessary at this time, so that the subject has a clear option of requesting that the recordings be destroyed at this point. Even though the recordings will be used only to score the subjects' behavior onto a coded data sheet, subjects should have the option of refusing to have the recording of their behavior preserved for even that long. In the event that the experimenter anticipates using some of the photographs to accompany a research report, even more care must be taken, and legal advice should be sought.

CHAPTER 9

ON THE AVOIDANCE
OF BIAS

The potential for systematic bias in experimental work is well documented, and the attendant problems have worried scientists in all fields for many years. In performing experimental operations, we humans are imperfectly standardized; in estimating their effects, we are imperfectly calibrated. More seriously, human errors are often nonrandom; that is, they tend to bias the results in a particular direction, thus casting doubt on the validity of the experiment.

There are two major varieties of bias that may intrude into social psychological experiments: bias due to the subject's perception of the **demand characteristics** of the experimental situation (Adair & Schachter, 1972; McDavid, 1965; Orne, 1962, 1969; Riecken, 1962; Rosenberg, 1966, 1969; Silverman, 1965; Weber & Cook, 1972) and bias due to the unintentional influence of the experimenter (Rosenthal, 1966, 1969). These are different but related problems. The possibility of either type of bias raises important questions about achieving validity in experimentation. Social psychological experiments in particular appear to be susceptible to bias because of the latitude experimenters frequently allow themselves in order to establish rapport with their subjects and because of the sensitivity of human subjects to subtle cues. In this chapter we describe these two types of bias and outline some methods that may be used to deal with them: either to eliminate them or at least to minimize their potential effects.

BIAS DUE TO DEMAND CHARACTERISTICS

Bias due to the demand characteristics of the experimental situation is a phenomenon closely related to the **placebo effect** in medical research. The term "placebo" (from the Latin "I shall please") refers to the ability of *inert* substances to produce changes in patients: changes that mimic the effects of "legitimate" treatments or medications. In testing the effects of new drugs, medical researchers typically give some subjects a drug and others a pill that looks like the drug but contains no active ingredients (a placebo). In a recent review, Linnie Price (1984) notes that the placebo effect has been shown to account for 30 to 40 percent of the efficacy of "active" medications; that is, 30 to 40 percent of subjects in medical research who are given placebos show improvement similar to that of subjects given "real" medications. Placebos have lowered the blood sugar levels of diabetics (Singer & Hurwitz, 1967); shrunk tumors in cancer patients (Klopfer, 1957); relieved postoperative pain (Beecher, 1955); and reduced serum cholesterol and mortality rates in coronary patients (Coronary Drug Project Research Group, 1980). Indeed, so powerful are the effects of placebos that some patients to whom they are administered actually develop classic symptoms of chemical dependence, including an inability to stop taking them, and withdrawal symptoms when the "medication" is withheld (Vinar, 1969). Thus, the trappings of the medical situation—the medication, the knowledge or rumors about its expected effects, the doctor's concern—seem to elicit a reaction that mimics the reaction to a real drug.

Similarly, in most social psychological experiments the subjects know that they are in an experimental situation. They are aware that they are being observed and that certain behaviors are expected of them. Thus, they respond not simply to the experimental operations but also to their own guesses or interpretations about the behaviors these experimental operations are supposed to elicit. As Henry Riecken (1962) has pointed out, the experimenter-subject relationship is one of unequal power and unequal knowledge. There is a one-sided distribution of information, whereby the experimenter attempts to conceal what might be defined as a "right answer." Even if the subjects are told specifically that there are no correct or incorrect answers, they may assume that there are answers that will enhance or diminish their value in the eyes of the experimenter, especially if they know that the experimenter is a psychologist. From the point of view of the subjects, the experiment may be seen as a game or contest in which they try to discover the true purpose. Their search for an explanation of the procedures may be motivated by a desire to make a good impression on the experimenter (Riecken, 1962; Rosenberg, 1965) or by an inclination to "help" the experimenter by ensuring that the hypothesis is supported by their performance. In any case, many subjects are actively searching for a hypothesis about what is going on in the experiment. More specifically, they may attempt to trace the connection between the events that happen to them and the experimenter's hypothesis. Unless the experimenter has taken special precautions to conceal the purpose of the experiment, bright, discerning subjects can often figure it out.

If the subjects believe that they have figured out the hypothesis, they may behave in a manner consistent with it, tailoring their responses to fit their view of the theory and attempting to cooperate with the experimenter. Alternatively, a few subjects may attempt to either express hostility or try to outwit the experimenter by performing in a manner that directly contradicts the hypothesis. Although there is little unambiguous evidence for either of these behaviors in social psychological experiments (Weber & Cook, 1972), there is a great deal of evidence indicating that subjects try to present themselves in the best possible light (Sigall, Aronson, & Van Hoose, 1970; Weber & Cook, 1972; and see Chapter 6). For example, during a clinical interview a subject may try to respond in a socially desirable manner (Masling, 1960). Of course, it is possible that in some experiments behavior that results in the most favorable self-presentation will also tend to confirm the experimenter's hypothesis. When the two motivations of "looking good" and "confirming the hypothesis" are pitted against each other, however, subjects typically choose to support their own self-image rather than the experimenter's hypothesis (Sigall, Aronson, & Van Hoose, 1970). In general, the subject's most important motive for discovering the experimenter's hypothesis is a desire to find out what behaviors are expected of the good, healthy, intelligent, and normal person so as to adjust his or her own behavior accordingly; a possible secondary motive is a desire to make the data useful by confirming the experimenter's hypothesis (Orne, 1969; Rosenberg, 1969).

Part of the presentation of a favorable image probably involves looking helpful and cooperative, that is, avoiding behavior that might brand one as a troublemaker. There is a host of experimental results documenting the docility and cooperativeness of subjects in experimental situations. Martin Orne (1962), attempting to find a set of operations that would lead the subject to refuse to cooperate, found that he was unable to do so. He designed a set of psychologically noxious, meaningless, and boring tasks and found that subjects would perform these tasks for long periods with few errors, little decrement in speed, and relatively little indication of hostility. In one situation, after subjects had performed a whole page of simple and uninteresting sums, the experimenter instructed them to tear up the answer sheet into 32 pieces, turn to the next page of addition problems, and continue working. Orne repeated this procedure, having the subjects tear up one answer sheet after another for several hours; none of the subjects showed any inclination to discontinue the activity. In another experiment, Orne and Frederick Evans (1965) found that subjects fearlessly complied with instructions to handle a poisonous snake or to reach barehanded into a beaker of fuming nitric acid. Similar evidence for the docility of subjects in experimental situations can be found in experiments by Albert Pepitone (1958), by Stanley Milgram (1973), and by Steven West and his associates (1975). Subjects seem to assume that there *is* a point to apparently pointless tasks, that apparently dangerous ones are really safe, and that immoral acts are someone else's responsibility. Thus to some extent their "usual" motivations are suspended in the laboratory setting. If the subjects extend this docility and cooperativeness to include specific behaviors that are consistent with the experimenter's hypothesis, the results of any such experiments may be meaningless, or, at best, irrelevant to any test of that hypothesis.

TECHNIQUES FOR MINIMIZING
THE EFFECTS OF DEMAND CHARACTERISTICS

There are several possible solutions to the problems raised by demand characterisics. Perhaps the best one is to follow the medical placebo model; one should try to design manipulations that appear essentially identical to the subjects in all conditions, just as placebo pills look identical to the pills containing the drug in a medical experiment. In this case any attempts that the subject might make to discover the experimenter's hypothesis cannot possibly have a systematic effect on the results of the experiment, since the demand characteristics and the performance designed to project a favorable image will be the same in all conditions. Such attempts on the part of the subject will simply increase random error. Unfortunately, in most social psychological experiments this solution is difficult to apply.

Giving the Subject a False Hypothesis

A more common attempt to solve this problem is the deception experiment. Here, the subject is given a plausible hypothesis about the purpose of the experiment, but it is unrelated or orthogonal to the true hypothesis. If subjects attempt to modify their behavior to support or refute this incorrect hypothesis, the results of the experimental test of the true hypothesis will not be affected in any systematic way. If subjects try to project a favorable self-image in terms of the perceived point of the experiment, these behaviors will also be irrelevant to the real hypothesis and can affect the results only by contributing to random error, or by affecting the scores of subjects in all conditions equally.

For an analogous procedure in medical research, imagine a situation in which the experimenter wishes to test a new formula designed to reduce anxiety. Concerned that the subjects might guess the true purpose and obligingly claim that they feel steady and serene, the experimenter might attempt to distract them from the real hypothesis by telling them that the drug is believed to prevent colds. The placebo effect should then result in reports of decreased incidence of colds, but it would be unlikely that subjects would show spurious reductions in their reports of anxiety, since their attention has been diverted from any expectations about this variable.[1]

It is important to realize that giving the subject a false, but credible, hypothesis is a much better procedure than not stating any hypothesis at all. For if there are loose ends to an experimental procedure, the subject will attempt to

---

[1]Ethical issues raised by this procedure are discussed in Chapter 3.

tie these up by devising a hypothesis. This hypothesis may *not* be orthogonal to the true hypothesis; indeed, it may even turn out to be identical or very similar to it, in which case any hypothesis-confirming behavior on the part of the subject would be a source of systematic bias. If the experimenter can tie the loose ends together for the subject by providing a plausible hypothesis that is far removed from the real hypothesis and unrelated to it, the subject's curiosity may be satisfied, thereby eliminating this source of bias. Indeed, this is the primary advantage of the use of deception in experiments. This procedure is really an attempt to provide a cognitive analogy to the placebo; all subjects receive identical explanations as to the purpose of the experiment, just as all subjects receive identical pills in the placebo procedure. Responses due to the "placebo effect" or to the subject's hypothesis about the desirable way to behave vis-à-vis the deceptive rationale should be common to both experimental and control groups. Thus, observed differences between groups will be due to the experimental treatment rather than to a placebo effect or an effect resulting from demand characteristics.

It should be noted that in practice, the suspicious subject may not take the false hypothesis at face value. Rather, the false hypothesis may offer the subject a new basis for speculating about the true purpose of the experiment. Thus, regardless of what the experimenter says, the subject may form personal, idiosyncratic hypotheses and make some responses on the basis of them. In a well-planned study, these responses will not be the ones in which the experimenter is interested. The experimenter may bring the dependent-variable measures in through the back door, while the subject is not thinking about them. If the experimenter's true hypothesis is unrelated to the cover story, it will probably be unrelated to the hypotheses generated by the subject, and the measure of the dependent variable will probably not be regarded as a significant element in the experiment.

For example, consider Stanley Schachter's (1959) experiments linking anxiety to the desire to affiliate with other people. Most of the subjects may have accepted Schachter's cover story to the effect that he was interested only in learning about physiological reactions to shock. But, since Schachter seemed to be going out of his way to frighten those subjects, some of the more suspicious ones in the high-anxiety condition might have developed hypotheses somewhat different from the cover story. For example, they might have guessed that the experimenter was trying to raise their anxiety level in order to see what effects anxiety would have on their responses to the shock. At the same time, it is doubtful that any of the subjects made the connection between the fact that the experimenter was deliberately raising their anxiety and the "incidental question" about whether they would prefer to wait alone or with other people. Thus, it can be immaterial whether the subject completely accepts the false hypothesis offered by the experimenter, so long as it prevents speculation about the *true* experimental hypothesis.

The most serious difficulty with this solution is, of course, that there is no foolproof way of being completely certain that the subject's hypothesis is really independent of the experimenter's hypothesis. Furthermore, even though the subject's hypothesis may be different from that of the experimenter, it may still have some effect on the response that the experimenter cares about. Take, for example, a typical attitude-change study like the classic Hovland and Weiss (1951) experiment, in which a given communication is attributed to either J. Robert Oppenheimer or *Pravda*. The subject may form the following hypothesis: "The experimenter is trying to see whether or not showing me some improbable statement that Oppenheimer made will change my opinion of Oppenheimer. Okay, I'll go along. I'll say that I do not like Oppenheimer as much as I formerly did." The willingness to criticize Oppenheimer, which comes as a result of the subject's attempt to cooperate, may in turn diminish the effectiveness of the communication, even though the subject had no direct hypothesis that the study dealt with the effect of source credibility on attitude change. The subject might mentally say, in effect, "If I'm not supposed to like Oppenheimer, and Oppenheimer said X, I guess I'm not supposed to like X." In this case the behavior that follows from the subject's hypothesis would be directly opposite to that predicted by the experimenter's hypothesis, and the results would be weakened by this subject's data. In much the same way, a subject's incorrect hypothesis could lead to behaviors that might *enhance* the predicted effect, again, for the *wrong* reason.

Of course, at the close of the experiment, the experimenter should probe into any actual hypotheses that the subject may have entertained during the course of the experiment and should specifically ask for the subject's appraisal of what behavior the experimenter expected in the experimental setting. Additional questions, such as questions about how the subject believes *most people* behave in the experimental situation, can help to clarify the subject's hypothesis about the purpose of the experiment. Several investigators (for example, Orne, 1969; Rosenberg, 1969) have suggested that the subject may be able to give more candid answers to these questions if the person conducting the postexperimental interview did not conduct the main experiment. In order to find out just which features of the experiment suggested which hypothesis to the subjects, one might stop the experiment at different points for different groups of subjects in order to ask them to comment on their impressions of the experiment so far (Orne, 1969). In this way it might be possible to locate the exact point at which demand characteristics become salient to the subjects.

It is possible, however, that even the most careful and sensitive probing might not reveal the reasons behind the subjects' behavior and thus would not tell the experimenter whether the results could have been artifactual. Moreover, if the experimenter discovers at the close of the experiment that many subjects did behave in an artifactual way, the problem has not been solved. However important it is to discover that experimental results are meaningless and that it is impossible to draw valid conclusions, knowledge gained in a postexperimental interview is knowledge that comes too late. Although such information is extremely important in designing a better experiment to be carried out at a *later* time, it cannot save the data at hand. In terms of understanding the phenomenon the experimenter started out to study, the prevention of bias is far preferable to its discovery after the fact. Thus, although postexperimental probing is very useful, no amount of this probing, however illuminating and effective, can take the place of a more reliable solution to the problem.

Removing the Dependent-Variable Measure from the Experimental Setting

An alternative solution to the problem of demand characteristics focuses on the measurement of the dependent variable. If this measurement takes place in a different context from the experimental treatment, the subject is less likely to associate the two. One strategy for removing the measurement of the dependent variable from the experimental setting is to convince the subjects that they are actually taking part in two unrelated experiments being run during the same block of time. For example, Milton Rosenberg (1965) brought subjects into the Education Department and asked them to write essays opposed to their own point of view. Subsequently, in the guise of a totally different experiment, their attitudes on the same issue were measured in the Psychology Department.

A more elaborate separation of the independent variable from the dependent variable was carried out in an experiment by Carlsmith, Barry Collins, and Robert Helmreich (1966). In this experiment, subjects were paid different sums of money to perform a very dull task. The dependent variable (the subject's evaluation of the task) was measured in a completely nonexperimental context, after the "experiment" had been completed. Posing as a consumer research specialist, a different experimenter asked the subjects to give their opinion of various pop records. The "consumer researcher" convinced them that people's general mood has a marked effect on their opinions about pop music and that it was therefore essential for him to find out how the subjects were feeling at the moment. In the course of collecting this information, he asked them what kinds of things they had done during the day and how much they had enjoyed them. Since all the subjects had recently participated in the "dull task" experiment, it was both simple and reasonable for the experimenter to get a rating of how much they had enjoyed the task. Since the context of the consumer research study was *psychologically* far removed from that of the original experiment, it was virtually impossible for any of the subjects to realize that the two procedures were related.

The technique of separating the measurement of the dependent variable from the experimental treatment by embedding them in different contexts has two major advantages with respect to controlling demand characteristics. First, it reduces the likelihood that the subjects will associate the two and thus have their responses influenced by their own hypotheses about the experiment. Second, when the dependent-variable measure is collected by a second experimenter who appears ignorant of the nature of the research, it reduces the biasing effect of the subjects' desire to look good in the eyes of the experimenter who actually conducted the experiment (Rosenberg, 1969).

Enlisting the Subject's Aid as an "Experimenter"

One technique that has proved highly successful in preventing subjects from speculating about the experimenter's hypothesis is to convince them that they are not subjects. This can be accomplished by enlisting a subject's aid as an "experimenter." For example, Aronson and Linder (1965) were interested in finding out whether our liking for other people depends on increases and decreases in their apparent esteem for us, and in mapping out the relationship between "being liked" and "liking in return." In essence, the subject was allowed to find out what another person thought of her on several separate occasions. These evaluations were the independent variable. The subject was then asked how much she liked the person she had overheard making the evaluations.

This kind of situation is a difficult one to study because the basic rudiments of the experiment are transparent. If the experiment were presented in a straightforward manner, virtually all subjects would recognize that the two were connected, at least in the experimenter's mind: "I heard her say how much she likes me, and now I am supposed to say how much I like her." In order to camouflage their purpose, Aronson and Linder enlisted the aid of the subject to help them run an experiment on instrumental verbal reinforcement. The evaluations that the subject overheard were part of a conversation in which the experimenter was supposedly reinforcing the evaluator for using plural nouns, and the subject's job was to keep track of the number of plural nouns the evaluator used. In this context, the manner in which the rudiments of the experiment were presented made it difficult for the subjects to suspect that they were actually the subjects in a rather simple experiment on interpersonal attraction.

Besides deflecting suspicion about the experimental hypothesis, Aronson and Linder's procedure probably served to reduce the subjects' concern for modifying their behavior to present themselves in the best possible light. Since they believed that someone else was the "real" subject in the experiment, they probably worried less about the potential significance of their own behavior. In general, any device that convinces the subjects that the experiment does not involve using their reactions to assess personality or mental health probably serves to reduce evaluation apprehension and the desire to project a blameless self-image.

Keeping the Subject Unaware of Being in an Experiment

In dealing with demand characteristics, one of our chief concerns is that the subject, having heard rumors about the gulf between appearance and reality in psychology experiments, will treat the situation as a kind of guessing game.

The definition of the situation as a game, in which the subject's job is to track down the elusive hypothesis, is bound to blunt the impact of the variables by distracting the subject's attention. In general, the experimenter should take every precaution to counteract the impression that the experiment is an experimenter-subject game. To some extent, all the techniques described in this chapter are useful for achieving this end. Given that the very idea of participation in a psychology experiment may suggest a gamelike situation to the subjects, one of the best techniques is to choose or create an experimental situation in which it is unlikely that the subjects will think that the things that are happening to them are part of an experiment. If the subjects are unaware that they are in an experiment, they will be unlikely to form hypotheses as to what the situation is "really" supposed to be about. The experiment by Harris (1974), described in Chapter 2, and by Crusco and Wetzel (1984) described in Chapter 7 provide excellent examples of this technique.

The essential feature is *not* the removal of the experiment to a naturalistic or field situation. Although a field experiment may make it less probable that demand characteristics will affect the subjects' behavior, in itself it is no guarantee. One need only recall the Hawthorne effect (Roethlisberger & Dickson, 1939) to realize that even in a natural setting, subjects' awareness that they are being observed can be a serious impediment to research.[2] The great advantage of the Harris (1974) and Crusco-Wetzel (1984) experiments is that their subjects did not know they were being studied, whereas in the Hawthorne study, although it took place in the real world, the subjects were fully aware that their behavior was being observed and investigated. Donald Campbell (1969) proposes the "disguised experiment" as one of the most promising ways of avoiding the problem of demand characteristics and suggests a number of natural settings in which such research can be carried out conveniently and unobtrusively: on the highway, at intersections, in public buildings, and so on.

Using Behavioral Measures

Avoiding easy and obvious response measures such as attitude scales provides another important solution to the problem of demand characteristics. You will recall that one reason for our preference for dependent variables that reflect behavioral commitment over purely verbal measures is that verbal measures are easily influenced by the subject's desire to help the experimenter or to look good, by inattention, or by cantankerousness. It is relatively easy for a subject to check plus 5 rather than plus 1 on an attitude scale if doing so might con-

---

[2]The Hawthorne effect may be one of those phantom phenomena that most people accept but no one has demonstrated. That is, although many scholars write of the Hawthorne effect, there is considerable controversy about its existence, even in the original study by Fritz Roethlisberger and William Dickson, and several different interpretations have been offered. [See the critique by Richard Franke and James Kaul (1978), articles by Jack Feldman and others (1982) in Vol. 37 of *American Psychologist*, and a discussion by Jerald Greenberg and Robert Folger (1988).]

ceivably help (or hurt) the experimenter or create a good impression. Such a large distortion of answers is less likely to occur if we investigate behaviors that are important to the subject and that are not so easily influenced by the demands of the situation.

For example, suppose that we are interested in measuring subjects' attraction to another person. We could measure the attractiveness of this person by getting the subject to fill out a series of rating scales. Or we could ask the subject to commit to carrying on a long-term relationship with the person, for example, by selecting the person as a roommate for the entire college semester. Since living with a person involves much more effort and commitment on the part of the subject, it is less likely that roommate selection will be influenced by the subject's desire to please the experimenter. The subject has too much to lose by the choice of an unacceptable roommate and not enough to gain by the temporary approval of the experimenter. Other things being equal, the greater the commitment involved in the dependent variable, the less likely it is to be due to cooperation or evaluation apprehension on the part of subjects. A field experiment by Bernie Silverman (1974) provides empirical support for this proposition. He provided incoming white college students with descriptions of other new students, systematically varying the race of the other students and the degree to which their attitudes and values were similar to the subjects'. Subjects in the experimental group were led to believe that their ratings would be used to determine their roommates in the upcoming year; subjects in the control group were led to believe that their ratings would have no lasting consequences. When there *were* consequences to the subjects' ratings, whites were evaluated more positively than blacks. However, when there were *no* consequences, subjects rated whites and blacks comparably. Subjects in both conditions might have been motivated to appear egalitarian, but for subjects in the experimental group, the advantages of appearing nonprejudiced were evidently outweighed by their concern for the consequences of their evaluations of other prospective students; after all, their ratings would determine with whom they would share a room 24 hours a day for at least a semester. Had ratings *alone* been used to assess racial attitudes, that is, without mention of the use to which the ratings would be put, the experimenter might have drawn the erroneous conclusion that race was not an important issue for these students.

Another advantage of some behavioral measures is that they can be obtained without the subject's awareness that anything is being measured. The amount of time the subject spends talking to a confederate, the subject's willingness to perform some favor, or choice of a seat close to or far from the confederate might serve, for example, as measures of interpersonal attraction that do not involve presenting the subject with an explicit question. A direct question from the experimenter is a natural cue that something is about to be measured and is likely to intensify the operation of any demand characteristics that may be present. If no question is asked, the subject is much less likely to know which behaviors are relevant, and because it is practically impossible for the subject to monitor the entire range of personal behavior, such observational measures may be less contaminated by the influence of demand characteristics.

Little is known about the correlation between a stated opinion and a serious commitment to behavior as functions of the same experimental treatment, and this correlation is undoubtedly different for different behaviors. For this reason we want to reemphasize that no blanket endorsement for behavioral measures over verbal measures is being implied. As stated previously, in certain situations a verbal measure may present a much closer approximation of the subject's beliefs or feelings than a behavioral measure can. Not only that, but sometimes the experimenter is simply not interested in behavior; instead, the subjects' ratings (confidence measures, subjective probability judgments, causal inferences, etc.) are the *only* dependent variables of interest.

Bias-Reducing Designs

We might add that there are certain kinds of experimental designs and procedures which, because of their inherent characteristics, may increase or decrease the possibility of bias due to acquiescence or cooperativeness on the part of the subject. One design which has been considered risky for the experimenter who is concerned with avoiding bias is the *pretest-posttest design* (see Chapter 4). This design often suggests a hypothesis to the subject. For example, if subjects are asked to state their attitude on an issue and then to read a communication about that issue, and afterward are asked to restate their attitude on the same issue, it may well become obvious to them that the communication is expected to have some effect on their attitude. There is less potential bias in an *posttest-only design,* because in the latter design, subjects are less likely to be sensitized to the question of interest to the experimenter.

The available evidence indicates that the results of pretest-posttest designs are likely to be biased *against* the hypothesis of attitude change, if anything (Campbell, 1969; Lana, 1969; McGuire, 1969). Robert Lana (1969), in a review of the literature on this topic, concludes that there is little evidence of pretest main effects or interactions with unidirectional communications, and that with two-sided communications, the most typical finding is a main effect in which the pretest serves to *inhibit* change. In other repeated-measures designs, however, especially when continuous feedback about the quality of performance is available to the subject, the subject's behavior may be shaped over time toward the behavior he or she thinks is characteristic of the intelligent, well-adjusted, normal person (Rosenberg, 1969).

Nonobvious Hypotheses

The effects of demand characteristics are sometimes minimized by a hypothesis that is not intuitively obvious. There has been a great deal of discussion about the advantages of ''nonobvious'' predictions, but we are not at all certain that nonobvious predictions are more valuable than obvious ones. We do suspect that such experiments can minimize the possibility of bias by making it more difficult for subjects to guess the true hypothesis. If this is to be claimed as a defense against experimental demands, however, it is necessary to run a control condition in which subjects are asked to guess the hypothesis and the direction of the results predicted by the experimenter. More elaborate versions of this control technique might involve actually giving the subjects the dependent-variable measure after describing the procedure to them, or asking them to behave as they think "real subjects" would behave, in order to try to deceive experimenters who are kept blind to which subjects are genuine and which are simulators (Orne, 1969). Of course, all these precautions are more useful if they are part of a well-organized pilot phase of the research than if they are components of the actual experiment, since flaws discovered in the pilot phase can be corrected before it is too late. Prevention is generally more satisfactory than diagnosis.

Few experimenters feel that their predictions are obvious; it is important to find out what their subjects think. As Orne (1969) points out, the fact that role-playing or simulating subjects behave like real subjects does not prove that the results of the experiment are a function of demand characteristics. It simply serves to illustrate how the demand characteristics operate in a given experimental setting and to raise the possibility that they constitute an alternative explanation of the results.

Stephen Weber and Thomas Cook (1972) also emphasize the value of nonobvious hypotheses, stating that "all experiments should be designed so that hypotheses are difficult to learn" (p. 291). In addition, they present evidence that subjects may not ordinarily discover the experimenter's hypothesis except in very simple situations, such as studies of conditioning or conformity based on paradigms that by now are well known to college students. If the experiment is a complex one, with many different groups and a conditional prediction—such as an interaction prediction—it is unlikely that the subjects will be able to figure out the grand design on the basis of their experience in only one condition.

Asking for the Subject's Help

Samuel Fillenbaum (1966) has suggested that it may be possible for the experimenter to use the docility of the subject to *reduce* the biasing effects of demand characteristics by making an honest and unsuspicious attitude the most important demand of the experiment. The experimenter's prestige and power can be used to convince subjects that the most desirable role for them to adopt during the experiment is that of the "faithful subject." According to Weber and Cook (1972, p. 275), "the faithful subject is someone who believes that a high degree of docility is required in research settings and who further believes that his major concern should be to scrupulously follow experimental instructions and to avoid acting on the basis of any suspicions he might have about the true purpose of the study."

In practice, the creation of a group of "faithful subjects" may involve telling the subjects beforehand that deception is involved and that the purpose of the study cannot be revealed to them at the outset. Cook and his colleagues (1970) found, for example, that subjects who were told that the purpose of the experiment had to be concealed behaved the same as did the successfully deceived subjects who were not given this introduction. Weber and Cook do not suggest that it is possible to elicit faithful behavior in all experimental situations, however. For example, when the subject has clear-cut cues that one course of behavior is "better," more normal, more appropriate, or more intelligent than the alternatives, it is improbable that the temptation to follow this course can be overcome by a plea to perform the role of faithful subject. This role is much easier to adopt in situations involving a low level of evaluation apprehension. In such situations, asking the subjects' help in generating accurate data, stressing the seriousness of the task and the importance of honest responses, and reminding the subjects of the worthlessness of a biased experiment may make a great difference in the validity of the results obtained. Rarely, however, is this technique a sufficient protection against demand characteristics.

BIAS DUE TO THE UNINTENTIONAL INFLUENCE OF THE EXPERIMENTER

A large body of research serves to remind us that the experimenter is not simply a passive administrator of prepackaged stimuli, but rather an active influence that contributes an unknown quantity of new stimuli to the situation. Experimenters differ in sex, skill, technique, personality, and many other factors, all of which can interact with the experimental operations to systematically bias results. F. J. McGuigan (1963), for example, used nine experimenters to test the effectiveness of four methods of learning with comparable groups of subjects. Some of the experimenters found no differences among the four methods; others found significant differences, but the order of the methods' effectiveness varied depending on the experimenter. Robert Rosenthal (1967) found that male experimenters behave in a more friendly manner than do female experimenters and that in general, experimenters are more likely to smile at female subjects than at male subjects. These results indicate that the experimenter can be an important variable in an experiment.

More disconcerting are the many examples from other sciences (cf. Wilson, 1952) that show how experimenters can bias data in extraordinarily subtle ways to support their hypotheses. Rosenthal and his associates have presented a body of systematic data exploring similar effects in social psychology (Rosenthal, 1966, 1969). The basic device used in Rosenthal's studies has been the suggestion of contradictory hypotheses to two groups of experimenters. When this is done, the data obtained from the subjects in each group lean significantly in the direction of the hypothesis the experimenter was given. In one experiment, for example, Rosenthal and Kermit Fode (1963a) devised a person-perception task using 20 photographs of faces. It had previously been determined that these photographs were neutral, in that none of them had been judged as portraying people who were particularly successful or particularly unsuccessful. The subject's task was to rate each photo along a success-failure continuum. Several of the experimenters running the study expected high ratings; several others expected low ratings. Those expecting subjects to rate the pictures high got significantly higher ratings than did those expecting low ratings. Indeed, there was no overlap between the distributions! More disconcerting than the data, however, is the fact that any cues given to the subject by the experimenter would have had to be extremely subtle; they were not readily apparent from sound films taken of similar experimental sessions.

Even more dramatic results were obtained in experiments involving learning in rats (Rosenthal & Fode, 1963b; Rosenthal & Lawson, 1964). In these studies each experimenter was randomly assigned a rat after being told that the animal had been specially bred for brightness or dullness. When the results were tabulated, it was found that the so-called bright rats learned more quickly than did the so-called dull rats. Similar results have been found in studies using planaria as subjects (e.g., Cordaro & Ison, 1963). In his 1969 review of the research on the effects of the experimenter's hypothesis, Rosenthal presents convincing evidence for the operation of **experimenter bias** in studies of animal learning, human learning, psychophysical judgment, reaction time, inkblot tests, structured laboratory interviews, and person perception. Oddly enough, the effects seem strongest in some of the ''harder'' areas and more variable in such areas as person perception, which might intuitively seem more susceptible to interpersonal influence.

The consistency of Rosenthal's data, as well as the wide variety of experimental situations he has employed and reviewed, argue against taking this problem lightly. The problem of experimenter bias is a serious one and should be taken into account by anyone planning an experiment. But some of the response to Rosenthal's data has been perhaps too extreme and too pessimistic. Our major reason for this belief is that virtually all Rosenthal's findings have occurred in contexts which are essentially different from those of the usual laboratory experiment and that the differences operate to *invite* bias. First, most of the experiments cited by Rosenthal (1966, 1969) are fairly simple, two-condition experiments in which a clear-cut expectancy is easily communicated to the experimenters. This is less frequently the case in social psychological experiments not specifically designed to investigate bias. Many social psychological experiments have several conditions, with complex hypotheses or with more than one ''hypothesis'' being pitted against the others. Rarely is an experimenter told how the data should come out. Thus, on the whole, it seems that in studies designed to demonstrate bias, the appropriate direction of bias is often clearer, and therefore the experimenters' expectations stronger, than they are in studies designed to test other hypotheses. Rosenthal himself has suggested that when the expectancy induced involves a simple response, the probability of bias may be higher than when the expectancy involves a more complex response (1969, p. 219).

Another difference between the experimenter-bias studies and many other social psychological experiments is that the former typically involve repeated measures of the same subjects. In this context, the experimenter has almost continuous feedback from the subject and is in an ideal position to shape the subject's behavior by reinforcing "correct" responses. In the more typical social psychological experiment, the dependent variable is measured only once, or if repeated measures are taken, the experimenter is usually unaware of the subject's responses and thus cannot bias the results through differential reinforcement. Rosenthal points out that operant conditioning is not sufficient to account for all of the results in experimenter bias, since in some studies the expectancy effects have been shown to be greater for the subject's very first response than for later responses (Rosenthal, 1966, pp. 289–293). Immediate feedback from subjects, however, may increase the experimenter's evaluation apprehension vis-à-vis his or her professor (many of these experiments have been conducted as part of the student-experimenter's course work) or supervisor, more so than would be the case if it were impossible for the experimenter to figure out how the subject was doing. Perhaps the experimenter whose results are strongly in the predicted direction on the first few trials is able to relax on subsequent trials, knowing that the data will probably come out "right." This might account for the greater effectiveness observed on the early trials. That the feedback *does* have an effect on the experimenter's behavior is illustrated by the finding that the bias effect increases *across* subjects when the data from the first few subjects confirm the hypothesis.

Finally, in Rosenthal's paradigm, each experimenter typically runs only one of the experimental conditions. For example, in the learning experiment, an experimenter ran either a "bright" rat or a "dull" rat. This does not occur in an actual experiment; instead, the experimenter usually runs subjects in all conditions. It may be that it is easier for an experimenter to bias a subject's behavior without being aware of it while running only one condition; experimenters who run more than one condition may be more likely to notice systematic differences in their behavior toward the subjects. Although Rosenthal (1966, 1969) has demonstrated that bias can exist even when the experimenter runs all the conditions, the results of such studies are not as straightforward as those of studies in which each experimenter runs a single condition. Often the bias effect does not occur. Probing more deeply, Rosenthal has found that when the same experimenters are given different expectancies about different groups of subjects, some experimenters produce the bias effect, and "a significant minority" obtain results that are just the opposite of the induced expectancies (Rosenthal, 1969, pp. 219, 243). These results are puzzling, and they indicate that the problem of experimenter bias in actual social psychological research may be rather more complicated than the simple hypothesis-confirming effect found in Rosenthal's earlier studies.[3]

TECHNIQUES FOR MINIMIZING
THE EFFECTS OF EXPERIMENTER BIAS

Using Naive Experimenters

Prevalent or not, it is important to devise techniques for eliminating this kind of bias. One technique that has been suggested involves keeping the experimenter (research assistant) unaware of the hypothesis. We find this an unsatisfactory solution, for two reasons. First, it probably is not effective. In one of Rosenthal's experiments (Rosenthal, Persinger, Vikan-Kline, & Mulry, 1963), it was shown that the research director could covertly communicate his expectations about the results to his assistants even when he did not describe the hypothesis to them. In short, assistants trained by each experimenter generated appropriately biased data even though they were not told the hypothesis. The authors of that research recommended the elimination of personal contact between the experimenter and assistants while they are being trained for a particular experiment, to rule out possibilities of covert communication. We suspect that this technique is likewise doomed to failure. The good researcher forms hypotheses; indeed, this is characteristic of all intelligent human beings. Thus, if not told the hypothesis, the research assistant, like a subject, attempts to discover one. Since most research assistants are more sophisticated than are most subjects (and usually have more information about the experiment), it is more likely that the assistant will arrive at the correct solution. Of course, even an incorrect hypothesis by the research assistant may bias the experimental outcome.

Moreover, either keeping the assistant in the dark or eliminating contact with the supervisor would reduce the value of the educational benefits derived from serving as an experimenter. Many experimenters are students, and full participation is the most effective way of learning how to conduct an experiment properly. Any technique involving the experimenter's ignorance of the hypothesis or a reduction of supervisory contact does the student a disservice.

Keeping the Experimenter Blind to the Subject's Condition

A more useful solution allows the experimenter to know the true hypothesis, but at the same time remain ignorant of the specific experimental condition to

---

[3]Some critics have argued that Rosenthal has exaggerated the prevalence and magnitude of the problem of experimenter bias. [See Barber & Silver (1968); see also Rosenthal & Rubin (1978), a review article followed by comments by 29 scholars.] Our own position is that experimenter bias occurs and that it can result in spurious confirmation of hypotheses. Until we have much better information on when it is likely to occur, our only recourse is to protect against experimenter bias in every experiment we run.

which each subject has been assigned. Thus in the Rosenthal-Fode experiment, this might involve telling the experimenters that genetically "bright" rats should learn faster than genetically "dull" rats, but *not* telling them which of the rats are bright and which are dull. In theory, this is a simple and *complete* solution to the problem of experimenter bias and should be employed whenever possible. In the example above this can be done easily by placing all the animals together and using a complex coding system or one that is invisible to the naked eye.

Again we can look to the medical research literature to find an analogous problem and solution. After the placebo effect was well understood, subjects were kept "blind" to the experimental treatment they received; that is, they were not told whether they had received a placebo or a drug. Further research revealed that even though the subjects didn't know whether they had received the drug, their responses could be influenced by the experimenter, who did have that knowledge. Thus subtle and unintentional biasing of the outcome led to the development of the so-called **double-blind experiment,** in which neither the subject *nor* the experimenter knows whether that subject is receiving a placebo or a drug.

The major drawback with this technique, of course, is that in social psychology it is not always possible to design an experiment in which the experimenter does not know the subjects' group membership. The placebo—whose contents are unknowable on inspection—is not a common experimental treatment. However, with some thought and ingenuity, it is certainly true that many more experiments can be run blind than is presently the case. This "double-blind" experiment is the ideal solution to experimenter bias.

Although in many situations it may be impossible to keep the experimenter blind to the subjects' status on all the relevant variables, a wide variety of techniques involve *partial* blindness. These techniques are usually less foolproof than the complete double-blind experiment, but they are always preferable to the situation in which the experimenter is not blind to anything. In general, the less the experimenter knows about how any particular subject is predicted to respond (or exactly which treatment he or she will receive), the less chance there is to bias the results in the predicted direction.

Two Experimenters, Each Half Blind   A partial implementation of the blind technique requires the experimenter to carry out the entire experimental procedure without knowing which treatment the subject will receive until the treatment is administered. That is, in most studies, the experimenter need not know what condition the subjects are in while making the introduction, giving the instructions, describing the research, setting up the task, and carrying out all the preliminary stages of the experiment up to the performance of the crucial manipulation. When the choice point is reached, a randomizing device can be used; the remainder of the experiment is, of course, not carried out in ignorance.

For example, in the severity-of-initiation study, it would have been easy to delay assigning subjects to conditions until the moment of the initiation; by reaching into a pocket and randomly pulling out one of three slips of paper, the experimenter could determine whether the subject would read the obscene words, the mild words, or no words at all. Thus all of the pretreatment instructions would be unbiased. This is only a partial solution, because the experimenter loses ignorance midway through the experiment. However, as Aronson and Carlsmith (1968) pointed out, if the experimenter had left the room immediately after administering the treatment and had assigned a different experimenter (ignorant of the subjects' experimental condition) to collect the data, this solution would be a good one. The use of multiple experimenters, each ignorant of some part of the experiment, offers a solution that is frequently feasible.

Since this solution was first proposed, it has become a standard technique for avoiding bias. Here is how it works: In an experiment by Aronson and Vernon Cope (1968), the subject was treated either harshly or pleasantly by the experimenter and was then allowed to overhear the *experimenter* being treated harshly or pleasantly by the research supervisor. The dependent variable was the subject's liking for the supervisor. In this experiment, both the experimenter and the supervisor were kept partially blind to the subject's condition. During the first part of the experiment, the experimenter, who was treating the subject either harshly or kindly, was unaware of the treatment that he would later be getting from the supervisor. Likewise, in the second part of the experiment, the supervisor, who was praising or berating the experimenter, was unaware of the experimenter's previous behavior toward the subject. Since the prediction was that the harsh supervisor would be liked when the experimenter had also been harsh and disliked when the experimenter had been pleasant, the supervisor was not in a position to bias the results. The supervisor could shape the subject's behavior in the direction of the hypothesis only by knowing how the experimenter had treated the subject, since the subject's predicted reaction to the supervisor depended on the earlier experience with the experimenter.

Automated Instructions   Another technique for implementing the blind experiment is through the use of taped instructions, or what Rosenthal (1966) terms the "reduced contact" technique. After greeting the subject and explaining the general nature of the experiment, the investigator can randomly decide on the experimental condition and conduct the rest of the experiment from another room via a set of standardized tapes. Or the treatment can be administered by computer. We have found that the use of tapes or computers can be easily justified to the subject simply by telling the truth, that is, that it is being done for the sake of greater control and standardization. As discussed in Chapter 7, the use of prepackaged treatments is not an ideal device, because it does reduce the impact of the treatment and sacrifices several important advantages of the live experimenter. But it can effectively preclude the primary *disadvantage* of a live experimenter—the possibility of experimenter bias—and therefore provides a useful precaution when other techniques are not feasible. Closed-circuit television provides a more powerful impact, and through the use of videotapes the experimenter can still be blind to the condition to which subjects have been assigned.

Running All Conditions Simultaneously An interesting and effective technique is to conduct the experimental session so that it includes subjects in all conditions of the experiment (for example, Aronson, Turner, & Carlsmith, 1963; Cottrell, 1965). For some subjects, Nicolas Cottrell first induced expectations of successful performance on a task; for other subjects he introduced expectations of failure. For half of the subjects in each of these two groups, he then confirmed this expectation, or disconfirmed it. He recited the general instructions to subjects in all the conditions simultaneously and then assigned subjects to conditions by randomly giving out written scores to each subject. This technique makes it almost impossible for the experimenter to bias the results in a systematic manner, since any biasing cues are emitted in the presence of subjects in all the experimental conditions and thus are extremely unlikely to influence the responses of subjects in only one group.

Experimenter Blind to One Variable in a Factorial Design When complete ignorance of the experimental conditions is not feasible, partial ignorance may be sufficient. Consider a design in which the treatments are crossed, such as the factorial. It is frequently possible to have the experimenter ignorant about one of the variables defining the subject's condition and knowledgeable about the other. For example, in a typical attitude-change experiment in which fear arousal (high versus low) and adequacy of fear-reducing remedies (adequate versus inadequate) are crossed factorially, the experimenter may know what the level of fear arousal is (having, for example, described the fearful consequences to the subject), but if the possible avenues of fear-reducing behavior are presented in a written communication, the experimenter need not know which communication the subject receives. If, as is the case in many social psychological experiments, the hypothesis is about an interaction between the two variables, and if no main effects are expected, this constitutes an effective blinding of the experimenter. Knowledge of the subject's position with respect to one experimental variable without knowledge of the other is not sufficient to predict where the subject should fall on the dependent variable. Even if one is concerned with more than just the interaction, ignorance of one variable precludes bias on all main effects and interactions involving that variable.

An example of this technique is provided by an experiment by Ellsworth and Carlsmith (1968). The experimenters predicted that the impact of a personal evaluation would differ depending on whether the evaluator were looking at or away from the person being evaluated. Thus if the evaluation were positive, the subject should respond to the evaluator more *positively* when the level of eye contact was high; if the evaluation were negative, the subject should respond more *negatively* with high eye contact. The design was a 2 × 2 factorial with high versus low eye contact and positive versus negative evaluation. The experimenter was kept blind to the nature of the evaluation by making complimentary (or derogatory) remarks about first-born (or later-born) children. Since she did not know whether the subject she was talking to was a first-born or a later-born child, the experimenter was ignorant of whether the remarks were positive or negative for the subject. The experimenter was necessarily aware of the eye-contact manipulation, but since the eye contact was hypothesized to have opposite effects depending on whether the evaluation was favorable or unfavorable, there was no way in which she could bias the results in favor of the hypothesis; any biasing cues would have worked *against* the hypothesis for half the subjects.

Of course, it may sometimes be possible for an experimenter to figure out the subjects' condition without being told, and when that happens the experimenter is no longer blind. For example, if first-borns in the eye contact experiment always agreed with statements favorable to first-borns, the experimenter might have guessed that they were in the positive feedback condition, and thus be able to bias their responses. It is important to check out whether the procedures designed to keep the experimenter blind really succeeded in doing so. In the eye contact experiment, for example, after running each subject the experimenter wrote down her guess about whether the subject was in the positive or negative feedback condition. Since these guesses were no more accurate than would be expected by chance, the authors could safely conclude that the results were not due to experimenter bias.

A Separate Experimenter for Each Subject In some experimental contexts it may be possible to recruit two subjects and let one actually perform the role of the experimenter. The reason that this technique provides some protection against experimenter bias is that the one-shot experimenter does not know about any of the other conditions in the experiment and thus has no information about the design, the variables, or the hypothesis. Earlier we argued that it is very difficult to keep an experimenter unaware of the hypothesis, because the experimenter runs subjects in all conditions and knows what the differences between the treatments are. If each experimenter runs only one subject in one condition, the likelihood that the experimenter will be truly blind to the hypothesis is much greater.

For example, Ellsworth and Lee Ross (1975) conducted an experiment designed to find out whether eye contact encouraged or discouraged intimate self-disclosure. Two subjects were signed up for each session. One subject was assigned to the role of speaker and the other subject was assigned to the role of listener. Unbeknownst to the speaker, the listener was instructed either to look directly into the speaker's eyes (in order "to communicate a sense of personal relationship") or to avoid eye contact (in order "to avoid embarrassing and inhibiting the talker"). Subjects were not told that the researchers were studying the effects of eye contact; all listeners were instructed to be as warm and accepting as possible, and their gaze instructions were just one of a number of techniques suggested to them to encourage intimacy. The main dependent variable was the intimacy of the speaker's disclosures.

Thus all listener-experimenters were given the hypothesis that their eye contact strategy (high or low) would encourage intimacy, and none knew (or guessed) that there were any other treatments involving eye contact. A drawback of this technique, of course, is that nothing about the experimenters can be held constant, so the amount of random error is unusually high. A corresponding benefit is that using many different experimenters greatly increases our confidence in the generality of the results.

Experimenter Blind to Incoming Data Rosenthal (1966, 1969) has found that the responses of the first few subjects tend to influence the experimenter's behavior toward subsequent subjects, so that the later subjects tend to behave like the earlier ones. Rosenthal suggests that "the results of behavioral research can, by virtue of early data returns, be determined partially by the performance of the first few subjects" (1969, p. 243).

The solution to this source of bias is simple: The experimenter should avoid looking at any of the data until all the subjects have been run. If the dependent variable is a questionnaire or is recorded automatically, it is relatively easy to avoid perusing each subject's response. If the dependent variable involves a direct face-to-face interaction, the experimenter can still be kept blind to the subject's response by having another person, who is blind to the subject's condition, measure the dependent variable. Using a second person in the role of observer or recorder of the dependent variable has other advantages as well. Not only does it keep the data from the experimenter—who therefore cannot unconsciously bias later subjects in the direction of the early returns—but it also can serve to reduce the subject's suspicion or evaluation apprehension about the measure *and* to prevent the experimenter from providing biasing cues to the subject at the time the measure is taken.

Combining Techniques

There is no reason that the experimenter should be restricted to just one of these techniques. Often, more than one may be needed to eliminate the possibility of bias completely. The experiment by Carlsmith, Lepper, and Landauer (1974) described in Chapter 3 illustrates the use of a variety of techniques, which taken together, effectively remove bias from the study. The hypothesis in this experiment was that children who are scared will be more obedient to a threatening adult but that children who are relaxed will be more likely to obey an adult who is warm and rewarding. There were two experimenters in the study; the first took the child through the preliminary stages of the experiment and showed a movie designed to elicit fear (or a control movie), and the second was the warm or threatening person who tried to get the child to obey.

The second experimenter, who tested for obedience by asking the child to pick up 150 tennis balls, illustrates the technique of *complete blindness to the subject's condition.* The experimenter's reputation as a threatening or rewarding person had been established earlier, when the child saw a *videotape* of this experimenter interacting in a friendly or punishing way with another child. In a later session, when asking the child to obey, the experimenter spoke in a standardized, neutral manner. Not knowing which videotape the child had seen, the experimenter thus did not know whether he elicited feelings of relaxation or fear in the child. Nor did the experimenter know whether the child had just seen the scary movie or the other one, because this experimenter did not arrive on the scene until after the movie was over. The experimenter simply walked in and asked the child to pick up the tennis balls. Thus, entirely blind to the subject's condition, the experimenter was incapable of behavior that could systematically bias the results.

The other experimenter was the man who showed the movie to the child: a frightening movie to children in the anxiety condition and a funny movie to those in the relaxation condition. This experimenter also kept the lights out for a little while in the anxiety condition and made a few remarks designed to heighten the child's awareness of his own fear. Thus this experimenter knew whether the child was anxious or not. He also knew whether the second experimenter had been given a tough image or a benevolent image by the earlier videotape presentation. It might have been better to keep this experimenter unaware of which videotape the child saw, so that he would have been *blind to one variable in a factorial design.* Since the effects of fear were predicted to be opposite in the tough and benevolent conditions, he would have been incapable of spuriously producing the hypothesized results.

The observers, who measured the child's obedience, were unaware of any aspect of the experimental condition; thus, *observer blindness* was complete. The behavior they measured—picking up tennis balls—was quite straightforward and required little subjective judgment and was also, of course, closer to the actual dependent variable of interest than a verbal statement of "intention to obey" would have been. The use of a *behavioral measure,* among its other virtues, is a further prevention against bias.

In sum, the possibility of systematic bias is forever present in social psychological research. However, this is no cause for despair. It is a rare experiment which, with some ingenuity, cannot be built in such a way as to allow the experimenter to be kept ignorant of at least one critical aspect of the subject's condition.

10

THE POSTEXPERIMENTAL INTERVIEW

The experiment does not end when the data have been collected. The experimenter will want to determine the subjects' reactions to the procedure and to provide them with a full explanation of the experiment. The postexperimental interview is not an unimportant "add-on"; rather, it provides the investigator with an invaluable opportunity to find out what the experiment meant to the individual subjects. It is an opportunity for the subjects to comment freely about how the experiment struck them, why they responded as they did, the alternatives they considered, and all other facets of their individual responses. This is the time for us to determine whether the subjects interpreted their experience as we intended. More important, the postexperimental interview provides the experimenter with an opportunity to fulfill an obligation to the subject: to explain all aspects of the procedure fully, to explore the meaning of the experience for the subject and the experimenter, and to discuss the scientific importance of the results.

If any deception has been employed, the experimenter now can verify that the subject believed the version of events presented in the cover story, or discover whether the subject had some doubts. If the subject *did* entertain any suspicion, the experimenter can systematically probe for further information needed to judge whether the suspicion was specific enough and accurate enough to raise questions about the validity of the data collected from that subject.

Whether or not deception is used, the experimenter should give the subject a full explanation of the experiment and make certain that the subject completely understands the purposes and the procedures before leaving the laboratory. If the experiment has involved any disquieting events, the experimenter can explain why those events were essential. If any deception has been involved, it is almost always best if the subject is informed of the deception and the reasons why it was necessary.[1]

It is impossible to exaggerate the importance of the postexperimental interview. A poorly conducted debriefing can be the most distressing part of the whole experiment, making the subject feel like an object or—worse yet—like a fool. Accordingly, the postexperimental interview should never be approached lightly.

Some researchers have suggested that caring, sensitive experimenters are born and not made—as if any potentially good experimenter has an intuitive sense of what constitutes a considerate debriefing. Moreover, they suggest, if potential experimenters do not know the difference between a glib and cavalier debriefing and one that is respectful and caring, then they shouldn't be experimenters in the first place. We disagree. We believe that this aspect of the experiment is as much a skill as is each of the preceding phases, and that a great deal of effort should go into teaching these skills. The art and skill of debriefing should be as important a part of research training as learning to find or create settings, to manipulate the independent variable, to measure the dependent variable, and to analyze the data. Therefore, we have devoted this chapter to a discussion of the "whys" and "how tos" of conducting the postexperimental interview.

The two major purposes of the interview are closely interwoven. For the remainder of this chapter we will focus our attention on debriefing following an experiment involving deception. Many of these remarks are equally applicable to the experiment with no deception, but the issues are *especially* critical when deception is involved.

CONDUCTING THE POSTEXPERIMENTAL INTERVIEW

If the experiment has involved deception, the experimenter must (1) probe gently to determine the precise nature of any suspicions the subject may have

---

[1]Even the standard of full and honest disclosure is only a guideline, not an absolute rule. In some cases, such disclosures may create feelings of confusion, anxiety, or persistent self-doubt that may be more dangerous for the subject than ignorance of the whole truth. In research with children, for example, the child may not be able to understand the explanation and may be made to feel confused and uncertain about an event that might have seemed vaguely interesting but not particularly important. Or the child may remember only that the experimenter lied. One good way to deal with this problem is to explain the experiment to a parent who knows the child well and so is in a better position to decide what to say about the experiment.

Other dangers may arise in experiments involving adult subjects. If a personality test is administered, for example, it may often be unwise to reveal the subjects' scores to them or even to disclose the purpose of the test. Personality tests may have a reliability that suffices for large-group experiments, but that should not be trusted for individual assessments. Even in experiments in which most subjects do receive a complete explanation, it may not be the best thing for some individuals. If a subject completely misunderstands the instructions and behaves inappropriately throughout the experiment, it may be very difficult to explain the experiment without making the subject feel like an idiot. These, and others like them, are delicate cases; the experimenter must always be sensitive to peculiarities of the procedures or of individual subjects that might raise questions about the advisability of complete debriefing. Like all other general rules in this book, the rule of full and honest disclosure has exceptions.

and (2) explain the deception in a considerate and gradual manner. In practice, these two aims are mutually consistent and can be realized simultaneously by the same general procedure.

Probing for Suspicion

In probing for suspicion, it is important to utilize a series of questions, introduced gradually. Why the need to move gradually? Why not simply ask if the subject suspected deception on the part of the experimenter? For a variety of reasons, subjects may be unresponsive to direct questions. First, a person who *did* guess the hypothesis might hesitate to admit it, out of a misplaced desire to spare the experimenter. Second, regardless of their feelings for the experimenter, most people are reluctant to admit that they can be fooled easily. Consequently, a subject who is suddenly told that deception was involved may imply that he or she suspected it all along. Thus, an abrupt procedure might fail to reveal some of the truly suspicious subjects, while falsely exaggerating the number of apparently suspicious subjects. As a result, the experimenter may be led to make inappropriate changes or to abandon a perfectly viable procedure. Moreover, abruptly stating that deception has been used is a harsh technique that could add unnecessarily to the subject's discomfort and elicit justifiable anger.

The best way to begin a postexperimental interview is to ask if the subject has any questions. If the subject has none, the experimenter should ask if the entire experiment was perfectly clear in its overall purpose and if all aspects of the procedure made sense. The subject can then be told that people react to things in different ways and that the experimenter would find it helpful to hear about the subject's feelings about and reactions to the experiment, the reasons for the subject's responses, and so on. Then, the experimenter should ask specifically whether the subject found any aspect of the procedure odd, confusing, or disturbing. Such a discussion may take a considerable length of time.

By this point in the interview, the subject is likely to have revealed any doubts or suspicions. Moreover, the experimenter should have all the information needed to discover whether the subject misunderstood the directions or failed to share the experimenter's assumptions about the meaning of the treatment. If no suspicions have been voiced, the experimenter can continue: "Do you think there may have been more to the experiment than meets the eye?" This question is almost a dead giveaway. Even a previously unsuspicious subject will probably begin to suspect that the experimenter was concealing something. In our experience, many subjects will take this opportunity to say that they did feel that the experiment, as described, appeared too simple, or too complex, or not ideally designed to test the hypothesis, or something. This is desirable. Whether or not the subjects really were suspicious, this question allows them to indicate that they are not completely naive; it gives them a chance to see themselves as less gullible than they otherwise might. The experimenter should immediately ask them to say some more about their suspicions, to elaborate on their questions about the procedure. The experimenter can then ask how these questions might have affected their behavior. From the subjects' answers to these questions, the experimenter can judge the extent to which their suspicions are likely to have affected their responses.

This is a fairly conservative technique; it will tend to overestimate the number of suspicious subjects, since some subjects may not arrive at any accurate suspicion until they have been exposed to a hint that deception may have been involved and have been forced by direct questioning to consider the nature of that deception. The criteria for excluding subjects' data should be rigid and should be set down before the experiment begins; an appropriate time is between the pilot subjects and the first "real" subject. And, of course, the decision to eliminate any particular subject from the data analysis should be made without knowledge of how that subject responded on the important measures.

Incidentally, it should be apparent that one implication of these recommendations is that subjects should be debriefed individually, even when two or more subjects have participated in the experiment. In the first place, it is difficult, if not impossible, to make accurate assessments of two subjects' reactions to the experiment if they are interviewed simultaneously. If one subject voices a suspicion, there is strong social pressure on the other to concur. Together, the two subjects are likely to arrive at a common interpretation of the experiment, which may not reflect what either of them felt at the time. Thus debriefing subjects in groups defeats the experimenter's purpose of making precise determinations of the degree of suspicion felt by each subject. In addition, this procedure defeats another primary purpose of the debriefing: the protection of the subject's feelings of competence through gradual revelation of the hypothesis. If two subjects are debriefed together, the less suspicious one may feel gullible and inferior when the other first voices any suspicions. The one who is slower to perceive the gist of the experimenter's gradual revelation of the purpose of the study may feel stupid and naive when the other understands it more quickly. The experimenter's remarks to the effect that most subjects typically believe the cover story will be vitiated if the subject sees another person whose perceptions differed. This kind of experience in group debriefing can make a subject feel foolish, and we have more than once heard students who have been debriefed in this way (not in our experiments) complain that "the debriefing was the worst part of the experiment."

Revealing Deception

When deception has been employed, debriefing in and of itself can cause subjects considerable embarrassment. Most people do not enjoy learning that they have been duped. Thus, even subjects who are perfectly convinced that the experimenter obtained no satisfaction deceiving them may *still* feel foolish, simply because they have been successfully deceived. For that reason, extreme care should be used in revealing the specifics of the deceptive techniques employed.

Once the experimenter has a full understanding of the subject's perception of the experiment, the debriefing process should be continued. Thus, the experimenter might say something like this: "You are on the right track; we were interested in some problems that we couldn't discuss with you in advance. One of our major concerns in this study is. . . ." The experimenter should continue by describing the problem being studied, specifying the reasons for its importance and explaining clearly exactly how the subject was deceived and why the deception was necessary. Further, the experimenter can reduce subjects' embarrassment by explaining that a great deal of time and effort went into constructing a situation that would be credible to everyone. By doing so, the experimenter assures the subjects that being duped or taken in does not in any way reflect on their perspicacity; rather, it is an indication that the experimenter had done his or her job right, and that the cover story was a credible one. The experimenter should include this information in the debriefing so that the subjects will realize that they were taken in by the effectiveness of the *situation* and *not* because of any gullibility or naivete of their own. Moreover, before terminating the experimental session, the experimenter should be certain that the subject fully understands all this.

A similar procedure is in order when the experimental treatments induce the subjects to behave in a "negative" manner—for example, to conform in the Asch experiment. Clearly, if the experiment is designed to produce this kind of behavior, and it is a good experiment, most subjects will be manifesting the unflattering behavior at least some of the time. The experimenter should point this out to each subject, stressing the fact that the person is not extreme in this direction; rather, the experimental operations must have been extremely powerful, since they induced the same kind of behavior from most of the people who served as subjects.

There is little doubt about the goal of the debriefing process. Most investigators would agree with Herbert Kelman's (1968, p. 222) recommendation that "in general, the principle that a subject ought not to leave the laboratory with greater anxiety or lower self-esteem than he came in with is a good one to follow." How can we be sure that this goal has been achieved? It is sometimes difficult to tell whether the subject still feels uncomfortable after the debriefing. It is conceivable that some subjects might feel that they must act like "good sports" or help the experimenter save face and so may pretend to be in good spirits while remaining in inner turmoil. The experimenter should not be taken in by such pretenses but rather should go out of his or her way to make it easy for the subject to express any misgivings about the experiment. A good way of getting a subject to reveal any lingering disturbances or uncertainty about the experiment is to solicit suggestions for improving the experiment. If subjects still feel uneasy about their behavior in the experiment, or uncertain of any of the things the experimenter said, it is invariably easier for them to attribute these doubts to some hypothetical future subject than to admit personal concern. For example, consider an experiment in which the treatment involves creating a feeling of temporary low self-esteem in the subject by administering a fake personality test and then revealing the "results" that portray the subject as a weak, unattractive person. At the end of the session, the experimenter will of course assure the subject that the negative personality description was made up long before the subject ever took the test, that the same description is given to all subjects in the negative condition, and that the subject would have been given the same feedback no matter what responses were made on the test. At this point, the subject might ask, "But what happens if you get a person who just happens to really correspond to the description you gave?" This might be the hypothetical question it appears to be. But as psychologists, we know that it is possible that this subject is expressing some personal anxiety and, although realizing that the test was a fake, is still concerned about the possible accuracy of the description. The experimenter should take such a statement as a cue for extra tact and extra time spent reassuring the subject. In describing how the hypothetical future subject might be dealt with, the experimenter might point out that the negative personality description was comprised of vague generalities that sound plausible and applicable to all subjects. The experimenter might even read over some of the items, pointing out that *everyone* believes that a person "feels shy in new situations" or "sometimes hurts people without meaning to" or whatever the negative statements might be. If the subject has really been expressing her own worries, the extra information should be reassuring, and she will have been spared the necessity of admitting personal concern openly.

The timing of the debriefing is frequently a relevant factor in the experimenter's attempt to prevent the subject from experiencing unpleasant aftereffects. Some experimenters prefer to wait until after all subjects have completed their participation in the experiment before informing any of them of the true nature of the research. The explanation of the experiment is often accomplished en masse through the use of a printed communication. This procedure has certain economic and methodological advantages, that is, it saves time and makes it impossible for a subject to reveal the experimenter's description of the experiment to any future subject. There may be some experimental circumstances in which delayed mass debriefing can be employed without ill effects. However, we do not recommend this kind of shortcut debriefing when there is any chance that a deception or its revelation might be painful for the subject. Moreover, even if no discomfort is likely to ensue, other aspects of an experiment may make it wise to debrief the subject immediately after the session. In a typical study of opinion change, for example, the subject's opinion may have changed because, in the experiment, a particular point of view was attributed to a prestigious person. It would be a breach of ethics for the experimenter to allow this changed opinion to affect the subject's behavior after leaving the laboratory. Clearly, the sooner the subject is debriefed, the better.

In addition, in many experimental situations, the subjects are students, and, as mentioned previously, one of the reasons for students to volunteer (and a major rationale for using them) is the educational value of the experience. If the experimenter personally provides a clear and detailed explanation of the experiment as soon as it ends, allows the subjects to ask questions, and spends time clearing up any ambiguities that may remain, the subject receives maximum educational benefit from the experience.

Our student experimenters have sometimes complained to us that it is impossible to provide the sort of careful, sensitive debriefing we recommend because the subjects aren't interested in listening to it. It is hard to establish rapport with a person who is gathering up books, mumbling monosyllabic answers, and glancing at the clock every five seconds. Unfortunately, not many subjects expect a full explanation of the experiment or a serious concern about their own reactions, perhaps because they so rarely get them. Thus, it is important to tell the subject at the outset that you are going to sit down and discuss the experiment in detail, and that this is one of the most important parts of the experiment. It is a good idea to say how long it will take. And in scheduling the experimental sessions make sure you include enough time for the postexperimental interview. If you schedule the subject for one hour and the experiment itself takes 55 minutes, you cannot possibly conduct a thorough interview, nor can you expect the subject to be motivated to cooperate.

We have placed heavy emphasis on the obligations of the experimenter to provide immediate feedback to the subject. These obligations are real and comprise the strongest arguments for such feedback. But it is important to point out that by omitting the lengthy interview with the subject which we have recommended, the experimenter is deprived of an important heuristic experience. Nothing is a richer potential source of information about the strengths and weaknesses of an experiment than subjects' responses to detailed debriefing.

It is conceivable that in some circumstances, the experimenter may feel that the debriefing should not be complete. For example, the underlying theory, the conceptual variables, or the overall design of the experiment might be so complex that it is difficult and unnecessary to convey a complete picture of it to the subjects. In such cases the complete picture may be so intricate as to merely confuse the subjects about those aspects of the experiment that have most relevance to them. In these circumstances the experimenter might simplify the explanation, presenting only those aspects of the experiment which are easily explained and which are most pertinent to the subjects' own experience. It would be a mistake, however, to hold back aspects of the deception; to do so would violate the subjects' trust in the one part of the experiment where they have a right to expect perfect honesty.

How can we tell if the debriefing has been successful? Experimenters frequently ask the subjects to write down their reactions to the experiment after the debriefing is over. To some extent this procedure is designed to be a check on the effectiveness of the debriefing and to assess the fully informed subject's perceptions of the ethics of the experiment. It is difficult to know how much confidence to place in subjects' responses to such questions, since some people may be reluctant to criticize the study or to indicate discomfort, but at least on this superficial level, the results of postexperimental checks are very encouraging. For example, recall that Bibb Latané and Judith Rodin (1969) ran a study in which subjects overheard a woman in the next room fall down and cry out in pain. Although the subjects didn't realize it, the experimenter's true concern was with the question of how people would respond to the woman's distress. In most of the conditions, a majority of subjects did not respond at all—not even to the extent of calling out to ask whether the woman needed help. After the subjects had been debriefed and informed of the true purpose of the experiment, the experimenters asked them to fill out an anonymous questionnaire about their reactions to the experiment. Ninety-nine percent of the subjects said that they had understood the true purpose of the experiment and that the use of deception was necessary to achieve this purpose. When asked about their personal reactions to the experiment and the *ethics* (as opposed to the necessity) of the deception, all of the subjects said that they would be willing to participate in similar experiments in the future and that the use of deception was justified. In addition, most of the subjects found the experiment interesting and stated that they were glad to have taken part. Although we cannot be sure that all subjects were telling the whole truth, it is unlikely that there was a great deal of unstated resentment. Moreover, it seems safe to assume that after the debriefing, most of the subjects felt that the experience had been worthwhile.

Enlisting the Subject's Aid

Because of demand characteristics inherent in conducting a direct assessment of subjects' perceptions and opinions about an experiment, it is often useful for the experimenter and instructive for the subject to make use of a more subtle measure: to enlist the subject's aid in improving the experiment. That is, before ending the debriefing, the experimenter can ask the subject for any suggestions about ways to improve the experimental procedure to make it more powerful, more credible, and more interesting for future subjects. This is the best way we know of for finding out about any of the negative aspects of the experiment. As we have pointed out repeatedly (see Chapter 9, for example), experimental subjects tend to be cooperative. In the worst circumstances, this may prevent them from admitting that the procedure caused them anguish, that the experiment had no meaning for them, or that it meant something other than what the experimenter thought it should mean. By specifically appealing to the subjects to help improve the experiment, the investigator can turn this cooperativeness to the advantage of the research and to the benefit of future subjects. In response to a genuine appeal, subjects may be only too pleased to cooperate by criticizing the experiment. These criticisms often lead to improvement and are an indispensable aid to the experimenter, especially in the pilot stages of the research. In addition, this procedure often allows the subjects sufficient latitude to admit that they were (or still are) upset by the procedure or the deception; if this should occur, the experimenter knows that further efforts must be made to bring the subjects to a full understanding of the reasons for the procedure and an acceptance of their own responses to it.

Finally, the experimenter tries to convince the subjects *not to reveal anything* about the experiment. This is a serious problem, because even if only a few subjects have been tipped off, the results can be invalid. Moreover, it is sobering to reflect on the fact that it is almost impossible to screen out sophisticated subjects in advance. It is not easy to successfully swear all subjects to secrecy; often, the subjects are drawn from a single class or school, and there is consequently a strong likelihood that they have friends who might subsequently volunteer for the experiment. These friends are almost certain to press former subjects for information. The experimenter can conduct the experiment in a manner designed to minimize intersubject communication by recruiting subjects from a variety of contexts, by running the whole study in as short a time as possible, by checking to make sure that later subjects are not roommates of early subjects (if a subject's roommate wants to participate, sign that person up for the next hour, so there will be no time for communication), and so on. In addition, the experimenter should attempt to forestall communication after the session, by graphically describing the waste of time and effort which result from including people who have prior knowledge about the procedure or the hypothesis of the experiment. In addition, the experimenter should provide a vivid account of the damage that can be done to the scientific enterprise by using data from such subjects. The experimenter should explain that because such information usually spreads rapidly, telling even one person might result in several subjects whose performance is either unusable or misleading.

The experimenter who has been sincere and honest in dealing with the subject during the postexperimental debriefing session can be reasonably confident that few subjects will break faith. To check on this, Aronson (1966) enlisted the aid of three undergraduates, each of whom approached three acquaintances who had recently participated in one of his experiments. The confederates explained that they had signed up for the same experiment, had noticed the friend's name on the sign-up sheet, and wondered what the experiment was all about. The experimenter had previously assured these confederates that their friends would remain anonymous. The results were encouraging. In spite of considerable urging, begging, and cajoling on the part of the confederates, none of the former subjects revealed the true purpose of the experiment; two of them went as far as providing the confederates with a replay of the cover story, but nothing else. Of course, not *all* experiments have given us such reason for optimism; some experimenters have found considerable leakage (e.g., Farrow, Lohss, Farrow, & Taub, 1975; Horka & Farrow, 1970; Lichtenstein, 1970; Walsh & Stillman, 1974). Differences in subjects' willingness to divulge information about an experiment could be a function of the nature of the deception employed; specifics of the experiment; when, where or by whom they were approached and asked for information; or the content, process, and degree of rapport established during the postexperimental session.

It will be easier for subjects to withstand pressure from curious friends if the experimenter gives them something to say. In urging the subjects to keep the true purpose of the experiment a secret, the experimenter can give examples of what they might say if asked about the experiment. For example, the experimenter can suggest that the task or some other superficial aspect of the procedure be described. Having something explicit to say spares the subjects the embarrassment of having to cut off friends with a prim, "I'd prefer not to discuss it," and also spares them the awkwardness of having to invent an innocuous description of the experiment.

What if the subject has been forewarned before entering the experimental room? That is, suppose that a subject *does* find out about the experiment from a friend who has participated previously. The new subject probably will not reveal this to the experimenter before the experiment, for fear of being disqualified from earning credit, money, points, love, or whatever incentive may have enticed the subject into the laboratory.[2] Moreover, if not prodded, the subject is unlikely to confess this after the experiment, because of reluctance to implicate the friend who, after all, broke a promise to the experimenter. Yet if the experimenter is unable to elicit this information, the results may be extremely misleading and the statement that no subjects were suspicious or sophisticated may be a serious error.

How can we be sure? Once again, the experimenter attempts to enlist the subject's cooperativeness, as well as the good will, which, it is to be hoped, has been built up during the postexperimental interview. First, as described above, the subject should be told clearly and forcefully the serious problems presented to science (and this particular research) if, unwittingly, the experimenter were to report erroneous data. The experimenter can then explain that although subjects are cautioned not to discuss the experiment, occasionally a former subject will reveal something by mistake. At this point, the experimenter can appeal to the subject to help out by mentioning now if she or he heard even a little about the experiment. The subject should, of course, be assured that the experimenter is uninterested in finding out *how* or *from whom* the information was transmitted. In the face of such a plea, few forewarned subjects will remain silent. We cannot overemphasize the importance of this kind of procedure as a safeguard against the artifactual confirmation of an er-

---

[2]Indeed, some researchers have taken advantage of subjects' tendencies to deceive experimenters about their knowledge. For example, David McMillen and James Austin (1971) were interested in the effects of having told a lie on people's willingness to help. When subjects were waiting to begin, a confederate entered the waiting room and told them about the alleged experiment. Fortunately for McMillen and Austin, and perhaps unfortunately for many other experimenters, 100 percent of the subjects—who were informed not only that the experiment involved taking a multiple-choice test, but also that most of the correct answers were "B"—lied to the experimenter and said they had heard nothing about the study!

roneous hypothesis due to the misplaced cooperativeness of the subject. A truly cooperative subject will probably cooperate with the experimenter in this regard also and will respond to a direct plea from the experimenter.

DEBRIEFING FOLLOWING FALSE FEEDBACK TO SUBJECTS

Many of the suggestions we made earlier are aimed at helping the experimenter to achieve the goal of restoring the subjects' self-esteem and sense of well-being and of making the experiment a worthwhile experience for them. The experimenter should not assume, however, that following all these suggestions in preparing a standardized debriefing speech will automatically ensure success in returning the subjects to their preexperimental state. Some experiments include false feedback to the subjects about their own abilities or performance. Such experiments require special care and caution in the postexperimental interview to ensure that the subjects not only understand that deception was involved but that they are also reassured that what the experimenter said to them about their own performance is devoid of information value. Some research suggests that a simple debriefing may be inadequate to erase the beliefs about ability that are induced by false feedback during an experiment (Ross, Lepper, & Hubbard, 1975). Recall from Chapter 9 that these investigators gave subjects a series of notes, some ostensibly written by people who had actually attempted suicide, others by people simulating suicide notes. The subjects' task was to guess which of the notes were real and which were simulated. Independent of actual performance, some subjects were told that they had done very well (24 out of 25 correct). Other subjects were told that they had done poorly (10 out of 25 correct). During a full debriefing, all subjects were told clearly that the feedback they had received was unrelated to their performance and had been determined randomly before the experiment began. Nevertheless, when later asked a series of questions about whether they thought they were really good at discriminating real from fake suicide notes, subjects still showed residual effects of the experimental treatments. That is, subjects who were told that they were successful at the task (even though it was later clearly explained that they were not in fact successful) still believed that they would be more successful in the future than did control subjects. Similarly, subjects who were told that they had done badly still expected to do badly in the future, even after a full debriefing.

The mechanisms underlying this "perseverance" phenomenon are still not well understood, and speculation about them goes beyond our purpose here. Nevertheless, the demonstration is an important one for any experimenter who gives subjects false feedback about performance, personality, or anything else. Fortunately, Lee Ross and his colleagues were also able to show that a fuller debriefing, one that explicitly discusses the perseverance process, can successfully undo the results of the experimental treatment. A thorough understanding of this "process debriefing," as they term it, is important for any experimenter. Basically, it consists of not only indicating that the feedback was incorrect and discussing the reasons for this but also providing a full explanation of the tendency for people to maintain their distorted perceptions about their abilities at the task, even after the original information that created the perceptions has been discredited.

When false feedback is related not to subjects' performance on a specific experimental task but rather to more enduring personality characteristics, "undeceiving" subjects may be especially difficult. Elaine Walster and her colleagues (1967) found evidence that debriefing was not always immediately effective and that some kinds of subjects may behave as though they still believe the manipulation, even after a longer delay. Apparently, the situation these researchers used to induce low self-esteem in their subjects triggered all sorts of thoughts and memories that activated other *real* feelings of low self-esteem in some subjects, and these feelings could not easily be removed by debriefing. The subjects seemed to realize that the experimenter had been lying in suggesting that they were inferior people; nevertheless, their own reactivated feelings of inferiority led them to feel that the experimenter's characterization had unwittingly hit on the truth. It was as though the subjects said to themselves, "I know he didn't mean it, but it's true anyway." This kind of resistant residual effect presents a very serious problem, especially since at the present time we have no reliable means of identifying in advance the subjects for whom regular debriefing procedures are likely to be ineffective.

At the very least, the experimenter should make every effort to determine the needs of each individual subject and should try to tailor the debriefing session to meet these needs. The information provided should be redundant, especially for any individualized feedback the experimenter might have given the subject on the basis of false personality tests and the like. The technique of gradually inducing the subject to recognize and describe the deception is probably one of the most effective means of ensuring that the subject fully understands it. A subject who is able to state the truth about an experiment is probably more likely to understand the truth than is one who simply hears it from the experimenter. If the debriefing session lasts longer than the experimenter expected, the next-scheduled subject should be canceled, so that the subject being debriefed doesn't leave with any remaining anxiety or confusion. Finally, the experimenter might do well to test the subject's understanding of the experiment in general and the treatment as it was applied in particular.

As we have pointed out repeatedly in this text, the experimental psychologist who concludes that research involving deception is the only valid method for elucidating the questions under study faces difficult ethical questions. Surely the quality and efficacy of the procedures used to explain the research and experimental procedures to the subject are indispensable for the justification of the use of such techniques. Research on this critical aspect of the entire experimental procedure is a welcome addition to our knowledge of how to carry it out most successfully and humanely.

WRITING IT UP

All the data are in. After a thorough and sensitive postexperimental debriefing, the last subject has left with self-esteem intact, confident that he or she has helped to extend our knowledge of human social behavior a little farther. The subject's job is done; as a researcher, your job continues. You have already arrived at a design appropriate to the research question, chosen or created a setting, decided on a suitable empirical realization of the independent variable, developed or chosen dependent-variable measures, and interacted with scores of subjects. *Finally,* you pour over your data, analyze and reanalyze, decide what they mean, and put pen to paper to write an article summarizing what you have learned about a particular aspect of social behavior. Thus, a research article represents the culmination of months of hard and exciting work. This article is a vehicle for communicating research findings to an audience of fellow scientists. It is also an opportunity for researchers to convince editors and reviewers of psychological journals that their ideas are interesting and well informed, that their research is methodologically sound, that their data analyses are appropriate and thorough, and that their interpretations of results are accurate and meaningful. In this chapter, we will provide recommendations for how to do that: how to prepare an article that is interesting, well written, and complete.

Readers who are new to the writing enterprise in psychology should read through the *Publication Manual* of the American Psychological Association (APA, 1983). This valuable reference provides detailed descriptions of the recommended organization and content of a psychological journal article from the title page to the appendices, including how to format references, tables, and figures. It also contains many useful tips for improving writing style and clarity. Of course, good psychological writing is first and foremost good *prose* writing, and many researchers are familiar with good books on clear writing. We would recommend William Zinsser's (1985) *On Writing Well* and William Strunk, Jr., and E. B. White's (1979) *The Elements of Style*.

BEFORE SITTING DOWN TO WRITE

Before you can explain your research to other people, you must be able to explain it to yourself. Clear writing requires clear thinking, and many of the problems people identify as problems in *writing* actually reflect gaps and ambiguities in their understanding of just what it is they want to say. So the first step is to figure out what the main point (or points) of your article will be. What do the results mean? What do we know now that we didn't know before? Why is it interesting? What is the "story" of your article?

Sitting in a chair and staring at a blank page or screen is not generally a productive way of finding answers to these questions. It is at least as likely to produce an anxiety attack as it is to produce an insight. Before most researchers lock their doors and pick up a pen and paper or switch on the word processor, they spend a considerable amount of time thinking about the results of their studies and talking with colleagues about them. Feedback from students and colleagues is valuable once a draft has been written but is even more valuable *before* a draft has been written. When results are puzzling, colleagues can provide hunches as to what they *might* mean, and suggestions for ways to determine what they *do* mean. Often, even when the data conform to an experimenter's predictions, colleagues can suggest a slightly different context into which the completed experiment fits or point to questions that beg to be answered in a follow-up study. So it is useful to talk to others about your study, and even to try presenting it in a more or less formal talk to a group of interested people. By trying to explain your research to others, you will learn where you need to improve your own understanding.

Ultimately, however, turning thoughts into sentences is a solitary enterprise, and you alone must decide what to write and for whom to write it. Your friends and colleagues are one source of useful feedback, and they can be used throughout the writing. A second source of useful feedback, oddly enough, is the act of writing itself. Although it is important to think out what you want to say before you start writing, you will find that the order "think, then write" is an oversimplified statement of what actually happens. By writing, you continue to discover what you don't understand and to clarify your ideas (Berthoff, 1988). In the course of writing, you may find that you have to carry out new data analyses, or check out references you had previously forgotten, or go back and revise earlier parts of the manuscript.

What to Write

How should you write up your data when your initial hypothesis was disconfirmed or only partially confirmed? As Daryl Bem (1987) points out, experimenters must choose between two alternatives in deciding what to write: what they would have written at the outset of a study *or* what they would write once the data have been collected and thoroughly analyzed. More often than not, the latter is the correct choice. Often subjects' behaviors and the data they generate do not conform to even the most sensible and insightful of hypotheses. Moreover, data may reveal patterns that are exciting and provocative, even if they were not anticipated at the outset of the study. For better or for worse, data are the reality with which experimenters work: one that sometimes conflicts with their expectations. Two implications follow.

First, a great deal of time should be invested in organizing, transforming, and analyzing the data. If initial patterns in the data do not support the hypothesis, data transformations (e.g., constructing composite indices from individual dependent-variable responses) or alternative statistical procedures may be in order, and internal analyses (see Chapters 5 and 7) often shed light on what would otherwise be a confusing set of findings. Of course, if initial patterns in the data *do* support the hypothesis, there is no reason to stop there. Data can be a rich source of surprises and additional hypotheses if they are exploited by a tenacious experimenter.

Second, because data sometimes yield surprising findings, it would be premature to write an article with the intention of filling in the blanks after the data have been analyzed. Far better to let the data influence the plot, at least to a limited extent. Often, the story an experimenter sets out to write has to be reworked and reframed once patterns in the data reveal themselves. Variables of primary interest may not prove as important as the experimenter predicted; variables of secondary interest at the outset of a study may prove to be more important or more interesting than the experimenter anticipated. As Bem (1987, p. 173) notes, it is better to restructure an article around unexpected findings, even to the point of forsaking the original hypothesis, than to lead readers on a meandering tour of "wrongheaded hunches only to show— *voilà!*—they were wrongheaded. A journal article should not be a personal history of . . . stillborn thoughts." People reading your article read it because they are interested in what you found, and your best current interpretation of the results you actually got: a story about human behavior. They are not particularly interested in a story about how you had a wrong idea and are now big enough to admit it.

Needless to say, we are *not* recommending that researchers pretend they were predicting outcomes that in actuality were unexpected. It is the obligation of the researcher to present the findings honestly and clearly, without concealing the unexpectedness of the results but without resorting to a historical account of a wrongheaded idea (for example, see Walster, Aronson, & Brown, 1966).

If the results are relevant to your initial hypothesis (e.g., they disconfirm it rather than confirm it, or they suggest a related but more complicated hypothesis), one simple solution is not to frame the introduction in terms of a hypothesis at all but simply to pose a question. If it turns out that the results provide interesting answers to a question that is *not* closely related to the one with which you started, then the introduction should be organized around the new question, the one that is actually answered, and the old question may simply be mentioned in a footnote.

Who Is the Audience?

Articles in social psychological journals are written *by* social psychologists, primarily *for* other social psychologists. Typically, readers and writers share comparable levels of methodological expertise and background knowledge about the question under investigation. For this reason, it is tempting to write solely for an audience of one's professional peers. This temptation should be resisted. First, psychology is a diverse discipline, and it is quite common for developmental or educational psychologists, for example, to be interested in social psychological research, and vice versa. Moreover, as social psychologists become more committed to applied research, it is important that they communicate their research findings to a wide range of people outside the immediate academic research community: to activists, physicians, educators, lawyers, policy makers, and others. Third, research articles are valuable teaching tools, and many undergraduate students read articles in the social psychological literature. Therefore, in the interest of comprehensibility, it is important that authors refrain from inundating readers with "buzzwords" or social psychological jargon intelligible to a select few. Finally, a good proportion of the most memorable articles in social psychology, and in psychology in general, are beautifully written. This is no coincidence. In social psychology, the data rarely "speak for themselves"; someone must speak for them. If the author is unwilling to take the trouble to explain why the research is interesting, it is highly unlikely that the reader will do so.

Our goal is to communicate our knowledge to as many people as are interested in our research: in essence, to teach anyone who wants to learn from us. A well-written journal article should teach psychologists and nonpsychologists alike something they didn't know before. Although not all readers may be well versed in the specifics of experimental design or data analysis, they should be able to understand the research question in general terms; they should be able to understand the basics of the experimental procedure and the answer it reveals; and, just as important, they should be convinced that the research was worth doing in the first place. Bem (1987, p. 174) sums it up nicely: "Direct your writing to the student in Psychology 100, your colleague in the Art History Department, and your grandmother."

WRITING THE ARTICLE

Students who have perused as few as two or three articles in the *Journal of Personality and Social Psychology, Journal of Experimental Social Psychology,* or *Personality and Social Psychology Bulletin* already have a feel for how the typical article is organized. They have probably noticed that some articles are more clearly and engagingly written than others. In this section, we will briefly discuss the organization of the typical empirical journal article and will provide suggestions on how to write a *good* article: one that is clear, accurate, complete, and interesting to a wide range of readers. Scientific writing need not be stiff, abstruse, or lean to the point of anorexia. Good writers of journal articles are good storytellers; they engage and provoke readers, educate them, sometimes amuse them, and—when it's really done well—leave readers with a feeling of "Gee whiz! I wish *I* had thought of that." Being dull or overly somber need not be a prerequisite for publishing in social psychological journals.

Getting Started: Organization

The general shape of a social psychology article has four sections: an *Introduction* in which you pose the problem, explain what is known about it and what you would like to add to that knowledge, and describe in general terms how you plan to achieve your goals; a *Method* section in which you describe exactly how you carried out the research; a *Results* section in which you present the results of the data analyses; and a *Discussion* section in which you step back and say what you think the results mean and how you have added to our knowledge. For very simple, small studies, the results and discussion may be collapsed into one section called, not surprisingly, *Results and Discussion*.

For some writers, this rough outline seems to be enough. They simply sit down and knock out a first draft. In fact, this draft is usually the result of days of musing, inventing, and shaping while driving, shaving, washing dishes, or ostensibly listening to someone else talk; it only *appears* to flow effortlessly onto the page without preparation.

Other writers need something on paper from which to work. An outline of what you want to say in each section can be very useful. In the introduction, for example, you want to get from a general question about human nature to the specific context you chose for your study: What are the steps that need to come between? Writing them down can help. Or, you might want to write down the three or four main points you want to include in a given section and then figure out how you will get from one to the next. Whatever form of outline you choose serves as a reminder, a means of moving you along from one idea to the next, and·a handy place to jot down additional thoughts you have about the points you want to include. It is meant to *facilitate* the writing of the paper, not be a paper in itself. Thus, unless it really helps you think, there is no point in writing down "I. Introduction. A. Opening paragraph.," and so on, following the classic outline form you learned in eighth grade. An outline is primarily helpful in forcing you to think about the organization of your paper in units larger than the single sentence and smaller than "Introduction," "Method," "Results," and "Discussion."

The Introduction

The purpose of the introduction to a journal article is to present an interesting question, to place a study within a larger context, and to give readers a sense of where the writer is headed. A well-written introduction begins by stating a problem, asking a question, or describing some social psychological phenom-enon—often in very general terms at the outset. It gradually becomes more focused as related work is described and evaluated and typically concludes with a specific rationale for the current study. A good introduction not only delineates a question or problem and informs readers about what has already been learned but also convinces them that the most logical and desirable ad-dition to the literature is the study they're now reading.

Introduce the Phenomenon of Interest   It is important in the beginning of the introduction to write in English prose, and to talk about people and their be-haviors, not researchers and their findings. It is not an exaggeration to say that by the time readers have scanned the first two paragraphs, they have either become intrigued and decided to read further, or they have yawned, stretched, and set the journal aside to engage in more rewarding activities.

Very few psychologists succeed in writing good opening paragraphs, and this is not surprising. After all, writing the first paragraph is all confounded with the agony of starting the paper. For many people, the first paragraph takes an embarrassingly long time and still ends up embarrassingly bad. Many articles published in our major journals would be better if the first paragraph were simply omitted. Table 11-1 shows the opening sentences of the first ten

TABLE 11-1

OPENING SENTENCES FROM THE FIRST TEN ARTICLES IN A RECENT ISSUE OF THE *JOURNAL OF PERSONALITY AND SOCIAL PSYCHOLOGY*

1 Each day we are required to make a number of predictions about the probable behavior, attitudes, and performances of other people.

2 Substantial research has shown that the lay person assigns other individuals to social categories by means of implicit theories of personality, and uses these categories to predict potential behaviors, emotional reactions, personality attributes, attitudes, and values.

3 Philosophers and social scientists have devoted a considerable amount of energy to understanding the experience of guilt.

4 Henley (1973, 1977), Goffman (1976, 1979) and others have suggested that gender differences in nonverbal behavior parallel gender differences in the power hierarchy of American society.

5 Patients' perceptions of control over the course, consequences, and treatment of a serious illness have received much scrutiny in the recent literature on cognitive adaptations to threatening events.

6 Many studies conducted over the past decade have revealed the potential deleterious effects of mindless information processing.

7 Much has been learned about the determinants of help giving (*three references*) and help seeking (*three more references*).

8 Floyd Allport (1924; Katz and Allport, 1931) coined the term *pluralistic ignorance* to describe the situation in which virtually all members of a group privately reject group norms yet believe that virtually all other group members accept them.

9 Group discussion often has the effect of inducing shifts in both individual opinions and group decisions.

10 To classify individuals by sex role orientation, Bem (1981a) used median splits on the Masculinity (M) and Femininity (F) scales of the Bem Sex-Role Inventory.

articles in an issue of the *Journal of Personality and Social Psychology* that happened to be lying on the desk of one of the authors when she was writing this section.

These sentences vary in quality, but it is unlikely that any of them would inspire a reader to go further unless that reader were already interested. Taken together, they illustrate several problems.

1 *Too many words.* Strunk and White's (1979) most persistent command is "Omit needless words." Note how this very sentence has been shortened from "Leave out words that aren't really necessary," "Don't use a lot of words where a few will do," or "It is important that psychologists and other social science writers attend to the quantity of words employed to convey relatively straightforward ideas, and that they devote the required attention to excising those that fail to make a significant contribution to the sentence as a whole." The use of too many words is particularly characteristic of first sentences, as they serve a sort of "revving the engine" function for the author. All the opening sentences in Table 11-1 could be shortened.

Some of these sentences present lists. The first sentence of an article is no place for a list. The *outline* is the place for a list; the opening sentence is the place for an *idea*.

2 *Psychological jargon.* In the interest of brevity, it is tempting to introduce psychological jargon too soon. Although this specialized language serves as a useful shorthand, there is nothing like consulting a psychology dictionary at every turn to frustrate even the most motivated of nonpsychologist readers. For example, it is often useful to write about such concepts as implicit personality theories, cognitive adaptations, sex role orientation in plain English first and to follow those descriptions with the appropriate social psychological shorthand.

3 *"Research has shown."* Most of these sentences begin not by talking about human behavior but by talking about previous researchers. There is a place for this in the introduction, but ordinarily it is not the first sentence. *You* have the responsibility of making your idea interesting, and pointing out that other social scientists have thought about the same issues is a rather feeble way of doing so. It is as though you're saying, "Lots of published articles address this topic, so it must be interesting." Or, "The point of this article is to place *me* in the company of (or in opposition to) Smedley, Schmolz, and Smelch." The reader is not particularly interested in where you fit into the spectrum of psychological opinion but rather in what your study is about. Finally, the very fact that three quarters of our articles begin with references to previous research suggests that it is an overused, if not worn out, technique. For that reason alone, it is unlikely to attract the reader's attention.

Table 11-2 presents the opening sentences of the first twelve articles assigned by one of us for a course on research methods. They were chosen not because they were well written but because they were important articles that illustrated the methodological issues in the course. Many of them are very well

TABLE 11-2
OPENING SENTENCES OF THE FIRST TWELVE ARTICLES
USED IN A RESEARCH METHODS COURSE

---

1 We shall here describe in summary form the conception and first findings of a program of investigation into the conditions of independence and submission to group pressure.

2 One of the most frequently reported components of agonistic or threat displays in primates is a steady, direct gaze at the object of aggression.

3 The jury is a uniquely democratic institution.

4 It is the purpose of this paper to provide empirical evidence on a number of issues created by the disqualification from capital juries of jurors who have scruples against the death penalty.

5 On February 27, 1967, the Associated Press carried the following story from Corvallis, Oregon: "A mysterious student has been attending a class at Oregon State University for the past two months enveloped in a big black bag."

6 The situation in which one agent commands another to hurt a third person turns up time and again as a significant theme in human relations.

7 Certain problems in psychological research require the experimenter to balance his career and scientific interests against the interests of his prospective subjects.

8 In a standard college dictionary, *null* is defined as "invalid, amounting to naught; of no value, effect or consequence, insignificant."

9 What happens to a person's private opinion if he is forced to do or say something contrary to that opinion?

10 If a boy who enjoys mowing lawns begins to receive payment for the task, what will happen to his intrinsic motivation for performing the activity?

11 The process by which man seeks to understand his environment—to discern the causes of events which surround him and explain the behavior of others toward him—has been of central concern to psychology for many years.

12 Why do you like him?

---

known, and their opening sentences are generally better than the opening sentences in Table 11-1. Doubtless the research is also generally better, but that is not the point. The point is that most of them make us want to read the next sentence, and they illustrate several techniques that are superior to the list, the jargon sentence, and "previous research has shown."

1 *The straightforward, no-nonsense description of what the article is going to do.* In the first sentence, Solomon Asch (1952) uses this technique to introduce his famous studies of conformity. Another example is sentence 4 (Zeisel, 1969): It looks deceptively simple, but in fact it is very hard to simply leap in and say, "I am going to tell you about X."

2 *The statement of the issue.* Authors of sentences 2, 6, 7, and 11 define the problem, although in 2 Ellsworth and her colleagues (1972) and in 11 Mark Lepper and his colleagues (1973) faintheartedly make a passing reference to other research, and Ellsworth uses needless words, including jargon. Nonetheless, this is the classic way to introduce your topic in a straightforward manner. This study is about staring as a threat signal, commanding a person to hurt another person, the conflict between the interest of science and the interest of research subjects, people's attempts to explain why things happen. Just say it:

There will be plenty of time in the next paragraph to show that you know that other important people have thought about the issue. "Just saying it" is of course extremely difficult and requires that you have a very clear idea about what "it" is. For that reason, sentences like this and their accompanying first paragraphs are often written last, after many tries, after the original first paragraph has been discarded. None of these sentences was written when the author first sat down before a blank page.

Note that the entire description of the problem need not be contained in a single sentence. Often it is more effective to take several sentences to lay out the problem in order to keep the first sentence from becoming overloaded with detail. For example, sentences 3 (Cowan, Thompson, & Ellsworth, 1984) and 4 (Zeisel, 1969) on our list are from articles that dealt with the same topic. The author of 4 lays out the issue in a single sentence; the authors of 3 choose a shorter, livelier, but less informative opening sentence, developing the issue in the remainder of the opening section.

3 *The example.* Sentences 5 (Zajonc, 1968) and 10 (Deci, 1971) illustrate a good way of capturing the reader's interest. Examples from the media, from literature, or from common experience can serve as vivid illustrations of the issue you have studied. In fact, Robert Zajonc (1968) tells you nothing of what the article is about, but of all the opening sentences in our table, his is probably the most likely to inspire the reader to continue. At the end of such an example, you sum up what it means psychologically and rephrase it as a research issue.

Related to the "example" technique is the use of a direct quote, an abstract statement by someone else that captures your question. For example, Charles Lord, Lee Ross, and Mark Lepper (1979, p. 2098) began their article with the following quote from Roger Bacon: "The human understanding when it has once adopted an opinion draws all things else to support and agree with it. And though there be a greater number and weight of instances to be found on the other side, yet these it either neglects and despises, or else by some distinction sets aside and rejects, in order that by this great and pernicious predetermination the authority of its former conclusion may remain inviolate."

The dictionary definition quoted in 8 is also an example of a quote from an authority, and, although it should not be used too often, it can be very effective, as in this example by Anthony Greenwald (1975). Dictionary definitions are often better written than most opening sentences in psychological journals.

4 *The question.* Your research was designed to answer a question. One of the most efficient ways of communicating to your reader what your question is is simply to ask it, as did the authors of sentences 9 (Festinger & Carlsmith, 1959), 10 (Deci, 1971), and 12 (Nisbett & Wilson, 1977). When they see a question, most people will become curious and read at least the next sentence.

Develop the Background Once the interesting phenomenon has been described, or the question raised, most writers provide a more detailed "state of the art" summary of relevant research. Commonly referred to as the *literature* *review,* this part of the introduction informs the reader of the contributions of other researchers. One of the hazards of being teachers and scholars is that we have a tendency to display our erudition, sometimes inappropriately. Thus, in effect, if a student or a colleague asks us the time, it is tempting to expound on a discussion of time zones and the history of time telling from the sundial to digital quartz watches. Colleagues and students may occasionally tolerate such detours, but readers almost never will. Although it is important to acknowledge the ideas and findings of other investigators, it is *more* important to limit discussion to research that is germane to the current study; research that is only tangentially related should be omitted.

Controversy is not uncommon in social psychology and makes the field exciting. Indeed, the purpose of many studies is to reconcile conflicting findings in the literature. Controversial issues should be treated evenhandedly. This is *not* to say that writers should withhold their informed opinions on an issue. However, if there are studies that conflict with other research results, or with the writer's hypothesis, they should be noted. The literature review is just that: a summary of our current state of knowledge vis-à-vis a particular question or problem, not a newspaper editorial.

State the Purpose of the Study After the question has been posed, and after relevant literature has been reviewed, the writer sets the stage for the study that follows. By reviewing the literature, you have moved from describing what the issue is to how psychologists have studied it. Thus, it should be relatively easy to move to a summary of where we stand on this issue *in psychology* and to a somewhat more operational version of the question that was posed in general terms at the outset. This section of the introduction—seldom more than a paragraph or two—provides for a smooth transition to the Method section that follows. One need not provide an exhaustive list of hypotheses 1, 2, 3, and 4, but one *should* provide a brief description of the study and a rationale for it. This brief overview is designed to familiarize readers with the specific question the study was designed to answer, the independent and dependent variables used, the design, and the procedure employed. In addition, a brief rationale is designed to convince readers that the question was worth asking in the first place.

Method

If the introduction establishes the underlying theme of the article, the Method section establishes the cast of characters and the plot line. That is, the Method section describes in detail the nuts and bolts of how the study was conducted. Who were the subjects? What did they experience? What was the setting like? How was the treatment administered? How was the dependent variable measured? How were subjects debriefed?

The Method section is for the most part a straightforward narrative that moves along in chronological order (with occasional digressions to describe the measuring instruments or special protections against bias or other features that are important in your particular research). The challenge of moving from general propositions to specific events or vice versa—that has to be faced in the Introduction and Discussion sections—is largely irrelevant here. Instead, the main challenge is to find a place to present detailed descriptions of those aspects of the study only you as the experimenter know about (e.g., the reliability of measures, pretest results, precautions against bias) without losing the flow of the events as they were experienced by the subjects.

Many authors write the Method section first, sometimes before the data have been completely analyzed. The story told in the introduction may depend on the actual results, but the Method section requires few modifications, even if the results are unexpected. Also, it is easiest to write a vivid, accurate description of the method if it is done shortly after the experiment is actually run. The Method section is typically divided into several subsections, as described below.

Overview of Method and Design   Unless the design is very simple, it is often a good idea to begin the Method section with an overview so that the reader becomes familiar with the design (i.e., what conditions were run), with the basic empirical realizations of the independent variable(s) and major dependent variable(s), and often with the purpose of the experiment as described to the subject. This is like a road map that keeps the reader from getting lost in a maze of details. The overview can be very brief, almost telegraphic, but it gives the reader a framework to keep in mind while reading through the details of the procedure.

For example: "Subjects, believing that they were participating in a study of ESP, listened to persuasive arguments about political issues. We instructed half the subjects to concentrate on the content of the arguments and half to concentrate on the speaker's style. In addition, half the arguments were about topics that were highly relevant to the subjects' own lives, while the other half were peripheral. Subjects' heart rates were measured while they listened, and their memory for the arguments was measured a week later." In but four sentences, the reader is informed that a 2×2 factorial design was used, and that there were two dependent variables in the study.

Subjects   This subsection—typically no longer than a paragraph or two—is designed to describe participants. Who served as subjects? Was there any particular reason for choosing this kind of person for the experiment? How many subjects were there? How were they selected? Were they paid? Did any subjects fail to complete the study? If so, why? To which experimental conditions were they assigned? It is also useful to describe relevant subject demographic characteristics such as age, institutional affiliation, and gender. This section is also a good place to note relevant information about the experimenter(s).

Apparatus (or Materials)   In some experiments, usually in the more biological areas of psychology, researchers include a special subsection describing the equipment used in the research: the make and model number of the polygraph, staining techniques, and particularly, any novel hardware designed for the particular study. A special subsection on apparatus rarely makes sense in the write-up of a social psychological study: first, because social psychologists seldom use complex equipment and second, and more important, because describing the equipment typically makes more sense as part of the explanation of the treatment, procedure, or measures. Thus, if the treatment is embedded in a computer game, it may be confusing to try to describe the computer program before describing the treatment itself. If unfamiliar instruments are used to measure the dependent variable, they are best described in the dependent variable subsection, along with their reliabilities.

Occasionally, the main purpose of the study is to present some new measuring device, such as a personality test, and to provide some evidence of its validity. In this case, a special section on the new test or method *does* make sense.

Procedure   The Procedure subsection provides a concrete, step-by-step description of how the experiment was executed. The reader already has an overview of the design; at this point the clearest way to proceed is to lead readers through the experiment as if they were subjects. What did you say to the subject about the purpose of the study? How did you explain what the tasks would involve? Your aim is to give readers a feel for what the experience was like for the subjects, so that readers can decide for themselves whether the procedures made sense and whether the events were engaging and meaningful. Readers should have enough information to judge whether the experimenter's conclusions about the subjects' interpretations of events and the meaning of their behaviors seem justifiable.

Often—especially in experiments with several independent variables—it is a good idea to write a brief subsection around each independent variable, and to place these subsections where they occur, chronologically, in the procedure. Stanley Schachter and Jerome Singer's (1962) fairly complicated experiment on the cognitive and physiological determinants of emotion (summarized in Chapter 4) is a beautifully written article that illustrates just how this may be done. The authors first describe the cover story given to subjects when they arrived and then the manipulation of arousal. Subjects were told that the experiment was a test of the effects of the vitamin compound "Suproxin"; the injection of "Suproxin" that immediately followed was in reality an injection of epinephrine (an arousing drug) or a placebo (no-arousal control group). This was the manipulation of the independent variable *arousal*.

Next, Schachter and Singer gave some subjects an *explanation* for their arousal, so that, according to the hypothesis, they would not think it was a sign of emotion. They set this section off with a subheading, "Manipulating an Appropriate Explanation," so the reader can easily see that the next part of the sequence of events experienced by the subject has to do with the *second* independent variable, "Information." When they get to the third independent variable, the euphoric or angry emotional context, they use another subheading, "Producing an Emotion-Inducing Cognition," with two further subheadings, "Euphoria" and "Anger," under which they describe in detail what happened to subjects. This technique makes a rather complex experiment easy to understand, and allows the authors to describe the actual events in great detail in a well-organized way; thus the reader does not lose sight of the design as a whole or of the point of the events.

Within each subsection, it is often a good idea to describe any verbal treatments verbatim. This makes it possible for readers to evaluate the adequacy of the experimental procedures, and to carry out an accurate replication if they so desire. It also makes the Method section vivid and interesting. For example, Schachter and Singer (1962), in describing their "Epinephrine Informed" condition, did not just say that they told the subjects about the side effects of the drug; they described verbatim what exactly they told subjects:

> *Epinephrine Informed* [note the subheading]. I should tell you that some of our subjects have experienced side effects from the Suproxin. These side effects are transitory, that is, they will only last about 15 or 20 minutes. What will probably happen is that your hands will start to shake, your heart will start to pound, and your face may get warm and flushed. Again, these are side effects lasting about 15 or 20 minutes.

Also note the label Schachter and Singer used to describe the treatment: These subjects were injected with *epinephrine* and were *informed* about its effects. It is a good idea to use concrete labels for each operation, variable, and treatment; this makes it easier for the reader to follow. For example, in the Aronson-Mills (1959) severity-of-initiation experiment, groups were labeled "control," "mild," and "severe." These labels are simple and easily remembered, and are more closely tied to the procedure than more abstract labels such as "high dissonance" or "low dissonance" groups or, worse yet, group 1 and group 2 or the labels you used for your computer analysis of the data. The Procedure subsection should be about concrete events such as reading dirty words aloud, *not* about abstractions such as cognitive dissonance. The connection between constructs and their empirical realizations can be made in the Discussion section; in the Procedure section of the article, readers want only a clear, concrete description of *what* was done and *how* it was done.

Likewise, when you get to the part of the procedure where you took your measures, use a subheading to alert the reader that you are now about to describe your important dependent variables, unless you have a very simple study with a single very simple measure. Here again, you should set off measures of different dependent variables with subheadings (e.g., Ratings of Defendants, Recommended Length of Sentence), and provide very specific descriptions of the behaviors you measured and/or actual examples of questionnaire items. Again, you thus enable the reader not only to evaluate your study, but also to see what it looked like from the point of view of the subject.

Information about the reliability of the measures, results of pretests, and equipment used can go here, where it fits the best. (Pretests of the independent variables, of course, should be described in the independent variable subsection.) It is often a good idea to describe the results of any measures designed as manipulation checks here (or in the independent variable section), rather than clutter up the Results section with methodological underbrush.

Precautions against Bias At some point you should report any precautions to eliminate experimenter bias, reduce demand characteristics, or control for artifactual effects. Often you can work these precautions in at the appropriate point during the narrative: "Experimenter 1, blind to the subject's expectations about her partner, explained how to play the game." This method has both elegance and modesty to recommend it, but if your precautions are numerous or complex, it may be difficult to achieve. If several experimenters were used, it may be wise, when you give your overview of the design, to introduce them and to explain which ones were blind to which aspect of the procedure. If precautions against bias were elaborate, you may need to add a separate subsection after the Procedure subsection, entitled "Precautions against bias." At any rate, whatever precautions you took to rule out artifactual influences should be described in the Method section.

Finally, it should be noted that despite some opposition to deception research in social psychology, deception experiments are common. For example, more than half of the studies published in the *Journal of Personality and Social Psychology*, the *Journal of Experimental Social Psychology,* and the *Personality and Social Psychology Bulletin* in 1983 contained deception: information designed to mislead subjects about the specifics of the study (see Adair, Dushenko, & Lindsay, 1985). Given this frequency, it is noteworthy that very few empirical articles address the ethical concerns and practices related to their methods. For example, only 9.6 percent of research articles published in the above journals in 1983 explicitly mentioned "informed consent," and fewer than 5 percent mentioned subjects' right to withdraw from the experiment. Moreover, given the fact that postexperimental debriefings serve both a methodological and ethical function, it is surprising that just over one-third of published studies surveyed by John Adair and his colleagues (1985) mentioned debriefing subjects. We hasten to add that this does not mean that the majority of researchers failed to debrief subjects or advise them of their right to withdraw from a difficult experiment—only that they did not report those aspects of the procedure in their write-ups. It goes without saying that from an ethical point of view, all these things are important: to secure informed consent, to remind subjects that they are free to discontinue participation at any time without prejudice, and to debrief subjects once the experiment is over. From a methodological point of view, one should describe the content of the debriefing session (including any suspicions voiced by subjects) and describe efforts made to ensure that subjects do not reveal the true purpose of a deception experiment to potential subjects. Moreover, the failure to report these procedures, in and of itself, has ethical implications in the sense that their omission might create the illusion in novice researchers that it is not important to perform them.

Results

This section of the journal article summarizes the data collected, and the statistical techniques used to analyze them. When most people think of the Results section, they think of descriptive and inferential statistics, tables, and figures. And rightly so. However, as Bem (1987) notes, it is important to remember that all the information contained therein (group means, significance levels, and so on) are joined by a narrative. Tables and figures, for example, are designed to *supplement* the text; they cannot do the job of a good writer in communicating research findings.

Ideally, you want to launch into your major results as soon as possible. You have posed your question and explained how you turned it into an experiment; now the reader will be curious to know what the answer is. Often, however, you will have a number of statistical analyses that have more to do with the success of your procedures than with the answer to your question: the reliabilities of your scales or your observers, the effects of methodologically important but conceptually dull variables such as the four experimenters who ran the study, the three orders of questions used in the questionnaire, the consequences of discarding data from subjects who were dropped because they were suspicious or somehow weird, the results of your manipulation checks, the combination of various measures into a composite index measures, and so on. Beginning the Results section with a catalog of digressions from the actual results is bound to be frustrating to many readers. However, most of this information should be presented *somewhere,* and the beginning of the Results section is a common choice.

Consider the possibility of moving some of this information to the Method section and some to footnotes. The Results section is often the most difficult to read, especially as statistical techniques become increasingly complex, and anything you can do to reach the interested reader who doesn't understand multidimensional scaling (or whatever techniques you have used) is worthwhile. Reliabilities can be reported when you describe the measures in the Method section, as can the effects of question order and any combination of individual scales into more general measures. Analyses of differences among experimenters, or between paid and volunteer subjects, or subjects recruited from different sources, or even male and female subjects (if gender is not a variable of specific interest) can be reported when you describe the subjects and the experimenters. Presumably this description can be very brief, since any differences will be trivial. If there are important differences, for example if your four experimenters got different patterns of results—you probably shouldn't be writing up the study in the first place. You might even describe the results of a successful manipulation check in a quick footnote when you describe the measure: "Subjects in the Fear condition rated themselves significantly higher ($M = 6.1$) on the fear scale than subjects in the No Fear condition ($M = 2.4$, $t = 2.58$, $p < .01$), so we can conclude that the fear treatment was successful.

Particularly with very complex analyses, you may not be able to move *all* the preliminaries away from the Results section, but it is a good idea to try. For those that remain, you might begin with a subheading such as "Preliminary Analyses" that alerts the reader that the *real* story is not yet beginning.

After the preliminaries are out of the way, writers can proceed to the main analyses. It is often useful to provide readers with an organizational overview of the analyses that follow: For example, in what order will the results be discussed? If the analytic techniques are common and familiar to most readers, an exhaustive description of the statistical procedures is unnecessary. For example, it is probably sufficient to write, "The significance of the difference between the group means was determined by an independent samples t-test"; one need not inundate readers with the theory and assumptions underlying the use of the general linear model. However, when reading about more esoteric or complicated analyses, readers often appreciate more extensive descriptions of the statistical tests, rationales for them, and references to more detailed descriptions of those techniques. If very few readers are likely to follow the statistical discussion, a long footnote or a special "statistical paragraph" may be useful.

When actually describing the data, describe the forest first, then the trees (Bem, 1987). That is, begin with the most important findings, and then proceed to secondary findings such as qualifications, elaborations, or variables of tangential interest. Throughout this section, it is important to sum up periodically and to tie the numbers to the questions you are asking. Moreover, because some readers are not as well versed in statistics as others, it is useful to preface numerical findings in English, and to follow the prose with numbers. For example, "Undergoing a severe initiation to join a group produced more favorable evaluations than undergoing no initiation at all. Subjects in the Severe Initiation condition rated the group discussion significantly higher than did subjects in the Control condition, $t(40) = 3.66$, $p < .001$. They also rated the participants significantly higher than subjects in the Control condition, $t(40) = 2.03$, $p < .05$." This strategy enables interested readers who don't know a t-value from a p-value to follow the text and to get the gist of the results without wading through incomprehensible statistics.

Tables and figures are valuable additions to the text, but they should not be used indiscriminately. They *can* be used to emphasize a simple but important point made in the text but are *more* useful in graphically illustrating complicated findings such as interactions among variables. Whenever possible, tables or graphs should tell their own story; readers should be able to read the title of the table or graph, look at the numbers, and immediately grasp what the data reveal. Thus, titles should be complete—even if they do look a little long—and groups should be identified with labels first used in the Method section. Notes at the bottom of the tables or figures can also remind readers what the numbers mean: "*Note*. Subject ratings of the discussion could range from a low of '0' to a high of '15.'"

The numbers in the tables or graphs—at least in the first, most important tables in which you present your basic findings—should represent real things: the actual number of times the subjects smiled, or helped, or conformed; or the actual ratings they made on the scale of liking, or belief, or depression. You may need to transform the data to standard scores or to perform more elaborate transformations, but you should begin by presenting the data in the form that most closely approximates what subjects actually said or did.

Although data are typically analyzed and summarized in the aggregate (i.e., scores of *groups* of subjects are compared with scores of other *groups* of subjects), results of statistical analyses can be illustrated with concrete examples. Of course, isolated vivid examples are not data used to support hypotheses— at least in experiments—but they serve two important functions: First, they enliven what is typically the most tedious part of the journal article; second, they often link numbers and statistics to concrete behaviors: behaviors that are the wellspring of statistics. For example, consider this description of the postexperimental interview: "Only one subject entertained definite suspicions; her results were discarded. None of the subjects expressed any resentment or annoyance at having been misled. In fact, the majority were intrigued by the experiment, and several returned at the end of the academic quarter to ascertain the results." This text provides a vivid description of spontaneous behaviors *and* lends credence to more objective measures such as ratings of subject suspicions or concerns about the experiment

In summary, readers need not roll their eyes or take a deep breath before tackling the Results section. It is the writer's responsibility to keep those eyes from rolling. When the forest precedes the trees and prose precedes numbers and statistics, when the writer provides a preview of coming attractions and frequent summaries, *and* when the writer makes appropriate use of tables, figures, and concrete examples, this section can be as interesting, clear, and engaging as the rest of the article.

Discussion

After results are summarized, writers are in a position to discuss their implications, especially as they relate to the original problem, question, or hypothesis. If the Method and Results sections are the place for "Just the facts, M'am," the Discussion section is the place for inferences and speculations, for placing results in a larger perspective, and, occasionally, for sticking one's neck out. Presumably, you have thought more about your study and the meaning of its results than any other human being, and the Discussion section allows you some scope to communicate those thoughts.

In a well-written journal article, this concluding section becomes a mirror image of the introduction. That is, the Discussion section typically starts with a clear and succinct description of what was learned in this particular study.

What hypotheses were supported? What hypotheses were not supported? Answers to these questions should be more than a reiteration of conclusions reached in the Results section. The Discussion section provides for a description of what statistically significant differences *mean* in more general terms. That is, the writer moves from a discussion of relationships among variables described in the Results section of the article to a discussion of relationships among abstract concepts.

After the results of the study have been summarized and interpreted, it is appropriate to compare results with those obtained by other investigators. In what ways has this study advanced our knowledge? Are the implications of this study at odds with previous investigations? If so, it is useful to speculate about the sources of surprising or atypical findings. Might they be accounted for by methodological shortcomings, by a different subject population, or by specifics of the experimental procedure? Writers need not obsess on every potential flaw or shortcoming. If you are surprised or puzzled by atypical or unexpected findings, say so, and invite readers to speculate as to their source; you need not expose readers to a comprehensive list of convoluted speculations, afterthoughts, and apologies. Too many Discussion sections spend far too much time in profitless obsession over the gaps and failures of the study at the expense of a clear consideration of its successes.

No single study answers all questions related to an issue or problem. Data often reveal patterns—whether or not the results support one's original hypotheses—that suggest new research directions. The successes and pitfalls of the current study often point to better ways to tackle a research problem: Alternative experimental procedures, alternative empirical realizations, even alternative methods of research might be suggested as useful means of advancing our knowledge.

As we first pointed out in this chapter, the writer's task is to convince readers—editors, reviewers, students, psychologists and nonpsychologists alike—that the study was worth doing in the first place. Thus, although it might appear magnanimous, humble, or insightful to point to better ways to answer the question or better questions to ask, as Bem (1987, p. 188) notes, it is preferable to "end with a bang, not a whimper." Just what has the researcher contributed that others haven't? What do readers know now about human social behavior that they didn't know before they read the article? What implications do these findings have for social psychological theorizing, our understanding of the human condition, world peace, or the price of beans in Bulgaria?

AFTER WRITING THE ARTICLE

It's done! After hours and hours of writing, editing, and revising, and after putting the article down for a week or two or three and picking it up again to edit and revise *some more*, is it at last time to submit the article to a social psychological journal? Not quite. After following all the recommendations delineated in this chapter and elsewhere, writers often believe they have a respectable manuscript. And sometimes they're right. However, writers are not the best judges of whether an article is interesting, clear, and well written. *Readers* are. For that reason, it is important to give a "final" draft to friends and colleagues to read with a critical eye. It is preferable that they have experience in writing for social psychological journals, but they need not be experts in the specific research area addressed by the article. Indeed, as useful critics of the writing itself, it is probably better if they are *not* well acquainted with the area, for the best index of the clarity of an article is the ease with which nonexperts understand the concepts and follow the line of reasoning.

Invite them to be merciless editors. Encourage them to scribble in the margins, correct syntax, and point out trouble spots. Questions and suggestions from just one intelligent colleague are valuable, for if even one reader says a sentence or paragraph or transition is unclear, it is by definition unclear, and should be changed. Questions and suggestions from two colleagues are *more* valuable; this arrangement simulates the situation when the article is finally submitted to the journal editor for review. If two colleagues agree on trouble spots, it's a safe bet that at least one reviewer will concur. Heed the feedback of these colleagues gracefully. Pride of authorship is an asset at the writing stage but an impediment at the revision stage.

If all goes well, writers join the ranks of the 15 percent of researchers whose articles are eventually accepted for publication. There are times, however, when things don't go well: when the editor of a particular journal decides not to publish the manuscript. Rejection hurts, and it is tempting to curse the reviewers and their mothers, and to file the rejected manuscript in the folder labeled "Pearls before Swine," or worse yet, in the trash can. It is very tempting to sit down immediately and write the editor a letter pointing out the manifest indications of bias, incompetence, or brain damage in the reviewers and carelessness in the editor's scrutiny of the reviews. Go ahead and do it if it makes you feel better, but *don't mail it*. A letter written within the first 24 hours of receiving a rejection notice will *not* fairly represent the reasonableness of your position. It *will* make you look like a hostile, arrogant, whining sore loser, as you will see for yourself if you read it over a week later.

No one is immune to rejection. Even the smartest of our colleagues have tasted that bitter pill. When rejections happen to our students or colleagues, we urge them not to become too discouraged. Editors are professionals and experts in the field, and their decisions are frequently justified. It is important to take the editor's and reviewers' comments seriously, but after addressing their concerns (or deciding not to) a writer should not hesitate to resubmit the article. Of course, whether writers choose to resubmit with some minor cosmetic surgery or go back to the drawing board and test the hypothesis in a different way depends on the nature of the criticism. Some experiments are fatally flawed methodologically; others make use of inappropriate statistical analyses; still others simply are not 100 percent clear or well written. If the last is the case, we encourage experimenters to revise their manuscripts, and to resubmit the revision along with a letter noting that some recommendations were heeded, and why some others were not. Manuscripts rejected the first time around are sometimes published after extensive revisions, whether or not authors are explicitly invited to revise and resubmit.

Not all writers possess this much chutzpah; that is, not all writers feel comfortable pleading their case with an editor who has decided against publishing their article. An alternative we often recommend is to view the first rejection as an educational experience: Use reviewers' comments and recommendations as guidelines for revision and submit the new and improved article to another journal. We are only half kidding when we tell students to mail an article to one journal and to address an envelope to a second journal in case the article is rejected by the first. Sometimes the trick to publishing a good article is to find the right audience, and articles deemed trivial or boring by the editor of one journal might be deemed exciting or provocative by the editor of another. Like many, it's an empirical question: one best answered by picking the article up, dusting it off, and submitting it again.

GLOSSARY

acquiescence response set   A response bias characterized by some respondents' tendency to agree with positively worded statements on questionnaires.

artifact   An extraneous variable produced by some aspect of the experimental procedure that occurs along with the treatment, and whose effects become confounded with the effects of the treatment.

behavioral measures   Measures of subjects' concrete, actual behaviors in the experimental setting (e.g., level of shock administered to a confederate; length of time subjects work to solve a puzzle; number of times drivers honk their horns).

behavioroid measures   Measures that require subjects to commit to a future behavior without actually having to perform it later (e.g., number of hours subjects agree to tutor a needy student; number of questionnaires subjects commit to help a confederate score).

between-subjects design   An experimental design in which each subject is exposed to one and only one of the experimental treatments, so that each condition of the experiment is composed of a different group of subjects.

carryover effects   Effects of an experimental treatment that affect subjects' responses to subsequent treatments (e.g., the effects of exposure to a credible communicator on subjects' later responses to a noncredible communicator). These effects are potential problems in *within-subjects designs*.

conceptual variable   A variable conceived at an abstract level, independent of concrete manifestations of that variable (e.g., aggression, conformity, self-esteem, attraction, frustration).

construct validity   The extent to which a concrete manifestation of an abstract concept (construct) is an accurate or true reflection of the underlying construct. Both dependent-variable measures and empirical realizations of the independent variable can be more or less valid representations of the abstract category or construct represented by the conceptual variable.

contrast effect   Effects of an experimental treatment in which subjects' exposure to a stimulus yields more extreme responses to subsequent stimuli.

control group   In an experiment, the group that receives no treatment.

correlation   A relationship between two variables.

correlation coefficient   A numerical index of the magnitude and direction of a correlation between two variables. Correlation coefficients range from $\Theta 1.00$ (a perfect positive correlation) to $\Sigma 1.00$ (a perfect negative correlation).

correlational studies   Studies in which the researcher has no control over the presumed antecedents of some phenomenon, and no ability to assign participants at random; studies in which the relationship between or among two or more variables can be measured, but cannot be controlled.

counterbalancing   In a repeated measures design, balancing the order in which subjects experience treatments or measures (e.g., treatment A—treatment B versus treatment B—treatment A).

criterion-related validity   The extent to which a score on a specific dependent-variable measure corresponds to scores on some independent, objective measure of the variable. Criterion-related validity is *concurrent* validity if the criterion is in the present and *predictive* validity if it is in the future.

cross-lagged panel technique   A statistical technique that enables researchers to draw tentative causal inferences from correlational data by studying the relationship between two variables at two or more points in time.

debriefing   The postexperimental interview in which the experimenter explains the purpose of the research to subjects, answers their questions, and responds to any lingering concerns they might express.

deception experiment   An experiment in which the investigator withholds the true purpose of the study from subjects. Deception may involve something as simple as withholding the hypothesis of the study or may involve more elaborate attempts to mislead subjects about the real purpose of the investigation.

demand characteristics   Subtle or not-so-subtle cues in the experimental setting that influence subjects' perceptions of what is expected of them, and that might systematically influence their behavior.

dependent variable   In an experiment, any aspect of a subject's behavior that is measured after the administration of a treatment; the expected effect of a treatment.

direct replication   A repetition of an experiment in which the conditions, procedures, measures, and so on are identical to those in the first experiment. Direct replications are designed to determine if a given experimental effect is reliable.

double-blind experiment   An experiment in which neither the experimenter nor the subject knows to which condition the subject has been assigned.

empirical realization   The translation of an abstract concept into concrete procedures or operations (e.g., "severe initiation" as reading a list of obscene words and literary passages aloud to an experimenter in order to join a discussion group).

equivalent time-samples design   A quasi-experimental design employing one group of subjects who are exposed to multiple treatments (usually assigned at random), each of which is followed by measures of the dependent variable(s) of interest.

experimental conditions   In an experiment, groups that are defined by treatments. In the simplest experiment, there are two conditions: an experimental condition (in which the treatment is administered) and a control condition (in which no treatment is administered).

experimental control   The ability of the experimenter to hold theoretically irrelevant factors constant in an experiment.

experimental group   In an experiment, the group or groups that receive treatment(s).

experimental impact   The degree to which events in the experimental setting are meaningful to and involving for subjects. Events that capture and hold subjects' attention are said to have experimental impact.

experimental realism   The extent to which experimental procedures have an impact on subjects; the extent to which events in the experimental setting are credible, involving, and taken seriously by subjects (contrasted with *mundane realism*).

experimenter bias   Systematic bias that threatens the validity of an experiment when experimenters' expectations are unconsciously or subtly communicated to subjects.

external validity   The degree to which results of a specific study can be generalized to other people, places, times, or empirical realizations of the independent variable.

face validity   The extent to which an instrument appears to measure what it purports to measure (e.g., a test that contains addition, subtraction, multiplication, and division problems is a face valid measure of arithmetic ability).

factorial design   An experimental design in which two (or more) treatments are administered simultaneously such that every level of one variable occurs with every level of other variable(s). The simplest factorial design is a 2×2 design, with two levels of two variables.

Guttman scale   An attitude scale in which opinion statements can be ordered so that respondent agreement with one statement implies agreement with all previous statements.

history effects   Events in the environment (other than the treatment of interest) that occur before the measurement of the dependent variable or between successive measurements of a dependent variable. These effects represent a potential threat to the internal validity of a study.

hypothesis   An assumption or prediction that is taken to be true for purposes of scientific investigation. Hypotheses often involve specific predictions about the relationships between two or more variables.

independent variable   In an experiment, the treatment or condition manipulated by the experimenter.

indirect measures   Measures for which the connection between the score itself and some other variable of interest involves some kind of hypothetical intervening process (e.g., recall errors as an indirect measure of attitudes; reaction time as an indirect measure of depth of information processing).

informed consent   The provision of sufficient information about an experiment to enable the subject to make an informed decision about whether to participate.

instrumentation effects   Changes in observers or measuring instruments over time. These effects represent a potential threat to the internal validity of a study.

interaction   In a factorial design, an outcome in which the effects of one factor (independent variable) is not the same at different levels of some other factor.

internal analysis   An analysis of the effects of nonmanipulated variables in an experiment. Experimenters are frequently interested in the effects of subject variables, or in the interactive effects of subject variables and treatments on dependent-variable measures.

internal consistency   An index of reliability, the extent to which items on a measuring instrument "hang together"; the extent to which scores on individual items are correlated with one another or with the total score.

internal validity   The extent to which a valid causal statement can be made about the effects of the independent variable on the dependent variable in a particular context.

interrupted time-series designs A general class of quasi-experimental designs in which the effect of the independent variable is assessed by comparing multiple observations of the same group of individuals: either before and after administration of one level of the treatment, or after the administration of different levels of a treatment (see *time-series experiment* and *multiple-group time-series design*).

interobserver reliability An index of reliability, the extent of correlation between the observations of two or more observers who have witnessed the same event.

judgment experiment An experiment in which subjects are asked to recognize, recall, classify, evaluate, or reason about stimulus materials. These experiments typically emphasize stimulus control over experimental impact.

Latin-square design A factorial experimental design in which only a fraction of the potential combinations of levels of treatment are included. This design is a partial solution to the problem of an excessive number of treatment groups when every level of every factor is paired with every level of every other factor.

Likert scale An attitude scale in which for each of a number of opinion statements, respondents indicate the extent to which they agree or disagree with the each statement, usually by checking numbers from 1 to 5 or 1 to 7.

manipulation check A measure administered to determine if the experimental treatment produced the internal state that constituted the conceptual variable (e.g., a questionnaire administered to determine if subjects in the High Fear condition really were feeling more fearful than subjects in the Low Fear condition).

matching A method of reducing error variance. Matching involves finding pairs (or groups) of subjects who are comparable on some dimension believed to be related to the independent variable, and assigning these subjects at random to experimental conditions.

maturation effects The effects of processes that unfold within subjects as a function of the passage of time, per se (e.g., growing tired, older, bored, hungry). These effects represent a potential threat to the internal validity of a study.

mortality effects The effects of a differential loss of subjects from experimental conditions. These effects represent a potential threat to the internal validity of a study.

multiple group time-series design A quasi-experimental design employing two groups of subjects, one of which receives a treatment embedded in a series of measurements of the dependent variable, and one of which receives no treatment.

multiple meaning The ambiguous meaning of an observed relationship between the independent and dependent variables. When treatments are meaningful and complex, it is often unclear which specific component of the treatment is responsible for observed changes in subjects' behaviors.

mundane realism The extent to which experimental events in a controlled setting are similar to events which occur in the "real" world (contrasted with *experimental realism*).

negative correlation A relationship between two variables in which an increase on the first variable is associated with a decrease on the second variable (e.g., the *higher* the amount of practice, the *lower* one's golf score).

nonequivalent control group design A widely used quasi-experimental design employing two existing groups of subjects, both of which receive a pretest and posttest, but only one of which receives the treatment.

one-group pretest-posttest design A pseudoexperimental design in which only one group of subjects is pretested, receives a treatment, and is then posttested.

one-shot case study A pseudoexperimental design in which only one group is exposed to treatment before dependent-variable measures are taken.

physiological measures   Measures of such bodily processes as blood pressure, heart rate, and pupil dilation that are usually beyond the conscious control of subjects.

pilot tests   Rehearsals of an experiment (or parts of an experiment) designed to detect any unforeseen technical problems.

placebo effect   A change produced by an inert substance or procedure presumed to have no effects (e.g., in drug research, subjects randomly assigned to receive a placebo often report feeling better).

positive correlation   A relationship between two variables in which an increase on the first variable is associated with an increase on the second variable as well (e.g., the *greater* the time spent in studying for an examination, the *higher* one's test score).

pretest sensitization   The possibility that pretesting, per se, sensitizes subjects to a topic or issue, thus systematically biasing their responses to subsequent tests or measures (see *testing effects*). Pretest sensitization may also interact with the treatment to produce invalid results.

pseudoexperiment   Nonexperimental designs in which the investigator has control over the administration of a treatment and the collection of dependent-variable measures, but which do not contain appropriate standards of comparison (i.e., control groups or control observations) to enable the researcher to assess the effects of the treatment. (See *one-shot case study, one-group pretest-posttest design, static-group comparison design*).

quasi-experiment   Any of a number of nonexperimental methods in which the researcher can control the administration of the treatment (when what is administered to whom, for example) and collect dependent variable measures but cannot assign subjects to conditions at random.

random assignment   Subjects are assigned to experimental conditions such that each subject has an equal probability of being assigned to any treatment or group and such that the assignment of one subject does not influence the assignment of any other subject.

random error   Error caused by extraneous and uncontrolled variables whose average influence on the outcome of an experiment is the same in all conditions. This type of error increases the baseline variability in *all* experimental conditions, and can mask the effects of the independent variable (e.g., such noise in the system as subject variables or minor events that occur during particular experimental sessions).

reactive measures   Measures that change the very phenomenon they were designed to assess. The mere measurement of the dependent variable may interact with the independent variable to produce spurious effects that would not obtain were a different measure used (see *pretest sensitization*).

reliability of measurement   The extent to which an instrument provides consistent measures (also see *internal consistency*).

replication   The repetition of an experiment (see *direct replication* and *systematic replication*).

role-playing studies   Alternatives to deception experiments in which subjects are asked to behave as if they were in a particular situation. Subjects collaborate with experimenters and play the role of someone who is not in an experimental setting or who does not know the true purpose of the research.

selection effects   The effects of initial systematic differences between or among groups of subjects prior to administration of the treatment. These effects represent a potential threat to the internal validity of a study.

self-selection   A situation in which subjects decide for themselves whether they will participate in a study or in which they assign themselves to one experimental condition over others.

semantic differential scale An attitude scale that assesses the connotative meaning of concepts (e.g., mother, birth control, desegregation) by asking respondents to rate the concept on a series of 7-point bipolar dimensions (e.g, good-bad, strong-weak, active-passive).

Solomon four-group design A true experiment designed to enhance external validity: two groups (one of which receives no treatment) receive only a posttest; two groups (one of which receives no treatment) receive both a pretest and a posttest. This elegant design enables the experimenter to assess the main and interactive effects of pretesting and the independent variable.

static-group comparison design A pseudoexperimental design employing two groups of subjects, only one of which receives a treatment before dependent-variable measures are collected from both groups.

subject variables Variables subjects bring with them into the experimental setting; personal variables over which the experimenter can exert no direct control (e.g., age, intelligence, socioeconomic status, gender).

systematic error Error caused by extraneous variables that tend to influence all scores in one condition in the same direction and to have no effect, or a different effect, on the scores in other conditions. This type of error can affect the size of the differences between or among conditions on dependent measures and distort the apparent effect of the independent variable.

systematic replication A repetition of an experiment in which the experimenter systematically varies some aspect of the original conditions, procedures, or measures in order to resolve ambiguities or add new information. Systematic replications provide for a clarification or extension of original findings.

testing effects The effects of collecting dependent-variable measures at one point in time on subsequent measures. These effects represent a potential threat to the internal validity of a study.

Thurstone scale An attitude scale consisting of an ordered series of opinion statements about a given object or issue, ranging from extremely unfavorable to extremely favorable.

time-series experiment (simple time-series design) A quasi-experimental design employing one group of subjects, in which a treatment is embedded (ideally at random) within a series of measurements of the dependent variable. Observations prior to treatment are compared with observations after treatment.

unobtrusive measures Measures that are unlikely to produce reactivity; these measures are often covert and indirect (e.g., voluntary seating patterns of blacks and whites as an index of racial attitudes; the number of accident insurance policies purchased at airports as an index of anxiety about flying).

validity In measurement, the extent to which differences revealed by a measure correspond to "real" differences in the conceptual variable (e.g., the extent to which subjects' ratings on a questionnaire correspond to their "true" underlying attitudes).

variable A measurable attribute that can assume different values among members of a class of subjects or events but that has only one value for any given member of that class at any one point in time (e.g., height, weight, gender, response latency, introversion, marital status).

within-subjects design An experimental design in which each subject is exposed to all treatments, so that each condition is composed of the same group of individuals.

Bibliography

Adair, J. G., Dushenko, T. W., & Lindsay, R. C. L. (1985). Ethical regulations and their impact on research practice. *American Psychologist, 40,* 59–72.

Adair, J. G., & Schachter, B. S. (1972). To cooperate or to look good?: The subjects' and experimenters' perceptions of each others' intentions. *Journal of Experimental Social Psychology, 8,* 74–85.

Aderman, D. (1972). Elation, depression, and helping behavior. *Journal of Personality and Social Psychology, 24,* 91–101.

Allport, G. W., & Postman, L. (1958). *The psychology of rumor.* New York: Henry Holt & Company. (Originally published, 1947).

Allport, G. W., & Vernon, P. E. (1933). *Studies in expressive movement.* New York: Macmillan.

American Psychological Association (1953). *Ethical standards of psychologists.* Washington, DC: Author.

American Psychological Association (1981). Ethical principles of psychologists. *American Psychologist, 36,* 633–638.

American Psychological Association (1982). *Ethical principles in the conduct of research with human participants* (rev. ed.). Washington, DC: Author.

American Psychological Association (1983). *Publication manual* (3rd ed.). Washington, DC: Author.

Aronson, E. (1961). The effect of effort on the attractiveness of rewarded and unrewarded stimuli. *Journal of Abnormal and Social Psychology, 63,* 375–380.

Aronson, E. (1966). Avoidance of inter-subject communication. *Psychological Reports, 19,* 238.

Aronson, E., & Carlsmith, J. M. (1962). Performance expectancy as a determinant of actual performance. *Journal of Abnormal and Social Psychology, 65,* 178–182.

Aronson, E., & Carlsmith, J. M. (1963). Effect of the severity of threat on the devaluation of forbidden behavior. *Journal of Abnormal and Social Psychology, 66,* 584–588

Aronson, E., & Carlsmith, J. M. (1968). Experimentation in social psychology. In G. Lindzey and E. Aronson (Eds.), *The handbook of social psychology,* (2nd ed., Vol. 2, pp. 1–79). Reading, MA: Addison-Wesley.

Aronson, E., & Cope, V. M. (1968). My enemy's enemy is my friend. *Journal of Personality and Social Psychology, 8,* 8–12.

Aronson, E., & Landy, D. (1967). Further steps beyond Parkinson's law: A replication and extension of the excess time effect. *Journal of Experimental Social Psychology, 3,* 274–285.

Aronson, E., & Linder, D. (1965). Gain and loss of esteem as determinants of interpersonal attractiveness. *Journal of Experimental Social Psychology, 1,* 156–171.

Aronson, E., & Mettee, D. K. (1968). Dishonest behavior as a function of differential levels of induced self-esteem. *Journal of Personality and Social Psychology, 9,* 121–127.

Aronson, E., & Mills, J. (1959). The effect of severity of intiation on liking for a group. *Journal of Abnormal and Social Psychology, 59,* 177–181.

Aronson, E., & Osherow, N. (1980). Cooperation, prosocial behavior, and academic performance: Experiments in the desegregated classroom. In L. Bickman (Ed.), *Applied social psychology annual* (Vol. 1, pp. 163–196). Beverly Hills, CA: Sage Publications.

Aronson, E., Stephan, C., Sikes, J., Blaney, N., & Snapp, M. (1978). *The jigsaw classroom.* Beverly Hills, CA: Sage Publications.

Aronson, E., Turner, J., & Carlsmith, J. M. (1963). Communicator credibility and communication discrepancy as determinants of opinion change. *Journal of Abnormal and Social Psychology, 67,* 31–36.

Aronson, E., Willerman, B., & Floyd, J. (1966). The effect of a pratfall on increasing interpersonal attractiveness. *Psychonomic Science, 4,* 227–228.

Asch, S. E. (1951). Effects of group pressure upon the modification and distortion of judgments. In H. Guetzkow (Ed.), *Groups, leadership, and men* (pp. 177–190). Pittsburgh: Carnegie Press.

Asch, S. (1952). Effects of group pressure upon the modification and distortion of judgments. In G. E. Swanson, T. M. Newcomb, and E. L. Hartley (Eds.), *Readings in social psychology.* New York: Holt, Rhinehart, and Winston.

Asch, S. E. (1965). Effects of group pressure upon the modification and distortion of judgments. In H. Proshansky and B. Seidenberg (Eds.), *Basic studies in social psychology* (pp. 393–401). New York: Holt, Rhinehart, and Winston.

Ax, A. F. (1953). The physiological differentiation between fear and anger in humans. *Psychosomatic Medicine, 15,* 433–442.

Back, K. W.. (1951). Influence through social communication. *Journal of Abnormal and Social Psychology, 46,* 9–23.

Bandura, A., & Walters, R. H. (1963). *Social learning and personality development.* New York: Holt.

Barber, T. X., & Silver, M. J. (1968). Fact, fiction, and the experimenter bias effect. *Psychological Bulletin* (Monograph Supplement), *70,* 1–29.

Barnes, R. D., Ickes, W., & Kidd, R. F. (1979). Effects of the perceived intentionality and stability of another's dependency on helping behavior. *Personality and Social Psychology Bulletin, 5,* 367–372.

Baumrind, D. (1964). Some thoughts on ethics of research: After reading Milgram's "Behavioral study of obedience." *American Psychologist, 19,* 421–423.

Baumrind, D. (1985). Research using intentional deception: Ethical issues revisited. *American Psychologist, 40,* 165–174.

Beecher, H. K. (1955). The powerful placebo. *Journal of the American Medical Association, 159*(17), 1603–1606.

Bem, D. J. (1965). An experimental analysis of self-persuasion. *Journal of Experimental Social Psychology, 1,* 199–218.

Bem, D. J. (1968). The epistemological status of interpersonal simulations: A reply to Jones, Linder, Kiesler, Zanna, and Brehm. *Journal of Experimental Social Psychology, 4,* 270–274.

Bem, D. J. (1987). Writing the empirical journal article. In M. P. Zanna and J. M. Darley (Eds.), *The compleat academic* (pp. 171–201). New York: Random House.

Berthoff, A. (1988). *Forming, thinking, writing* (2nd ed.). Portsmouth, NH: Boynton/ Cook Publishers.

Bock, R. D. (1963). Multivariate analysis of variance of repeated measurements. In C. W. Harris (Ed.), *Problems in measuring change* (pp. 85–103). Madison: University of Wisconsin Press.

Borgida, E., & Nisbett, R. E. (1977). The differential impact of abstract vs. concrete information on decisions. *Journal of Applied Social Psychology, 7,* 258–271.

Brehm, J. W., & Cole, A. H. (1966). Effect of a favor which reduces freedom. *Journal of Personality and Social Psychology, 3,* 420–426.

Bridgeman, D. (1981). Enhanced role-taking through cooperative interdependence: A field study. *Child Development, 52,* 1231–1238.

Brock, T. C., & Becker, L. A. (1966). "Debriefing" and susceptibility to subsequent experimental manipulations. *Journal of Experimental Social Psychology, 2,* 314–323.

Brown, R. (1962). Models of attitude change. In R. Brown, E. Galanter, E. H. Hess, and G. Mandler (Eds.), *New directions in psychology* (Vol. 1, pp. 1–85). New York: Holt, Rhinehart, and Winston.

Brunswik, E. (1956). *Perception and the representative design of psychological experiments* (2nd ed.). Berkeley: University of California Press.

Buck, R. (1984). *The communication of emotion.* New York: The Guilford Press.

Byrne, D. (1961). Interpersonal attraction and attitude similarity. *Journal of Abnormal and Social Psychology, 62,* 713–715.

Byrne, D. (1969). Attitudes and attraction. In L. Berkowitz (Ed.), *Advances in experimental social psychology* (Vol. 4, pp. 35–89). New York: Academic Press.

Byrne, D. (1971). *The attraction paradigm.* New York: Academic Press.

Byrne, D. & Nelson, D. (1965). Attraction as a linear function of proportion of positive reinforcements. *Journal of Personality and Social Psychology, 1,* 659–663.

Byrne, D. & Rhamey, R. (1965). Magnitude of positive and negative reinforcements as a determinant of attraction. *Journal of Personality and Social Psychology, 2,* 884–889.

Campbell, D. T. (1957). Factors relevant to validity of experiments in social settings. *Psychological Bulletin, 54,* 297–312.

Campbell, D. T. (1969). Prospective: Artifact and control. In R. Rosenthal and R. Rosnow (Eds.), *Artifact in behavioral research* (pp. 351–382) New York: Academic Press.

Campbell, D. T., & Fiske, D. W. (1959). Convergent and discriminant validation by the multitrait-multimethod matrix. *Psychological Bulletin, 56,* 81–105.

Campbell, D. T., & Stanley, J. C. (1966). *Experimental and quasi-experimental designs for research*. Chicago: Rand McNally.

Cannell, C. F., & Kahn, R. L. (1968). Interviewing. In G. Lindzey and E. Aronson (Eds.), *The handbook of social psychology* (2nd ed., Vol. 2, pp. 526–595). Reading, MA: Addison-Wesley.

Carlsmith, J. M., Collins, B. E., & Helmreich, R. L. (1966). Studies in forced compliance: I. The effect of pressure for compliance on attitude change produced by face-to-face role playing and anonymous essay writing. *Journal of Personality and Social Psychology, 4,* 1–13.

Carlsmith, J. M., Ebbesen, E. B., Lepper, M. R., Zanna, M. P., Joncas, A. J., & Abelson, R. P. (1964). Dissonance reduction following forced attention to the dissonance. *Proceedings of the 77th Annual Convention of the American Psychological Association, 4,* 321–322.

Carlsmith, J. M., Ellsworth, P., & Whiteside, J. (1968). *Guilt, confession and compliance*. Unpublished manuscript, Stanford University.

Carlsmith, J. M., & Gross, A. E. (1969). Some effects of guilt on compliance. *Journal of Personality and Social Psychology, 11,* 232–239.

Carlsmith, J. M., Lepper, M. R., & Landauer, T. K. (1974). Children's obedience to adult requests: Interactive effects of anxiety arousal and apparent punitiveness of the adult. *Journal of Personality and Social Psychology, 30,* 822–828.

Carlsmith, L. (1973). Some personality characteristics of boys separated from their fathers during World War II. *Ethos, 1,* 466–477.

Christensen, H. T., & Carpenter, G. R. (1962). Value-behavior descrepancies regarding premarital coitus in three Western cultures. *American Sociological Review, 27,* 66–74.

Christensen, L. (1988). Deception in psychological research: When is its use justified? *Personality and Social Psychology Bulletin, 14,* 664–675.

Cialdini, R. B., Borden, R. J., Thorne, A., Walker, M. R., Freeman, S., & Sloan, L. R. (1976). Basking in reflected glory: Three (football) field studies. *Journal of Personality and Social Psychology, 34,* 366–375.

Cialdini, R. B., Cacioppo, J. T., Bassett, R., & Miller, J. A. (1978). Lowball procedure for producing compliance: Commitment then cost. *Journal of Personality and Social Psychology, 36,* 463–476.

Cialdini, R. B., Darby, B. L, & Vincent, J. E. (1973). Transgression and altruism: A case for hedonism. *Journal of Experimental Social Psychology, 9,* 502–516.

Cook, T. D., Bean, J. R., Calder, B. J., Frey, R., Krauetz, M. L., & Reisman, S. R. (1970). Demand characteristics and three conceptions of the frequently deceived subject. *Journal of Personality and Social Psychology, 14,* 185–194.

Cook, T. D., & Campbell, D. T. (1979). *Quasi-experimentation: Design and analysis issues for field settings*. Boston: Houghton Mifflin.

Cook, T. D., Leviton, L. C., & Shadish, W. R., Jr. (1985). Program evaluation. In G. Lindzey and E. Aronson (Eds.), *The handbook of social psychology* (3rd ed., Vol. 1, pp. 699–777). New York: Random House.

Cooper, J. (1976). Deception and role playing: On telling the good guys from the bad guys. *American Psychologist, 31,* 605–610.

Cooper, J., & Fazio, R. H. (1984). A new look at dissonance theory. In L. Berkowitz (Ed.), *Advances in experimental social psychology* (Vol. 17, pp. 229–266). New York: Academic Press.

Cooper, J., & Fazio, R. H., & Rhodewalt, F. (1978). Dissonance and humor: Evidence for the undifferentiated nature of dissonance arousal. *Journal of Personality and Social Psychology, 36,* 280–285.

Cordaro, L., & Ison, J. R. (1963). Observer bias in classical conditioning of the planarian. *Psychological Reports, 13,* 787–789.

Coronary Drug Project Research Group (1980). Influence of adherence to treatment and response to cholesterol on mortality in the coronary drug project. *New England Journal of Medicine, 303,* 1038–1041.

Cottrell, N. B. (1965) Performance expectancy as a determinant of actual performance: A replication with a new design. *Journal of Personality and Social Psychology, 2,* 685–691.

Cowan, C., Thompson, W., & Ellsworth, P.C. (1984). The effects of death qualification on jurors' predisposition to convict and on the quality of deliberation. *Law and Human Behavior, 8,* 53–79.

Crano, W. D., & Brewer, M. B. (1986). *Principles and methods of social research.* Newton, MA: Allyn & Bacon.

Cronbach, L. J. (1975). Beyond the two disciplines of scientific psychology. *American Psychologist, 30,* 116–127.

Croyle, R., & Cooper, J. (1983). Dissonance arousal: Physiological evidence. *Journal of Personality and Social Psychology, 45,* 782–791.

Crusco, A. H., & Wetzel, C. G. (1984). The Midas touch: The effects of interpersonal touch on restaurant tipping. *Personality and Social Psychology Bulletin, 10,* 512–517.

Crutchfield, R. S. (1955). Conformity and character. *American Psychologist, 10,* 191–198.

Darley, J. M., & Latané, B. (1968). Bystander intervention in emergencies: Diffusion of responsibility. *Journal of Personality and Social Psychology, 8,* 377–383.

Davidson, A. R., & Jaccard, J. J. (1979). Variables that moderate the attitude-behavior relation: Results of a longitudinal survey. *Journal of Personality and Social Psychology, 37,* 1364–1376.

Dawes, R. B., McTavish, J., & Shaklee, H. (1977). Behavior, communication, and assumptions about other people's behavior in a commons dilemma situation. *Journal of Personality and Social Psychology, 35,* 1–11.

Dawes, R. M., Singer, D., & Lemons, F. (1972). An experimental analysis of the contrast effect and its implications for intergroup communication and the indirect assessment of attitude. *Journal of Personality and Social Psychology, 21,* 281–295.

Dawes, R. M., & Smith, T. L. (1985). Attitude and opinion measurement. In G. Lindzey and E. Aronson (Eds.), *The handbook of social psychology* (3rd ed., Vol. 1, pp. 509–566). New York: Random House.

Deci, E. L. (1971). Effects of externally mediated rewards on intrinsic motivation. *Journal of Personality and Social Psychology, 18,* 105–115.

Dement, W. C. (1972). *Some must watch while some must sleep.* Stanford, CA: Stanford Alumni Association.

Deutsch, M. (1949). An experimental study of the effects of cooperation and competition upon group process. *Human Relations, 2,* 199–231.

Deutsch, M., & Gerard, H. B. (1963). A study of normative and informational influences upon individual judgment. *Journal of Abnormal and Social Psychology, 51,* 629–636.

Doob, A. N. (1967). *Some determinants of aggression.* Unpublished doctoral dissertation, Stanford University.

Doob, A. N., Carlsmith, J. M., Freedman, J. L., Landauer, T. K., & Tom, S., Jr. (1969). Effect of initial selling price on subsequent sales. *Journal of Personality and Social Psychology, 11,* 345–350.

Duncan, S., Jr. (1969). Nonverbal communication. *Psychological Bulletin, 72,* 118–137.

Dunnette, M. D., Campbell, J., & Jaastad, K. (1963). The effect of group participation on brainstorming effectiveness for two industrial samples. *Journal of Applied Psychology, 47,* 30–37.

Eagly, A. H., & Crowley, M. (1986). Gender and helping behavior: A meta-analytic review of the social psychological literature. *Psychological Bulletin, 100*(3), 283–308.

Eagly, A. H., & Steffen, V. J. (1986). Gender and aggressive behavior: A meta-analytic review of the social psychological literature. *Psychological Bulletin, 100*(3), 309–330.

Edelman, R. I. (1970). Some variables affecting suspicion of deception. *Journal of Personality and Social Psychology, 15,* 333–337.

Edelmann, R. J. (1987). *The psychology of embarrassment.* Chichester, England: John Wiley & Sons.

Ekman, P. (1985). *Telling lies: Clues to deceit in the marketplace, politics, and marriage.* New York: W. W. Norton & Company.

Ekman, P., & Friesen, W. V. (1969). Nonverbal leakage and clues to deception. *Psychiatry, 32,* 88–105.

Ekman, P., & Friesen, W. V. (1975). *Unmasking the face.* Englewood Cliffs, NJ: Prentice-Hall.

Ekman, P., Friesen, W. V., & O'Sullivan, M. (1988). Smiles when lying. *Journal of Personality and Social Psychology, 54,* 414–420.

Ekman, P., Friesen, W. V., O'Sullivan, M., & Scherer, K. (1980). Relative importance of face, body, and speech in judgments of personality and affect. *Journal of Personality and Social Psychology, 38,* 270–277.

Ellsworth, P., & Carlsmith, J. M. (1968). Effects of eye contact and verbal content on affective response to a dyadic interaction. *Journal of Personality and Social Psychology, 10,* 15–20.

Ellsworth, P., & Carlsmith, J. M. (1973). Eye contact and gaze aversion in an aggressive encounter. *Journal of Personality and Social Psychology, 28,* 280–292.

Ellsworth, P. C., Carlsmith, J. M., & Henson, A. (1972). Staring as a stimulus to flight in humans: A series of field experiments. *Journal of Personality and Social Psychology, 21,* 302–311.

Ellsworth, P. C., Friedman, H. S., Perlick, D., & Hoyt, M. E. (1978). Some effects of gaze on subjects' motivation to seek or avoid social comparison. *Journal of Experimental Social Psychology, 14,* 69–87.

Ellsworth, P., & Langer, E. J. (1976). Staring and approach: An interpretation of the stare as a nonspecific activator. *Journal of Personality and Social Psychology, 33,* 117–122.

Ellsworth, P., & Ross, L. D. (1975). Intimacy as a response to a direct gaze. *Journal of Personality and Social Psychology, 11,* 592–613.

Eron, L., & Huesmann, L. R. (1980). Adolescent aggression and television. *Annals of the New York Academy of Sciences, 347,* 319–331.

Eron, L., & Huesmann, L. R. (1986). The role of television in the development of prosocial and antisocial behavior. In D. Olweus, J. Block, and M. Radke-Yarrow (Eds.), *Development of antisocial and prosocial behavior: Research, theories, and issues* (pp. 285–314). Orlando, FL: Academic Press.

Exline, R. V. (1971). Visual interaction: The glances of power and preference. *Nebraska Symposium on Motivation* (pp. 163–206). Lincoln: University of Nebraska Press.

Farrow, J. M., Lohss, W. E., Farrow, B. J., & Taub, S. I. (1975). Intersubject communication as a contaminating factor in verbal conditioning. *Perceptual and Motor Skills, 40,* 975–982.

Fast, J. (1970). *Body language.* New York: M. Evans.

Feldman, J. (1982). Ideology without data. *American Psychologist, 37,* 857–858.

Feldman, S., & Kleck, R. E. (1970). *Nonverbal behavior as a function of impression sets.* Unpublished manuscript.

Feller, W. (1968). *An introduction to probability theory and its applications.* New York: Wiley.

Festinger, L. (1957). *A theory of cognitive dissonance.* Stanford CA: Stanford University Press.

Festinger, L., & Carlsmith, J. M. (1959). Cognitive consequences of forced compliance. *Journal of Abnormal and Social Psychology, 58,* 203–210.

Festinger, L., Riecken, H. W., & Schachter, S. (1956). *When prophecy fails.* Minneapolis: University of Minnesota Press.

Festinger, L., Schachter, S., & Back, K. (1950). *Social pressures in informal groups: A study of human factors in housing.* New York: Harper & Row.

Festinger, L., & Thibaut, J. (1951). Interpersonal communications in small groups. *Journal of Abnormal and Social Psychology, 46,* 92–99.

Fillenbaum, S. (1966). Prior deception and subsequent experimental performance: The "faithful" subject. *Journal of Personality and Social Psychology, 4,* 532–537.

Forster, E. M. (1951). What I believe. *Two cheers for democracy* (pp. 77–78). London: Edward Arnold.

Forward, J., Canter, R., & Kirsch, N. (1976). Role-enactment and deception: Alternative paradigms? *American Psychologist, 31,* 595–604.

Franke, R. H., & Kaul, J. D. (1978). The Hawthorne experiments: First statistical interpretation. *American Sociological Review, 43* 623–643.

Freedman, J. L. (1965). Long-term behavioral effects of cognitive dissonance. *Journal of Experimental Social Psychology, 1,* 145–155.

Freedman, J. L. (1969). Role-playing: Psychology by consensus. *Journal of Personality and Social Psychology, 13,* 107–114.

Freedman, J. L. (1988). Television violence and aggression: What the evidence shows. In S. Oskamp (Ed.), *Applied social psychology annual* (Vol. 8, pp. 144–162). Newbury Park, CA: Sage Publications.

Freedman, J. L., & Fraser, S. C. (1966). Compliance without pressure: The foot-in-the-door technique. *Journal of Personality and Social Psychology, 4,* 195–202.

Freedman, J. L., Wallington, S., & Bless, E. (1967). Compliance without pressure: The effect of guilt. *Journal of Personality and Social Psychology, 7,* 117–124.

Freund, P. A. (1967). Is the law ready for human experimentation? *American Psychologist, 22,* 394–399.

Fultz, J., Batson, C. D., Fortenbach, V. A., McCarthy, P. M., & Varney, L. L. (1986). Social evaluation and the empathy-altruism hypothesis. *Journal of Personality and Social Psychology, 50,* 761–769.

Funder, D. C. (1987). Errors and mistakes: Evaluating the accuracy of social judgment. *Psychological Bulletin, 101*(1), 75–90.

Gerard, H. B., & Mathewson, G. C. (1966). The effects of severity of initiation on liking for a group: A replication. *Journal of Experimental Social Psychology, 2,* 278–287.

Gergen, K. J. (1973). Social psychology as history. *Journal of Personality and Social Psychology, 26,* 309–320.

Gonzales, M. H., Aronson, E., & Costanzo, M. (1988). Using social cognition and persuasion to promote energy conservation: A quasi-experiment. *Journal of Applied Social Psychology, 18,* 1049–1066.

Greenberg, J., & Folger, R. (1988). *Controversial issues in social research methods.* New York: Springer-Verlag.

Greenberg, M. S. (1967). Role-playing: An alternative to deception? *Journal of Personality and Social Psychology, 7,* 152–157.

Greenwald, A. (1975). Consequences of prejudice against the null hypothesis. *Psychological Bulletin, 82,* 1–20.

Greenwald, A. G. (1976). Within-subjects designs: To use or not to use? *Psychological Bulletin, 83,* 314–320.

Greenwald, A. G., Pratkanis, A. R., Leippe, M. R., & Baumgardner, M. H. (1986). Under what conditions does theory obstruct research progress? *Psychological Review, 93,* 216–229.

Gregory, W. L., Burroughs, W. J., & Ainslie, F. M. (1985). Self-relevant scenarios as an indirect means of attitude change. *Personality and Social Psychology Bulletin, 11,* 435–444.

Gruder, C. L., Cook, T. D., Hennigan, K. M., Flay, B. R., Alessis, C., & Halamaj, J. (1978). Empirical tests of the absolute sleeper effect predicted from the discounting cue hypothesis. *Journal of Personality and Social Psychology, 36,* 1061–1074.

Guttman, L. (1944). A basis for scaling qualitative data. *American Sociological Review, 9,* 139–150.

Haire, M. (1950). Projective techniques in marketing research. *Journal of Marketing, 14,* 649–656.

Hall, E., & Hall, M. (1971, June). The sounds of silence. *Playboy, 18*(6), 138–140, 148, 204–206.

Hansen, C. H., & Hansen, R. D. (1988). Finding the face in the crowd: An anger superiority effect. *Journal of Personality and Social Psychology, 54,* 917–924.

Harlow, H. F. (1958). The nature of love. *American Psychologist, 13,* 673–685.

Harris, M. (1974). Mediators between frustration and aggression in a field experiment. *Journal of Experimental Social Psychology, 10,* 561–571.

Hartmann, G. W. (1936). A field experiment on the comparative effectiveness of "emotional" and "rational" political leaflets in determining election results. *Journal of Abnormal and Social Psychology, 31,* 99–114.

Hastorf, A. H., & Cantril, H. (1954). They saw a game: A case study. *Journal of Abnormal and Social Psychology, 49,* 129–134.

Heberlein, T. A., & Black, J. S. (1976). Attitudinal specificity and the prediction of behavior in a field setting. *Journal of Personality and Social Psychology, 33,* 474–479.

Helmreich, R. E., Aronson, E., & LeFan, J. (1970). To err is humanizing—sometimes: Effects of self-esteem, competence, and a pratfall on interpersonal attraction. *Journal of Personality and Social Psychology, 16,* 259–264.

Holmes, D. S., & Bennett, D. H. (1974). Experiments to answer questions raised by the use of deception in psychological research. *Journal of Personality and Social Psychology, 29,* 358–367.

Horka, S. T., & Farrow, B. J. (1970). Methodological note on intersubject communication as a contaminating factor in psychological experiments. *Journal of Experimental Child Psychology, 10,* 363–366.

Hovland, C. I., Lumsdaine, A. A., & Sheffield, F. D. (1949). *Experiments in mass communications.* Princeton, NJ: Princeton University Press.

Hovland, C. I., & Sherif, M. (1952). Judgmental phenomena and scales of attitude measurement: Item displacement in Thurstone scales. *Journal of Abnormal and Social Psychology, 42,* 215–239.

Hovland, C. I., & Weiss, W. (1951). The influence of source credibility on communication effectiveness. *Public Opinion Quarterly, 15,* 635–650.

Huesmann, L. R., Lagerspetz, K., & Eron, L. (1984). Intervening variables in the TV violence-aggression relation: Evidence from two countries. *Developmental Psychology, 20,* 746–775.

Jones, R. A., Linder, D. E., Kiesler, C. A., Zanna, M. P., & Brehm, J. W. (1968). Internal states or external stimuli: Observers' attitude judgments and the dissonance theory—self-persuasion controversy. *Journal of Experimental Social Psychology, 4,* 247–269.

Jourard, S. M. (1968). *Disclosing man to himself.* Princeton, NJ: Van Nostrand.

Katz, D. (1971). Social psychology: Comprehensive and massive. *Contemporary Psychology, 16,* 273–282.

Kaufmann, H. (1970). *Aggression and altruism: A social psychological analysis.* New York: Holt, Rinehart, and Winston.

Kelley, H. H. (1967). Attribution theory in social psychology. In D. Levine (Ed.), *Nebraska Symposium on Motivation* (pp. 192–238). Lincoln: University of Nebraska Press.

Kelman, H. C. (1953). Attitude change as a function of response restriction. *Human Relations, 6,* 185–214.

Kelman, H. C. (1967). Human use of subjects: The problem of deception in social psychological experiments. *Psychological Bulletin, 67,* 1–11.

Kelman, H. C. (1968). *A time to speak: On human values and social research.* San Francisco: Jossey-Bass.

Kelman, H. C., & Hovland, C. I. (1953). "Reinstatement" of the communicator in delayed measurement of opinion change. *Journal of Abnormal and Social Psychology, 48,* 327–345.

Kiesler, C. A., Collins, B. E., & Miller, N. (1969). *Attitude change: A critical analysis of theoretical approaches.* New York: Wiley.

Kimmel, A. J. (1988). *Ethics and values in applied social research.* Newbury Park, CA: Sage Publications.

Klopfer, B. (1957). Psychological variables in human cancer. *Journal of Projective Techniques, 21,* 331–340.

Krout, M. H. (1935). Autistic gestures: An experimental study in symbolic movement. *Psychological Monographs, 46*(4, Whole No. 208).

Kruglanski, A. W. (1975). The human subject in the psychology experiment. In L. Berkowitz (Ed.), *Advances in experimental social psychology* (Vol. 8, pp. 101–147). New York: Academic Press.

Kuckenberg, L. (1963). *Effect of early father absence on statistical aptitude.* Unpublished doctoral dissertation, Harvard University.

Kulik, J., & Brown, R. (1979). Frustration, attribution of blame, and aggression. *Journal of Experimental Social Psychology, 15*, 183–194.

Lana, R. E. (1969). Pretest sensitization. In R. Rosenthal and R. Rosnow (Eds.), *Artifact in behavioral research* (pp. 119–141). New York: Academic Press.

Landauer, T. K., Carlsmith, J. M., & Lepper, M. (1970). Experimental analysis of the factors determining obedience of four-year-old children to adult females. *Child Development, 41*, 601–611.

Landy, D., & Aronson, E. (1968). Liking for an evaluator as a function of his discernment. *Journal of Personality and Social Psychology, 9*, 133–141.

Landy, D., McCue, K., & Aronson, E. (1969). Beyond Parkinson's law: III. The effects of protractive and contractive distractions on the wasting of time on subsequent tasks. *Journal of Applied Psychology, 53*, 236–239.

Langer, E. J. (1975). The illusion of control. *Journal of Personality and Social Psychology, 32*, 311–328.

Langer, E. J., Blank, A., & Chanowitz, B. (1978). The mindlessness of ostensibly thoughtful action: The role of "placebic" information on interpersonal interaction. *Journal of Personality and Social Psychology, 36*, 635–642.

LaPiere, R. T. (1934). Attitudes versus action. *Social Forces, 13*, 230–237.

Latané, B., & Darley, J. M. (1966, September). *Bystander intervention in emergency situations*. Paper presented at a meeting of the American Psychological Association, New York.

Latané, B., & Darley, J. M. (1968). Group inhibition of bystander intervention in emergencies. *Journal of Personality and Social Psychology, 10*, 215–221.

Latané, B., & Rodin, J. (1969). A lady in distress: Inhibiting effects of friends and strangers on bystander intervention. *Journal of Experimental Social Psychology, 5*, 189–202.

Lefkowitz, M., Blake, R. R., & Mouton, J. S. (1955). Status factors in pedestrian violation of traffic signals. *Journal of Abnormal and Social Psychology, 51*, 704–705.

Lefkowitz, M. M., Eron, L. D., Walder, L. O., & Huesmann, L. R. (1972). Television violence and child aggression: A follow-up study. In G. A. Comstock and E. A. Rubenstein (Eds.), *Television and social behavior* (Vol. 3: *Television and adolescent aggressiveness*). Washington, DC: United States Government Printing Office.

Lehman, D. R., Lempert, R. O., & Nisbett, R. E. (1988). The effects of graduate training on reasoning: Formal discipline and thinking about everyday-life events. *American Psychologist, 43*, 431–442.

Lepper, M. R., Greene, D., & Nisbett, R. E. (1973). Undermining children's intrinsic interest with extrinsic reward: A test of the "overjustification" hypothesis. *Journal of Personality and Social Psychology, 28*, 129–137.

Leventhal, H., & Niles, P. (1964). A field experiment on fear-arousal with data on the validity of questionnaire measures. *Journal of Personality, 32*, 459–479.

Lewinsohn, P. M., Mischel, W., Chaplin, W., & Barton, R. (1980). Social competence and depression: The role of illusory self-perceptions. *Journal of Abnormal Psychology, 89*, 203–212.

Lichtenstein, E. (1970). "Please don't talk to anyone about this experiment": Disclosure of deception by debriefed subjects. *Psychological Reports, 26*, 485–486.

Likert, R. A. (1932). A technique for the measurement of attitudes. *Archives of Psychology, 22*, 5–55.

Lindquist, E. F. (1953). *Design and analysis of experiments in psychology and education*. Boston: Houghton Mifflin.

Lord, C. G., Ross, L., & Lepper, M. (1979). The effects of prior theories on subsequently considered evidence. *Journal of Personality and Social Psychology, 37,* 2098–2109.

Maccoby, E. E., Dowley, E., Hagen, J. W., & Degerman, R. (1965). Activity level and intellectual functioning in normal pre-school children. *Child Development, 2,* 280–289.

Mahl, G. F. (1964). Some observations about research on vocal behavior. *Disorders of Communication, 42,* 466–483.

Mahl, G., & Schultze, G. (1964). Psychological research in the extralinguistic area. In T. A. Sebeok, A. S. Hayes, and M. C. Bateson (Eds.), *Approaches to semiotics* (pp. 51–124). London: Mouton.

Manucia, G. K., Baumann, D. J., & Cialdini, R. B. (1984). Mood influences on helping: Direct effects or side effects? *Journal of Personality and Social Psychology, 46,* 357–364.

Markus, H., & Zajonc, R. (1985). The cognitive perspective in social psychology. In G. Lindzey and E. Aronson (Eds.), *The handbook of social psychology* (3rd ed., Vol 1, pp. 137–230). New York: Random House.

Marlowe, D., Frager, R., & Nuttall, R. L. (1965). Commitment to action taking as a consequence of cognitive dissonance. *Journal of Personality and Social Psychology, 2,* 864–868.

Masling, J. (1960). The influence of situational and interpersonal variables in projective testing. *Psychological Bulletin, 57,* 65–85.

Masters, W. H., & Johnson, V. E. (1966). *Human sexual response.* Boston: Little, Brown.

McDavid, J. W. (1965). Approval-seeking motivation and the volunteer subject. *Journal of Personality and Social Psychology, 2,* 115–117.

McGraw, K. (1987). Guilt following transgression: An attribution of responsibility approach. *Journal of Personality and Social Psychology, 53,* 247–256.

McGuigan, F. J. (1963). The experimenter. A neglected stimulus object. *Psychological Bulletin, 60,* 421–428.

McGuire, W. J. (1967). Some impending reorientations in social psychology. *Journal of Experimental Social Psychology, 3,* 124–139.

McGuire, W. J. (1969). Suspiciousness of experimenter's intent. In R. Rosenthal and R. Rosnow (Eds.), *Artifact in behavioral research* (pp. 13–57). New York: Academic Press.

McMillen, D. L., & Austin, J. B. (1971). Effect of positive feedback on compliance following transgression. *Psychonomic Science, 24,* 59–64.

McNemar, Q. (1962). *Psychological statistics.* New York: Wiley.

Mehrabian, A. (1969). Significance of posture and position in the communication of attitude and status relationships. *Psychological Bulletin, 71,* 359–372.

Milgram, S. (1963). Behavioral study of obedience. *Journal of Abnormal and Social Psychology, 67,* 371–378.

Milgram, S. (1964). Issues in the study of obedience: A reply to Baumrind. *American Psychologist, 19,* 848–852.

Milgram, S. (1966, September). *Four studies using the lost letter technique.* Address given at a meeting of the American Psychological Association, New York.

Milgram, S. (1973). *Obedience to authority: An experimental view.* New York: Harper & Row.

Miller, A. G. (1972a). Role-playing: An alternative to deception? *American Psychologist, 27,* 623–636.

Miller, A. G. (1972b). *The social psychology of social psychological research.* New York: Free Press.

Miller, N. E. (1957). Experiments on motivation. *Science, 126,* 1271–1278.

Mills, J. (1958). Changes in moral attitudes following temptation. *Journal of Personality, 26,* 517–531.

Mischel, W. (1968). *Personality and assessment.* New York: Wiley.

Mischel, W., Ebbesen, E. B., & Zeiss, A. R. (1972). Cognitive and attentional mechanisms in delay of gratification. *Journal of Personality and Social Psychology, 21,* 204–218.

Mook, D. G. (1983). In defense of external invalidity. *American Psychologist, 38,* 379–387.

Moore, B. S., Underwood, B., & Rosenhan, D. L. (1973). Affect and altruism. *Developmental Psychology, 8,* 99–104.

Morgan, J. J. B. (1945). Attitudes of students towards the Japanese. *Journal of Psychology, 21,* 219–227. Cited in C. Selltiz, M. Jahoda, M. Deutsch, and S. W. Cook (Eds.)(1963), *Research methods in social relations.* New York: Holt, Rinehart, and Winston.

Murray, H. A. (1963). Studies of stressful interpersonal disputations. *American Psychologist, 18,* 28–36.

Murray, T. H. (1982). Ethics, power, and applied social psychology. In L. Bickman (Ed.), *Applied social psychology annual* (Vol. 3, pp. 75–95). Beverly Hills, CA: Sage Publications.

Neale, J. M., & Liebert, R. M. (1986). *Science and behavior: An introduction to methods of research* (3rd ed.). Englewood Cliffs, NJ: Prentice-Hall.

Nisbett, R. E., & Ross, L. (1980). *Human inference: Strategies and shortcomings of social judgment.* Englewood Cliffs, NJ: Prentice Hall.

Nisbett, R. E., & Wilson, T. (1977). Telling more than we can know: Verbal reports on mental processes. *Psychological Review, 84,* 231–259.

Orne, M. (1962). On the social psychology of the psychological experiment. *American Psychologist, 17,* 776–783.

Orne, M. (1969). Demand characteristics and the concept of quasi-experimental control. In R. Rosenthal and R. Rosnow (Eds.), *Artifact in behavioral research* (pp. 143–179). New York: Academic Press.

Orne, M. T., & Evans, F. J. (1965). Social control in the psychological experiment: Antisocial behavior and hypnosis. *Journal of Personality and Social Psychology, 1,* 189–200.

Osgood, C. E., Suci, G. J., & Tannenbaum, P. H. (1957). *The measurement of meaning.* Urbana: University of Illinois Press.

Pallak, M. S., & Pittman, T. S. (1972). General motivational effects of dissonance arousal. *Journal of Personality and Social Psychology, 21,* 349–358.

Parker, S. D., Brewer, M. B., & Spencer, J. R. (1980). Natural disaster, perceived control, and attributions of fate. *Personality and Social Psychology Bulletin, 6,* 454–459.

Pepitone, A. (1958). Attributions of causality, social attitudes and cognitive matching processes. In R. Tagiuri and L. Petrullo (Eds.), *Person perception and interpersonal behavior* (pp. 258–276). Stanford, CA: Stanford University Press.

Piliavin, J. A., Dovidio, J., Gaertner, S., & Clark, R. D. III (1981). *Emergency intervention.* New York: Academic Press.

Piliavin, J. A., & Piliavin, I. M. (1972). The effect of blood on reactions to a victim. *Journal of Personality and Social Psychology, 23,* 253–261.

Piliavin, J. A., Piliavin, I. M., & Rodin, J. (1975). Costs, diffusion, and the stigmatized victim. *Journal of Personality and Social Psychology, 32,* 429–438.

Piliavin, I. M., Rodin, J., & Piliavin, J. A. (1969). Good Samaritanism: An underground phenomenon? *Journal of Personality and Social Psychology, 13,* 289–299.

Porter, N., & Geis, F. (1981). Women and nonverbal leadership cues: When seeing is not believing. In C. Mayo and N. Henley (eds.), *Gender and nonverbal behavior.* New York: Springer-Verlag.

Pratkanis, A. R., Greenwald, A. G., Leippe, M. R., & Baumgardner, M. H. (1988). In search of reliable persuasion effects. III. The sleeper effect is dead. Long live the sleeper effect. *Journal of Personality and Social Psychology, 54,* 203–218.

Price, L. (1984). Art, science, faith, and medicine: The implications of the placebo effect. *Sociology of Health and Illness, 6,* 61–73.

Regan, D. T., Williams, M., & Sparling, S. (1972). Voluntary expiation of guilt: A field experiment. *Journal of Personality and Social Psychology, 24,* 42–45.

Rhodewalt, F., & Comer, R. (1979). Induced-compliance attitude change: Once more with feeling. *Journal of Experimental Social Psychology, 15,* 35–47.

Riecken, H. W. (1962). A program for research on experiments in social psychology. In N. F. Washburne (Ed.), *Decision, values and groups* (Vol. 2, pp. 25–41). New York: Pergamon Press.

Ring, K. (1967). Experimental social psychology: Some sober questions about some frivolous values. *Journal of Experimental Social Psychology, 3,* 113–123.

Roethlisberger, F. J., & Dickson, W. J. (1939). *Management and the worker.* Cambridge, MA: Harvard University Press.

Rogosa, D. (1980). A critique of cross-lagged correlations. *Psychological Bulletin, 88*(2), 245–258.

Rosenberg, M. J. (1965). When dissonance fails: On eliminating evaluation apprehension from attitude measurement. *Journal of Personality and Social Psychology, 1,* 28–42.

Rosenberg, M. J. (1966). Some limits of dissonance. In S. Feldman (Ed.), *Cognitive consistency* (pp. 135–170). New York: Academic Press.

Rosenberg, M. J. (1969). The conditions and consequences of evaluation apprehension. In R. Rosenthal and R. Rosnow (Eds.), *Artifact in behavioral research* (pp. 279–349). New York: Academic Press.

Rosenberg, M. J., & Abelson, R. P. (1960). An analysis of cognitive balancing. In M. J. Rosenberg, C. I. Hovland, W. J. McGuire, R. P. Abelson, & J. W. Brehm (Eds.), *Attitude organization and change: An analysis of consistency among attitude components* (pp. 112–163). New Haven, CT: Yale University Press.

Rosenthal, R. (1966). *Experimenter effects in behavioral research.* New York: Appleton-Century-Crofts.

Rosenthal, R. (1967). Covert communication in the psychology experiment. *Psychological Bulletin, 67,* 356–367.

Rosenthal, R. (1969). Interpersonal expectations: Effects of the experimenter's hypothesis. In R. Rosenthal and R. Rosnow (Eds.), *Artifact in behavioral research* (pp. 181–277). New York: Academic Press.

Rosenthal, R., & Fode, K. L. (1963a). Psychology of the scientist: V. Three experiments in experimenter bias. *Psychological Reports, 12,* 491–511.

Rosenthal, R., & Fode, K. L. (1963b). The effect of experimenter bias on the performance of the albino rat. *Behavioral Science, 8,* 183–189.

Rosenthal, R., & Lawson, R. (1964). A longitudinal study of the effects of experimenter bias on the operant learning of laboratory rats. *Journal of Psychiatric Research, 2,* 61–72.

Rosenthal, R., Persinger, G. W., Vikan-Kline, L., & Mulry, R. C. (1963). The role of the research assistant in the mediation of experimenter bias. *Journal of Personality, 31,* 313–335.

Rosenthal, R., & Rubin, D. B. (1978). Interpersonal expectancy effects: The first 345 studies. *The Behavioral and Brain Sciences, 3,* 377–415.

Ross, L., Bierbrauer, G., & Hoffman, S. (1976). The role of attribution processes in conformity and dissent. *American Psychologist, 31,* 148–157.

Ross, L., Greene, D., & House, P. (1977). The "false consensus" effect: An egocentric bias in social perception and attribution processes. *Journal of Experimental Social Psychology, 13,* 279–301.

Ross, L., Lepper, M. R., & Hubbard, M. (1975). Perseverance in self perception and social perception: Biased attributional processes in the debriefing paradigm. *Journal of Personality and Social Psychology, 32,* 880–892.

Ross, L. D. (1987). The problem of construal in social inference and social psychology. In N. E. Grunberg, R. E. Nisbett, J. Rodin, and J. E. Singer (Eds.), *A distinctive approach to psychological research: The influence of Stanley Schachter.* Hillsdale, NJ: Lawrence Erlbaum Associates.

Rubin, Z. (1970). Jokers wild in the lab. *Psychology Today, 4*(7), 18–24.

Schachter, S. (1951). Deviation, rejection, and communication. *Journal of Abnormal and Social Psychology, 46,* 190–267.

Schachter, S. (1959). *The psychology of affiliation: Experimental studies of the sources of gregariousness.* Stanford CA: Stanford University Press.

Schachter, S., & Singer, J. E. (1962). Cognitive, social and physiological determinants of emotional state. *Psychological Review, 69,* 379–399.

Schachter, S., & Wheeler, L. (1962). Epinephrine, chlorpromazine, and amusement. *Journal of Abnormal and Social Psychology, 65,* 121–128.

Scherer, K. R., & Ekman, P. (1977). *Handbook of methods in nonverbal research.* Cambridge: Cambridge University Press.

Schneider, D. J., Hastorf, A. H., & Ellsworth, P. C. (1979). *Person perception* (2nd ed.). Reading, MA: Addison-Wesley.

Schulman, J. L., & Reisman, J. M. (1959). An objective measure of hyperactivity. *American Journal of Mental Deficiency, 64,* 455–456.

Schultz, D. P. (1969). The human subject in psychological research. *Psychological Bulletin, 72,* 214–228.

Schuman, H., & Kalton, G. (1985). Survey methods. In G. Lindzey and E. Aronson (Eds.), *The handbook of social psychology* (3rd ed., Vol. 1, pp. 635–697). New York: Random House.

Scott, W. A. (1968). Attitude measurement. In G. Lindzey and E. Aronson (Eds.), *The handbook of social psychology* (2nd ed., Vol. 2, pp. 204–273). Reading, MA: Addison-Wesley.

Sears, R. R., et al. (1967). *Privacy and behavioral research.* Washington, DC: Executive Office of the President.

Selltiz, C., Jahoda, M., Deutsch, M., & Cook, S. W. (1963). *Research methods in social relations.* New York: Holt, Rinehart, and Winston.

Shaw, M. E., & Wright, J. M. (1967). *Scales for the treatment of attitudes.* New York: McGraw-Hill.

Sherman, S. J., Cialdini, R. B., Schwartzman, D. F., & Reynolds, K. D. (1985). Imagining can heighten or lower the perceived likelihood of contracting a disease: The mediating effect of ease of imagery. *Personality and Social Psychology Bulletin, 11,* 118–127.

Shils, E. A. (1959). Social inquiry and the autonomy of the individual. In D. Lerner (Ed.), *The human meaning of the social sciences* (pp. 114–157). New York: Meridan.

Sidman, M. (1960). *Tactics of scientific research: Evaluating experimental data in psychology.* New York: Basic Books.

Sigall, H., Aronson, E., & Van Hoose, T. (1970). The cooperative subject: Myth or reality? *Journal of Experimental Social Psychology, 6,* 1–10.

Silverman, B. I. (1974). Consequences, racial discrimination, and the principle of belief congruence. *Journal of Personality and Social Psychology, 29,* 497–508.

Silverman, I. (1965, September). *Motives underlying the behavior of the subject in the psychological experiment.* Paper presented at a meeting of the American Psychological Association, Chicago.

Silverman, I., Shulman, A. D., & Wiesenthal, D. L. (1970). Effects of deceiving and debriefing psychological subjects on performance in later experiments. *Journal of Personality and Social Psychology, 14,* 203–212.

Singer, D. D., & Hurwitz, D. (1967). Long-term experience with sulfonylureas and placebo. *New England Journal of Medicine, 227,* 450–456.

Smith, C. A., & Ellsworth, P. C. (1985). Patterns of cognitive appraisal in emotion. *Journal of Personality and Social Psychology, 48,* 813–838.

Smith, M. B. (1967). Conflicting values affecting behavioral research with children. *American Psychologist, 22,* 377–382.

Smith, S. S., & Richardson D. (1983). Amelioration of deception and harm in psychological research: The important role of debriefing. *Journal of Personality and Social Psychology, 44,* 1075–1082.

Soble, A. (1978). Deception in social science research: Is informed consent possible? *Hastings Center Report, 8,* 40–46.

Sommer, R. (1969). *Personal space.* Englewood Cliffs, NJ: Prentice-Hall.

Stoner, J. A. F. (1961). *A comparison of individual and group decisions involving risk.* Unpublished master's thesis, Sloan School of Management, Massachusetts Institute of Technology.

Strack, F., & Martin, L. L. (1987). Thinking, judging, and communicating: A process account of context effects in attitude surveys. In H. J. Hippler, N. Schwarz, and S. Sudman (Eds.), *Social information processing and survey methodology,* (pp. 123–148). New York: Springer-Verlag.

Stricker, L. J. (1967). The true deceiver. *Psychological Bulletin, 68,* 13–20.

Stricker, L. J., Messick, S., & Jackson, D. N. (1969). Evaluating deception in psychological research. *Psychological Bulletin, 71,* 343–351.

Strunk, W., Jr., & White, E. B. (1979). *The elements of style* (3rd ed.). New York: Macmillan.

"Student." (1931). The Lanarkshire milk experiment. *Biometrika, 23,* 398–406.

Swann, W. B., Jr. (1984). Quest for accuracy in person perception: A matter of pragmatics. *Psychological Review, 91,* 457–477.

Taylor, D. W., Berry, P. C., & Block, C. H. (1958). Does group participation when using brainstorming facilitate or inhibit creative thinking? *Administrative Sciences Quarterly, 3,* 23–47.

Thurstone, L. L. (1931). *The measurement of social attitude.* Chicago: University of Chicago Press.

Thurstone, L. L., & Chave, E. J. (1929). *The measurement of attitude.* Chicago: University of Chicago Press.

Tversky, A., & Kahneman, D. (1973). Availability: A heuristic of judging frequency and probability. *Cognitive Psychology, 5,* 207–232.

Tversky, A., & Kahneman, D. (1974). Judgment under uncertainty: Heuristics and biases. *Science, 185,* 1124–1131.

Underwood, B. J. (1957). *Psychological research.* New York: Appleton-Century-Crofts.

Underwood, B., Froming, W. J., & Moore, B. S. (1977). Mood, attention, and altruism: A search for mediating variables. *Developmental Psychology, 13,* 541–542.

United States Public Health Service (1969). *Protection of the individual as a research subject.* Washington, DC: U.S. Government Printing Office.

Vinar, P. (1969). Dependence on a placebo: A case report. *British Journal of Psychiatry, 115,* 1189–1190.

Wallace, J., & Sadalla, E. (1966). Behavioral consequences of transgression. *Journal of Experimental Research in Personality, 1,* 187–194.

Walsh, W. B., & Stillman, S. M. (1974). Disclosure of deception by debriefed subjects. *Journal of Counseling Psychology, 21,* 315–319.

Walster, E., Aronson, E., & Brown, Z. (1966). Choosing to suffer as a consequence of expecting to suffer: An unexpected finding. *Journal of Experimental Social Psychology, 2,* 400–406.

Walster, E., Berscheid, E., Abrahams, D., & Aronson, E. (1967). Effectiveness of debriefing following deception experiments. *Journal of Personality and Social Psychology, 4,* 371–380.

Ward, W. C., & Jenkins, H. M. (1965). The display of information and the judgment of contingency. *Canadian Journal of Psychology, 19,* 231–241.

Webb, E. J., Campbell, D. T., Schwartz, D., & Sechrest, L. (1966). *Unobtrusive measures: Nonreactive research in the social sciences.* Chicago: Rand-McNally.

Weber, S. J., & Cook, T. D. (1972). Subject effects in laboratory research: An examination of subject roles, demand characteristics, and valid inference. *Psychological Bulletin, 77,* 273–295.

Webster's New Universal Unabridged Dictionary (2nd ed.) (1983). New York: Dorset & Baber.

Wegner, D. M., Wenzlaff, R., Kerker, R. M., & Beattie, A. E. (1981). Incrimination through innuendo: Can media questions become public answers? *Journal of Personality and Social Psychology, 40,* 822–832.

Weick, K. E. (1968). Systematic observational methods. In G. Lindzey and E. Aronson (Eds.), *The handbook of social psychology,* (2nd ed., Vol. 2, pp. 357–451). Reading, MA: Addison-Wesley.

Weick, K. E. (1985). Systematic observational methods. In G. Lindzey and E. Aronson (Eds.), *The handbook of social psychology,* (3rd ed., Vol. 1, pp. 567–634). New York: Random House.

West, S. G., & Gunn, S. P. (1978). Some issues of ethics in social psychology. *American Psychologist, 33,* 30–38.

Willis, R. H., & Willis, Y. A. (1970). Role playing versus deception: An experimental comparison. *Journal of Personality and Social Psychology, 16,* 472–477.

Wilson, E. B. (1952). *An introduction to scientific research.* New York: McGraw-Hill.

Wilson, T. D. (1985). Strangers to ourselves: The origins and accuracy of beliefs about one's own mental states. In J. H. Harvey and G. Weary (Eds.), *Attribution in contemporary psychology.* New York: Academic Press.

Zajonc, R. B. (1968). Attitudinal effects of mere exposure. *Journal of Personality and Social Psychology Monograph, 9*(2), Part 2, 1–28.

Zeisel, H. (1969). *Some data on juror attitudes toward capital punishment.* Monograph, Center for Studies in Criminal Justice, University of Chicago Law School.

Zinsser, W. (1985). *On writing well: An informal guide to writing nonfiction* (3rd ed.). New York: Harper & Row.

Name Index

Subject Index